BRIDGES ACROSS HUMANITY

'Understanding religion as an essential task of meaning-making, Akhil Gupta's book offers readers a glimpse of the commonalities across diverse historical and cultural contexts, making new and vibrant connections for contemporary life. Allowing readers to explore common existential ideas, this text creates a scaffold for meaning-making that helps us in our common quest for better, more peaceful lives as individuals, and as a global community.'

—**Tiffany L. Steinwert,**
Dean for Religious and Spiritual Life, Stanford University

'Every page of this book comprises inspiring wisdom from our world's diverse religions—and also the material to build bridges between them.'
—**Eboo Patel**, author of *We Need To Build* and
Founder and President of Interfaith America

'There isn't a more potent driving force in human affairs than religion. As this book convincingly proves, there are more similarities than differences across seemingly diverse faiths. Perhaps if we understood these common foundations, we could better live and work together in harmony.'
—**Hamilton (Tony) James**, Former Executive Vice-Chairman,
The Blackstone Group

'A riveting journey across the world's major religions, this book shows the commonalities that exist among us—and how those similarities must serve as the roadmap to a shared, prosperous future.'
—**Jacqueline Novogratz**, bestselling author of *The Blue Sweater and Manifesto for a Moral Revolution: Practices to Build a Better World*

'Akhil Gupta convincingly demonstrates how meaning-making in relation to the ultimate questions of life is a universal human experience; indeed, it is what actually makes us human. The allegory of the blind men and the elephant comes vividly alive in the author's comprehensive canvassing of common themes across all religions and spiritual traditions. If only we keep aside our differences and listen to each other with empathy, we might all have a better sense of why we are here and what we should be doing—not just to preserve ourselves and our planet, but also to truly flourish.'

—**Rev. Scotty McLennan** (M.Div., J.D.),
Minister and former Dean for Religious Life at Stanford University

BRIDGES ACROSS HUMANITY

Different Religions, Similar Teachings

AKHIL GUPTA

RUPA

Published by
Rupa Publications India Pvt. Ltd 2023
7/16, Ansari Road, Daryaganj
New Delhi 110002

Sales centres:
Bengaluru Chennai
Hyderabad Jaipur Kathmandu
Kolkata Mumbai Prayagraj

The views and opinions expressed in this book are the author's own and the facts are as reported by him which have been verified to the extent possible, and the publishers are not in any way liable for the same.

P-ISBN: 978-93-5702-071-8
E-ISBN: 978-93-5702-048-0

Second impression 2023

10 9 8 7 6 5 4 3 2

Printed in India

Contents

Foreword

Bridges across humanity are very ambitious undertakings, so very comprehensive that one might have feared it would be predictable or merely skimming the surface. But this is not the case. Akhil Gupta and his team have worked very hard on each chapter and each brings intelligent and informed possibilities to the fore. Each chapter poses similarities and some differences in a way that invites conversation and further exploration of what any given chapter proposes.

Akhil's personal voice is everywhere in the book, as he reminisces on the importance of learning about interfaith generosity when he was a child, all the way up to his years of study and learning at Stanford and Harvard amid and after his successful business career. In the first chapter, 'Only One Universal God', Akhil mentions how his early life affected his view of religions:

> I was born in Old Delhi which, to this day, remains one of the most religiously pluralistic places in the world. As a child, I was exposed to the living traditions of many religions and used to be fascinated by the diversity and the commonalities across religions. In adulthood, these commonalities were reinforced through more text-based theological evidence as I looked more closely at the scriptures of all major religions.

In the preface he remembers a formative experience on his 10th birthday:

> My parents celebrated it in an unusual way. Rather than showering gifts on me, my mother took me to feed the poor people outside

> the temples of six different faiths: a Sikh Gurdwara, a Hindu Temple, a Jain Temple, a Christian Church, a Jewish Synagogue and an Islamic Mosque. As I handed over two pieces of bread and some very appetizing curry to each person, I did not see Muslim or Hindu or Christian faces—I only saw grateful human faces.

The experience was formative and not to be forgotten:

> Even though it was a fleeting exchange—a small act of kindness and the acknowledgment of gratitude—I can still vividly remember the deep human connection I felt that day and the profound sense of joy it gave me. When we returned home, my father read from the scriptures of these six major faiths. He told us that there is only one God who has been manifested on the earth in different times, be it Krishna, Christ, Mohammed, Moses, Guru Nanak, Buddha, Mahavir, or many others. The words: '*Ekam sat vipra bahudha vadanti*' (truth is one but called differently by many) from the Rig Veda (I.164.46) still ring in my ears. He ended our prayer by saying, *Sarve Janah sukinoh bhavantu* (May all the peoples of the world be happy and prosperous).

Much later in the book, tucked away in the chapter called 'Music', Akhil notes that growing up in Chandni Chowk, a densely populated area in Old Delhi, he "had the good fortune to participate in ritual worships of multiple religions and have witnessed the all-consuming enchanting effect music can have." His neighbourhood was "a true cultural melting pot where people of multiple faiths co-existed harmoniously in close quarters. Our neighbourhood was surrounded by temples of all faiths." He listened, but also joined in:

> I recall waking up to the soul-stirring 'azan' (call for prayers for Muslim) from a nearby mosque. On my way to school, I often met a group of devout Sikhs doing their early rounds of 'prabhat-feri' and joined them in singing hymns until I had to part ways to head for my school but the beautiful 'Shabads' kept echoing all the way. I occasionally accompanied my dad to attend 'Urs Sharif' at Khwaja Nizamuddin Aullia's shrine and rocked back and forth to the beats of 'naat' and 'qawwalis'. My dad and I

> both favoured Sufi music and dad would often hum the newly learned verses at home.

His mother would take him to satsangs in which he joyfully participated:

> During my middle school summer holidays, my mom would ask me to accompany her to late night 'satsangs' (religious meetings) at a nearby park. Although at that age toys and games were more enticing, I willingly joined mom to listen to Mukund Hari Baba, a religious sage who had an amazing flair to tell the famous stories of prominent devotees using simple harmonium which created music that felt ethereal even to me despite my young age. During holidays, dad and mom used to take us to various pilgrimage places. They later told me stories of how I used to skilfully dance and copy rhythmic gyrations of the ISKCON temple devotees in Vrindavan. I recall enjoying the 'kirtan' and the upbeat music but have no recollection of me dancing, perhaps due to a self-imposed amnesia to suppress embarrassment. What I do vividly recall is watching a religious performance of twirling dervish and feeling an unfamiliar but trance like state of peace.

His horizons expanded further during his studies at Stanford University and his sense of the commonality of all religions only deepened. As Akhil puts it, "I respect all religions, but I do not consider myself very religious. Still, even though I questioned the merits of many rituals, the music helped evoke the amalgamation of strong feelings of joy, peace, calm and tranquillity at a cellular level and left a lasting imprint on my mind."

Akhil's time at Harvard in 2015 and thereafter only deepened and expanded his early and growing convictions about the unity of religions, as he attended a variety of courses throughout the university—mine included, as he kindly notes—and widened his understanding of things he knew instinctively:

> I was like a kid in a candy store, giddy from all the knowledge I was gathering and digesting. I stayed at Harvard for three more years as a guest, courtesy of Harvard Divinity School, with several privileges to continue to soak in Harvard's intellectual

environment. The dots started to connect and the task for the rest of my life became clear.

Thence came together the idea of this book:

> I decided to share the deep insights I gathered during these years focusing on human flourishing and the role of religion in our lives with the masses. This book is an attempt at the latter. I am convinced that the various religious traditions of the world need not be in conflict with one another, nor do the other domains of human knowledge like science need to be in conflict with religion.

All of this led to Akhil's 'Universal Enlightenment & Flourishing (UEF)' project, and then this current volume.

How are we to understand and, more importantly, use this book? Throughout the book, Akhil shows himself to not only be well disposed toward interreligious openness, but also to have a strong rational disposition, submitting every point to a helpful questioning. He clearly respects all traditions: that people believe in certain ways, and what they believe, is to be respected. But it is also true that the inquiring observer can reinterpret what people believe in terms of a human search for meaning. Specific faith claims must be honoured, but not allowed to push aside anyone else's faith claim. "Let us be reasonable," Akhil requests. This is a plausible approach that will gain respect in our pluralistic environment, even if explaining faiths always runs the risking of explaining them away as well. But the key is that Akhil wants us to think, question and do the work ourselves of sifting through similarities and differences.

The book is full of small glimpses of historical information with many names and dates, and important points are supported by quotations from many sources. Yet the book is not simply a depository of information such as might be found in textbooks or online and does not replace other sources of information. The purpose is a rather practical one: to invite readers into an informed and practical conversation about religions seen and heard together in accord with 54 different themes.

This is not a very long book and you could rush through the whole of it quickly if you were so inclined. But there is no need for that. It will be more useful as a kind of workbook; intellectual and spiritual exercises that help readers give concrete reality to their intuition that the religions are connected. The 54 themes educate readers on how to think variously about the harmony and common ground of traditions and working through the relationships among religions slowly and thoughtfully. You might even plan to read and stay with one chapter a week through the 52 weeks of the year with the two extra reserved for times of leisure or travel. You can read consecutively as Akhil unfolds his vision in 54 different ways. Or you might want to skip around, exploring the different themes as you might find suitable on any given day.

I cannot help but observe too that this is a courageous book, a brave effort to insist on commonality, mutual respect, and openness of mind and heart in a time when the world is torn apart by many divisive forces when too many assert that religions are past and over with or, worse, that religions are a major causes of the problem. In turn, some believers feel that exerting power over people of other faiths is divine will. Akhil stubbornly believes in a shared source and finality of religions, shared values for a better life. What people of faith have in common outweighs even the undeniable differences and certainly puts to the side any notion that religions are meant to compete and quarrel, or use majority status and political power to intimidate people of small faith communities. Even if we admit that differences are real, he says:

> I am convinced, however, that we are not as familiar as we should be with the deep *commonalities* that exist in our religions. These become clearer if we interpret the stories metaphorically rather than literally. We hope that after reading this book you will see our particularities in a new light, which just might expunge some degree of exclusivism in the world. In turn, we can all develop more affinity with the other and approach each other with a sense of curiosity, appreciating the beauty of diversity.

Or as Akhil puts it at the end of Chapter 11, 'Metaphorical versus Literal Interpretations':

> The problem we face today is that, when taken literally, the ancient scriptures and beliefs that were composed thousands of years ago are impossible to reconcile with the present. We live and worship within a fact-based approximation of reality. All religions have fundamentalist factions that continue to cling to

literalist interpretations of ancient texts, thus creating a variety of alternative and competing realities. This naturally leads to bigotry, conflict and violence. Each religion must reckon with this problem if we are to restore religion to its original mission and intentions of peace. As our world and our species continue to evolve, so too must the lessons we take away from religious materials.

Having achieved much in life—in business, in friendships, as a lifelong learner—Akhil has now given a gift to all of us, a book that invites all people of good will to listen, learn, practice together towards a better world in which faith, love and confidence in the transcendent reality of the divine are forces for peace and human flourishing.

For this powerful book, so intensely wrought, Akhil Gupta and his associates are to be warmly thanked and congratulated.

Francis X. Clooney, S.J.
Parkman Professor of Divinity
Harvard University
President CTSA 2022-2023

Preface

Spring 2015, Harvard Kennedy School. I was attending a class on religion and world politics with Brian Hehir, a professor and McArthur Fellow known for his Socratic style of teaching. He started the class by asking a question: 'Is the role of religion in people's lives likely to increase, decrease, or remain the same?' Sixty per cent of the class said that it would decrease at a rapid rate, thirty-five per cent said it would be the same and only five per cent said that it was likely to increase. I was in the 'rapidly decrease' camp when I raised my hand.

Professor Hehir quizzed me, challenged me, but I was able to defend my views, citing predictions that the influence of religions in our affairs would constantly decline with the proliferation of secular democracies around the world, the spread of modern literacy and advances in science and technology. Professor Hehir said, 'I will come back and ask you the same question at the end of the course.' And he did.

Through the course, Professor Hehir convinced us that religion is still playing a very important role in our lives. It was in this class that I became fully aware of the extent of violence that has been committed in the name of religion. Particularly appalling to me was its prevalence in the world, through history, of intra-religious warfare. I couldn't believe that millions of Catholic and Protestant Christians had slaughtered each other over such minor religious differences when it was clear that both sides ultimately believed in and worshipped the same God—a God whose primary commands concern loving one another and even loving one's enemy. The same can be said of Sunni and Shia Muslims. The violence of extreme forms of Islam is inimical to Muhammad's teachings and in contravention of the teachings of Islam.

I contrasted all this with my childhood experiences in India, which I want to illustrate with one particularly memorable anecdote: my tenth birthday. My parents celebrated it in an unusual way. Rather than showering gifts on me, my mother took me with her to feed the poor people outside the temples of six different faiths: a Sikh temple, a Hindu temple, a Jain temple, a Christian church, a Jewish synagogue and an Islamic mosque. As I handed over two pieces of bread and some very appetising curry to each person, I did not see Muslim or Hindu or Christian faces—I only saw grateful human faces. Even though it was a fleeting exchange—a small act of kindness and the acknowledgement of gratitude—I still vividly remember the deep human connection I felt that day, and the profound sense of joy it gave me. When we returned home, my father read from the scriptures of these six major faiths. He told us that there is only one God who has been manifested on earth in different times, be it Lord Krishna, Jesus Christ, prophet Muhammad, prophet Moses, Guru Nanak, the Buddha, Mahavir or many others. The words '*Ekam sat vipra bahudha vadanti*' (Truth is one, but the wise men know it as many) from the Rig Veda (I.164.46) still ring in my ears. He ended our prayer by saying *Sarve janah sukhinoh bhavantu* (May all the peoples of the world be happy and prosperous).

A few years later, I was reading a book given to me by my father. It was written by Dr Radhakrishnan, a former president of India who also inaugurated the Center for the Study of World Religions at Harvard Divinity School. In the book, Radhakrishnan wrote about how he recognized himself as an heir to the entirety of human civilization and not just Hindu civilization. This struck a chord within me and it continues to resonate in my life today. These two events—two beautiful gifts handed to me by my mother and father—enriched my life immeasurably by teaching me how to cherish and harness the diversity in the world around me.

Back to 2015. I was at Harvard as a fellow at the Advanced Leadership Initiative (ALI). The ALI fellowship provided me with an amazing platform that allowed me to audit classes across the university without any grades or assignments. Over two years I took over thirty courses. I did this not for any kind of certificate or other end-result, but simply because I believe in learning as an autotelic activity, one that is valuable and fulfilling as an end unto itself. I was like a kid in a candy store, giddy from all the knowledge I was gathering and digesting. I stayed at Harvard for three more years as a guest, courtesy of Harvard Divinity School, with several privileges to continue to soak in Harvard's intellectual environment. The dots started to connect and the task for the rest of my life became clear. I decided to share the deep insights I gathered during these years focusing on human flourishing and the role of religion in our lives. This book is an attempt at the latter.

I am convinced that the various religious traditions of the world need not be in conflict with one another, nor do other domains of human knowledge like science need to be in conflict with religion. In fact, our lives would be richer and more meaningful if we practised our religion interreligiously. This book will primarily focus on the religions of the world, with a secondary emphasis on the complementary nature of the natural and social sciences in crafting a full picture of the world, our place in it as human beings, and how to live a fulfilling life.

The class on religion and world politics triggered my interest to get a basic understanding of all belief systems and their evolution over time. I took a variety of classes on many religions, including several on Islam, Buddhism and Hinduism. I also read works from history, evolutionary biology, psychology, anthropology of religion and neuroscience. After taking these diversified courses, I not only felt enlightened, but was also inspired to share my learnings with the general populace.

I decided to start a non-profit institute called Universal Enlightenment & Flourishing (UEF), of which I am still the active director. I decided to take what I learned in my classes at Harvard and share my experiences and learning of the deeply common nature and destiny that we have.

One of the first big projects of UEF has been the writing of this book on common themes across all religions. My goal was to write a book that would broaden and deepen our understanding of religions. It dawned on me that many others might be able to benefit from a more critical examination, just as I have. Most of us do not have enough understanding of our own religions, much less that of others. This is only natural, as we are not taught about religions in grade school, at least not from a critical perspective, and most of us do not have the free time in our adult lives to pursue this kind of study on our own as there is simply too much religious literature to comb through.

Until now.

The beauty of this book is its curation of a wide collection of quotes and insights from the world's major religions, distilling the main substance of human wisdom into actionable insights.

My connection to Harvard enabled me to gather a small team of researchers and writers to help me with this book, as well as other UEF projects. Among them is Allen Simon, a graduate of Harvard Divinity School who has been working on the book since 2018. He was very sceptical at first, wondering what the value of such a book would be among all the other existing literature on religions. But soon, he came to see the uniqueness of our approach (narrated below) and became more passionate about the project. He has devoted about five years towards doing some deep and unique research.

Early on in the research process, we were both surprised to learn just how many common themes we found across all religions. When I first conceived of this book, I thought I would be able to write about maybe ten to fifteen common themes, but in the end, we identified, researched and wrote about more than fifty. These similarities that we found are amazing from one point of view, but completely unsurprising if we view all religions as different expressions of the same meaning-making endeavour of humanity that manifests itself in different historical and cultural contexts.

In other words, although real differences across belief systems exist, they exist primarily due to historical and geographical contexts. The most important and prominent tenets of religions do not change across time and place, such as loving one's neighbour, or striving to quiet and tame the mind. There are many popular authors today who write about religion through a comparative lens. Karen Armstrong, for example, argues that all religions share a common core and are fundamentally one; Steven Prothero essentially argues the opposite. Richard Dawkins and Steven Pinker find little to no redeeming value in religion and view it as something akin to proto-science that ought to be replaced by 'real' science.

As we will see, each of these perspectives has its fair share of predecessors. Several notable intellectuals of the twentieth century, like William James, Aldous Huxley and Joseph Campbell, argued for this idea of a common core in all religions; Huxley termed it 'the perennial philosophy'.[1] Another notable proponent of the perennial philosophy is Huston Smith, whose *The World's Religions*[2] was the first book that I read after I started to get re-engaged in the study of different religions at Harvard. It is still one of the most popular and influential books on world religions ever written.

But the approach taken by most books is to keep the descriptions of different religions in silos. We are approaching it differently. We take the major themes and show how most religions have some variant of the same theme. By taking this horizontal approach (taking a theme and showing how it is part of various religions and other wisdom systems), we aim to create bridges across different religions for our readers, encouraging them to ponder over each theme and go back and forth into different religions as many times as they like. This will deepen the cross-religious experience and hopefully be a lot more effective in illustrating the central thesis of our book.

If we look at religion as a major meaning-making[3] technology that we, as humans have used across all civilizations, it gives us a logical reason to respect all religions. Our shared way of making meaning manifests differently due to our differing contexts and is also dependent on the extent to which we have developed our cognitive toolkit. We will revisit meaning-making in more detail in the last chapter, as this is one of the major insights we want to share with you. Through this book we want to help people love and celebrate the beautiful diversity that exists among us and see this diversity as an opportunity rather than a threat.

When I started to entertain the idea of digging deeper into these commonalities, I was cautioned by my friends in different divinity schools: 'Don't forget about the particularities of each religion.' I took that advice seriously. I respect and appreciate the diverse particularities we find in religions just as I appreciate diversity in all aspects of our existence.

---

[1]Aldous Huxley, *The Perennial Philosophy* (New York, London: Harper & Brothers, 1945).

[2]Huston Smith, *The Illustrated World's Religions* (New York: HarperCollins, 1995).

[3]Robert Kegan, *The Evolving Self: Problem and Process in Human Development* (Cambridge, Mass: Harvard University Press, 1982).

I am convinced, however, that we are not as familiar as we should be with the deep *commonalities* that exist in our religions. These become clearer if we interpret the stories metaphorically rather than literally. We hope that after reading this book you will see some particularities in a new light, which just might expunge some degree of exclusivism in the world. In turn, we can all develop more affinity with the other and approach each other with a sense of curiosity, appreciating the beauty of diversity.

There is a well-known story in Indian religious texts, including texts of Hinduism and Buddhism, about an elephant and a group of blind men. Because they are blind, the men must rely on their sense of touch to examine the elephant. Since they are all touching different parts of the animal—the trunk, the tail, the tusks, etc.—they all come to very different conclusions as to the identity of what they're touching. And thus, the elephant can only be seen for what it is by the blind men if they each share and piece together their findings.

This is how we should understand religion: each of the major prophets were dealing with limited information and resources based on their historical and geographical contexts. Furthermore, their insights had to be constrained in ways that would be communicable to their own people, rather than the people of other continents where they were unable to travel. Nevertheless, their teachings all contain truths about humanity and the universe, and if we, today, pooled together these different, smaller truths, we collectively would be closer to the bigger truth.

Today, in a world of globalization, religious communities wrestle with the question of how their collective identities are to service this ongoing cultural diversification. They struggle to maintain their age-old traditions in the face of pluralism. In the words of Diane Moore of Harvard University:

> Religions have functioned throughout human history to inspire and justify the full range of agency from the heinous to the heroic. Their influences remain potent at the dawn of the 21st century in spite of modern predictions that religious influences would steadily decline in concert with the rise of secular democracies and advances in science. Understanding these complex religious influences is a critical dimension of understanding modern human

affairs across the full spectrum of endeavors in local, national, and global arenas.[4]

My dream is that this book will be a first step to help all of us to appreciate the diversity of different ethical systems and inform our own convictions by learning with and from others. By learning about others, we learn more about ourselves. Montaigne believed that human learning came from interacting with different people and their foreign lands, in a sense, by 'rubbing our brains against other people's'. And Francis X. Clooney, S.J., Parkman Professor of Divinity, Harvard University, explains how, 'When we go to other parts of the world and see things that might change our lives, we still come back home. It is just that "home" is now a little different, too. Why can't we do that intellectually and religiously as well?'[5] I hope your time with this book will be just such a journey that changes the way you see your world.

Put in the language of our present-day circumstances, in the midst of a once-in-a-lifetime deadly pandemic, there is another virus that has corrupted our hearts and minds. Its symptoms include prejudice based on race, rank, region, various 'isms', bigotry, extremist forms of religion, and other related social problems. In a broader sense, these are all manifestations of the problem of self versus the other. So long as a critical mass of us remain unvaccinated against the virus causing this problem, we will not have a healthy society and we will not be able to fully flourish as a species. As writer and documentarian Raoul Martinez notes, what we need is 'a potent antidote to the worst excesses of arbitrary identification; to the sorts of narrow, entrenched, dogmatic worldviews that drive us to kill and die for flags, symbols, Gods, and governments whose connection to us is no more than accidental.'[6]

---

[4]Diane L. Moore, 'Diminishing Religious Literacy: Methodological Assumptions and Analytical Frameworks for Promoting the Public Understanding of Religion', in *Religious Literacy in Policy and Practice*, ed. Adam Dinham and Matthew Francis (UK: Policy Press, 2016), 27.

[5]Francis X. Clooney, interview by Wendy McDowell, Harvard Divinity School, December 2009.

[6]Raoul Martinez, *Creating Freedom: The Lottery of Birth, the Illusion of Consent, and the Fight for Our Future* (New York: Vintage Books, 28 November 2017), 28.

I see UEF as working towards the development of a vaccine against the insidious virus that prevents us from extending unconditional love towards one another.

How to read this book (and how not to)

Let us start with the 'how not'. This book should not be read as a comprehensive survey of all the world's religions and all of the most important scriptures, beliefs, and practices therein. This is a near-impossible task for a single book of this length to tackle. Similarly, the shared themes we are extracting from the religious materials we choose to examine are not comprehensive—there are many more such themes we could have highlighted. Our thematic selections are meant to be those most relatable and most relevant to our present-day globalized world.

When we point out similarities, we are not trying to claim equivalences: these are two different things. The existence of similarities does not deny the existence of differences, and vice versa. Furthermore, conscious of the moral and political implications of comparing material from a variety of both Western and non-Western traditions, we are not arguing for the superiority of any one individual or group of individual religious traditions over others; that would be perfectly counter-productive to the efforts of this book. We are not arguing that any one religion is more 'true' than any others, nor are we interested in arguing in favour of any other particular view of the ultimate objective truth of reality—this is not a metaphysical or theological book.

This book should be read as a somewhat instructive guidebook for how to be more conscious of these comparative threads that we are constantly weaving across cultural boundary lines and how to ask the right kinds of questions about what those comparisons tell us not just about the unfamiliar other, but also about ourselves.

This book should also be read with the intention of thinking more deeply about the common religious themes that we have identified, using a plurality of resources from various traditions. Fostering cross-cultural dialogue is an important part of this book, but the self-investigative and self-transformative potential of this book lies in how deeply you think about how the actual content of the materials—what the religions are actually saying about each of these themes—and how those insights can potentially be relevant for you and your lived existence, whether you are religious or not.

As you read this book, which contains ideas and beliefs from various religious traditions, you will inevitably encounter things with which you fundamentally (maybe even vehemently) disagree. Pretend that is not the case. You will get more out of it that way. In other words, pretend everything that these religious texts are saying is true. If you read in this way, you will have an easier time with temporarily inhabiting another world and another mode of consciousness different from your own. If afterwards your opinions and beliefs remain unchanged, you may at least have gained a better sympathetic understanding for why a particular religious tradition holds the beliefs and practices that it does. As the scholar of comparative theology Michelle Voss Roberts puts it:

> When I read the texts of two traditions together, they suggest things to me as a reader that they would not if read alone. They resonate together and strike chords within me, but there is no rule to determine how this will happen for me or for anyone else.[7]

We want to make these texts talk to one another, and we want you to listen in on this conversation, but we also want you to jump in when possible and join in the conversation. If you talk to the texts, they will talk back. Or, as a widely used metaphor in the study of religion would have it, when you look in the mirror the reflection will look back at you. Perhaps you will see something you had not seen before. Finally, we hope to show that at this point in human history we have amassed enough knowledge and wisdom across many aspects of life and the universe to be able to put together comprehensive schemes of understanding the world and our place in it in a meaningful way that will allow us to live more intelligently and peacefully, so as to promote human flourishing in the world.

---

[7]Michelle Voss Roberts, *Tastes of the Divine* (New York: Fordham University Press, 2014), 14.

The World's Major Religions

Christianity

Christianity is the most popular religion in the world with 2.4 billion followers. It began during the first century CE in the Roman Empire, following the death of Jesus of Nazareth, whom Christians believe to be the son of God, foretold as the Messiah in the Hebrew Bible. Christianity's primary scripture, the Holy Bible, comprises of both of the Hebrew Bible (which Christians call the Old Testament) and the New Testament, which records the life of Jesus as well as new laws and commandments. Throughout its history, Christianity has undergone two major schisms: first, between the Catholic and Orthodox churches, and then, between Catholicism and Protestantism, which itself has branched off into many sects.

Islam

Islam is the world's second-most-popular religion with 1.8 billion followers. Islam's founding prophet Muhammad lived from 570 CE to 632 CE, when the religion began to spread from his native Mecca to the Middle East and Africa. The holy book, the Qur'an, is believed to be the living word of God dictated by the angel Gabriel to Muhammad; the text is also seen by Muslims as the final revelation, following the Old and New Testaments. And so, the Qur'an teaches Muslims to show special respect to Jews and Christians (or the people of the book). These three religions are grouped together as the Abrahamic religions, as Abraham was the first prophet to form a covenant with God. Following Muhammad's death, Islam split into two factions over succession: the Sunnis and the Shias. A third minority sect, known as Sufi Islam, went the way of mysticism.

Judaism

Judaism began in the Middle East and was started by the founding prophet Abraham, who is believed to have lived around 2000–1700 BCE. Judaism is often seen as the world's first major and enduring monotheistic religion, i.e. a religion that believes in only one God. The core scriptural texts are collected into a body of works known as the Tanakh or Hebrew Bible, which includes the Torah. These books recount the history of the Jews, God's chosen people, as their faith is repeatedly tested through trial and hardship. Hence, Jews emphasize their shared ethnic and cultural identity and ancestry. This is why Judaism has a relatively low global population, as Jews are encouraged to marry within the community and conversion is a rare and laborious process.

Baha'i

The Baha'i faith, like Judaism, has a small presence across the globe. Unlike Judaism, Baha'i is a very new faith, having formed in the nineteenth century in Persia. The central founding figure is the prophet Bahá'u›lláh, who recorded his revelations in the sacred texts, the Kitáb-i-Aqdas and the Kitáb-i-Íqán. Central to the theology of the faith is the idea of progressive revelation—that the same one God has operated throughout human history, sending various prophets to different places on earth. Hence, all the major prophets of each religion are thought to be messengers of the same God and all religions are to be respected as different expressions of the same truths. In addition to the Baha'i texts, followers are encouraged to study the scriptures of all major religions.

Hinduism

Hinduism began on the Indian subcontinent around five thousand years ago, although proto-forms of the religion had existed long before that in the region. This is why it is deemed the oldest religion in the world. Hinduism is somewhat unique in having no particular founder or prophet. Theologically, Hinduism is also unique in the nuanced balance held between monotheism and polytheism. Generally, Hindus believe in one God, who can have a plurality of forms. So, a vast pantheon of Hindu deities represents different characteristics of God. It is sometimes said that there are as many 'Hinduisms' as there are Hindus. Hinduism has a vast literature of scriptures, including the Vedas, the Upanishads, the Puranas, and two lengthy epics—the Ramayana and the Mahabharata, which contains the Bhagavad Gita.

Sikhism

Sikhism was a reformist religion founded in the fifteenth century CE in India by Guru Nanak, with the famous proclamation: 'There is no Hindu. There is no Muslim.' This statement reflects the Sikh belief in unity and equality of humankind, and the conviction that no single religion holds exclusive access to the truth. It is a monotheistic religion, believing in one God, and its main holy text is called the Guru Granth Sahib. Sikhs treat this holy text both as a scripture laying down their central tenets of belief and practice, but also as a living Guru. The Sikh appearance is easily identifiable by the distinctive head-covering, as well as the five other required markers: uncut hair, a wooden comb, an iron bracelet, a cotton undergarment and an iron dagger, all of which must be carried at all times.

Jainism

Jainism is an ancient Indian religion, dating back to at least the sixth century BCE—during which time the last major prophet of the faith, Mahavira, lived. The Jain scriptures are known as Agamas and were transmitted orally. The defining feature of the faith is strict adherence to the principle of 'ahimsa' or non-violence. Conservative Jains carry small brooms and wear face masks so as to not accidentally kill any tiny creatures (which might be too tiny to see) by sitting on them or breathing them in, respectively.

Buddhism

Buddhism came into being by branching off from Hinduism. This process started in the fifth century BCE by the founder Siddhārtha Gautama, who later became 'the Buddha' (the Awakened One). Many Buddhist concepts are drawn from Hinduism—including reincarnation, karma, and enlightenment—and practices, like meditation, are also common to both. However, the distinct insight the Buddha offered revolved around the concept of 'dukkha' (translated as 'suffering' that characterizes the human condition). In his Four Noble Truths, the Buddha taught (1) Life is fundamentally characterized by suffering, (2) The cause of suffering is desire, (3) An end to suffering is possible, and (4) The eightfold path is the process by which one gets enlightenment and escapes suffering by ending the cycle of reincarnation. Like Hinduism, Buddhism has a vast literature but no central text.

Confucianism

Confucianism is, of course, named after Confucius (born in 551 BCE), the famed Chinese teacher and philosopher most known for his many aphorisms and pieces of sage wisdom, which can be found in the central Confucian text, The Analects. Other key texts include the I Ching and the Five Classics (both of which pre-date Confucius), as well as the Doctrine of the Mean, the Great Learning, and the Book of Mencius, written by his followers. It is impossible to overestimate the profound impact that Confucius had on the course of Chinese history as these texts have functioned as the backbone of the Chinese educational system for thousands of years and Confucian virtues constitute the moral, ethical and political culture of the nation.

Taoism

Taoism arose in China around the same time as Confucianism. Whereas Confucianism emphasized structure with its strict social rules, routines and rituals, Taoism responded against this rigidity with concepts like 'wu wei', meaning effortless action, or to essentially let oneself be guided by the patterns and phenomena of nature, following the mysterious 'Tao' or the Way. Taoism also emphasizes a belief in non-dualism, in which the many seemingly opposing forces in the universe (light and dark, male and female, birth and death, etc.) are actually complementary, famously visualized through the yin yang symbol. While Taoism does not have a founder, three texts attributed to three foundational individuals stand out the most: the Tao Te Ching by Lao Tzu, the Book of Chuang Tzu, and the Book of Lieh Tzu.

1

Only One Universal God

Some would deny any legitimate use of the word God because it has been misused so much. Certainly it is the most burdened of all human words. Precisely for that reason it is the most imperishable and unavoidable.[1]

—Martin Buber

In all theistic religions, whether they are polytheistic or monotheistic, God stands for the highest value, the most desirable good. Hence, the specific meaning of God depends on what is the most desirable good for a person.[2]

—Erich Fromm

I remember when my classmate from Stanford Business School, Dan Rudolph, then the Chief Operating Officer of Stanford Business School, visited me in India from California with his family. His two daughters, seven and nine years old respectively, who were raised in a devout Christian family, got quite fascinated by Hindu mythology.

---

[1]Martin Buber, *I and Thou* (New York: Simon & Schuster, 1996), 123-24.

[2]Erich Fromm, *The Art of Loving*, Fiftieth Anniversary Edition (New York: HarperCollins, 2006), 59.

They carried home small figurines of Lakshmi (the Goddess of wealth), Saraswati (the Goddess of knowledge) and Ganesha (the God of fortune). Later one day, when one of the daughters was going to school in California, her mom anxiously wished her good luck for her test. She reassured her mother with the open-hearted, playful confidence younger children so often display: 'Mom, nothing to worry about. I've got Ganesha in one pocket and Saraswati in the other pocket so I'm completely taken care of!' In our innocence, and as children, we can quite easily and naturally incorporate the concepts of different religions and mythologies into our lives.

I was born in Old Delhi which, to this day, remains one of the most religiously pluralistic places in the world. As a child, I was exposed to the living traditions of many religions and used to be fascinated by the diversity and the commonalities across religions. In adulthood, these commonalities were reinforced through more text-based theological evidence as I looked more closely at the scriptures of all major religions.

Initially, this lesson came to me through the teachings of my parents and a particular scriptural passage from the Rig Veda: *'Ekam sat vipra bahuda vadanti'* (Truth is one, but the wise men know it as many).[3] This is echoed in the Qur'an, which affirms that the same truth is being spoken in 'monasteries, churches, synagogues, and mosques, in which the name of God is commemorated in abundant measure.'[4] Similarly, Guru Nanak, the founder of Sikhism (the fifth largest religion in the world with twenty-five million followers), taught that, 'There is one God, named truth, the creator, without fear, without hate, timeless in form, beyond birth, self-existent, (known by) the grace of the Guru.'[5]

In brief, regardless of whether or not the specific term 'God' is used, all religions revolve around the search for some ultimate first principle of existence—whether or not this first principle is depicted as a single conscious being, a plurality of conscious beings, or as an impersonal force; these are all human-made metaphors for the same *something* that

---

[3]Wendy Doniger, trans, *The Rig Veda* (New York: Penguin, 2005), I.164.46.

[4]Qur'an, 22:40 (Yusuf Ali).

[5]Guru Nanak, *Guru Granth Sahib*, Ang 1, *Sikhism: A Very Short introduction,* trans. Eleanor Nesbitt (Oxford: Oxford University Press, 2016), 22-24.

cannot be perceived by us directly.

Thus, it is only natural for the same God to be understood differently across all religions, as all appearances are simply metaphorical approximations meant to illustrate certain aspects of God. Each religion has its own beliefs about *how* God should be imagined and worshipped, but this does not mean we are all imagining a *different* God.

In the Laṅkāvatāra Sūtra, this concept is explained beautifully by the Buddha:

> Objects are frequently known by different names according to different aspects that they present—the god Indra is sometimes known as Shakra, and sometimes as Purandara. These different names are sometimes used interchangeably and sometimes they are discriminated, but different objects are not to be imagined because of the different names, nor are they without individuation. The same can be said of myself as I appear in this world of patience before ignorant people and where I am known by uncounted trillions of names. They address me by different names not realizing that they are all names of the one Tathagata.[6]

In Hinduism, God is thought to be far too mysterious and all-encompassing to be accurately depicted within a single representation. So instead, Hindus depict God in the form of a vast pantheon of beings ('Gods') with both human-like and animal-like qualities that each represent the different ways through which God is manifested throughout the universe. This allows each Hindu to form their own personal connection to God based on each person's subjective preference for one or more of these representations over others. Devdutt Pattanaik, an Indian mythologist and author, sums this up well: 'The idea of 330 million Hindu deities is a metaphor for the countless forms by which the divine makes itself accessible to the human mind.'[7] Because we are all different, we all imagine God in different ways, and

---

[6]'Lankavatara Scripture' (12:4) in *A Buddhist Bible*, ed. Dwight Goddard, trans. D.T. Suzuki (Boston: Beacon Press, 1994), 344.

[7]Devdutt Pattanaik, *Myth = Mithya: A Handbook of Hindu Mythology* (India: Penguin Books India, 2008), 5.

Hindus are very conscious of this fact in their rituals of worship. The particular conception of God that each person chooses to implement in pursuing this shared goal of seeking connection with God is akin to one liking the colour yellow while another likes green. The God or Goddess you choose to focus on is simply a personal choice; it doesn't indicate any kind of superiority or inferiority in one's particular form of belief or worship. What matters is the intention and practice itself. While a particular deity can help you deepen your intention in worship, it doesn't make your God or Goddess *better* than anyone else's God or Goddess.

Hinduism is, therefore, considered to be an example of a style of worship known as 'henotheism', in which the existence of a single and overarching God is recognized alongside the more direct worship of lesser Gods and Goddesses; there are many examples of henotheism outside of Hinduism also. One example we can point towards is the Yoruba religious tradition of West Africa, where everyone strives towards connection with the Supreme God, Olorun (also known as Olodomare). This is done primarily through fostering a personal connection with one of the 'Orishas', or anthropomorphic intermediate Gods that embody different qualities of Olorun. Another example of this is the ancient Egyptian religious movement of 'Atenism', which briefly existed alongside the otherwise polytheistic religious culture of the region and is often viewed as the earliest example of monotheism in human history. Excerpts from the 'Great Hymn to the Aten', composed in the fourteenth century BCE, certainly displays a striking resemblance to scriptural texts from the Abrahamic monotheistic religions:

> O sole god, like whom there is no other!
> Thou didst create the world according to thy desire,
> Whilst thou wert alone: All men, cattle, and wild beasts,
> Whatever is on Earth, going upon (its) feet,
> And what is on high, flying with its wings.[8]

---

[8]'The Hymn to the Aton' *The Ancient Near East – Volume 1: An Anthology of Texts and Pictures*, ed. James B. Pritchard, trans. John A. Wilson (New Jersey: Princeton University Press, 1958), 227-230.

But perhaps the most familiar example of henotheism for a Western audience is the religious landscape of ancient Greece, where each polis (city state) was typically dedicated to a particular God or Goddess, like Athens, which was named after the patron Goddess of the city, Athena. Likewise, three of the major strains of Hindu worship—Vaishnavism, Shaivism and Shaktism—involve preferential focus on the Gods Vishnu and Shiva, and the Goddess Shakti, all of whom are anthropomorphically depicted in the forms of statues and murals within their corresponding temples, just as statues of Athena and other Gods and Goddesses were common focal points in ancient Greek religion. These local Gods are paradoxically worshipped as though they are *the* God, but still, the existence of *One*—Zeus and Brahman, respectively, in these cases—is not forgotten.

Even the God of the Western monotheistic religions is not confined to a single representation. In the Hebrew Bible, God tells Moses that 'You cannot see my face, for man may not see me and live.'[9] Because of this, God must take on the forms of things that are more familiar to human beings: a burning bush, a pillar of fire, a pillar of a cloud, a booming voice or a whisper. Furthermore, there are passages from other works of Jewish literature that closely echo the Hindu concept of seeing God in many forms, like the following, from the Jewish Talmudic writings: '[T] he Holy One said: Because you see Me in many guises, do not imagine that there are many Gods.'[10] So even scripturally, God is said to recognize the fact that human beings cannot possibly comprehend his true nature except by means of indirect representation, or through a plurality of forms.

The words of scriptures, prophets, and other messengers of God remind us that religions are aware of their own metaphorical nature. Nevertheless, God is understood to be One, as reflected in the most important Jewish prayer, *'Sh'ma Yisrael Adonai Eloheinu Adonai Eḥad,'* which translates to 'Hear, O Israel, Yahweh is our God. Yahweh is one.'[11]

---

[9]Exodus 33:20 (World English Bible).

[10]Yalkut Shimoni, Yitro, 286 in Hayyim Nahman Bialik and Yehoshua Ḥana Rawnitzki, *The Book of Legends: Sefer Ha-Aggadah*, trans. William Gordon Braude (New York: Schocken Books, 1992), 79.

[11]Deuteronomy 6:4 (World English Bible).

Similarly, the most central component of worship for Muslims is the frequent affirmation of God's oneness (known as 'Tawhid') through recitation of the phrase, 'La illaha illallah' (no God but Allah). This is also expressed clearly in the Qur'an: 'And your God is one God; there is no God but He, the most gracious the most merciful.'[12] And still, Muslims too represent God in a plurality of forms—not visually, but through the ninety-nine names for God in the Qur'an, which once again represent different qualities of the same one God. Rounding out the three Abrahamic religions, all Christians believe that God is one, but many sects also believe in the doctrine of the Holy Trinity: that this one God is manifested as the Father, the Son (Jesus Christ) and the Holy Spirit.

But what about the so-called 'non-theistic' religious traditions like Confucianism, Daoism and Buddhism? Actually, there are cases to be made here as well for the acknowledgement of one God. The main reason why the concept of God seems to be absent from these religions has to do with the degree of emphasis placed on God itself. As opposed to the Western monotheisms, in which everyday worship is centred around God, actual lived religion (as in the above-named religions) has very little to do with God directly. God is seen as too transcendent to foster a clear relationship with, and so, worship focuses more on spirits, ancestors and cosmic forces of cause and effect.

As scholar of religion Todd Tremlin observes, 'In religions that teach the existence of some ultimate power or impersonal divinity—the forces of Tao, Brahman, and Buddha-nature, the creator Gods of many African tribes and of early American deists—such ideas are almost completely ignored in favor of more personal and practical deities.'[13] For instance, Heaven ('Tian', which literally translates to 'sky') is the term used in Chinese religious traditions for an abstract and impersonal power that is sometimes seen as analogous to God. In the Analects of Confucius, one of his companions remarks that 'Life and death are a matter of destiny; wealth and honor rest with Heaven'.[14] Heaven is not represented

---

[12]The Qur'an, 2:163 (Yusuf Ali).

[13]Todd Tremlin, *Minds and Gods: The Cognitive Foundations of Religion* (Oxford: Oxford University Press, 2006), 123.

[14]Confucius, *The Analects*, trans. Annping Chang (New York: Penguin, 2014), 181.

anthropomorphically, and hence is not a popular target of day-to-day worship. However, it is still thought to be very powerful and influential with respect to human life.

A closer analogue to God in Confucius' day might be the anthropomorphic God called 'Shang-di', or simply, 'Di', a supreme God ruling over a pantheon of other anthropomorphic deities that were thought to directly affect people's welfare. But neither Tian nor Di—powerful and important as they are—find their way prominently into the mainstream religiosity of China, then or now. In the case of ancient China during the emergence of Daoism and Confucianism, scholar Ruth H. Chang describes the phenomenon of focusing attention on local Gods rather than the one God:

> While the official religion focused on a supreme Heaven, people outside the ruling court, however, mainly worshipped local cults and deities. They were more concerned with the practical abilities of divinity, and their conception of gods and spirits concentrated on things that affected people's welfare. Making propitiation was of greater importance than understanding where the powers came from, or why the powers even existed at all.[15]

From personal experience, I can confidently say that this description could just as well apply to the religious landscape of India.

Finally, Buddhism is normally seen as completely atheistic, rejecting the existence of God. Specifically, however, the Buddha rejected the idea of a *creator* God. So Buddhists do reject the existence of a personal or conscious God who created the universe, but, as popular author and Buddhist monk Nyanaponika Thera explains, they still recognize the truth of experiences that people associate with God.

> The lives and writings of the mystics of all great religions bear witness to religious experiences of great intensity, in which considerable changes are effected in the quality of consciousness [...] This relative unification of mind is then interpreted as a union or communion with the One God [...] The psychological

[15]Ruth H. Chang, 'Understanding Di and Tian: Deity and Heaven from Shang to Tang Dynasties' in *Sino-Platonic Papers*, ed. Victor H. Mair, no. 108 (September 2000), 29.

facts underlying those religious experiences are accepted by the Buddhist and are well-known to him; but he carefully distinguishes the experiences themselves from the theological interpretations imposed upon them.[16]

Thus, Buddhism recognizes and affirms those experiences across religions which are normally described as a communion with God, even acknowledging the commonality of the experience across religions. But what other religions call God, Buddhism simply declines to call by any name other than psychological experience, abiding in the unknowable mystery of any ultimate source of experience and creation. The difference lies only in the way we make meaning differently out of the same experiences, which is largely just a result of our differing cultural contexts.

We all stand on the same earth and below the same sun and moon, which provide us with the same light. We are born the same way, in our mother's womb, as a result of the union between the egg of our mother and the sperm of our father and, according to the National Human Genome Research Institute, 99.9 per cent of our genes are identical.[17] We all have the same anatomy, the same internal systems—the digestive, circulatory, endocrinal, excretory, respiratory and immune systems, which are the same across the human species. The basic structure of our brains and nervous system is the same. The chemical composition that runs through our veins is within the same expected range, regardless of skin colour, ethnicity, etc. We have the same emotions—joy, anger, sadness, curiosity, fear, etc.—and similar facial expressions correspond to those emotions. The instinctive love a mother feels for her child has always been the same across all human civilizations. If there was a different God responsible for creating each of the world's major civilizations, wouldn't we expect to see different structures of life in those populations? It should, therefore, be a natural corollary for all religions to agree that human beings across the world, and throughout history, have all been worshipping the same

[16]Nyanaponika Thera, *Buddhism and the God-Idea,* online edition (Buddhist Publication Society, 2008), 6-7.

[17]National Human Genome Research Institute, accessed on 9 July 2022, https://www.genome.gov/about-genomics/fact-sheets/Genetics-vs-Genomics.

God and that we were all created by the same God; we are children of the same God, though we still may have our differences over how this God should be worshipped.

The unity and affinity between humankind can and should be a reality because we are all children of the same God. However, a lack of religious literacy and genuine interfaith dialogue has created a rift between us, fuelled by the misguided impression that differences across religions can never be reconciled. There are several vested interests that want to create a separate identity for people of different faiths and spread false narratives of one God being superior to another. Our commonalities become clearer when we remind ourselves of our shared biology and cognitive structures, as well as the fact that many ideas and stories from across religions are meant to be interpreted metaphorically rather than literally. More on this in later chapters.

2

Ordered Universe

We are predisposed to see order, pattern, and meaning in the world, and we find randomness, chaos, and meaninglessness unsatisfying. Human nature abhors a lack of predictability and the absence of meaning. As a consequence, we tend to 'see' order where there is none, and we spot meaningful patterns where only the vagaries of chance are operating.[1]

—Thomas Gilovich

As a biological species, human beings, at all times and places, have been equipped with essentially the same cognitive and neurological makeup, and thus our brains are all inclined to perform certain operations like, for instance, seeing order in the universe. The ability to see order in the world is and always has been vital to our biological survival. Our ancestors' abilities to study and interpret the stars in the night sky enabled them to develop better navigational skills, to better understand the passage of time and to predict time-dependent phenomena like the changing of the seasons.

In addition to this survivalist need, we have an existentialist need to establish order where there is none. Due to the infinite nature of reality and the comparative limitations of our cognitive apparatus, our minds

[1]Thomas Gilovich, *How We Know What Isn't So* (UK: Simon & Schuster, 2008), 9.

are constantly trying to make some sense of what is around us and to identify causal relationships that might make existence more meaningful and predictable; our minds simply find meaninglessness and chaos unpalatable. A human life without meaning and some sense of order is a life defined by terror, anxiety and existential dread.

This compulsion for order has catalysed the creation of society, nations, corporations, all of which are institutions created in order to fill the void of chaos and meaninglessness that we would otherwise be prone to experiencing. We see this in rhythmic poetry and music. We see it in the way we look for railway timetables or in the regularity of our daily newspaper. Something as small as packing a child's bag every morning provides us with some order in our day.

Religion has been, above all, a meaning-making endeavour. Hence, identifying and explaining order in the universe should be one of the most prevalent common themes across religions. And that is exactly what we find when we look across different belief systems. In fact, William James, known as the 'father of American psychology', defined religion as 'the belief that there is an unseen order, and that our supreme good lies in harmoniously adjusting ourselves thereto'[2] and philosopher Peter Singer has defined religion as 'an audacious attempt to perceive the entire universe as a humanly significant system of order'.[3] These two descriptions raise an interesting and perennial question about order in the universe and in our meaning-making efforts. Are we imposing an order that does not really exist on to an otherwise chaotic world, or are we, in fact, identifying a harmonious order that does independently exist? Ultimately, the answer may very well be that both are true. There is a system of order that permeates the universe and that we too are part of that order and thus the way we make meaning often does accord closely with this more fundamental natural order.

One of the most basic features of order in the universe, which has been identified across religions, is the division between the human

---

[2]William James, *The Varieties of Religious Experience* (Cambridge, MA: Harvard University Press, 1985), 51.

[3]Peter L. Berger, *The Sacred Canopy: Elements of a Sociological Theory of Religion* (New York: Open Road Integrated Media, 2011), 38.

world (earth) and the divine world of deities (heaven). In Hinduism, the Rig Veda describes these two parts of the universe as two halves of an egg, with the sun as the yolk in the middle.[4] This example is a good place to start because it reproduces several basic elements shared across religions: heaven and earth as two balanced halves, a third interstitial space between these two and an emphasis on celestial bodies like the sun.

People in the west might be more familiar with the story of Genesis from the Judaeo-Christian traditions as an example of an ordered universe governed by complementary pairs.

> God said, 'Let there be lights in the expanse of the sky to divide the day from the night; and let them be for signs to mark seasons, days, and years; and let them be for lights in the expanse of the sky to give light on the earth;' and it was so. God made the two great lights: the greater light to rule the day, and the lesser light to rule the night. He also made the stars. God set them in the expanse of the sky to give light to the earth, and to rule over the day and over the night, and to divide the light from the darkness. God saw that it was good.[5]

Once again, the basic order of the cosmos is one of balanced duality. There are the pairs, such as heaven and earth, light and dark, day and night as well as stars (of which the sun, of course, is one) as mediating between day and night. This same idea of God creating the universe through ordered principles is taken up again in the Qur'an:

> It is He who made the sun to be a shining glory and the moon to be a light (of beauty), and measured out stages for her; that ye might know the number of years and the count (of time). Nowise did God create this but in truth and righteousness. (Thus) doth He explain His signs in detail, for those who understand.[6]

---

[4]Wendy Doniger, *Hinduism, The Norton Anthology of World Religions: Vol. 1.* ed. Jack Miles (New York: W.W. Norton & Company, 2015), 235.
[5]Gen 1:14-18 (World English Bible).
[6]Qur'an, 10:5 (Yusuf Ali).

Here, God is said to have established order to guide us and to help us understand and survive in our chaotic environment, as well as to understand God himself through feelings of awe. This is why, for much of Western civilization, maths and science went hand in hand with religion. Maths and science were seen as holy endeavours because they were the tools that allowed us to decipher the clues left to us by God. These clues were meant to help us understand the mysteries of the universe. The New Testament teaches that 'For the invisible things of him since the creation of the world are clearly seen, being perceived through the things that are made, even his everlasting power and divinity, that they may be without excuse'[7]. Similarly, Baha'u'llah, the prophet of the Baha'i faith, said that '[Nature's] manifestations are diversified by varying causes, and in this diversity there are signs for men of discernment. Nature is God's Will and is its expression in and through the contingent world.'[8] Because the order in the universe is seen as God's creation, the quest to discover the physical laws of nature can be seen as a quest towards better understanding God himself.

Of course, some scientific discoveries that were perceived to run contrary to the words of the Holy Bible were met with heavy resistance from the Catholic church, but even in many of these cases, the individuals credited with the discoveries were clergymen themselves. This is true, for instance, of both Nicolaus Copernicus—famed for his heliocentric model of the solar system—and Gregor Mendel—the monk who uncovered the role of genes in determining hereditary traits in biological organisms. As a more modern example, famed physicist Albert Einstein, though not a traditionally religious person, once remarked, 'I believe in Spinoza's God who reveals himself in the orderly harmony of what exists, not in a God who concerns himself with fates and actions of human beings.'[9] Einstein's very sense of spirituality was thus intertwined with his scientific view of the world, filled with as much awe and wonder as he experienced

[7]Romans 1:20 (World English Bible).

[8]*Tablets of Bahá'u'lláh Revealed After the Kitáb-i-Aqdas*, Baha'i Reference Library (US: Bahá'í Publishing Trust, 1988), 142, http://reference.bahai.org/en/t/b/TB/tb-10.html

[9]'Professor Einstein Declares His Faith in Spinoza's God', The Archive of the Jewish Telegraphic Agency, 28 April 1929, https://www.jta.org/1929/04/28/archive/professor-einstein-declares-his-faith-in-spinozas-God

the order in the universe. There is nothing inherently contradictory between science and religion, as each pursues the laws of the universe in different ways. Almost all of the backlash against scientific discovery from religious institutions has had more to do with politics and power than actual theology or the pursuit of truth.

We have come to understand as a species that the galaxies, stars, planets and life forms strewn throughout the otherwise disordered darkness of the universe—along with those of the past and the future—are all governed by a consistent set of laws determining their life cycles and their relationships with one another. And throughout history, religions and other belief systems have wondered who or what is responsible for the existence of these laws, as well as which laws of the universe are most relevant to our own lives. In the Bhagavad Gita, Lord Krishna, who is an avatar of the God Vishnu, tells the hero, Arjuna, that, 'Under my guidance, Nature brings forth all beings, all things animate or inanimate, and sets the whole universe in motion.'[10] In other words, the order we see in nature and the universe can be traced back to Vishnu, who is one representation of God. In Hinduism, along with other religions native to India (like Buddhism and Jainism), the concept of order in the universe is referred to as 'dharma'. As Robert Wright explains:

> Even naturalistic, 'secular' Buddhism does, I'd argue, posit a kind of 'unseen order'. As enlightenment begins to dawn, reality, which had seemed all chopped up, turns out to possess an underlying continuity, a kind of infrastructure of interconnection. Some people call it emptiness, others call it unity, but all agree that it looks less sharply fragmented than it looked before they got the picture.[11]

Turning to the religions of China, Confucianism and Taoism both sought to rectify the rift between the social order and the universal order of nature, from which we, as a species, had divorced ourselves. However, the two religions approach this common issue in different

---

[10]The Bhagavad Gita, trans. Stephen Mitchell (New York: Harmony Books, 2000), 9:10.
[11]Robert Wright, *Why Buddhism is True: The Science and Philosophy of Meditation and Enlightenment* (UK: Simon & Schuster, 2017), 262.

ways. In the *Analects,* Confucius makes use of the Chinese term 'wen' to signify something like harmony or order. Here's how translator D.C. Lau explains the term's meaning:

> In the first place, wen signifies a beautiful pattern. For instance, the pattern of the stars is the wen of heaven, and the pattern of the skin of a tiger is its wen. Applied to man, it refers to the beautiful qualities he has acquired through education.[12]

For Confucius, a life structured around rituals and education was how humanity could cultivate its own form of 'wen,' thus allowing the species to stitch itself harmoniously into the greater fabric of the universe. Ritual and educational structure was also a way of establishing peace through imposing a common moral order on a civilization that had recently been embroiled in long chaotic years of civil war. Taoist philosophy, however, sees ritual and man-made institutions as part of the problem.

But while Confucianism and Taoism disagree when it comes to the question of social order, they share a common framework for the natural order of the universe: the balance between the twin forces of 'yin' and 'yang'. The yin yang symbol that many of us are familiar with depicts a circle with one half white and one half black; each half having a kind of yolk at its centre to draw a comparison to the Vedic conception of the basic order in the universe we saw earlier. Taoism and Confucianism see all the phenomena in the entire universe as various expressions of these twin forces of yin and yang, manifesting themselves in a myriad of ways: light and dark, day and night, sun and moon, male and female, hard and soft, hot and cold, etc. As the Taoist sage Lao Tzu explains:

> Have and have not create each other
> hard and easy produce each other
> long and short shape each other
> high and low complete each other
> note and noise accompany each other
> first and last follow each other.[13]

---

[12]Confucius, *The Analects*, trans. D.C. Lau (London, England: Penguin Books, 1971), 37.
[13]Lao Tzu, *Tao te ching*, trans. Red Pine (Port Townsend: Copper Canyon Press, 2009), Chapter 2, 4.

Rather than being at odds with one another, the components of each pair are seen as complementary, each one's existence depending on the other. A proper understanding of how yin and yang interact was thought to be essential for human beings to make sense of the world around them. This is why both Confucianism and Taoism have rich histories of divination (or fortune-telling) practices. The framework of yin and yang was thought to be a powerful predictive tool since it described the order of the universe so accurately and seamlessly.

To provide another example of the worlds of science and religion overlapping in their quests to make meaning of the same world, consider the pioneering quantum physicist Neils Bohr, who was so struck by the parallelism he found between the complementarity of yin-yang and the behaviours of complementarity observed between particles at the quantum level that he designed a family coat of arms with the yin-yang symbol emblazoned in the centre.

Even an anthropomorphic species like ours has realized that there is an extraordinary order in the universe that exists independent of us—the tides, the stars or, closer to home, the ways in which our cells divide and multiply. There is order in the web of diverse lifeforms that have existed for far longer than we have. It was by apprehending the logical order running through the amazing biodiversity of the Galapagos Islands that Charles Darwin was able to formulate his theories of natural selection. There was order to be seen in the ways that different species of birds were uniquely adapted to their own specific environments, each having differently shaped beaks to suit their respective needs.

Across time and place, we are constantly finding new ways to describe the order we see in the universe. We are constantly adjusting our worldviews and behaviours accordingly. This diversity of beliefs and ideas across cultures and religions turns the mysteries of the universe into something beautiful and exciting, rather than something terrifying.

Is there some fundamental order in the universe? Is there some higher power behind it all? Do we truly have free will if the universe is predetermined in this way? Or is all this perceived order something that exists primarily in our minds? What should our response be to this sense of order around us? These are the questions that *all* religions have grappled with.

My own stance is that seeing the universe as ordered helps me see myself from a broader perspective, recognizing my own limited knowledge. I do not understand death, but I have faith that death is part of the natural order of the universe and is an important feature of how my life is meant to be. I was not responsible for my birth, nor will I be for my death, but I am at peace with the idea that I will die one day, following the order in the universe. For me, faith is less about having blind and dogmatic beliefs about unanswerable questions and more about trusting the natural order of things beyond my control. The faith I have in the ordered universe brings me peace in life. While I do maintain my own beliefs about things, they have changed and evolved throughout life due to new experiences and interactions with people who are very different from me. Scholar of religion, Marianne Moyaert writes, 'Mature faith is post critical faith. This faith is grounded in the conviction that truth emerges in the space opened up in the dialogue between conflicting perspectives.' [14] This is the kind of faith I try to cultivate in my own life.

[14]Marianne Moyaert, *In Response to the Religious Other: Ricoeur and the Fragility of Interreligious Encounters* (London: Lexington Books, 2014), 95.

3

Interconnectedness

When I look up in the universe, I know I'm small, but I'm also big. I'm big because I'm connected to the universe and the universe is connected to me.[1]

—Neil deGrasse Tyson

Let the good in me connect with the good in others, until the world is transformed through the compelling power of love.[2]

—Rebbe Nachman of Breslov

To see the universe as ordered is to see all things as interconnected. In space, a new star system is born just like a phoenix out of the fiery remnants of a dead star. The earth, and all life on it, is composed of these same remnants. This is what cosmologist Carl Sagan meant when he famously quipped, 'We are all star stuff.'[3] Our

---

[1]Neil deGrasse Tyson, *Your Ego and the Cosmic Perspective,* Big Think, YouTube, 2:38, 25 May 2013, https://www.youtube.com/watch?v=x3sPsbv3fnY.

[2]Rebbe Nachman of Breslov, *The Gentle Weapon: Prayers for Everyday and Not-so Everyday Moments: Timeless Wisdom from the Teachings of the Hasidic Master, Rebbe Nachman of Breslov,* ed. Moshe Mykoff and S. C. Mizrahi, Breslov Research Institute (Woodstock, Vermont: Jewish Lights Publishing, 1999), 47.

[3]Carl Sagan, *Cosmos,* Season 1, Episode 1, 'The Shores of the Cosmic Ocean', directed by Adrian Malone (PBS, 28 September 1980).

own star, the sun, evaporates water from lakes and rivers and oceans; the condensation then coalesces into clouds that replenish these bodies of water in an interconnected chain of events known as the water cycle. Our sun also gives life to plants, which are eaten by herbivores, and herbivores themselves are eaten by carnivorous predators, and finally, upon their death, these predators are decomposed back into the soil to provide nutrients for plants.

The careful observations of nature made by Charles Darwin almost two hundred years ago gave birth to the field of evolutionary biology, which has since come to uncover a mountain of scientific evidence to confirm that we are part of the same unbroken biological chain of life's diverse proliferation on earth. Darwin's findings gave new meaning to older wisdom and traditions that had once come to similar conclusions. In the Qur'an, for instance, it is said, 'There is not an animal (that lives) on the earth nor a being that flies on its wings but (forms part of) communities like you. Nothing have we omitted from the book and they (all) shall be gathered to their Lord in the end,'[4] and, 'O mankind! We created you from a single (pair) of a male and a female, and made you into nations and tribes, that ye may know each other (not that ye may despise each other).'[5] The Taoist sage Chuang Tzu similarly proclaimed, 'Heaven and Earth were born at the same time I was, and the ten thousand things are one with me.'[6] The Big Bang Theory has become widely adopted in the scientific community and provides similar implications: we are all part of the primordial dust that originated from the same singular source. The whole logic of the cosmos is in each of us, in every fragment of dust, in every organism along the various interwoven chains of life's evolution.

And yet, how many of us can claim to be deeply aware of all this on a daily basis? The full extent of life's interconnectedness is not always something easily apparent to us. It takes a truly grand and expansive perspective to appreciate it all. C.S. Lewis wrote, 'If you could see humanity spread out in time, as God sees it, it would not look like a lot

---

[4]The Qur'an, 6:38 (Yusuf Ali).

[5]Qur'an, 49:13 (Yusuf Ali).

[6]*Zhuangzi: Basic Writings*, trans. Burton Watson (New York: Columbia University Press, 2003), 38.

of separate things dotted about. It would look like one single growing thing—rather like a very complicated tree. Every individual would appear connected with every other.'[7] He likely had in mind passages from the New Testament that stated, 'We, who are many, are one body in Christ, and individually members of one another,'[8] and 'from whom all the body, being fitted and knit together through that which every joint supplies, according to the working in measure of each individual part, makes the body increase to the building up of itself in love.'[9]

In Hinduism, atman, the innermost true self, is said to be the same among all creatures, which are all transient expressions of the same one ultimate reality, brahman. The concepts of atman and brahman are expressed beautifully and repeatedly in the Bhagavad Gita, in which it is written, 'Those who possess this wisdom have equal regard for all. They see the same self in a spiritual aspirant and an outcast, in an elephant, a cow and a dog.'[10] Furthermore, this identical self we share with all beings connects us all. In the Brihadaranyaka Upanishad, this is expressed in a beautiful metaphor: 'As all the spokes are held together in the hub and felly of a wheel, just so in this Soul all things, all Gods, all worlds, all breathing things, all selves are held together.'[11]

In Buddhism, our interconnectedness is expressed through the concept of *pratītyasamutpāda* (dependent co-origination or dependent arising). This is a concept that is central to Buddhist philosophy, which argues that all living and non-living things around us—that we perceive as separate and distinct entities—have no real independent existence. Instead, all things arise only through their interrelatedness to other things, or a dependent arising. For instance, there is no singular thing you can point to that makes you 'you'. It is rather the continual aggregation of many different parts that makes you 'you', and this aggregation is only temporary. When we die, our bodies become broken back down

---

[7]C.S. Lewis, *The C.S. Lewis Signature Classics* (New York: HarperCollins, 2017), 146-47.

[8]Romans 12:5 (World English Bible).

[9]Ephesians, 4:16 (World English Bible).

[10]*The Bhagavad Gita*, Second Edition, trans. Eknath Easwaran (Tomales, CA: Nilgiri Press, July 2007), 5:18-19.

[11]*The Thirteen Principal Upanishads*, Brihadaranyaka Upanishad 2. 5. 14, trans. Robert Ernest Hume (UK: Oxford University Press, 1921), 104.

into separate components that then get absorbed into other living and non-living things. The same can be said of our non-material components like consciousness. The illusion of an enduring consciousness is what propagates the illusion of a self, which in turn, propagates the illusion of the world itself. In the words of the Buddha:

> And what is the origination of the world? Dependent on the eye and forms there arises eye-consciousness. The meeting of the three is contact. From contact as a requisite condition comes feeling. From feeling as a requisite condition comes craving. From craving as a requisite condition comes clinging/sustenance. From clinging/sustenance as a requisite condition comes becoming. From becoming as a requisite condition comes birth. From birth as a requisite condition, then aging and death, sorrow, lamentation, pain, distress, and despair come into play. This is the origination of the world.[12]

Buddhists teach that it is craving, or desire, that causes us to be constantly reincarnated on earth; this craving is also the cause of all of our suffering. Specifically, it is the craving that arises from our mistaken notion of having a separate and enduring self. This concept exists prominently in the history of Western antiquity as well. The Ancient Greek philosopher Anaximander reasoned, 'All things originate from one another and vanish into one another, according to necessity [...] under the dominion of time.'[13] And the clearest analogue to the Buddhist idea of *pratītyasamutpāda* is the Ancient Greek philosophical idea of 'the ship of Theseus', wherein we are invited to ponder whether or not a ship that has had each of its individual parts replaced at one time or another can still be said to be the same ship. If not, at what point does it cease to be the same ship? Similar thought experiments are invoked by Buddhists to challenge the assumption that the individual self is an enduring discrete thing that is appropriate for us to identify ourselves with.

---

[12]Thanissaro Bhikkhu, trans, 'Saṁyutta Nikāya', 12:44, *Dhamma Talks*, accessed on 14 July 14 2022 https://www.dhammatalks.org/suttas/SN/SN12_44.html.

[13]Roberto Mangabeira Unger, *The Religion of the Future* (Cambridge, Massachusetts: Harvard University Press, 2014), 13.

To use a more real-world example, modern science has revealed to us that our cells are constantly being shed and replaced by fresh cells. This happens at different rates in different parts of our body, but it happens everywhere. After roughly seven to ten years, *all* of our cells have been completely replaced. This means that there is not a single cell in your body currently that existed ten years ago! If this is true, can you still claim to be the same person? Most of us would intuitively say yes—after all, people can still recognize us as the same person from ten years ago; we retain the same set of memories, and we *feel* a sense of continuity.

And in the Avataṃsaka-sūtra, we get another Buddhist metaphor in the form of of Indrajāla (Indra's net). As author Vasuman Ravichandran explains in an article:

> Indra, the chief of gods, lives on top of Mount Sumeru. One of the artifacts he is said to possess, is a net of infinite dimension, with a glittering jewel at each of its infinite vertices. Upon examining the polished surface of one of these jewels, you see the infinite reflections of the other jewels, each of which contain the reflections of all the others, ad infinitum.[14]

Different versions of this view have, in fact, served as a cornerstone of belief systems since ancient times, such as Confucianism. As explained by Huston Smith: 'Apart from human relationships there is no self. The self is a center of relationships.'[15] As with the case of Indra's net, Confucian philosophy argues that each individual person is simply a node in a vastly interconnected net or web, which owes its existence only to the intersecting relationships between nodes. This is such a profound idea. To think that the very sense of our existence is completely dependent upon one another, that our relationships, our interactions, and our common humanity are the true essence. This underlies our being underneath the artificial ego that we take on in our adult lives. As Smith believed, it is easier to see the commonalities of our belief systems if we recognize our interconnectedness, and it

[14]Vasuman Ravichandran, *Indrajala: The Infinite Web,* Medium, 25 June 2020, https://vasuman.medium.com/indrajala-the-infinite-web-5e08a0499f87.

[15]Huston Smith, *The Illustrated World's Religions* (New York: HarperCollins, 1995), 113.

is easier to see our interconnectedness if we take time to think about our commonalities.

The famous South African theologian and social reformer Desmond Tutu expressed our social interconnectedness in his own cultural terms by explaining the meaning of the Bantu word ubuntu.

> Ubuntu is very difficult to render into a Western language. It speaks of the very essence of being human. When we want to give high praise to someone we say, 'Yu, u nobuntu'; 'Hey, so-and-so has ubuntu.' Then you are generous, you are hospitable, you are friendly and caring and compassionate. You share what you have. It is to say, 'My humanity is caught up, is inextricably bound up, in yours.' We belong in a bundle of life. We say, 'A person is a person through other persons.' It is not, 'I think therefore I am.' It says rather: 'I am human because I belong. I participate, I share.'[16]

Understanding our interconnectedness in this way is conducive to the health of any community, especially our global pluralistic society, because it frees us from feelings of competition and the pride that comes from attachment to the individual ego. The Jewish philosopher Martin Buber wrote that, 'Egos appear by setting themselves apart from other egos. Persons appear by entering into relation to other persons.'[17]

The many peoples of the earth are now socially connected like never before. In the words of the recently deceased Stephen Hawking, 'We are all now connected by the Internet, like neurons in a giant brain.'[18] Technologies like the Internet, a product of our modern life, hold the potential to actually connect us and show us our interconnectedness. We see this with the emergence and ever-expanding popularity and importance of social media. In our modern era of globalization, we are perhaps now waking up to what the Baha'i prophet Baha'u'llah had in mind when he declared that, 'The earth is but one country, and mankind its citizens.'[19] This is not some ideal vision, but a fundamental

---

[16]Desmond Tutu, *No Future Without Forgiveness* (New York: Doubleday, 1999), 29.

[17]Martin Buber, *I and Thou* (New York: Simon & Schuster, 1996), 112.

[18]Stephen Hawking, Twitter post, 2 January 2016, https://twitter.com/thescientist_sh/status/683421747522174976?lang=en.

[19]Baha'u'llah, *Tablets of Baha'u'llah Revealed after the Kitab-i-Aqdas* (Haifa: Baha'i World Centre, 1978), 167.

reality. There is no turning the clock back. We can no longer deny our interconnectedness.

And while the globalizing forces of our modern technologies are bringing us together and building bridges between different cultures, this need not cause a dissolution of our differences. Rather, when we recognize our interconnectedness, we have all the more reason to embrace our diversity. Astrophysicist Enrico Ramirez-Ruiz expressed this well in a story he shared during a recent TED Talk:

> Chichimecas believe that our essence was assembled in the heavens. And on its journey towards us, it actually fragmented into tons of different pieces [... and] those pieces fell into other people. And only by sharing them you will become more complete.[20]

In the language of the Hebrew Bible, 'Iron sharpens iron; so a man sharpens his friend's countenance.'[21] It is time for us to fully awaken to this reality of our interconnectedness and to realize that our wholeness and individual welfare depend on the welfare of others. Realizing this, it is only logical that we should choose love for the other over hate.

Nature recently impressed some crucial lessons upon us through the COVID-19 pandemic. We learned from this global event that we are interconnected and interdependent. We learned that the health of one depends upon the health of all. We can no longer afford to remain unconscious of this fact. Lise Kingo, the Chief Executive Officer of United Nations Global Compact (a voluntary UN pact between 170 countries and over 10,000 businesses to foster sustainable and socially responsible living), puts it well: 'We are interconnected with and interdependent on each other in ways we did not fully understand before.'[22] Our freedoms can't be absolute or independent from society. This pandemic has made us recognize that humankind is no master of this world—we are simply its witnesses and stewards. Caring for other species and the environment

---

[20]Enrico Ramirez-Ruiz, 'Your body was forged in the spectacular death of stars', *TED@NAS,* November 2019, https://www.ted.com/talks/enrico_ramirez_ruiz_your_body_was_forged_in_the_spectacular_death_of_stars?language=en

[21]Proverbs 27:17 (World English Bible).

[22]Lise Kingo, 'What the world could look like after COVID-19', *GreenBiz,* 10 April 2020, https://www.greenbiz.com/article/what-world-could-look-after-covid-19.

is just as vital as caring for one another. The health of people, animals and the environment in which we all live is inextricably linked.

The solidarity built during the wrath of the pandemic can help us deal with some of humanity's greatest challenges, such as climate change, as well as lingering social issues, like racism and bigotry, along with interreligious conflict. Again, Kingo captures these thoughts well: 'I can't help but think of COVID-19 as a fire drill for future global challenges. Will we be better prepared to respond to the climate emergency and other urgent sustainability challenges as a result of this experience?'[23]

As separate individuals, we may feel insignificant, but as interconnected beings, we are the world. We are connected with one another across time and space. True knowledge brings us to the acceptance of our insignificance as individuals, but it also shows us our immortality through our interconnectedness. Scholar of religion Marianne Moyaert writes, 'The human subject is not self-sufficient and solitary but can only fully develop its humanity by reaching out to others and becoming part of a historico-cultural web of relationships. Human beings are essentially directed toward one another for flourishing.'[24] Award-winning author Jeremy Lent puts this into a global perspective and brings us some much-needed optimism for the future:

> By continuing to see humans as essentially separate from nature and from each other, we've found ourselves on a path either to collapse or a bifurcation of humanity. What is ultimately required is a shift towards a new way of finding meaning from our existence—a new global consciousness, based on an underlying and all-infusing sense of connectedness.[25]

The timing for such a shift could not be better when we consider the immense progress we are making in all scientific disciplines, especially neuroscience and astrophysics; we are getting to know our

---

[23]Ibid.

[24]Marianne Moyaert, *Response to the Religious Other: Ricoeur and the Fragility of Interreligious Encounters* (London, UK: Lexington Books, 2014), 39.

[25]Jeremy Lent, *From Disconnection to Connectedness*, 2016, Jeremy Lent: Author and Integrator, accessed on 9 July 2022, https://www.jeremylent.com/sustainable-flourishing.html.

world from the inside and outside. We have scaled heights: education has spread through economic progress, accumulative knowledge has been built (through human cooperation) in the physical and social sciences, we have achieved freedom from repressive authorities through democratization and found individual agency through liberation, and finally, we have achieved interconnectedness through the internet. All of this can be leveraged to be able to spread the true wisdom of our interconnectedness.

Returning to the subject of biology and evolution with which we began, we can see this effect through yet another notable observation by Charles Darwin. He said, 'All living things have much in common, in the chemical composition, their germinal vesicles, their cellular structure and the laws of growth and reproduction. Therefore, I should infer that probably all the organic beings which have ever lived on the earth have descended from someone primordial form.'[26] In fact, this inference has turned out to be spot-on, just as geneticist and environmental activist David Suzuki notes:

> By studying DNA, molecular biologists have verified that all living organisms are genetically related [...] Through our evolutionary history, we are related to all other beings present and past—they are our genetic kin. When we see other species as our relatives rather than as resources or commodities, we will have to treat them with greater care and respect.[27]

With a growing awareness of these facts, how can we be cruel to animals, or destroy our environment? How can we go on killing people because of our prejudices and fears of the other, or because of our differences in belief? It is only ignorance of our interconnectedness that leads to these atrocities.

People from all different religions can be allies in making change. To borrow a precept from the New Testament, 'that I with you may be

---

[26]Charles Darwin, *On the Origin of Species: By Means of Natural Selection Or the Preservation of Favored Races in the Struggle for Life* (New York: Cosimo Inc., 2007), 303.

[27]David Suzuki, *The Sacred Balance: Rediscovering Our Place in Nature* (Vancouver: Greystone Books, 2009), 196-97.

encouraged in you, each of us by the other's faith, both yours and mine'.[28] Or, as Pope Francis said in his 2017 TED Talk, 'The future is, most of all, in the hands of those people who recognize the other as a "you" and themselves as part of an "us". We all need each other. Quite a few years of life have strengthened my conviction that each and everyone's existence is deeply tied to that of others.'[29] To be spiritual is to believe in the interconnectedness of everything that is or ever was, both in time and space. Albert Einstein spelled out a vision of what we must do with this information.

> [The human] experiences himself, his thoughts and feelings, as something separated from the rest—a kind of optical delusion of his consciousness [...] Our task must be to free ourselves from this prison by widening our circles of compassion to embrace all living creatures and the whole of nature in its beauty.[30]

With insights about this interconnectedness strewn through the traditions of human history, we can hopefully begin to dig ourselves out of the ignorant trenches we have been living in for so long.

---

[28]Romans 1:12 (World English Bible).

[29]His Holiness Pope Francis, 'Why the only future worth building includes everyone', trans. Elena Montrasio and filmed in Vatican City, *TED2017*, https://www.ted.com/talks/his_holiness_pope_francis_why_the_only_future_worth_building_includes_everyone/transcript?language=en.

[30]Walter Sullivan, 'The Einstein Papers. A Man of Many Parts', *The New York Times Archives*, 29 March 1972, https://www.nytimes.com/1972/03/29/archives/the-einstein-papers-a-man-of-many-parts-the-einstein-papers-man-of.html.

4

Love

[L]ove [is] the Divine energy.[1]

—C.S. Lewis

In brotherly love there is the experience of union with all men, of human solidarity, of human at-onement. Brotherly love is based on the experience that we are all one. The differences in talents, intelligence, knowledge are negligible in comparison with the identity of the human core common to all men.[2]

—Erich Fromm

The idea of love has come under intense debate and speculation throughout history. It is the most used and abused word in human history. We often confuse love with physical relationships and, thereby, only allow ourselves to see one manifestation of love. We even conflate the words love and relationship. Love is more than just being in a relationship, or lust, or romantic love, although romantic love is indeed a type of love. The classical Greek thinkers distinguished

---

[1]C.S. Lewis, *The Four Loves* (Mariner Books: New York, 2012), 827.

[2]Erich Fromm, *The Art of Loving*, Fiftieth Anniversary Edition (New York: HarperCollins, 2006), 44.

between seven types of love: eros (erotic or sexual love), philia (love of friends and friendship), storge (familial love), ludus (playful love), pragma (practical love based on duty), philautia (self-love) and agape (universal love). The highest forms of love would have us give ourselves entirely without the expectation of reciprocity. To quote the early Christian Paul of Tarsus (5–64/7 CE), from one of his letters to his early Christians at Corinth: 'Love is patient and is kind. Love doesn't envy. Love doesn't brag, is not proud, doesn't behave itself inappropriately, doesn't seek its own way, is not provoked, takes no account of evil; doesn't rejoice in unrighteousness, but rejoices with the truth; bears all things, believes all things, hopes all things, and endures all things.'[3] Paul, writing in Greek, uses the word agape. Here and elsewhere, Paul is extolling the virtues and describing the character of true universal love—love for all.

Most of us are familiar with the religious injunction to love our neighbours as we love ourselves. This, of course, is expressed clearly and famously by Jesus, who decrees, 'A new commandment I give to you, that you love one another. Just as I have loved you, you also love one another. By this everyone will know that you are my disciples, if you have love for one another.'[4] The supreme importance of loving one another is impressed upon us not just in Christianity, but in fact, by all religious traditions throughout human history.

Love may begin as a relationship with a specific person, but it ultimately must grow into a worldview that informs the way we interact with everyone and everything around us. As social psychologist Erich Fromm describes it, 'Love is not primarily a relationship to a specific person; it is an attitude, an orientation of character which determines the relatedness of a person to the world as a whole, not toward one "object" of love.'[5]

In the Jewish Talmudic writings, we see examples like 'This is what the Holy One said to Israel: My children, what do I seek from you? I seek

[3]1 Corinthians 13:4-7 (World English Bible).

[4]John 13:34-35 (World English Bible).

[5]Erich Fromm, *The Art of Loving*, fiftieth anniversary edition (New York: HarperCollins, 2006), 43.

no more than that you love one another and honor one another.'[6] Just as any good parent would want for all of their children to get along, we are told that God's greatest wish is for all of humanity to love one another, given that we are all bound as one family through a common ancestry.

The main concern of all religions is to get people to love one another, but each religion goes about describing, promoting and implementing this goal in slightly different ways. As a species, we may not have always lived up to this ideal, but it has always been written into our sacred scriptures and has been uttered by our wisest sages and prophets.

To love all of humanity, we start by learning to love small circles at a time—our immediate family, our friends, our close neighbours. The same is true of loving God—if we do not know how to love one another, then we do not even know what love is. In the Qur'an, it is suggested that the love between spouses is meant to bring us closer to loving God: 'And among His signs is this, that He created for you mates from among yourselves, that ye may dwell in tranquillity with them, And He has put love and mercy between your (hearts): verily in that are signs for those who reflect.'[7] The common message expressed here is that in loving those who are closest to us, our circle of love can gradually be expanded.

A lot of the hate present in the world comes from loving too selectively. Instead of seeing people as intrinsically worthy of love, we limit our love to the groups and individuals that are most like ourselves, at the expense of hating others. But as the Baha'i prophet Baha'u'llah declared, 'Ye were created to show love one to another and not perversity and rancour. Take pride not in love for yourselves but in love for your fellow-creatures.'[8] Just as all religions explicitly promote the importance of love, they also explicitly denounce the follies of hate. The Buddha advised his followers:

> Let no one deceive another
> or despise anyone anywhere,

---

[6]Seder Eliyyahu Rabbah, 26 in Hayyim Nahman Bialik and Yehoshua Hana Rawnitzki, *The Book of Legends: Sefer Ha-Aggadah*, trans. William Gordon Braude (New York: Schocken Books, 1992), 646.

[7]Qur'an 30:21 (Yusuf Ali)

[8]Baha'u'llah, *Tablets of Baha'u'llah Revealed after the Kitab-i-Aqdas* (Haifa: Baha'i World Centre, 1978), 138.

or through anger or irritation
wish for another to suffer.

As a mother would risk her life
to protect her child, her only child,
even so should one cultivate a limitless heart
with regard to all beings.
With good will for the entire cosmos,
cultivate a limitless heart:
Above, below, and all around,
unobstructed, without enmity or hate.[9]

Just as a mother loves her child unconditionally and with all her heart, so too should we strive to extend the fullness of our love to each and every sentient creature, without judgement or prejudice. Our own imperfections prevent us from loving everyone as they are.

Father Francis Clooney, a present-day priest of the Jesuit order, is a great exemplar of how to love expansively and unconditionally. He is also a professor who teaches classes on Hinduism and comparative theology at the Harvard Divinity School. Here I reproduce his translation of the wisdom of the Good Samaritan story from the Bible for our modern world.

> Today, this could be a person who is black or white, Christian or Jew or Muslim, native-born or just-arrived, police or criminal or innocent bystander. It doesn't matter. It is just a human being, and the test for the priest, the Levite, and the Samaritan, is how they react when they encounter another person, simply as a human being.[10]

Behind all of these artificial identity categories is the more important and authentic character of our shared humanity. And this is why it is

---

[9]Thanissaro Bhikkhu, trans, 'Sutta Nipāta,' 1:8, *Dhamma Talks*, accessed on 14 July 2022, https://www.dhammatalks.org/suttas/KN/StNp/StNp1_8.html.

[10]Francis X. Clooney, SJ, 'The Good Samaritan: in a time of violence, Jesus calls us to be neighbors to everyone who needs us', *Harvard.edu blog*, 10 July 2016, https://projects.iq.harvard.edu/francisclooney/blog/good-samaritan-time-violence-jesus-calls-us-be-neighbors-everyone-who-needs-us.

only logical to love everyone. Succinctly, St Augustine says that the guiding principle for each one of us should be, 'Love, and do what you will: [...] let the root of love be within, of this root can nothing spring but what is good.'[11]

In Hinduism, our common essence is expressed through the concepts of 'atman' and 'brahman'. We are all born with different personalities, characteristics and circumstances in life and we come to identify ourselves with them. But underlying all of this is a deeper self (atman) which unites us all as equal parts of the same ultimate oneness (brahman) permeating the universe. It is said that we are all waves of atman in the same ocean of brahman—each of us is a transient expression of the same one reality. Nisargadatta Maharaj, an Indian guru, put this poetically. 'The consciousness in you and the consciousness in me, apparently two, really one, seek unity and that is love.'[12] It is through love that we can see past our superficial differences to recognize our common essence, which is why it is said in the Bhagavad Gita, 'This supreme Lord who pervades all existence, the true Self of all creatures, may be realized through undivided love.'[13]

To invoke Erich Fromm again, love manifests 'as spontaneous affirmation of others, as the union of the individual with others on the basis of the preservation of the individual self', and 'is based on the experience that we are all one. The differences in talents, intelligence, knowledge are negligible in comparison with the identity of the human core common to all men.'[14] To revisit the brahman-ocean analogy, it is because we are all part of the same 'ocean' that we are able to so freely exchange our 'minerals'. Loving your neighbour in this way means seeing what *you* uniquely have to *give*, as well as recognizing what you will *receive*

---

[11]St Augustine, 'Homily 7 on the First Epistle of John', trans. H. Browne, *Nicene and Post-Nicene Fathers, First Series*, Vol. 7, Ed. Philip Schaff (Buffalo, NY: Christian Literature Publishing Co., 1888), Revised and edited for New Advent by Kevin Knight, http://www.newadvent.org/fathers/170207.htm.

[12]Sri Nisargadatta Maharaj, *I Am That*, (Mumbai, India: Chetana Publishing, 1973), 81.

[13]The Bhagavad Gita, Second Edition, trans. Eknath Easwaran, (Tomales: Nilgiri Press, 2007), 8:22.

[14]Erich Fromm, *The Art of Loving*, Fiftieth Anniversary Edition (New York: HarperCollins, 2006), 44.

from millions and billions of people. Learning, and sharing your acquired knowledge and experiences with the next generation, is an act of love. Hinduism prescribes three main possible pathways towards spiritual attainment: jnana yoga (the pursuit of knowledge), karma yoga (selfless action) and bhakti yoga (loving devotion). True knowledge leads to right karma which ultimately leads to love.

We all benefit from having more love in the world, and conversely, we all lose when hate prevails. Thousands of years ago, the Taoist sage Lao Tzu wrote:

> Is it not because of their selflessness
> Whatever [sages] seek they find.[15]

In fact, one of the longest running studies in the world has proven that there just might be some connection between selflessness (or love) and longevity. Since 1938, Harvard has been conducting 'The Study of Adult Development', tracking the physical and emotional well-being of more than 700 men who grew up in Boston in the 1930s and 1940s.[16] It is one of the longest and most comprehensive longitudinal studies of its kind, closely following subjects from their late teens and early twenties to their eighties and nineties. Robert Waldinger, director of the study, later explained in a TED Talk, 'The clearest message that we get from this 75-year study is this: Good relationships keep us happier and healthier. Period.'[17] Love, quite simply, is good for us. Luckily, most of us are in a position to demonstrate love for everyone in our daily lives.

Tyler J. VanderWeele, a professor at the Harvard T.H. Chan School of Public Health and director of the Human Flourishing Program at Harvard University, has similar things to say about this line of research.

---

[15]Lao Tzu, *Tao te ching*, trans. Red Pine (Washington: Copper Canyon Press, 2009), Chapter 7, 14.

[16]Harvard Study of Adult Development, accessed on 10 July 2022, https://www.adultdevelopmentstudy.org/.

[17]Robert Waldinger, 'What makes a good life: lessons from the longest study on happiness', *TEDxBeaconStreet*, November 2015, accessed on 10 July 2022, https://www.ted.com/talks/robert_waldinger_what_makes_a_good_life_lessons_from_the_longest_study_on_happiness/transcript.

> [Love] fulfills one of the deepest human yearnings for connection with others. It is no wonder, then, that the experience of love appears to affect so many health and well-being outcomes. Love is not often considered in our medical and public health discussions as to what shapes health. But perhaps that should change as more and more research points to its profound importance.[18]

Striving to love selflessly, then, is not just about following a religious commandment. Regardless of which religious tradition you subscribe to (if any), love truly is an essential component of well-being and flourishing. By loving others, we are in fact also loving ourselves in the truest sense. 'Let's stop thinking about giving as just this moral obligation and start thinking of it as a source of pleasure,' says social scientist Elizabeth Dunn.[19]

Neuroscientific studies have yielded similar insights. One study, published in the journal Annals of Behavioral Neuroscience proposes the following:

> [F]indings in neuroscience suggest that the perceived separateness is an illusion created by our brain. Nevertheless, the brain itself is endowed with the capacity to overcome this separateness by Universal Love. Spirituality is about rewiring the brain to realize this capacity. Most spiritual practices, both religious and non-religious, represent different methods to achieve this goal.[20]

Supporting this idea, another study, from the *Clinical Psychology Review*, suggests rewiring the brain to unlock more of our innate capacity for universal love to understand the effects of Loving-Kindness Meditation (LKM) and Compassion Meditation (CM).

---

[18]Tyler J. VanderWeele, 'How Parental Love Impacts Flourishing Later in Life', *Psychology Today*, 28 June 2019, https://www.psychologytoday.com/us/blog/human-flourishing/201906/how-parental-love-impacts-flourishing-later-in-life.

[19]Elizabeth Dunn, 'Helping others makes us happier—but it matters how we do it', *TED2019*, April 2019, https://www.ted.com/talks/elizabeth_dunn_helping_others_makes_us_happier_but_it_matters_how_we_do_it.

[20]Rohana Ulluwishewa, 'Spirituality, Universal Love and Sustainable Behaviour', *Annals of Behavioral Neuroscience, Volume 1*, September 2018, https://www.researchgate.net/publication/327932215_Spirituality_Universal_Love_and_Sustainable_Behaviour.

> Neuroimaging studies suggest that LKM and CM may enhance activation of brain areas that are involved in emotional processing and empathy [...and] may provide potentially useful strategies for targeting a variety of different psychological problems that involve interpersonal processes, such as social anxiety, marital conflict, anger, and coping with the strains of long-term caregiving.[21]

This suggests that even just focusing on love and compassion is enough to improve personal health across several different metrics.

It takes no great leap of the imagination to see how this could have broader implications for improving human society. Ralph Waldo Emerson once mused, 'The power of love, as the basis of state, has never been tried.'[22] Just imagine, if states were governed on the basis of love—caring for everyone's needs and well-being—rather than power or greed or personal ambition.

Looking through literature from across time and place, we see that human imagination does not lack the ideal of a world in which love triumphs and governs our entire lives. And yet, we have found this quite difficult to implement in action. But we still should not give up hope for a future where love does indeed triumph as the supreme governing value of our species. As envisioned by Pierre Teilhard de Chardin, a Catholic Jesuit priest who wrote extensively about the future of humanity, 'The day will come when, after harnessing the ether, the winds, the tides, gravitation, we shall harness for God the energies of love. And, on that day, for the second time in the history of the world, man will have discovered fire.'[23]

---

[21]Stefan G. Hofmann, Paul Grossman, and Devon E. Hinton, 'Loving-Kindness and Compassion Meditation: Potential for Psychological Interventions', *Clinical Psychology Review*, 31 November 2011, https://www.ncbi.nlm.nih.gov/pmc/articles/PMC3176989/.

[22]Ralph Waldo Emerson, *The Collected Works of Ralph Waldo Emerson* (Musaicum Books, 2018).

[23]Pierre Teilhard De Chardin, 'The Evolution of Chastity' (1934) in *Toward the Future*, trans. René Hague (San Diego, California: Harcourt, 1975), 86-87.

5

Flawed Human Condition

The human desire to transcend the limitations of the physical is a completely natural one. To journey from the boundary-based individual body to the boundless source of creation—this is the very basis of the spiritual process.[1]

—Sadhguru

The human being is an open possibility, incomplete and incompletable. Hence he is always more and other than what he has brought to realization in himself.[2]

—Karl Jaspers

We like to think of ourselves as special when compared to other creatures. But the reality is that we, too, are bound by our material limitations—or, at least, this is how we experience the world around us. We are severely limited in our sensory capacities, only experiencing a very narrow range of the full spectrum of sights, sounds and smells that exist all around us, escaping our

[1]Jaggi Vasudev (Sadhguru), *Inner Engineering: A Yogi's Guide to Joy,* (New York: Spiegel & Grau, 2016), 92.

[2]Karl Jaspers, *General Psychopathology: Volume 2,* trans. J. Hoenig and Marian W. Hamilton (Baltimore: Johns Hopkins University Press, 1997), 766.

awareness. We can't be in two places at once and our lives are too short to experience any more than a fraction of even this limited bounded world. There are limits to our knowledge and perceptions of the world around us.

The fact is that we are endowed with limited cognitive ability compared to the infinite and complex reality we face. What compounds this is that we also develop cognitive biases as we grow up in our respective societies, like confirmation bias, negativity bias, anchoring bias, and so on. For each of us, what we believe to be the absolute truth is merely built on a database of conditioning and information, including that of our genes.

Religions remind us of how incomplete our perceptions of reality are and, in some cases, teach us ways to make these perceptions more complete. We are inherently flawed beings, and that is a reality that all religions have acknowledged and confronted in a variety of ways. But this fact does not have to plunge us into despair nor should it console us with false promises. Rather, the value in understanding this common theme across religions is to be able to uncover the tangible actions and attitudes that can actually improve our flawed condition.

In his book *The Religion of the Future*, Harvard professor Roberto Unger posits four major features of our flawed condition: mortality, groundlessness, insatiability and belittlement. The first two are unavoidable and unchangeable—we can prolong life, but we cannot prevent death; we can search for the ground upon which we stand and the ultimate purpose for which we were created, but we will never arrive at a definitive answer. This compounds the difficulty of dealing with our insatiability, as we have a hard time with questions that have no answers. Unger describes how the world religions address these flaws in terms of three broad categories: by (1) 'overcoming the world', which is emphasized in Hinduism, Buddhism and Taoism. He proposes that our flaws are rooted in our illusory understanding of the world itself, and which can be overcome through contemplative practices that rewire the mind; by (2) 'humanizing the world', a concept primarily represented by Confucius, which focuses on imposing an artificial social order on a world that is otherwise chaotic and without order; by (3) 'struggling with the world', as exemplified by the Abrahamic religions, which refers to the corrupted nature of earthly life and is meant to test our character by constantly tempting us with sin (from which we must refrain in order to achieve salvation). Literal understandings of these doctrines seem to primarily respond to mortality, groundlessness and insatiability, but if we interpret them more metaphorically, we can see how they can help us reduce our sense of belittlement and live a meaningful life.

Belittlement is what Unger seizes on as the most promising term of what religion can offer us, since it refers to our *attitude* towards our condition, which is something we can repair. This is why Unger calls for a greater focus on this theme.

> What we are to do about our susceptibility to belittlement has always been a theme in the religious consciousness of humanity. For the more than twenty-five hundred years that witnessed the emergence, and influence of the present world religions, it has, however, remained largely a subterranean theme.[3]

So what is belittlement? It is the sense of smallness and insignificance we feel in relation to the great chorus of life around us, along with the feelings of alienation that we feel at a deep existential level. We crave purpose, not just as individuals but also as members of the most intelligent, self-aware species. Humans are the only lifeforms (that we know of) that have a huge amount of excess psychic energy compared to others—in other words, whereas animals are constantly caught up in meeting their basic biological needs, we have more leisure to apply our thoughts to other endeavours. There is an irony here. We are the most advanced form of life, but somehow, the most unfinished and hence flawed. We do not know how to deploy our psychic energy productively in a way that satisfies us; that is the cause of our flawed condition. By contrast, we envy the creatures around us who seem to know and love their roles, and who seem to thrive in our absence. What, then, is our role? Why are we here? What is it that we are meant to contribute to this chorus? Why do we feel like castaways in our own home? Why are we so fractured and flawed in comparison to the harmony of the natural world?

---

[3]Roberto Mangabeira Unger, *The Religion of the Future* (New York: Verso, 2016), 26.

The first step each of these religious traditions have taken in responding to these questions is by attempting to explain how or why we were created in such a flawed manner in the first place. A major commonality we see in the responses to this question is the narrative of some kind of 'fall' from a more perfect original state. For many people, the first example that might come to mind is the biblical narrative of Genesis from the religions of Judaism, Christianity and Islam: the original sin of Adam and Eve of eating forbidden fruit in the Garden of Eden, which resulted in their expulsion, thus dooming our species to be stripped of immortality and made to live in a harsher and more chaotic environment on earth. There are, in fact, very similar narratives in other religions, such as Taoism. Translator Martin Palmer describes the Taoist sage Chuang Tzu's conception of humanity's fall: 'He pictures a perfect world when all were equal and none had any sense of being greater or lesser. They just followed their innate nature. He then depicts the fall from this age of primal, innate, natural living.'[4]

However, the situation is not hopeless. Chuang Tzu, along with a subsequent line of Taoist sages and thinkers, believed that people could recapture some of this innate nature by striving for simplicity in life and by learning through careful observation about the world as it truly is, beyond the prejudices of human socialization. They even believed it was possible to attain immortality by cultivating the 'Tao' and harmonizing the forces of yin and yang.

Another 'fall' narrative comes from the Hindu tradition, as described by Indian writer Vilas Sarang.

> [T]he One caused himself to fall into two pieces; 'cause to fall' is in Sanskrit pat. The one caused himself to fall into two pieces, a husband and a wife, which, in Sanskrit, is pati and patni. A husband and a wife were born.[5]

Hindus believe that they are potentially divine. They use the phrase,

---

[4]Martin Palmer, *The Book of Chuang Tzu,* Penguin Classics edition, trans. Martin Palmer (New York: Penguin Books, 2006), xxiii.

[5]Wendy Doniger, *Hinduism, The Norton Anthology of World Religions: Vol. 1,* ed. Jack Miles (New York: W.W. Norton & Company, 2015), 691.

'Aham Brahmasmi', which translates to 'I am Brahman, the Creator'. Hindus believe in a true self (or soul) that is immortal, but through the corrupting force of 'maya' (illusion), these very souls end up attached to artificial ego selves. Clinging to this ego self is what keeps us trapped in *samsara*, the endless cycle of birth and death in both Hindu and Buddhist thought. Across religions, this fall is one way of accounting for the existence of birth and death, our feelings of groundlessness, and the insatiable desires of our ego selves, which also contribute to our feelings of belittlement.

But for every fall narrative there is a prescribed path back to a more whole state of being. Hindus developed the four yogas—karma (action), bhakti (devotion), jnana (knowledge), raja (meditation)—the practice of which leads to the realization of our divine potential. In Islam and Christianity, our flawed condition is a form of punishment from God, but we can reverse this through good deeds and faith. The Qur'an says, 'We have indeed created man in the best of molds, then do we abase him (to be) the lowest of the low—except such as believe and do righteous deeds: for they shall have a reward unfailing.'[6] And in the Christian tradition, Athanasius, the fourth-century bishop of Alexandria, stated, 'the Son of God became man so that we might become God.'[7]

The promises of escaping or transcending death are, of course, metaphysical speculations, but the flaws in our thoughts, attitudes and behaviour can be understood and overcome if illuminated. In the biblical book of Romans, Paul muses, 'We know that the law is spiritual, but I am fleshly, sold under sin. For I don't know what I am doing. For I don't practice what I desire to do; but what I hate, that I do.'[8] And in the Qur'an it is written, 'Truly man was created very impatient;—fretful when evil touches him and niggardly when good reaches him;—not so those devoted to prayer.'[9] If we think of fall narratives as metaphorical, they can be read as reminders not to 'fall' back into the selfish and individualistic

[6]Qur'an 95:4-6 (Yusuf Ali).

[7]St. Athanasius, 'On the Incarnation,' in *English Translation of the Cathechism of the Catholic Church for the United States of America,* 1997, accessed on 10 July 2022, https://www.catholicculture.org/culture/library/catechism/cat_view.cfm?recnum=2153.

[8]Romans 7:14-15 (World English Bible).

[9]The Qur'an, 70:19-22 (Yusuf Ali).

impulses that are remnants of our evolutionary past. Instead, we can behave with the understanding that, to borrow a phrase from Unger's book, we are 'incomplete in ourselves, we complete ourselves through service to others'.[10] If we see ourselves as separate individuals, then of course we will feel a constant sense of belittlement. We will needlessly strive in vain to overcome it by pursuing selfish desires, which will bring us only moments of fleeting pleasure. As Pope Francis explains, it is love that allows us to escape this hamster wheel of worldly desires: 'If you are looking for meaning in life but, not finding one, you throw yourself away with "imitations of love", such as wealth, career, pleasure, or an addiction, let Jesus look at you, and you will discover you have always been loved.'[11] We can escape belittlement by recognizing that we are each, unique parts of the rich tapestry of the human species, and that our best selves are only attainable through loving and learning from one another.

Another religion that heavily stresses on the importance of overcoming worldly and selfish desires is Buddhism. Buddha's primary message was that life is fundamentally characterized by suffering, and that all suffering is ultimately caused by desire. This may sound bleak, but Buddhist monk and translator Bhikkhu Bodhi alludes to a famous Buddhist allegory to explain why religions that primarily emphasize love and empathy are sometimes misunderstood as pessimistic or fatalistic for focusing so much on human flaws.

> If a man does not know that his house is on fire, he lives there enjoying himself, playing and laughing. To get him to come out we first have to make him understand that his house is on fire. In the same way the Buddha announces that our lives are burning with old age, sickness and death. Our minds are flaming with greed, hatred and delusion. It is only when we become aware of the peril that we are ready to seek a way to release.[12]

---

[10]Unger, Roberto Mangabeira, *The Religion of the Future* (Cambridge: Harvard University Press, 2014), 93.

[11]Pope Francis, Twitter Post, 27 June 2020, https://twitter.com/pontifex/status/1276840197691371522.

[12]Bikkhu Bodhi, *Nibbana (Nirvana)* (1981) in 'Why did the Buddha teach the Noble Truth of suffering?' YouTube video, 29 September 2021, https://www.youtube.com/watch?v=m8zEWml3000

All too often, we go through life in denial of our inherent flaws, both physical and mental. Until we pay attention to these flaws, we will never achieve an understanding of which ones are correctable and the mechanisms by which they can be corrected. The seemingly pessimistic aspects of Buddhism are meant to convey a sense of urgency so we may deal with these matters sooner rather than later, just as we would if our house was on fire.

There is no shame in making mistakes. We all make mistakes! We should only be ashamed if we continue to make the same mistakes without learning. This is what Confucius meant when he said, 'To fail to cultivate virtue, to fail to practice what I have learned, not to direct my steps toward what is right when I know what that is, and to make mistakes and not be able to correct them—these are the things that worry me.'[13] A similar message is expressed in the Old Testament: 'a righteous man falls seven times and rises up again; but the wicked are overthrown by calamity.'[14] Even as children, we correct flaws in our behaviour by learning from mistakes. We touch a hot stove out of curiosity and learn not to do this again; we run around without being careful, tripping and scraping our knees, then become cautious.

The great religious prophets and scriptures urge us to apply the same reasoning to our psychological and spiritual lives, correcting our flaws through proper guidance. And we can learn to do this early in life with the right kind of education, as the Baha'i leader, Shoghi Effendi, explains,

> In fact Bahá'í education, just like any other system of education, is based on the assumption that there are certain natural deficiencies in every child, no matter how gifted, which his educators, whether his parents, schoolmasters, or his spiritual guides and preceptors, should endeavour to remedy [...]The child when born is far from being perfect. It is not only helpless, but actually is imperfect.[15]

---

[13]Confucius, *The Analects*, trans. Annping Chin. (New York: Penguin, 2014), 7:3.
[14]Proverbs, 24:16 (World English Bible).
[15]From a letter dated 9 July 1939 written on behalf of Shoghi Effendi to an individual believer in *A Compilation on Bahá'í Education*, Baha'i Reference Library,(Bahá'í World Centre: Research Department of the Universal House of Justice, August 1976), 49-50, http://reference.bahai.org/en/t/c/BE/be-123.html.

As adults, we can learn how to train ourselves, staying vigilant with a kind of inner wakefulness. When we feel anger or jealousy or hate, for instance, we can investigate where those feelings are coming from and which experiences seem to trigger them; we can decide whether those feelings make our lives (and that of others) better or worse.

Religious practices (like prayer, meditation, yoga and various rituals) are designed with such purposes in mind. They help us mitigate and correct our flaws over time. Philosopher Pierre Hadot has commented on the spiritual and philosophical traditions of ancient Greece.

> All schools agree that man, before his philosophical conversion, is in a state of unhappy disquiet. Consumed by worries, torn by passions, he does not live a genuine life, nor is he truly himself. All schools also agree that man can be delivered from this state. He can accede to genuine life, improve himself, transform himself, and attain a state of perfection.[16]

Many different religions, philosophies, systems of psychology and education are predicated upon this basic assumption: there are remedies for our natural flaws, like selfishness and unrestrained passion. The flaws in us, which hinder us from loving, are the most serious, but they are also the most correctable. The cosmic force responsible for our creation—call it God, call it nature—is responsible for endowing us not only with flaws, but with the capacities necessary for overcoming many of these flaws. Namely, through our capacity for empathy. Indeed, it is our species' unique capacity for empathy which has driven our evolution, enabling us to band together in social groups, and thus allowing us to survive in a world filled with physically stronger and superior predators. Were it not for empathy, our species might have died out long ago. And if we are to continue surviving into the future, empathy must still be our greatest tool for overcoming the flaws that hold us back. Maybe it is even our incompleteness that provides us with purpose, the purpose to strive towards perfection collectively. It is the process of doing so and not the end-point that is called life.

---

[16]Pierre Hadot, *Philosophy as a Way of Life*, ed. Arnold I. Davidson, trans. Michael Chase (Malden: Blackwell, 1995), 102.

Why have God and nature made us as such unfinished products? A human must be nurtured by parents for a very long time relative to other animals. This is evolution at work. We are a work in progress. We can evolve to see what heights can be achieved by life on earth.

6

Death

Knowledge is not going to solve our problems. You may know, for example, that there is reincarnation, that there is a continuity after death. You may know, I don't say you do; or you may be convinced of it. But that does not solve the problem. Death cannot be shelved by your theory, or by information, or by conviction. It is much more mysterious, much deeper, much more creative than that.[1]

—Jiddu Krishnamurti

Of all the common threads in this book, there is virtually nothing that is more universal than death. We are all born, and we all must die. Because it is such a universal phenomenon, it is no surprise that all religions take death very seriously. Many people presume, in fact, that death and our fear of death is the reason we have developed religions in the first place. It has become popular in certain circles to dismiss religion merely as a set of false promises designed solely to alleviate people's anxieties and fears about death and other existential concerns. But anthropologist Pascal Boyer counters this by pointing out the assumption '[t]hat mortality is unbearable or makes human existence intrinsically pointless is a culture-specific speculation

[1]Jiddu Krishnamurti, *The First and Last Freedom* (New York: HarperCollins, 1975), 91.

and by no means provides universal motivation'.[2]

Death is indeed inevitable, at least for now, unless there is a major breakthrough in medical research. But we do have a choice in how we respond to death's inevitability. The examples in this chapter will show that religious attitudes towards death consist of much more than just unconvincing consolations. Rather, the great prophets and scriptures urge us to confront death directly, to embrace all its reality and mystery, without trying to ignore it, without trying to explain it away. It can be the very thing that gives our life meaning. Hence, all religions address death to help foster an acceptance. They mean to teach us what it is, what happens to us after the fact, how we should deal with it and how we should live our lives leading up to it.

Many religions believe that death should inform how we live our lives. The Qur'an, for example, treats death as a test of character: 'Blessed be He in whose hands is dominion; and He over all things hath power; He who created death and life, that He may try which of you is best in deed: and He is the exalted in might, oft-forgiving.'[3] Paul the Apostle, in the Christian tradition, taught that 'if you live after the flesh, you must die; but if by the Spirit you put to death the deeds of the body, you will live'.[4] Of course, there is more than one way to interpret these passages. Literally speaking, Paul is referring to the belief that Christ will resurrect those dead individuals who lived righteous lives. This accords closely with the Qur'anic passage earlier, in which life and death are used to test us on earth. We are constantly developing attachments to things here on earth, but nothing lasts forever. Training ourselves to let go of such attachments helps us to have a more realistic and healthier outlook on life and death, and can even enable us to employ death (in a symbolic sense) as a force for good in our lives.

Pierre Hadot describes how pivotal a role death played in the ancient Greek conception of 'the good life', with each of the major philosophical schools encouraging people to live with the constant awareness of

---

[2]Pascal Boyer, *Religion Explained: The Evolutionary Origins of Religious Thought* (New York: Basic Books, 2001), 21.

[3]The Qur'an, 67:1-2 (Yusuf Ali).

[4]Romans 8:13 (World English Bible).

mortality: 'Plato, for example, had defined philosophy as an exercise for death, understood as the separation of the soul from the body.'[5] Hadot also writes that 'Training for death is training to die to one's individuality and passions, in order to look at things from the perspective of universality and objectivity.'[6]

Echoing this idea of expanding our perspective beyond our limited sense of individuality, philosopher Bertrand Russell at eighty-one wrote the following in his essay *How to Grow Old:*

> Make your interests gradually wider and more impersonal, until bit by bit the walls of the ego recede, and your life becomes increasingly merged in the universal life. An individual human existence should be like a river—small at first, narrowly contained within its banks, and rushing passionately past rocks and over waterfalls. Gradually the river grows wider, the banks recede, the waters flow more quietly, and in the end, without any visible break, they become merged in the sea, and painlessly lose their individual being.[7]

This is similar to the Hindu belief that the atman (individual soul) merges into paramatman—the infinite, ultimate self characterized by selflessness. The Hindu tradition provides a good place to start if we are to understand how we conceive of death across religions. Death is understood as an illusion. In the Bhagavad Gita we are taught that, 'The self is not born nor does it ever die. Once it has been, this self will never cease to be again. Unborn, eternal, continuing from the old, the self is not killed when the body is killed.'[8] The 'you' that the Bhagavad Gita is referring to is the real self—not our bodies, not our minds, but the universal atman inside us all. Similarly, the Baha'i leader 'Abdu'l-Bahá maintained that 'Through his ignorance, man fears death; but the death he shrinks from is imaginary and absolutely unreal; it is

[5]Pierre Hadot, *Philosophy as a Way of Life*, ed. Arnold I. Davidson, trans. Michael Chase (Malden: Blackwell, 1995), 68.

[6]Ibid, 94-95.

[7]Bertrand Russell, 'How to Grow Old,' *Portraits From Memory And Other Essays* (New York: Simon & Schuster, 1956), 52.

[8]*The Bhagavad Gita*, trans. Laurie L. Patton (New York: Penguin, 2014), 2:20.

only human imagination.'[9] The Qur'an similarly advises, 'And say not of those who are slain in the way of God: "They are dead." Nay they are living though ye perceive (it) not.'[10] In the Bible, in Genesis, it is famously proclaimed, 'For you are dust, and you shall return to dust.'[11]

The Taoist sage Lieh-tzu exemplifies how this insight can change our lives for the better by relativizing life and death. In the process we are able to view death as a great leveller that makes us all equal, which allows us to loosen our attachments and live more freely and consciously, rather than being ruled by fears, anxieties or the arbitrary metric of success and failure.

> In a hundred years, everyone we know will be just a pile of bones. What is there to gain in life, and what is there to lose in death?' The ancients knew that life cannot go on forever, and death is not the end of everything. Therefore, they are not excited by the event of life nor depressed by the occurrence of death. Birth and death are part of the natural cycle of things.[12]

We are all the same in death, and to realize this is to realize that we are not so different in life either. Scholar of religion Yuki Miyamoto writes, 'The dead provide resources for disrupting boundaries, not only through their otherworldly existence, but also by calling into question nationalistic, mythical, and heroic narratives.'[13]

The deeper meaning behind these passages is that what we commonly understand as birth and death are actually illusory representations of those phenomena. We are tempted to view birth as the emergence of something out of nothing, and of death as a transformation of something into nothing. Zen master Shunryu Suzuki elucidates this point further: 'You may think that when you die, you disappear, you no longer exist.

---

[9]Abdu'l-Bahá, *The Promulgation of Universal Peace*, second edition, (Bahá'í Publishing Trust, 1982), 88, Baha'i Reference Library, accessed on 10 July 2022, http://reference.bahai.org/en/t/ab/PUP/pup-38.html.

[10]The Qur'an, 2:154 (Yusuf Ali).

[11]Genesis 3:19 (World English Bible).

[12]*Lieh-tzu: A Taoist Guide to Practical Living*, trans. Eva Wong (Boston: Shambhala, 2001), 32.

[13]Yuki Miyamoto, *Beyond the Mushroom Cloud: Commemoration, Religion, and Responsibility After Hiroshima* (New York: Fordham University Press, 2012), 77.

But even though you vanish, something which is existent cannot be non-existent.'[14] Death is a natural part of our existence. Having faith (whatever your faith tradition might be) means accepting death. Death is an integral part of the process of life and the evolution of the universe.

Personally, just this fact alone makes me accept the prospect of my own death gracefully. Do you know that more than 100 billion people have lived and died before us? I surrender to the inscrutable wisdom of the universe in which mysterious birth and mysterious death are a part of the gameplan. Yet, considering our mind and our cognitive activities and limitations, death is the ultimate cause of fear which I need to overcome constantly.

As journalist Michael Easter explains, 'Roughly seven out of ten Westerners say they feel uncomfortable with death. Only half of people over 65 have considered how they want to die.'[15]

He goes on to explain a particularly compelling case study of a more positive attitude towards the deaths of Bhutan. It is a feature of their educational and socialization programmes and it has resulted in a populace that embraces the reality of death and uses that awareness to live more meaningful and compassionate lives.

> The understanding that we're all going to die is hammered into Bhutan's collective conscience [...] Bhutanese arts often center around death; paintings of vultures picking the flesh from corpses, dances that reenact dying.[16]

The implications of such a programme are profound and do not depend on any particular metaphysical beliefs or belief systems. Death itself, and the fear of it, are universal to the human experience. This means that an awareness of it and of the rituals surrounding it, can be universally therapeutic ways of making meaning, regardless of the specific practices, beliefs or religious identity involved.

---

[14]Shunryu Suzuki, *Zen Mind, Beginner's Mind* (Boston: Shambhala, 2011), 46.

[15]Michael Easter, *The Comfort Crisis* in Michael Easter, 'The Secret to Happiness? Thinking About Death,' Outside, 13 May 2021, https://www.outsideonline.com/outdoor-adventure/exploration-survival/secret-happiness-think-about-dying-comfort-crisis-easter/.

[16]Ibid.

7

Afterlife

> *[T]he fact that early humans did decorate corpses, lay out the bodies in particular postures or bury people with flowers, aligned horns or tools would support the notion that some ritualization of death is a very ancient human activity.*[1]
>
> —Pascal Boyer

The question of what happens after death is one of the most prominent expressions of human curiosity. Several proposed answers to this question have been offered to make meaning of the universal phenomenon of death. It is timeless and perplexing, and we will never cease to think about this question and we will likely never receive a clear answer. Many philosophers argue that there can be no religion without some provisional answer to this existential question about death and afterlife, especially since other disciplines of knowledge (like science) cannot address it either. Essentially, religions are almost forced to address this big question to reduce the uncertainty and ambiguity surrounding questions about why we must die.

Not surprisingly, all religions have some sort of postulation about what happens after death, and that has huge implications for the complex

---

[1]Pascal Boyer, *Religion Explained: The Evolutionary Origins of Religious Thought* (New York: Basic Books, 2001), 203.

beliefs and principles of conduct that comprise each religion. After all, assuming we do continue to exist in some form after death, we all want to achieve the most favourable circumstances in the afterlife. In some respect life after death (for those who believe in it, which included my father) is more important than life on earth, as it is free from the limitations of our physical reality.

The Abrahamic religions, Judaism, Christianity and Islam, believe that we have one life on earth, after which there is an eternal afterlife. According to these faiths, those who are righteous in life will be resurrected after death. As the Hebrew Bible explains, 'Many of those who sleep in the dust of the earth will awake, some to everlasting life, and some to shame and everlasting contempt. Those who are wise will shine as the brightness of the expanse. Those who turn many to righteousness will shine as the stars forever and ever.'[2]

Generally speaking, in all three traditions, it is believed that the soul continues after death. Additionally, there is a foretold date, the day of resurrection or judgement. On this day, the souls of the dead will be judged according to their deeds in life and receive the appropriate rewards or punishments. The concept of a 'day of judgement', when people's fates will be determined according to how they lived, carries over across all three traditions. In the Christian Bible: 'I am the resurrection and the life. He who believes in me will still live, even if he dies.'[3] Meanwhile, the wicked 'will go away to eternal punishment, but the righteous to eternal life.'[4] And the Qur'an teaches that, 'Every soul shall have a taste of death: and only on the Day of Judgment shall you be paid your full recompense. Only he who is saved far from the fire and admitted to the garden will have attained the object (of life): for the life of this world is but goods and chattels of deception.'[5]

Interpretations vary across these traditions and even across the various intra-religious sects: some claim that the physical bodies of the righteous dead will be resurrected, while others claim that only the souls

[2]Daniel 12:2-3 (World English Bible).
[3]John 11:25 (World English Bible).
[4]Matthew 25:46 (World English Bible).
[5]Qur'an, 3:185 (Yusuf Ali).

survive death, some claim that good and bad souls will go to heaven and hell respectively, while others claim there is only heaven and no hell to speak of. In any case, the general belief is that the righteous will meet a better eternal fate than the sinful, which means that we should do everything we can now to live good lives here on earth. For instance, by being kind and charitable to others.

Comparing this to the religions of India, like Hinduism and Buddhism, the specific concepts and narratives differ quite a bit, but the overall message and implications are actually quite similar in many ways. Hindus, for instance, speak of a soul that never dies, which is reminiscent of the enduring quality of the soul in the Abrahamic traditions. The Buddha has taught similarly.

> When the Aggregates arise, decay and die, O bhikkhu, every moment you are born, decay, and die. This, even now during this lifetime, every moment we are born and die, but we continue. If we can understand that in this life we can continue without a permanent, unchanging substance like Self or Soul, why can't we understand that those forces themselves can continue without a Self or a Soul behind them after the non-functioning of the body?[6]

Again, this is broad enough that it remains fairly well in agreement with the Abrahamic religions: the assertion here is simply that the 'self' we identify with may, in some form, carry on beyond the death of the physical body. Explanations, however, diverge a bit from the Abrahamic traditions. Hindus, Buddhists, Jains and Sikhs all believe in reincarnation, i.e., the idea that we live many lives on earth, and therefore, experience many deaths and rebirths in a process known as samsara. The long-term goal is to escape samsara so that our souls no longer return to earth, while the short-term goal is simply to achieve more meritorious births while we remain in samsara. This is accomplished by doing good deeds while on earth (a feature in common with the Abrahamic traditions). Our sum of good and bad deeds, stretched out across our numerous incarnations on earth, determines our karma, which in turn determines the nature of our

[6]Walpola Rahula, *What the Buddha Taught* (New York: Grove Press, 1974), 33.

next reincarnation. This can range from being a lowly insect to a human being, and in many cases, there are even states of reincarnations that go beyond these two poles like ghostly states or demigods and Gods.

My father had a difficult life, but he accepted all his hardships, believing they were the result of his past life, and so long as he endured those consequences gracefully in this life, his next life would be beautiful. When I asked him, 'if there is a God, then why do billions suffer?', this concept of karma was always his answer. He was a very well read and erudite man who had deep roots in his faith.

A person's state of mind at the time of death is thought to be pivotal in many schools of Hindu and Buddhist thought. In the Bhagavad Gita, for instance, the Hindu God, Krishna, states, 'Those who remember me at the time of death will come to me. Do not doubt this. Whatever occupies the mind at the time of death determines the destination of the dying.'[7] And, in Buddhism, *The Tibetan Book of the Dead* details the process whereby the living help to guide a dying person by reciting certain phrases that serve as directions for the conscious soul as it travels towards its next state of existence. This concept of a journeying soul that must be guided is also a common one across religions, going back to very ancient civilizations. According to scholar Ruth Chang, 'It was common in Han tombs to paint images of either the occupants travelling to paradise or to another world in the after-life, and the travel was often done on a mythical animal. Sometimes there is also a figure that guides one to the next life.'[8] Further back, ancient Egyptians also believed in Gods depicted as mythical animals, some of whom had important roles in the afterlife. Anubis, a God with the head of a jackal or wolf, would judge dead souls by weighing their hearts to determine whether they had lived righteously or not. If they had, they would be guided to the afterlife, but if not, their hearts would be eaten by Ammit, the God with a crocodile head, thus denying them an afterlife. And so, the element of judgement in the afterlife existed even before the Abrahamic traditions,

---

[7]Eknath Easwaran, trans. *The Bhagavad Gita*, second edition (Tomales, CA: Nilgiri Press, July 2007), 8:5-6.

[8]Ruth H. Chang, 'Understanding Di and Tian: Deity and Heaven from Shang to Tang Dynasties,' in *Sino-Platonic Papers*, no. 108, ed. Victor H. Mair (September 2000), 32.

marking an important commonality that spans across religions, both ancient and modern.

The ancient Greeks, who had a great deal of interaction and cultural exchange with both ancient Egyptians and ancient Hindu civilizations, share traits with these conceptions of the afterlife. Like the ancient Egyptians, the ancient Greeks believed in a mythical guide figure: Charon, the ferryman, who would row the souls of the dead across the mythical river Styx, to lead them to their afterlife in the underworld. Hindus also believe that souls are guided through communion with a river, although in this case it is a river on earth, rather than in the mythical underworld. Hindus believe that cremating dead bodies by the river Ganges can help to free souls from samsara, and in any case, it is a symbolic action that nicely corresponds with Hindu doctrines of the soul (atman) as arising out of and merging back into a state of oneness (brahman). In all of these narratives, the general meaning being expressed is that death is not the final state of a person's being. It is not the end of a soul's journey, but rather the beginning of a new phase of the journey. As one metaphorical expression from the Baha'i faith puts it, 'We may compare the body to a vehicle which has been used for the journey through earthly life and no longer needed once the destination has been reached.'[9]

This brings us to one of the most universal dimensions of the afterlife, which is the disposal of dead bodies. Anthropologist Pascal Boyer describes the ubiquity of burial rituals as follows: 'From embalming to cremation, all sorts of techniques are used to do something with the corpse. But the point is, something must be done. This is a constant and has been so for a long time.'[10] Countless civilizations, cultures and religions have come and gone throughout human history, but all have taken the matter of how to dispose of dead bodies seriously. After all, the physical remains of a dead person are the only aspect of the afterlife that we, as the living, have direct evidence of. There are practical reasons

[9]From a letter of the Universal House of Justice to an individual believer (6 June 1971), in *Lights of Guidance*, ed. Helen Bassett Hornby (New Delhi, India: Baha'i Publishing Trust, 1988); Baha'i Library Online: http://bahai-library.com/hornby_lights_guidance_2.html&chapter=1#n666

[10]Pascal Boyer, *Religion Explained: The Evolutionary Origins of Religious Thought* (New York: Basic Books, 2001), 203.

for disposing of a dead body that are applicable at the physical level—removing the stench of decay and the spread of disease—but we also care for the dead body to provide ourselves with the solace that comes from caring for a loved person one last time. Hindus actually cremate their dead, as they believe that the body is like a dress that you strip away at death, bringing along your eternal soul into a new life clothed in a new body. As the Bhagavad Gita puts it, 'As a person sheds worn-out garments and wears new ones, likewise, at the time of death, the soul casts off its worn-out body and enters a new one.'[11]

Ultimately, we have no final answers about what happens to a person's soul or consciousness after death.

This has been poetically expressed by the Taoist sage Chuang Tzu: 'We can point to the wood that has burned, but when the fire has passed on, we cannot know where it has gone.'[12] What we do know is that we can choose how to live our lives, and how to treat others in our lives, while we are still around. In this way, thinking about death—even without any definitive answers—is an important part of working towards living a fuller life. The religious focus on death and the afterlife that we see across traditions is not just making predictions about what happens when we die; it has more to do with reminding us to live more consciously and to express our love for others as much as possible.

---

[11]Eknath Easwaran, trans, *The Bhagavad Gita*, Second Edition (Tomales, CA: Nilgiri Press, July 2007), 2:22.

[12]Martin Palmer, trans. *The Book of Chuang Tzu*, Penguin Classics edition (New York: Penguin Books, 2006), 24.

8

Salvation

Put bluntly, doctrines of the soul and salvation may be so widespread and so consistent across human cultures because they reflect something fundamentally accurate about human nature.[1]

—Jeffrey J. Kripal

Doctrines of salvation typically deal with the eternal resting place of our souls. Much of our anxieties about death come from our uncertainty about what follows from it. Where do we go after we die? More importantly, is there a heaven and a hell, a pleasant realm in the afterlife and an unpleasant one? Does the way we live our lives affect the condition of our afterlife, and vice versa? We want to reunite with the loved ones we lose throughout the course of our lives, and we crave assurance that there is some inherent meaning or purpose to our existence, that one day, we will all transcend our frail mortal conditions to become something more than human. In very broad strokes, the types of answers to the question of salvation can be divided into two: salvation 'to' and salvation 'from'. In the Western monotheistic traditions, salvation involves ascending to a heavenly realm to spend eternity in a pleasant afterlife with God and

[1]Jeffrey J. Kripal, *Comparing Religions*, illustrated edition (West Sussex, UK: John Wiley & Sons, 2014), 295.

our loved ones. Whereas in Eastern traditions, like those of Hinduism and Buddhism, salvation involves escape from the cycle of birth and death (samsara) through what's alternatively known as moksha, mukti or nirvana.

In the Bhagavad Gita, the God Krishna says to the hero, Arjuna, 'no one who does good work will come to an evil end. Reaching the heaven of the righteous, after uncountable years that man will be born again to parents who are upright and wealthy.'[2] In religions like Hinduism, where belief in reincarnation is present, salvation is a kind of ongoing process—doing good in life grants us access to a pleasant realm in the afterlife, from which we then enter into pleasant circumstances in our new life on earth, and so on, until one day we achieve the ultimate salvation (moksha, mukti or nirvana) or release from the cycle of birth and death.

The general principle that good deeds in life result in pleasant afterlife states holds true for the Abrahamic religions as well, but seeing as they do not believe in reincarnation, there is only one chance to get things right. In Christianity and Islam, the good go to heaven and the bad go to hell, as described in the following passage from the Qur'an: 'Nay those who seek gain in Evil and are girt round by their sins they are Companions of the Fire therein shall they abide (forever). But those who have faith and work righteousness they are Companions of the Garden therein shall they abide (forever).'[3] In Judaism, there is no hell, but there still is the possibility of missing out on salvation, since only the good are granted access to heaven. Admission into heaven requires that we live a life characterized not only by good deeds, but also by devotion and reverence for God, as is also the case with Christianity. So it is said in the Biblical book of Romans that 'if you will confess with your mouth that Jesus is Lord, and believe in your heart that God raised him from the dead, you will be saved'.[4] It is passages like these that Martin Luther drew upon when he sparked the Protestant Reformation in the middle of the twentieth century. Traditionally, in Catholicism, salvation could

---

[2] *The Bhagavad Gita.* trans. Stephen Mitchell (New York: Harmony Books, 2000) 6:40-41.
[3] Qur'an, 2:81-82 (Yusuf Ali).
[4] Romans 10:9 (World English Bible).

only be achieved through the rites and rituals of the church and clergy. Protestants, however, believe that salvation is a matter of personal devotion and faith in Jesus Christ as the saviour.

There is an interesting parallel to this in a form of Buddhism that likely had some direct influence from Christianity. It is known as 'Pure Land Buddhism', and it is widespread in East Asia. Pure Land Buddhism is similar to Christianity in that both religions believe that our salvation is dependent upon our devotion to a human-saviour figure, and that this salvation involves entering into an eternal heavenly resting place after death. For Christianity, this figure is, of course, Jesus Christ, and in Pure Land Buddhism, it is a bodhisattva, known as Amida Buddha. Amida (or amita in Sanskrit) translates into 'infinite', which is why the Japanese monk, Shinran, notes that the 'supreme Buddha is formless, and [...] In order to make us realize that the true Buddha is formless, it is expressly called Amida Buddha'.[5] Described as infinite and formless, we might also draw a similarity between Jesus and Amida, as beings who lived fully human lives on earth while also being fully divine.

So far, all of this is very doctrinal and literal, but if we are looking for metaphorical readings of these same doctrines of salvation, there are resources for that as well. Consider the following theological interpretation of Christian salvation by C.S. Lewis.

> The point is not that God will refuse you admission to His eternal world if you have not got certain qualities of character: the point is that if people have not got at least the beginnings of those qualities inside them, then no possible external conditions could make a 'Heaven' for them.[6]

At the causal level, we are all children of God. God does not intend to damn us, but rather to grant us happiness on earth and beyond. We all inherit the same basic capacities as members of the same species, and this includes the capacity and inclination to cultivate the kind of qualities that are conducive to improving our own lives

---

[5]Shinran, 'On Jinen Honi,' in Masao Abe, *A Study of Dogen: His Philosophy and Religion* (Albany: SUNY Press, 1992), 166.

[6]C.S. Lewis, *The C.S. Lewis Signature Classics* (New York: HarperCollins, 2017), 73.

and the lives of others. Qualities like love, selflessness, generosity, curiosity, self-control and so forth.

In the Baha'i faith, there is a similar belief that the character traits we cultivate on earth are carried with us into the next life, and this is why they believe it is so important to take our earthly lives seriously and to constantly seek to improve ourselves. Our earthly lives are said to be a stage in our soul's journey that give us the opportunity to grow and mature, taking with us into the afterlife all the lessons we learned on earth. This conviction in the everlasting value of our achievements and quests towards truth and virtue while on earth is further echoed by Confucius who said: 'If a man in the morning hear the right way, he may die in the evening without regret.'[7] The point is that learning and self-improvement are worthy pursuits right up until the day you die, and quite possibly beyond as well.

Salvation as the cultivation of conditions within our own being is similar to other Eastern notions of enlightenment, as in Hinduism, Buddhism and Taoism, to name a few. The Zen master Shunryu Suzuki taught that 'when your practice is calm and ordinary, everyday life itself is enlightenment'.[8] And the Taoist sage Lieh Tzu notes, 'Enlightenment is a very normal experience, attainable by everyone. Therefore, there is nothing mysterious or secretive about it.'[9] Elaborating on this concept and some parallels across other religions is Eckhart Tolle.

> Most ancient religions and spiritual traditions share the common insight—that our 'normal' state of mind is marred by a fundamental defect. However, out of this insight into the nature of the human condition—we may call it the bad news—arises a second insight: the good news of the possibility of a radical transformation of human consciousness. In Hindu teachings (and sometimes in Buddhism also), this transformation is called enlightenment. In the teachings of Jesus, it is salvation, and in Buddhism, it is the

---

[7]James Legge, *Confucian Analects, The Great Learning, The Doctrine of the Mean,* (Pantianos Classics, 2017), 4:8.

[8]Shunryu Suzuki, *Zen Mind, Beginner's Mind* (Boston: Shambhala, 2011), 43.

[9]*Lieh-tzu: A Taoist Guide to Practical Living,* trans. Eva Wong (Boston: Shambhala, 2001), 117.

> end of suffering. Liberation and awakening are other terms used to describe this transformation.[10]

Enlightenment, in a variety of religious traditions, is salvation, attainable by anyone, that can occur in our lives in the present if we locate persistent illusions that keep us clinging to unhealthy desires and attachments.

This brings us to our final point and the most important takeaway from this common thread of salvation. It is best expressed by Robert Wright: 'Any religion whose prerequisites for individual salvation don't conduce to the salvation of the whole world is a religion whose time has passed.'[11] In his own time, Jesus may have only offered salvation for his own people, and the same can be said of Muhammad or the Buddha, and so on. But they also encourage the spread of their teachings. And the point of this was not to say that only Christians or Muslims or Buddhists could earn salvation, but that all people could. It was not until about a little over a half century ago, during the Second Vatican Council that the Catholic Church formally acknowledged, for the first time, that salvation was attainable for believers of other faiths. For two thousand years, the Church had claimed to be the exclusive path towards salvation, but now it seems to be moving away from such outdated exclusivist and ethnocentric ideas.

It would be hard to imagine one of these prophets in our present age—with access to modern transportation, technology and knowledge of geography—restricting their messages and guarantees of salvation only to certain countries or nations of people, and not others. Imagine if any of those prophets came to earth today, would they be confining their activities to only one region? Salvation, like all of our common threads across religions, should be seen as a set of shared human questions, hopes and experiences containing a vision for a better future. As former President of Czechoslovakia Vaclav Havel said, 'The salvation of this human world lies nowhere else than in the human heart, in the human

---

[10]Eckhart Tolle, *A New Earth: Awakening to Your Life's Purpose* (New York: Penguin, 2005), 13.

[11]Robert Wright, *The Evolution of God*, (New York: Little, Brown and Company, 2009), 307.

power to reflect, in human modesty, in human responsibility. Without a global revolution in the sphere of human consciousness, nothing will change for the better.'[12] Focus on the world within can bring about change in the outer world, and eventually, even on collective human society.

[12]Vaclav Havel, 'Address to US Congress', The Vaclav Havel Library Foundation, 22 February 1990, https://www.vhlf.org/havel-quotes/speech-to-the-u-s-congress/.

9

Belief in Other Worlds

The uniquely human capacity for detached, creative thought, which includes the ability to conceive of imaginary beings and alternative worlds, stands behind literature, art, science, and, of course, religion.[1]

—Todd Tremlin

Like many other people, I've always been fascinated by the stars. I have often marvelled at the fact that we now know each of these to be suns very much like our own, around which orbit numerous planets similar to those in our own solar system. For most of human history, our ancestors would have had no way of knowing this and could only speculate over the question of whether or not there were other worlds out there.

Modern astronomy has now revealed to us that there are hundreds of billions of other galaxies in our universe, each containing as many as one trillion stars! These are unfathomably large numbers. Things only get more mind-boggling when we realize that most of these stars are orbited by planets much like those in our own solar system. Just how many of these exoplanets are earth-like is still a matter of ongoing discovery,

[1]Todd Tremlin, *Minds and Gods: The Cognitive Foundations of Religion* (Oxford: Oxford University Press, 2006), 104.

but already a couple dozen planets have been identified as potentially similar in makeup to our own. The question of whether or not life exists elsewhere in our universe is still an open one, but it is certainly starting to seem more and more plausible with each such discovery.

Religions are complex systems of knowledge transmission and storytelling which, throughout history, have showcased the full range of the human imagination. One dimension of this involves speculating on the existence and description of other worlds besides our own. Historian of religion Jeffrey Kripal mentions this.

> Human beings cannot endure chaos for long—that is, complete disorder and non-meaning. And so they are always and everywhere constructing a cosmos—that is, an ordered system of meaning, structure, and purpose.[2]

Today, we see this in many forms: we have identified numerous planets in the universe resembling our own, and many others that look entirely alien; we are constantly musing over the possibility and probability of extraterrestrial life, and even here on earth, the artificial human environments we have created constitute a world unto itself that is very different from the natural world our ancestors were born into.

Early forms of religion, like animism and totemism, located Gods and spirits in the natural world, but since then, the major world religions have suggested that other worlds are more likely to be dwelling places for Gods. One common proclivity has been to point to the sky. Before modern science and astronomy, human beings often saw the stars and planets either as Gods, or as entities associated with Gods. The ancient Greeks pointed towards the peak of Mount Olympus—which reached into the sky—as the dwelling place of the Gods. In India, many holy shrines are on top of a mountain. Similarly, *tian* is a Chinese term that can mean either 'sky' or 'God'. 'Heaven', in many religions, is typically thought to exist somewhere above earth.

The Abrahamic religions constantly make reference to another world as the dwelling place of God, like when Jesus told his followers,

---

[2]Jeffrey J. Kripal, *Comparing Religions*, illustrated edition (West Sussex: John Wiley & Sons, 2014), 112.

'My Kingdom is not of this world.'[3] Furthermore, there are scriptural references from these religions that describe earth as just one among many worlds created by God. In the Qur'an, for instance, 'God is He who created seven firmaments and of the earth a similar number. Through the midst of them (all) descends His command: that ye may know that God has power over all things, and that God comprehends all things in (His) knowledge.'[4] A Jewish Talmudic passage takes this to a hyperbolic extreme, noting that God created thousands of worlds!

> God carries everything beneath His arms. With His right arm he carries the heavens, and with His left arm he carries the earth. How much do God's arms carry? The left carries the 18,000 worlds that surround this world. The right carries 120,000 worlds of the World to Come.[5]

Of course, as noted earlier, we have since then scientifically proven that this is just the tip of the iceberg—in truth, there are trillions of other worlds in the universe, and according to many theoretical physicists, there may even be an infinite number of universes! This picture of a dizzying number of other worlds in the universe has been anticipated by many ancient religious traditions and scriptures, as in the case of the Buddhist text, the *Avatamsaka Sutra*.

> What worlds are there herein? I'll tell you. In these seas of fragrant waters, numerous as atoms in unspeakably many Buddha-fields, rest an equal number of world systems. Each world system also contains an equal number of worlds. Those world systems in the ocean of worlds have various resting places, various shapes and forms, various substances and essences, various locations, various entryways, various adornments, various boundaries, various alignments, various similarities, and various powers of maintenance.[6]

---

[3]John 18:36 (World English Bible).

[4]The Qur'an, 65:12 (Yusuf Ali).

[5]*Tree of Souls: The Mythology of Judaism,* ed. Howard Schwartz (Oxford: Oxford University Press, 2007), 23.

[6]Thomas Cleary, *The Flower Ornament Scripture: A Translation of the Avatamsaka Sutra,* (Boston:Shambhala Publications, 1993).

There is also a short Hindu poem that notes the cosmological reality of a plurality of other worlds.

> Insects in a fig
> Cannot imagine
> Worlds other than the fig.
>
> There are so many fig-trees
> In these woods:
> And so many more
> Vast clusters of stars.[7]

The point is that we should not be so egocentric as to think that the world with which we are familiar is the only one that exists. In Hindu mythology, there are three worlds: vaikunth (where you are with the lord), heaven (where you are happy) and hell (where you are punished). You are allocated one of the three after your death based on your karma. As the Indian mythologist Devdutt Pattanaik notes, the ancient Greeks had a similar conception of different realms for the Gods and for mortals in the afterlife.

> The goal for the Greeks was Elysium, meant for individuals who lived extraordinary lives. It was the final destination of mythic heroes such as Achilles, Odysseus, Theseus, Jason and Perseus. Those who lived ordinary unremarkable lives were sent to the Asphodel Fields after death. Those who angered the gods were thrown into Tartarus, condemned to do monotonous tasks, like Sisyphus who was condemned to roll a rock up a mountain all day, only to find it rolling back down at night. This was hell: doing monotonous mundane chores endlessly. The gods lived on Mount Olympus, controlling everything. These Olympians achieved their exalted position after overthrowing older gods, the Titans, and so constantly feared overthrow at the hands of humans, who they kept in check through the Fates. To be extraordinary, and win a place in Elysium, humans had to defy the Gods.[8]

---

[7]Wendy Doniger, *Hinduism, The Norton Anthology of World Religions: Volume 1*, ed. Jack Miles (New York: W.W. Norton & Company, 2015), 462.

[8]Devdutt Pattanaik, *Myth=Mithya: Decoding Hindu Mythology* (UK: Penguin, 2008).

The aforementioned poem raises another important aspect of the common thread of belief in other worlds: the sheer mystery they represent. For instance, the Taoist sage Lieh Tzu said that, 'The vital spirit is an allotment from heaven, the physical body is the allotment of earth. The celestial is clear and diffused, the earthly is opaque and condensed. When the vital spirit leaves the body, each returns to its reality. Hence the term ghost. Ghosthood means return, returning to the true home.'[9] Two of life's greatest mysteries: that of the existence of other worlds, and the questions surrounding where we go after we die. And Lieh Tzu is not the only one to speak of these two as deeply interrelated.

Another example comes from 'Abdu'l-Baha, eldest son of the Baha'i prophet Bahá'u'lláh, who similarly described earthly life and the afterlife as a kind of continuous journey.

> That world beyond is a world of sanctity and radiance; therefore it is necessary that in this world he should acquire these divine attributes. In that world there is need of spirituality, faith, assurance, the knowledge and love of God. These he must attain in this world so that after his ascension from the earthly to the heavenly Kingdom he shall find all that is needful in that life eternal ready for him.[10]

The Baha'i notion of the afterlife is one that emphasizes continuity with our present life. What we do on earth matters because all of the virtues we cultivate in life carry over into our afterlife, in the next world. Even though the exact nature of this other world is mysterious, our purpose on earth is rather clear.

Belief in other worlds is an important and common thread across religions because it deeply informs how we choose to live our lives in the here and now. We may not ever know where we go when we die, and we may never have definitive proof of heaven or any other divine

---

[9]Lieh Tzu, *The Book of Master Lieh,* trans. Thomas Cleary (2009).

[10]'Abdu'l-Bahá, *Foundations of World Unity*, sixth printing (US: Bahá'í Publishing Trust, 1979), 63, Baha'i Reference Library: http://reference.bahai.org/en/t/c/FWU/fwu-19.html.

or supernatural worlds, but we do know that our earth is just one world among a virtually infinite array of others in the universe. If we cultivate a steady awareness of these facts, it can instill in us a sense of wonder that brings a new level of meaning into our lives, as well as a sense of humility that might make us live more selflessly. We can start to see meaning as something infusing the entirety of existence, rather than something pertaining only to our individual selves.

10

Revelation

The powerful revelations that stand at the beginnings of great communities, at the turning-points of human time, are nothing else than the eternal revelation.[1]

—Martin Buber

As Martin Buber suggests, revelation is such an important and common thread across religions because it is what stands at the historical beginning of any religion. Followers of major religions believe that all their prophets had divine truth revealed to them. God delivered the ten commandments to Moses on Mount Sinai; the angel Gabriel transmitted the words of Qur'an to Muhammad; the Srutis of Hinduism are likewise known as 'revealed' texts—from Krishna to Arjuna, for instance. And the Buddha has his awakening or Satori (awakening) as the Zen Buddhists call it, understood as an opening of the third eye. Revelations are like initial sparks that have ignited new religious traditions and other belief systems throughout human history. These are subsequently kindled and kept alive through prophets, sages, disciples, rituals, scriptures, temples and institutions, all of which trace their origins back to that same starting point. Because of this central role that they play in the unfolding of any religion,

[1]Martin Buber, *I and Thou* (New York: Simon & Schuster, 1996), 166.

revelations typically also contain information about the future.

Religious revelations typically consist of imparted wisdom transmitted directly from God or some other divine source to the human world, through one or more specially chosen prophets. A good place to start is with the final book of the New Testament, 'Revelations', and which contains the famous statement, '"I am the Alpha and the Omega," says the Lord God, "who is and who was and who is to come, the Almighty."'[2] Alpha and omega are the first and last letters of the classical Greek alphabet, respectively, and this declaration emphasizes God's omnipotence and identity as the divine source of creation.

The following passage from the Bhagavad Gita is a similar example of God revealing that he is the ultimate master of reality. The hero, Arjuna, is granted a rare revelatory experience by Krishna, an avatar of the God Vishnu. 'The whole universe, all things animate or inanimate, are gathered here—look!—enfolded inside my infinite body. But since you are not able to see me with mortal eyes, I will grant you divine sight.'[3] It is an important feature of Hindu religious practice to seek out a direct revelatory experience (*darshan*) like the one described in this passage. But we should realize that the point of this is not just to have an exciting experience, but to be transformed in such a way that we are able to directly perceive the interconnectedness of the entire cosmos, which should, in turn, change the way we think and behave in the world for the better.

Buber has also said, 'The encounter with God does not come to man in order that he may henceforth attend to God but in order that he may prove its meaning in action in the world. All revelation is a calling and a mission.'[4] Once again, revelations are only the spark—the fire they ignite must be continually fanned. Ultimately, all revelations are concerned with the vision of a better future and with the unity of all humankind. The Baha'i leader Shogi Effendi, for instance, interprets the revelation of his own tradition.

---

[2]Revelation 1:8 (World English Bible).

[3]*The Bhagavad Gita*, trans. Stephen Mitchell, (New York: Harmony Books, 2000), 11:7-8.

[4]Martin Buber, *I and Thou* (New York: Simon &Schuster, 1996), 164.

> The Revelation of Bahá'u'lláh, whose supreme mission is none other but the achievement of this organic and spiritual unity of the whole body of nations, should, if we be faithful to its implications, be regarded as signalizing through its advent the coming of age of the entire human race.[5]

Thus, revelations are not just about the transmission of literal truths or fixed doctrines. They are attempts to galvanize our species toward the *pursuit* of truth, which is an ongoing process, and a clarion to act upon the recognition of our interconnectedness in order to live in a truly flourishing society.

Zen master Shunryu Suzuki reinforces this point about resisting literal or dogmatic interpretations of particular revelations, emphasizing instead the importance of self-reflection and searching for truth from within: 'Wisdom is not something to learn. Wisdom is something which will come out of your mindfulness.'[6] We are, therefore, the catalysts for our own revelations. Confucius taught similarly, 'A man is worthy of being a teacher who gets to know what is new by keeping fresh in his mind what he is already familiar with.'[7] Whenever we are presented with something new, we should always reflect upon how it accords with what we already know.

The injunction to reflect upon revelations is a key concept found across religions. Belief in revelations means unquestionable authority with respect to the content of the revelation. It accords huge powers to the priests to enforce the tenets of revelation on the followers. This is why God in the Qur'an notes of religious prophets, '(We sent them) with clear signs and books of dark prophecies; and we have sent down unto thee (also) the message; that thou mayest explain clearly to men what is sent for them, and that they may give thought.'[8] Just because a message—even

---

[5]Shoghi Effendi, *The World Order of Bahá'u'lláh*, first pocket-size edition (US: Bahá'í Publishing Trust: 1991), 163, Baha'i Reference Library, http://reference.bahai.org/en/t/se/WOB/wob-42.html

[6]Shunryu Suzuki, *Zen Mind, Beginner's Mind* (Boston: Shambhala, 2011), 106.

[7]Confucius, *The Analects*, Penguin Classics edition, trans. D.C. Lau (London, England: Penguin Books, 1971), 2:11.

[8]Qur'an, 16:44 (Yusuf Ali).

from God—is presented clearly, that does not mean we have to accept it literally and unquestioningly. Scriptures contain all sorts of metaphors, parables, paradoxes and other mysterious phrases. We must understand religious revelations as constantly unfolding sources of wisdom to be revisited and reinterpreted based on what we have come to learn from other sources. In the Tao Te Ching, Taoist sage, Lao Tzu, writes:

> [The Tao is] distant and dark
> But inside is an essence
> An essence that is real
> Inside which is a heart
> Throughout the ages
> Its name hasn't changed[9]

Truth is differently expressed by so many because it is so elusive. All we can do is approach truth and God, while accepting that there are some things we may never be able to ascertain or describe in full detail. The essence of this wisdom is in all of us, which is why the messages across religions share so many similarities.

One way to look at revelations, either those of our own belief systems or those of others, is as definitive truths. But another way is to look at them as powerful catalysts for our own intrinsic wisdom-seeking and meaning-making faculties. As the Sufi leader Hazrat Inayat Khan writes, 'To a Sufi, revelation is the inherent property of every soul. There is an unceasing flow of the divine stream, which has neither beginning nor end.'[10] This is one way through which we can reconcile the differences in revelations from different religions, all of which contain the same essence as they are coming directly from the one God that has spoken to the prophets of all religions.

---

[9]Lao-Tzu, *Tao te ching,* trans. Red Pine (Washington: Copper Canyon Press, 2009), Chapter 21, 42.

[10]Hazrat Inayat Khan, *The Sufi Message Volume 1: The Way of Illumination* (Delhi: Motilal Banarsidass, 2011), 56.

11

Metaphorical versus Literal Interpretations

Spiders can't help making flying-traps, and men can't help making symbols.[1]

—Aldous Huxley

From the ancient cave drawings of Lascaux to the complex language systems that have existed on earth, humanity has been defined by an impressive array of symbolic thought and communication models. Recognizing this, we see that many of the elements constituting religions are highly symbolic. Everything, from dietary restrictions and prescribed clothing to rituals and devotional practices, has a deeper meaning behind the literal content of the objects or actions.

The same is true for religious scriptures. Communication always involves interpretation. When the ancient prophets gave lectures and sermons to their disciples, the messages were meant to be meditated upon deeply so that their full meaning could reveal itself. Similarly, when we read the scriptures today, as crystallized forms of these original teachings, we always have the choice to interpret the words literally or metaphorically. The great prophets, who delivered the foundational revelations and teachings of major religious traditions, lived during a time

[1]Aldous Huxley, *Island* (New York: Harper Perennial Modern Classics, 2009), 220.

when literacy rates were extremely low. The written word was relatively scarce and education was a luxury of a select few. For the masses, the only way they could be taught was orally, through storytelling, with deeper truths encoded in easy-to-understand metaphors and parables.

The same can be said of the physical and visual artefacts of religions. Many of us are likely familiar with the visual trope of the Abrahamic God as a great man in the sky with a big grey beard, an image that has been reinforced through a long history of Western artistic depictions of God. But as the art historian Ernst Gombrich notes, it was clear to the artists and their patrons that, 'God is not a man with a beard, but that among all sensible things of which man can have an experience on earth, a beautiful and dignified fatherly ruler of infinite splendor is the most fitting metaphor our mind can grasp [...] The Church warns the faithful not to take any of these symbols literally but only as sensible analogies to higher meanings.'[2] Most religions anthropomorphize God in one way or another. Our mental and sensory capabilities as human beings have clear limitations. So too do each of our respective language systems. When the concepts and phenomena we are trying to contemplate exceed these limitations, we can't help but turn to metaphorical depictions of things to make them more familiar. Another example of this can be found in explanation by the historians Louise Bruit Zaidman and Pauline Schmitt Pantel. 'The fact that the Greeks sculpted such statues of their Gods does not imply a belief that the Gods resembled men or had bodies that were in every respect human; what the Greeks did believe was that the beauty, youth or perfection of a real human body evoked qualities of the divine.'[3]

Interpreting scripture metaphorically does not mean disbelieving in its authenticity or value, or rejecting its core messages. Mahatma Gandhi's favourite text was the Bhagavad Gita, which is part of the epic, Mahabharata. And yet he was clear about the importance of reading it metaphorically.

---

[2]E. H. Gombrich, "The use of art for the study of symbols", *American Psychologist*, 20(1), 1965, 34–50.

[3]Louise Bruit Zaidman and Pauline Schmitt Pantel, *Religion in the Ancient Greek City*, trans. Paul Cartledge (Cambridge: Cambridge University Press, 1992), 217.

> I do not regard the Mahabharata as a historical work in the accepted sense [...] The persons therein described may be historical, but the author of the Mahabharata has used them merely to drive home his religious theme.[4]

The literal narrative of the Mahabharata is a tale of a bloody war between two sets of family members, but Gandhi treasured it as one of the greatest inspirations for his own messages of peace and non-violence, maintaining that this was the true deeper meaning of the text.

Indeed, many prophets and scriptures explicitly urge us to interpret texts metaphorically. The Baha'i believes in the prophets and scriptures of all major religions as messages from the same God, and yet, 'Abdu'l Baha, one of the faith's most important figures, maintains, 'The holy books are full of significance and must never be taken literally.'[5] That is, if we interpret all of scripture literally, then we will fail to grasp its full significance. Therefore, reading scripture metaphorically is actually the most devout form of worship.

Similarly, a Talmudic passage from the traditions of Judaism says, 'We have been taught that R. Judah said: He who translates a verse literally is a liar, and he who adds [his own words] to it is a blasphemer and reviler.'[6] Through the devotional practice of 'midrash' (textual interpretation), Jewish scripture is constantly being interpreted and reinterpreted in an ongoing process of new meanings being suggested for the same ancient words. This is how the Talmudic literature came to be. The Torah itself is intentionally written without any vowels. This is to allow for an infinite range of interpretation so that there are truly as many valid interpretations of the Torah as there are readers of it.

God is said to communicate through metaphors and symbols. Most of the Qur'an's passages are written from the first perspective of

---

[4]Mahatma Gandhi, in Wendy Doniger, *Hinduism, The Norton Anthology of World Religions: Vol. 1,* ed. Jack Miles (New York: W.W. Norton & Company, 2015), 643.

[5]'Abdu'l-Bahá, *'Abdu'l-Bahá on Divine Philosophy,* ed. Elizabeth Fraser Chamberlain (Boston: Tudor Press, 1918), 40, Baha'i Library Online: http://bahai-library.com/abdulbaha_divine_philosophy&chapter=all

[6]Babylonian Talmud, Kiddushin 49a in Hayyim Nahman Bialik and Yehoshua Ḥana Rawnitzki, *The Book of Legends: Sefer Ha-Aggadah,* trans. William Gordon Braude (New York: Schocken Books, 1992), 451.

God (signified by the pronoun 'We'), and the highly poetic nature of its composition cements the proposition that God speaks in metaphors and that scripture should be read as such: 'And such are the parables we set forth for mankind, but only those understand them who have knowledge. God created the heavens and the earth in true (proportions): verily in that is a sign for those who believe.'[7]

Huston Smith, the great scholar of comparative religion, backs this up by describing the Sufi sect of Islam as particularly exemplary practitioners of metaphorical interpretation.

> The principle method the Sufis employ for penetrating God's veils is symbolism. In using visible objects to speak of invisible things, symbolism is the language of religion in the way numbers are the language of science.[8]

Those who we consider 'mystics' are often heralded as the most devout of religious worshippers, and therefore, metaphorical interpretation is not at all at odds with having deep faith. For instance, one of the most famous mystical texts, *The Interior Castle*, comes from the Christian saint, Teresa of Avila, who used all sorts of metaphors to describe the relationship between God and the inner states of the soul.

> The silkworm, which is fat and ugly, then dies, and a little white butterfly, which is very pretty, comes forth from the cocoon. Now if this were not seen but recounted to us as having happened in other times, who would believe it? Or what reasonings could make us conclude that a thing as nonrational as a worm or bee could be so diligent in working for our benefit and with so much industriousness?[9]

For Saint Teresa, the most authentic state of spiritual transformation (which she tries to capture in writing) can only be expressed through symbolism and metaphor since, like the case of a caterpillar's

---

[7]The Qur'an 29:43-44 (Yusuf Ali).

[8]Huston Smith, *The Illustrated World's Religions* (New York: HarperCollins, 1995), 174.

[9]Teresa of Avila, *The Interior Castle*, trans. Kieran Kavanaugh and Otilio Rodriguez (New Jersey: Paulist Press, 1979), 91-92.

metamorphosis, it cannot be explained through ordinary reasoning to someone who has not experienced the phenomenon at first hand.

There is a metaphor in the Hebrew Bible. 'Yahweh, you are our Father. We are the clay and you our potter. We all are the work of your hand.'[10] This example from the Abrahamic traditions express the transformational effects of religious devotion, which is a common message of metaphors from many other religious traditions as well. For instance, in the Hindu Upanishads, we find metaphors like, 'As butter lies hidden within milk, The Self is hidden in the hearts of all. Churn the mind through meditation on it.'[11] The Buddha, who was influenced by his own Hindu upbringing, also turns to metaphorical language to express the value of cultivating one's inner states. In The Dhammapada, a collection of his teachings, we see statements like, 'As irrigators lead water where they want, as archers make their arrows straight, as carpenters carve wood, the wise shape their minds.'[12]

Lao Tzu, the foundational Taoist sage, was also fond of using metaphors. He uses a slew of naturalistic metaphors to describe the characteristics of a sage.

> Genuine, unformed was he! Like uncarved wood.
> Merged, undifferentiated was he! Like muddy water.
> Broad and expansive was he! Like a valley.[13]

One of the most important recurring metaphors in ancient Taoist texts is that of 'uncarved wood', used to describe a kind of pregnant emptiness. It is a reference to the mark of a wise person. Having an empty and open mind signals flexibility and the ability to be ready for anything, ready at any point to radically change your own beliefs when presented with new knowledge and experiences.

We find this sentiment echoed by Marianne Moyaert.

---

[10]Isaiah 64:8 (World English Bible).

[11]*The Upanishads,* trans. Eknath Easwaran (Tomales: Nilgiri Press, 2007), 289.

[12]*The Dhammapada,* trans. Eknath Easwaran, second edition (Tomales: Nilgiri Press, 2007), 80.

[13]Lao-Tzu, *Tao te ching,* trans. Red Pine (Washington: Copper Canyon Press, 2009), Chapter 15, 30.

> Individuals who have strong symbolic interpretation of religion have less need for closure and are more open to experiences of otherness, lending the promise of enrichment to encounters with others. This faith understanding entails a symbolic way of thinking that sees conflicting interpretations not as a problem to be solved but as opening up a horizon of innovation with respect to meaning.[14]

This should be the main lesson that we learn from metaphor as a common thread across religions. Metaphorical thinking is a tool we can use to better understand viewpoints other than our own. We can find value in them and, therefore, embrace diversity. Emile Durkheim, the founding figure in sociology, expressed it in his writings on religion.

> No doubt, when all we do is consider the formulas literally, these religious beliefs and practices appear disconcerting, and our inclination might be to write them off to some sort of inborn aberration. But we must know how to reach beneath the symbol to grasp the reality it represents and that gives the symbol its true meaning. The most bizarre or barbarous rites and the strangest myths translate some human need and some aspect of life, whether social or individual.[15]

Surely, much of our fear of the other is due to an overemphasis on literal examinations of seemingly bizarre rites and myths, which point to something more universal when viewed symbolically. This misplaced focus on differences and otherness stems, in a large part, from the misguided tendency to read scripture literally. In most cases, the scriptures were never intended to be read this way. Rather, the literal words of scripture are merely stepping stones that lead to the truly important lessons and insights they are meant to convey.

The Medieval Jewish philosopher Maimonides sought to eliminate

---

[14]Marianne Moyaert, "From Religious Violence to Interreligious Hospitality", in *Paul Ricoeur in the Age of Hermeneutical Reason: Poetics, Praxis, and Critique,* ed. Roger W. H. Savage (London: Lexington Books, 2015), 25.

[15]Emile Durkheim, *The Elementary Forms of Religious Life,* trans. Karen E. Fields (New York: The Free Press, 1995), 2.

the confusion we consider how and when we should interpret scripture metaphorically, arguing that 'One should accept the truth from whatever source it proceeds'.[16] In other words, we need not go on defending certain portions of scripture as true *if* new advancements in our knowledge of the world paints a different picture. The great religious texts of the world were intended to be living documents, and the authors and orators of parables knew this well.

The problem we face today is that, when taken literally, the ancient scriptures and beliefs that were composed thousands of years ago are impossible to reconcile with the present. We live and worship within a fact-based approximation of reality. All religions have fundamentalist factions that continue to cling to literalist interpretations of ancient texts, thus creating a variety of alternative and competing realities. This naturally leads to bigotry, conflict and violence. Each religion must reckon with this problem if we are to restore religion to its originally peaceful mission and intentions. As our world and our species continue to evolve, so too must the lessons we take away from religious materials.

My father imparted to me a powerful metaphor, which has served as the guiding philosophy of my life and has enabled me to navigate several difficult situations in life and find meaning in doing so. He taught me to be like the lotus flower, which grows and receives nourishment from mud but remains above it.

---

[16]Maimonides, foreword to *The Eight Chapters Of Maimonides On Ethics,* trans. Joseph I. Gorfinkle (New York: Columbia University Press, 1912), 35-36.

12

Teaching by Parables

We know that human minds are narrative or literary minds.[1]

—Pascal Boyer

Writing is a relatively recent invention as compared to storytelling. Storytelling has been with us from our earliest beginnings. Before written scriptures, religious ideas were transmitted orally; before the existence of the religions we know today, hunter-gatherers and tribal communities would gather around the fire to share stories. Storytelling might very well be our earliest recorded form of meaning-making.

Because storytelling is etched so deeply into the history of our species, it remains a powerful form of communicating ideas today, and is one of the most compelling facets of our religions. This can be seen not only in the collective infancy of our species, but in our own individual early lives as well. For most of us, some of the earliest stories we remember hearing in our childhood were religious parables, stories that contain some lesson or piece of wisdom that cannot be transmitted through direct reasoning.

A Jewish parable from the Talmudic writings provides a good illustration of the importance of parables themselves.

---

[1]Pascal Boyer, *Religion Explained: The Evolutionary Origins of Religious Thought* (New York: Basic Books, 2001), 204.

> Consider the king who has lost a gold coin or a precious pearl in his house. May he not find it by the light of a wick worth no more than an issar? Likewise, do not let the parable appear of little worth to you. By its light, a man may fathom words of Torah.[2]

Parables, then, are the keys to unlocking much of the meaning contained in more abstract ideas from the various religious traditions of the world.

Prophets and sages of all religions taught their congregation through the use of parables. This fact is reflected in the scriptures that they and their followers left behind. In the first book of the New Testament, the Gospel of Matthew, 'Jesus spoke all these things in parables to the multitudes; and without a parable, he didn't speak to them.'[3] Jesus also tells his followers, 'To you is given the mystery of God's Kingdom, but to those who are outside, all things are done in parables, that "seeing they may see, and not perceive; and hearing they may hear, and not understand; lest perhaps they should turn again, and their sins should be forgiven them."'[4]In one of the most famous such parables, the parable of the sower, Jesus tells his disciples about a farmer who scatters seeds such that they end up falling on various terrains,some of which are fertile and allow the seeds to take root, while others do not. He explains that this parable represents the fact that not everyone will be receptive to his teachings. Furthermore, he explains that the reason he speaks to crowds by telling them parables is that most people are unreceptive to his messages otherwise.

Similarly, in the Lotus Sutra, an important Buddhist text that is full of extended metaphors and parallels, the Buddha reminds his followers: 'We employ countless expedient means, discussing causes and conditions and using words of simile and parable to expound the teachings.'[5] The Buddha's explanation for why he teaches in parables is essentially the

---

[2]Shir HaShirim Rabbah, 1:1 in Hayyim Nahman Bialik and Yehoshua Ḥana Rawnitzki, *The Book of Legends: Sefer Ha-Aggadah*, trans. William Gordon Braude (New York: Schocken Books, 1992), 3.

[3]Matthew 13: 34 (World English Bible).

[4]Mark 4:11-12 (World English Bible).

[5]Burton Watson, trans, *The Lotus Sutra* (New York: Columbia University Press, 1993), 31.

same as Jesus's. Most people simply do not possess the understanding to grasp the fullness of the teachings when explained with ordinary language. The Buddhist concept of 'expedient means' is predicated upon the belief that a teacher should use whatever means are most expedient to teach particular individuals or groups, which often necessitates the use of metaphors, half-truths, and even downright lies.

Perhaps the most famous parable from the Lotus Sutra involves the Buddha describing a scene where a couple of small children are playing inside a house that is on fire. Because of their age, they do not grasp the seriousness of the situation. Thus, the adult trying to save them cannot lure them out through ordinary reasoning: instead, he entices them with promises of special toys and gifts, and that proves to be more successful. Likewise, most people have not undergone the rigorous spiritual practice that led to the Buddha's enlightenment. They do not fully grasp the seriousness of the suffering that is caused by desire and samsara, the endless cycle of birth and death. Furthermore, they do not realize that reincarnation as a human being provides a being with an incredibly rare opportunity to make progress towards escaping samsara. Therefore, in order to most effectively enable such people to make the most of this limited opportunity—thus delivering them from the burning house that is samsara—they must first be taught messages that they will be most receptive to, before eventually being taught the fuller truths.

The famous philosopher Friedrich Nietzsche sums up this line of reasoning from both Jesus and the Buddha noting that, 'An educator never says what he himself thinks, but always only what he thinks of a thing in relation to the requirements of those he educates.'[6] Most people require indirect and entertaining forms of education in order to begin to grasp the meaning of an important set of information, and this is where parables come in. Parables take us beyond the limitations of ordinary language and can even span the gaps of communication that might occur between different languages. The Bible and the Tao Te Ching are the two most translated books in the world. Just think of how many people from such different backgrounds, speaking different tongues, have continued

[6]Friedrich Nietzsche, *The Will to Power: An Attempted Transvaluation of All Values: Vol II Books III and IV* (Redditch, UK: Read Books Ltd, 2013), 250.

to find meaning in the parables from these texts.

In Plato's famous cave allegory, a group of prisoners are chained to a rock in a cave such that they are facing a wall in the cave. They have never seen what lies beyond the cave. Indeed, they do not even suspect that there is a world beyond the cave. They see shadows flickering on the wall and do not realize that the shadows are being cast by physical objects and people beyond the cave. One prisoner is eventually able to escape, sees the outside world, and excitedly comes back to explain it to his prisoner companions, but they do not believe him and soon turn angry and violent.

This story illuminates the importance of teaching through parables, demonstrating that attempting to teach people who are unprepared through plain language is not only ineffective, but may actually be harmful, since it can alienate and even enrage the recipient of the message. One need only look at the case of Jesus's crucifixion to see the full severity of preaching messages to a crowd that is unprepared to hear.

Having reflected upon the purpose and theory behind parables, we can look at a few more parables to see some of the common types of content they encode. Many parables across religions, for instance, are meant to bolster faith in God, as in the following example from the Qur'an.

> Or (take) the similitude of one who passed by a hamlet all in ruins to its roofs. He said: 'Oh! how shall God bring it (ever) to life after (this) its death?' But God caused him to die for a hundred years then raised him up (again). He said: 'How long didst thou tarry (thus)?' He said: '(perhaps) a day or part of a day.' He said: 'Nay thou hast tarried thus a hundred years; but look at thy food and thy drink; they show no signs of age; and look at thy donkey: and that we may make of thee a sign unto the people look further at the bones how we bring them together and clothe them with flesh!' When this was shown clearly to him he said: 'I know that God hath power over all things.'[7]

From the Taoist sage Chuang Tzu a very different kind of parable is used to bolster faith in a very different kind of higher power—the Tao,

[7]Qur'an 2:259 (Yusuf Ali).

which is the prevailing way that things take their course in nature. When studied and cultivated by humans, the Tao can allow us to live better, longer and more harmonious lives. In the following parable, cultivation of the Tao is manifested in a special skill exhibited by a chef.

> My senses are idle. The spirit
> Free to work without plan
> Follows its own instinct
> Guided by natural line,
> By the secret opening, the hidden space,
> My cleaver finds its own way.
> I cut through no joint, chop no bone. [...]
> Prince Wan Hui said,
> 'This is it! My cook has shown me
> How I ought to live
> My own life!'[8]

This parable seeks to express a certain characteristic of the Tao, which in itself cannot be described directly, illustrating through one particular skill that there is value in following the Tao.

In other cases, parables are used to illustrate and teach behavioural virtues, such as patience, in this Confucian example from the Book of Mencius.

> Let us not be like the man of Sung. There was a man of Sung, who was grieved that his growing corn was not longer, and so he pulled it up. Having done this, he returned home, looking very stupid, and said to his people, 'I am tired to-day. I have been helping the corn to grow long.' His son ran to look at it, and found the corn all withered.[9]

Finally, I share a parable that is popular across the religions of India, which urges us, as human beings, to see the purpose of our lives to be the spreading of compassion among other beings.

---

[8]*The Way of Chuang Tzu*, trans. Thomas Merton (New York: New Directions, 2010), 45-47.
[9]Mencius, 'The Book of Mencius,' trans. James Legge in Barnes & Noble, *The Art of War and Other Classics of Eastern Thought* (New York: Sterling, 2013), 2.2:16.

A hunter watched as the saint carefully and gingerly lifted the creature out of the water, only to fling it back in as he convulsed in pain from each fresh sting. Finally, the hunter said to the sadhu, 'Forgive me for my frankness, but it is clear that the scorpion is simply going to continue to sting you each and every time you try to carry it to safety. Why don't you give up and just let it drown?' The sadhu replied: 'My dear child, the scorpion is not stinging me out of malice or evil intent. Just as it is the water's nature to make me wet, so it is the scorpion's nature to sting. He doesn't realise that I am carrying him to safety. That is a level of conscious comprehension greater than what his brain can achieve. But, just as it is the scorpion's nature to sting, so it is my nature to save. Just as he is not leaving his nature, why should I leave my nature? My dharma is to help any creature of any kind—human or animal. Why should I let a small scorpion rob me of the divine nature which I have cultivated through years of sadhana?'[10]

We tend to get so hung up on just how different the content of the stories from various religions is that we fail to see the underlying commonality in the purpose and function of these stories. They all attempt to help us create meaning in our lives and to live more gracefully and harmoniously with one another.

The widespread and common use of parables across religions makes perfect sense if we see religion as a meaning-making endeavour, since parables allow people to find their own meanings out of stories and lessons that have been passed down generations and transported across continents. Through metaphorical interpretation, we can locate a part of ourselves in religious parables from foreign times and places. As the Zen Buddhist and translator Robert Aitken suggests, '[One should] read religion as parable, as folklore, as poetic presentation of your own history and nature.'[11]

---

[10]Swami Chidananda, 'The saint and the scorpion', *The Times of India,* 16 May 2011, https://timesofindia.indiatimes.com/the-saint-and-the-scorpion/articleshow/6451408.cms.

[11]Robert Aitken, *The Gateless Barrier: The Wu-Men Kuan (Mumonkan)*, trans. Robert Aitken (New York: North Point Press, 2016), 31.

13

Chariot Imagery

I saw in a flash that my situation was just like that of the horse: fate was lashing me with its whip, and all I was aware of was my suffering. I hated the invisible power that was tormenting me, but I had not understood that it was all being done so that I should learn to perform some task, take some spiritual hurdle so to speak.[1]

—Gustav Meyrink

Whenever I fly in or out of Bali—the only part of Indonesia that remains predominantly Hindu—I always take a moment to admire the imposing statue of Krishna ensconced in a chariot with Arjuna. It is a reference to the beloved Hindu scripture, the Bhagavad Gita. Like the story it represents, the statue has a dual meaning. Its exterior expresses nobility and military glory, but its deeper meaning has more to do with conquest of the mind than the conquest on the battlefield.

During a recent visit to Greece, I also got to see the remains of a charioteer statue in the museum at the Temple of Delphi. Again, the figure appears triumphant, but also very calm and stoic, in total of control of both body and mind, which was of course the ideal image of the civilized man in ancient Greece.

---

[1]Gustav Meyrink, *The Green Face*, trans. Mike Mitchell (Sawtry: Dedalus, 2004), 138.

Around the time that most of the world religions in this book originated, chariots were a prominently used tool of transportation, especially among royalty and the upper classes. Therefore, it is not surprising that chariots also became a common metaphorical tool across many religions. Even more striking is the fact that the particular *meaning* behind this metaphor is remarkably consistent across religions, namely, among the prophets and scriptures of these religions. The chariot represents the components of the human mind and the willpower needed to control it.

Before we get to this, however, it is worth pointing out some of the stories of Gods and prophets in which literal chariots play an important role, as here too we can find similarities. The most famous chariot story in the Hebrew Bible, or in the Old Testament, is one where the prophet Elijah is taken up to heaven in God's chariot, a magnificent vehicle pulled along by flaming horses: 'As they continued on and talked, behold, a chariot of fire and horses of fire separated them, and Elijah went up by a whirlwind into heaven.'[2] The presence of the chariot highlights what a special event this is, as Elijah is one of only two people (the other being Enoch) in the Bible to have ascended to heaven without dying.

Interestingly, we find a very similar story in Hinduism—a religion as distinct from Judaism as any. In the Mahabharata, the famously long epic that contains the Bhagavad Gita as part of its grander narrative, Arjuna's oldest brother, Yudhishthira, is taken in a chariot to dwell in the realm of the Gods, the only human to do so.

> Then Dharma and Indra and the Maruts and the two Ashvins and all the other gods and celestial sages made Yudhishthira mount the chariot, and along with them, in their own chariots, went the perfected beings that go wherever they wish to go [... Yudhishthira] flew swiftly upwards in that chariot, encompassing heaven and earth with blazing glory.[3]

[2]2 Kings 2:11 (World English Bible).

[3]Wendy Doniger, *Hinduism, The Norton Anthology of World Religions: Vol. 1*, ed. Jack Miles (New York: W.W. Norton & Company, 2015), 159.

Just like Elijah, Yudhishthira is taken up to heaven to live alongside Gods. Incidentally, in the Bhagavad Gita, Krishna—an avatar of the God Vishnu—disguises himself as Arjuna's charioteer. The Hindu scriptures also provide us with a good place to start when discussing the metaphorical use of chariot imagery, since the following quote from the Katha Upanishad may very well be the first instance of this in a major religious text.

> Know the Self as lord of the chariot, the body as the chariot itself, the discriminating intellect as the charioteer, and the mind as reins. The senses, say the wise, are the horses; selfish desires are the roads they travel. When the Self is confused with the body, mind and senses, they point out, he seems to enjoy pleasure and suffer sorrow.[4]

The process of training and cultivating the mind, which is certainly one of the most important avenues towards spiritual attainment expressed in the Upanishads, is likened to the skill required to control and steer a chariot—a difficult yet rewarding skill to have. The chariot represents the body, which is propelled along by horses, which represent the senses. The atman—the higher self within us all that connects us with the divine—controls the chariot with the reins, which are like the mind. The key is to not let the horses, or the senses, have complete control of the chariot. Rather, the senses can and should be tamed through disciplining the mind.

In a very different cultural context, the use of the chariot metaphor to illustrate the difficulty and importance of taming the mind finds expression in the writings of Plato, particularly in his *Phaedrus* dialogue.

> We will liken the soul to the composite nature of a pair of winged horses and a charioteer. Now the horses and charioteers of the gods are all good and of good descent, but those of other races are mixed; and first the charioteer of the human soul drives a pair, and secondly one of the horses is noble and of noble breed, but the other quite the opposite in breed and character.

[4] *The Upanishads,* 1.3.3-4, trans. Eknath Easwaran (Tomales: Nilgiri Press, 2007), 81.

> Therefore in our case the driving is necessarily difficult and troublesome.[5]

This passage has actually been quite influential in the study of the mind, since it informed the famous tripartite model of mind that Sigmund Freud—a student of the classics—proposed several thousands of years later. In Freud's language, the noble horse is the super ego, which represents our moral conscience; the wild horse is the id, which represents our baser instincts; and the charioteer is the ego, which drives the chariot of the mind by balancing out the use of these two 'horses', getting them to move together instead of in two different directions.

Scholar of religion Jen Schlieter describes the similarities of the chariot imagery found in both early Hindu and ancient Greek philosophy.

> [C]hariots were depicted as vehicles of gods such as the sun, i.e. as a symbol of cosmic stability; they were, moreover, used as symbols of royal power and social prestige, e.g. of kings and warriors (in the Iliad Vedic hymns, and poetic literature); and, finally, chariots served as metaphors for the 'person', the 'mind' and the 'way to liberation'.[6]

There is some historical evidence to suggest that there may have been some direct contact between the early Hindu and ancient Greek civilizations, which may account for some of this similarity, but given that human civilization itself depends on our capacity to tame our minds, it is not surprising to see that many other religions and cultures have employed the same metaphor.

In a collection of tales from the tradition of Sufi Islam, we see another very similar metaphor of the charioteer. Here too it is used to represent

---

[5]Plato, Phaedrus, 246a in, *Plato in Twelve Volumes*: *Vol. 9*, trans. Harold N. Fowler (Cambridge: Harvard University Press, 1925), accessed via Tufts' Perseus Digital Library, accessed 10 July 2022, http://www.perseus.tufts.edu/hopper/text?doc=Perseus%3Atext%3A1999.01.0174%3Atext%3DPhaedrus%3Apage%3D246.

[6]Jens Schlieter, 'Master the Chariot, Master Your Self: Comparing Chariot metaphors as Hermeneutics for Mind, Self and Liberation in Ancient Greek and Indian Sources,' in *Universe and Inner Self in Early Indian and Early Greek Thought*, ed. Richard Seaford (UK: Edinburg University Press, 2016), 168.

the conscious rational part of the mind that is responsible for taming the less rational parts of the mind.

> Picture a charioteer. He is seated in a vehicle, propelled by a horse, guided by himself. Intellect is the 'vehicle', the outward form within which we state where we think we are and what we have to do. The vehicle enables the horse and man to operate. The horse, which is the motive power, is the energy which is called 'a state of emotion' or other force. This is needed to propel the chariot. The man, in our illustration, is that which perceives, in a manner superior to the others, the purpose and possibilities of the situation, and who makes it possible for the chariot to move towards and to gain its objective.[7]

Once again, another important part of this shared metaphor is that the chariot—which represents the mind—has a purpose, a destination. We can think of this destination as our own attitudes and behaviours, our ways of being in the world. These are then shaped by intention and willpower, or the charioteer. We are responsible for channelling all parts of our mind—intellect, emotion, instinct, etc.—towards a singular goal. And for all religions, the ultimate goal is for us is to express love in our actions and interactions with others, to help each other flourish as human beings. This emotion is encapsulated in the teachings of Christian Baptist preacher Charles Spurgeon who writes, 'The axle of the wheels of the chariot of Providence is Infinite Love, and Gracious Wisdom is the perpetual charioteer.'[8]

Similarly, in the tradition of Confucius, who also made use of chariot imagery and its metaphors, the goal is to strive towards the ideal of 'junzi', often translated as 'gentleman' or a respectable person (male or female) characterized by the core virtue of 'ren' (benevolence). The attainment of this goal is structured around a traditional model of education comprising of six arts, one of which is, in fact, charioteering. Confucius reveals the metaphorical value behind this art in the Analects when he remarks, 'I do

---

[7]Idries Shah, *Tales of the Dervishes: Teaching Stories of the Sufi Masters Over the Past Thousand Years* (London: The Octagon Press, 1982), 207.

[8]Charles Haddon Spurgeon, *Gleanings Among the Sheaves* (New York: Sheldon and Co., 1869), 71.

not know how a man without truthfulness is to get on. How can a large carriage be made to go without the cross-bar for yoking the oxen to, or a small carriage without the arrangement for yoking the horses?'[9] Part of what it means to be benevolent and well-intentioned towards others, is the demonstration of trustworthiness. Confucius illustrates the central importance of this character trait by likening it to an essential mechanical component of a carriage (essentially, a chariot).

As Zen master Shunryu Suzuki points out, the Buddha also employed ox cart metaphors, albeit in this case with a slightly different focus. 'Buddha said the same thing about the good ox driver. The driver knows how much load the ox can carry, and he keeps the ox from being overloaded. You know your way and your state of mind. Do not carry too much!'[10] The focus of the metaphor is on the mind and how to train it, but in this case, the Buddha's insight into the training of the mind is that it must be taken on gradually and carefully. This follows from the Buddha's overall philosophy of spiritual education as evinced by his eightfold plan, which is very step-oriented.

And finally, the Taoist sage, Lieh Tzu, expresses many of the key themes seen from our other examples in his description of a charioteer's training. The charioteer must govern their intentions by training the mind, yoking together the different parts of the mind and body, and must do so efficiently.

> Your body responds to your mind, the reins respond to the movements of your body, and the horses respond to the pressure from the reins. In this way, without expending any energy, you can drive a chariot over long distances and not feel tired.[11]

Of all the recurring types of images across the literature of most religions, chariot imagery is worth highlighting. After all, it is impossible to extract the meaning-making value from religion if we do not have a firm grasp on the reins of our primary meaning-making instrument—the mind.

---

[9]Confucius, 'Analects' in *Confucian Analects, The Great Learning, The Doctrine of the Mean*, trans. James Legge. (Pantianos Classics, 2017), 2:22.

[10]Shunryu Suzuki, *Zen Mind, Beginner's Mind* (Boston: Shambhala, 2011), 43.

[11]*Lieh tzu: A Taoist Guide to Practical Living*, trans. Eva Wong (Boston: Shambhala, 2001), 154-55.

14

Prophets as Shepherds

Yahweh is my shepherd:
I shall lack nothing.
He makes me lie down in green pastures.
He leads me beside still waters.
He restores my soul.
He guides me in the paths of righteousness for his name's sake.[1]

—The Hebrew Bible

In many religious traditions, the major prophets are described as shepherds—either literally or metaphorically, and often, as both. It's not difficult to understand why. First of all, the major religions came into being when human society was predominantly pastoral and agricultural. Secondly, a shepherd's life is suggestive of many attributes we normally associate with the religious life. It suggests a humble beginning, the countryside that is away from the excesses of the city, a slow-paced life that allows time for deep thought and reflection, patience and gentleness. The development of all these character traits early in one's life would certainly provide fertile soil for growth into a wise and compassionate adult. The deeper, more spiritual and metaphorical side to this is that God is often described as the shepherd

[1]Psalm, 23:1-3 (World English Bible).

of humanity, and thus prophets, as messengers of God, are meant to serve this role. This association perhaps persists most obviously in the title of the 'pastor' in Christian churches; the Latin translation of the term literally means 'shepherd'.

We see an example of God as the shepherd in the psalms of the Hebrew Bible: 'Yahweh is my shepherd: I shall lack nothing. He makes me lie down in green pastures. He leads me beside still waters. He restores my soul. He guides me in the paths of righteousness for his name's sake.'[2] Like sheep that need to be herded back into their pen for safety, God is said to keep us on the right path, to guide us through life, through its many alternative paths. And most importantly, God, across religions, is seen as the shepherd, not just of some, but of all, humanity. As the Baha'i leader 'Abdu'l-Bahá writes:

> The shepherd is one and all people are of his flock. The world of humanity is one and God is equally kind to all. What then is the source of unkindness and hatred in the human world? This real shepherd loves all his sheep. He leads them in green pastures. He rears and protects them. What then is the source of enmity and alienation among humankind?[3]

The fact is that humanity consists of a large and diverse flock. Religions can believe in one God while still recognizing that different prophets needed to be appointed at different times and places to watch over their own respective communities on that very God's behalf.

In the Hebrew Bible, for instance, God anoints Moses as a prophet upon witnessing the care Moses shows for each and every sheep in a flock. As one story from the Jewish Talmud recounts, God tells Moses, 'Because you showed such compassion in tending the flock of a mortal, as you live, you shall become shepherd of Israel, the flock that is Mine.'[4] Other

---

[2]Psalm 23:1-3 (World English Bible).

[3]'Abdu'l-Bahá, *Foundations of World Unity,* sixth printing (US: Bahá'í Publishing Trust, 1979), 81, Baha'i Reference Library, http://reference.bahai.org/en/t/c/FWU/fwu-23.html.

[4]Exodus Rabbah, 2:2, Hayyim Nahman Bialik and Yehoshua Ḥana Rawnitzki, *The Book of Legends: Sefer Ha-Aggadah,* trans. William Gordon Braude (New York: Schocken Books, 1992), 62.

examples of prophets from major religions working as shepherds in their youth are Muhammad, Confucius and Krishna (also known as 'Govinda' or 'Gopala', translated as cowherd). All three prophets came to deeply care about the welfare of their people. Muhammad united an impressive number of disparate tribes into one community through his teachings of Islam; Confucius sought audience amidst students and political leaders alike to share his wisdom on conduct and governance; and Krishna is an avatar of the God Vishnu, who is also known as the 'preserver'.

These prophets can, and should be, seen as not only the shepherds of people in their own time, but also models of behaviour and character traits for us today to strive towards as well. The Muslim Prophet Muhammad, for instance, taught that 'Each of you is a shepherd, and all of you are responsible for your flocks.'[5] All of us have people in our lives who depend on us for love and support, and we too should seek to provide such guidance to those who might need our help.

Jesus, for example, placed great emphasis on the importance of tending to the weak and sick. He maintained that these afflicted people are the ones that God loves most, as they need it more than others. Jesus, therefore, also described himself as a shepherd on many occasions. 'I am the good shepherd. The good shepherd lays down his life for the sheep',[6] and, 'I am the door. If anyone enters in by me, he will be saved, and will go in and go out, and will find pasture.'[7] Jesus often claimed to be 'the gate' or 'the way' to emphasize that in following him people would be following God. They would thus find their way to the Kingdom of Heaven.

Like a good shepherd, however, Jesus did not force people to act in a certain way—he simply provided a model through the life he lived and the teachings he preached. Zen master Shunryu Suzuki likewise emphasizes the importance of gentleness and non-interference when guiding people. He too uses the analogy of shepherding. 'To give your sheep or cow a large, spacious meadow is the way to control him. So it is with people: first let them do what they want, and watch them. This

---

[5]Muhammad al-Bukhari, *Al-Adab Al-Mufrad*, Book 10, Hadith 212, Sunnah.com,https://sunnah.com/adab:212.

[6]John 10:11 (World English Bible).

[7]John 10:9 (World English Bible).

is the best policy.'[8] Nobody likes being told what to do. People become rigid and defensive when forced to behave in a certain way. Consider the rebellious nature of teenagers, who struggle to find expression in their newfound independence, while simultaneously being bound to many sets of rules and restrictions at home, school and elsewhere.

And finally, the Taoist sage Lieh Tzu uses another shepherding analogy to promote gentleness in teaching and leading.

> Have you seen a shepherd at work? He can control several hundred sheep by getting a child to prod them gently from behind with a bamboo stick. The entire flock will move in the direction he wants them to go. On the other hand, if you try to lead each sheep, you will not be able to get the flock moving.[9]

The meaning is twofold: one, that it is simply not efficient or even feasible to attend to one individual at a time if the goal is to change people's behaviour at large; and two, that people do not respond well to direct modes of teaching and leadership. Rather, people are most responsive when they are not fully aware or conscious of the means by which they are being taught, like the sheep who are prodded from behind rather than led by the shepherd in front of them. We see this in cases of leadership by example, as with figures like Jesus or Gandhi or Martin Luther King Jr. We see it in storytelling as well. In all cases, the point is to 'show, not tell'.

The prophet is a leader—not a domineering personality but a caring one. Prophets, like shepherds, use gentle methods to lead people towards the right path and to keep them united as a single flock. The prophet as shepherd shows us that we are all one and that love and compassion is the way to follow. We need leaders to bring us together, but if this is done through force and violence then it should not be seen as love and compassion. If it is being done without tact, then it will not be effective. Shepherding is a strong metaphor for the role that modern leaders in all walks of life must perform for our world to live in harmony.

---

[8]Shunryu Suzuki, *Zen Mind, Beginner's Mind* (Boston: Shambhala, 2011), 15.
[9]*Lieh-tzu: A Taoist Guide to Practical Living,* trans. Eva Wong (Boston: Shambhala, 2001), 204.

15

The Mysterious Births of Prophets

The tendency [in myth] has always been to endow the hero with extraordinary powers from the moment of birth, or even the moment of conception.[1]

—Joseph Campbell

The birth of prophets and other founding figures of religion are momentous occasions. They are thus recorded as grand, often supernatural, even fantastical narratives in the literature of their respective traditions. Their arrival signals not only the entry of a new teacher into the world, but also an entirely new way of viewing the world, being in the world and of building a new community of people.

Of course, one of the most famous myths of a mysterious birth comes from Christianity—the birth of Jesus of Nazareth as recounted in the New Testament. 'Now the birth of Jesus Christ was like this: After his mother, Mary, was engaged to Joseph, before they came together, she was found pregnant by the Holy Spirit.'[2] In Christianity, this birth is known as the 'immaculate conception'.

A kind of immaculate conception also appears in one of the popular narratives of the Buddha's birth, recounted by author Barbara O'Brien.

[1]Joseph Campbell, *The Hero with a Thousand Faces,* The Collected Works of Joseph Campbell Series edition (Novato, CA: New World Library, 2008), 274.

[2]Matthew 1:18 (World English Bible).

> A magnificent white bull elephant bearing a white lotus in its trunk approached Maya and walked around her three times. Then the elephant struck her on the right side with its trunk and vanished into her.[3]

The Buddha's birth was special as he seemingly entered his mother's womb by way of this special elephant. And the white elephant, a symbol in Buddhist and Hindu traditions signifying holiness and nobility, foretells the destiny of the Buddha, as well as also explaining Krishna's proclamation in the Bhagavad Gita that: 'I was born from the nectar of immortality as the primordial horse and as Indra's noble elephant. Among human beings, I am the king.'[4]

And in fact, there is another similarity between the mysterious birth narratives of these two religious founders: the appearance of a special light to signal their entrance into the world. In the case of Jesus, it was the Zoroastrian Magi who are said to have interpreted a special star in the sky as evidence that a great new king had been born. 'Where is he who is born King of the Jews? For we saw his star in the east, and have come to worship him.'[5] And as recounted in the Lotus Sutra, the evidence of the Buddha's birth was likewise apparent from far away due to the sudden illumination caused by a special light.

> A wonderful sign of this kind
> has never been seen or heard of in the past.
> It is because some heavenly being of great virtue has been born,
> or because the Buddha has appeared in the world.[6]

It is as though the appearance of a light in the sky, seen from faraway lands, is meant to broadcast the news of the birth of a prophet. It is seen as an event that has significance across the world, claiming that

---

[3]Barbara O'Brien, 'The Birth of the Buddha', *Learn Religions,* 27 March 2018, https://www.learnreligions.com/the-birth-of-the-buddha-449783.

[4]*The Bhagavad Gita,* trans. Eknath Easwaran (Tomales: Nilgiri Press, 2007), 10:27.

[5]Matthew 2:2 (World English Bible).

[6]*The Lotus Sutra,* trans. Burton Watson, (New York: Columbia University Press, 1993), 129.

these individuals enter into the world not just for the benefit of their own people but for all of humankind.

The special appearance of light is, in fact, one of the most common elements of mysterious birth narratives. In Washington Irving's famous biography of the Islamic Prophet Muhammad, we see close parallels to these examples from Christianity and Buddhism.

> [Muhammad's] mother suffered none of the pangs of travail. At the moment of his coming into the world a celestial light illumined the surrounding country, and the new born child, raising his eyes to heaven, exclaimed: 'God is great! There is no God but God, and I am his prophet!'[...] In the same eventful night the sacred fire of Zoroaster, which, guarded by the Magi, had burned without interruption for upward of a thousand years, was suddenly extinguished, and all the idols in the world fell down.[7]

The Magi are attentive to Muhammad's birth, just as they were to Jesus's birth several centuries earlier. Furthermore, Muhammad immediately declares his purpose and mission, just as the Buddha did.

Turning to the Chinese religious traditions of Taoism and Confucianism, both inherited the same existing ancient myths of the 'August Emperors', mythological rulers of ancient China said to have been demigods. We see some of these same recurring motifs in accounts of their births.

> The Chinese chronicles record that when the earth had solidified and the peoples were settling in the riverlands, Fu His, the 'Heavenly Emperor' (2953–2838 B.C.), governed among them [...] He had been born of a miraculous conception, after a gestation of twelve years; his body being that of a serpent, with human arms and the head of an ox. Shen Nung, his successor, the 'Earthly Emperor' (r. 2838–2698 B.C.) was eight feet seven inches tall, with a human body but the head of a bull. He had been miraculously conceived through the influence of a dragon [...] Huang Ti, the 'Yellow Emperor' (r. 2697–2597 B.C.), was the third of the august

[7]Washington Irving, 'Mahomet and His Successors', in *The Works of Washington Irving: Vol. 3* (New York: Pollard & Moss, 1882), 9.

> Three. His mother, a concubine of the prince of the province of Chao-tien, conceived him when she one night beheld a golden dazzling light around the constellation of the Great Bear.[8]

Furthermore, the legendary founder of Taoism, Lao Tzu (which means 'Old Master') was so named due to a legend. It claimed that he had been in his mother's womb for sixty-two years after she was impregnated when she gazed upon a shooting star.

Another example of an important religious figure with a mysterious birth narrative is Patanjali, the Indian sage who authored the Yoga Sutra. He is said to have come into the world as a newborn serpent that fell into the hands of his human mother; her hands were held out in a gesture of worship towards the sun when he fell into them. The two parts of his name encode this myth: 'pata' can mean 'serpent' or 'falling', and 'anjali' means 'hands cupped in worship'.[9]

These stories of mysterious births are told in retrospect. They are narrated as marked with signs that highlight their supreme importance in human history. Historian of religion Jeffrey Kripal agrees.

> Founding myths, above all, work to set apart their subjects from the ordinary lot of humanity. They thus often include stories of special births, which function to mark the founder or saint as someone different and destined for great things. Hence one story of the Buddha's birth describes how, upon exiting his mother's womb, he immediately took seven steps and then announced that this was his final birth, in which he would save the world. Similarly, according to a version of Mahavira's birth narrative, Mahavira was first conceived in the womb of a brahman or Hindu priest but was then transferred to the womb of a member of the warrior caste.[10]

---

[8]Joseph Campbell, *The Hero with a Thousand Faces,* The Collected Works of Joseph Campbell Series edition (Novato, CA: New World Library, 2008), 272-73.

[9]Wendy Doniger, *Hinduism, The Norton Anthology of World Religions: Vol. 1*, ed. Jack Miles (New York: W.W. Norton & Company, 2015), 132.

[10]Jeffrey J. Kripal, *Comparing Religions,* illustrated edition (West Sussex: John Wiley & Sons, 2014), 134.

This story of Mahavira—a major prophet in Jainism, the oldest living religion in the world—is not the lone story of a prophet or deity being transferred to a different womb. A Hindu legend about Krishna, for instance, recounts how Krishna was transferred from the womb of his mother to that of another of his father's wives in order to escape an attempt on his life from his uncle, the tyrant ruler Kamsa. In another tale from the Puranas, Krishna's father, Vasudeva, escapes from prison with the newborn Krishna and manages to secretly swap him with another baby in a nearby village so that he can grow up under the care of this other baby's oblivious parents, safe from Kamsa. This story of Krishna's birth is actually quite similar to the narratives in the Abrahamic traditions, in which both Moses and Jesus had to be taken away in their infancy to evade attempts on their lives.

The Book of Exodus recounts how the Pharaoh, who had enslaved the Israelites, ordered that all their male children be thrown into the Nile River at birth, out of fear that they might one day rise up against him. Ironically, Moses' mother was able to save him by carefully placing him in a basket and leaving the woven basket in the Nile. Moses was found and raised—even more ironically—by the Pharaoh's daughter.

> A man of the house of Levi went and took a daughter of Levi as his wife. The woman conceived and bore a son. When she saw that he was a fine child, she hid him three months. When she could no longer hide him, she took a papyrus basket for him, and coated it with tar and with pitch. She put the child in it, and laid it in the reeds by the river's bank. His sister stood far off, to see what would be done to him. Pharaoh's daughter came down to bathe at the river. Her maidens walked along by the riverside. She saw the basket among the reeds, and sent her servant to get it. She opened it, and saw the child, and behold, the baby cried. She had compassion on him, and said, 'This is one of the Hebrews' children.'[11]

Of course, it was Moses who, eventually, under God's command, was able to lead his people out of Egypt. This provides another example

[11]Exodus 2:1-6 (World English Bible).

of how a unique birth narrative anticipated the important role a future prophet would be called upon to play.

In the New Testament, Joseph was warned by an angel of a plot by yet another tyrannic ruler to take his infant son, Jesus's life.

> Now when they had departed, behold, an angel of the Lord appeared to Joseph in a dream, saying, 'Arise and take the young child and his mother, and flee into Egypt, and stay there until I tell you, for Herod will seek the young child to destroy him.' He arose and took the young child and his mother by night and departed into Egypt, and was there until the death of Herod, that it might be fulfilled which was spoken by the Lord through the prophet, saying, 'Out of Egypt I called my son.'[12]

In each of these cases of mysterious births and miraculous escapes, even the antagonists of the stories seem to sense something special about these newborns. Divine intervention then not only ensures their conception and birth, but also their survival into adulthood, demonstrating to believers of these religious traditions that their prophets had a direct connection with God.

Prophets come into this world with a special mission or purpose.

Surely, if we believe that God is repeatedly incarnated on earth, we should not be surprised by the many commonalities we see in the messages of various religions; they are ultimately just different manifestations of the same God coming to earth, again and again, in different times and places. If we look beneath the literal surface of these birth narratives, we can see how much they echo one another.

Furthermore, we need not take any of these stories literally—instead, we should all heed the words of the great figures of human history; the messages they spread did enlighten people and bring them together, they did foster love and a sense of interconnectedness with one another. We should all feel the essence of these messages. What sense, then, is there in trying to argue that these myths prove any kind of superiority of one religion over another?

---

[12]Matthew 2:13-15 (World English Bible).

16

Deification of Prophets

In short, religions that reach great stature have a tendency to rewrite their history in the process. They cast themselves as distinctive from the get-go, rather than as growing organically out of their milieu. They find an epoch-marking figure—a Moses, a Jesus, a Muhammad—and turn him into an epoch-making figure.[1]

—Robert Wright

Deification of prophets after their death is common. These celebrated individuals are elevated to a status that is fundamentally beyond the human. Like with the mysterious birth narratives, these stories are left to interpretation; we can accept the literal meaning that there are Gods who appear on earth and walk among us in human form, or we can understand them as expressions of deep reverence for prophets, exemplars of good behaviour and wisdom. I used to believe, for instance, that Lord Krishna, an avatar of Vishnu, literally incarnated and walked around on earth as a human being. And though I have come to interpret this more metaphorically later in life, many Hindus—including my mother—do indeed continue to believe in this literal version, just as most Christians believe that Jesus was and is a living incarnation of the Abrahamic God.

[1]Robert Wright, *The Evolution of God,* (New York: Little, Brown and Company, 2009).

It is no wonder that religious communities would think of their prophets as such special beings. They give birth to new worldviews, communal practices and structures that transcend vast geographical and generational expanses. Stories of their deification keep religions alive even after their founders have passed away. The followers of prophets across religions have also always had a vested interest in deifying their leader—by pronouncing these figures as Gods, the teachings attributed to them become absolute and unquestionable. This is the way followers are recruited, and unfortunately, it also opens the door to abuse of power as religious leaders seek to gain control over their followers by appealing to authoritative scriptures that cannot be argued against, or by claiming to be in direct contact with these prophets or God. As authors David Gooding and John Lennox note, something similar to this occurred in the case of Alexander the Great, who 'did get himself proclaimed as the son of the Egyptian God, Ammon; and he did eventually propose, for political reasons, that both his Greek and his oriental subjects should worship him as a God'.[2] However, the great prophets did not declare themselves to be Gods; they were deified after their death.

One exception to this is Jesus Christ, who declared himself to be the son of God. Christians, therefore, believe him to be the son of God or even God himself, both fully human and fully divine. He was, therefore, deified in his own lifetime as God-incarnate and his divine nature was said to be revealed through many of his actions in life, especially by his resurrection after death, which was witnessed by some of his closest followers as they visited his tomb and saw him emerging from it. 'So they took away the stone from the place where the dead man was lying. Jesus lifted up his eyes, and said, "Father, I thank you that you listened to me. I know that you always listen to me, but because of the multitude standing around I said this, that they may believe that you sent me."'[3] Similarly, in Hinduism, Krishna, a major character in the Mahabharata, and Rama, a major character in the Ramayana, are two of the most famous avatars of Vishnu—incarnate forms of the God posing as a human on earth.

---

[2]David Gooding and John Lennox, *The Bible and Ethics* (Coleraine, N. Ireland: Myrtlefield House, 2015), 120.

[3]John 11:41-42 (World English Bible).

Another example of a prophet deified after death is Confucius. This is interesting because Confucius was not even thought of as a prophet during his life. Indeed, though he was much loved by his students, he, along with his teachings, did not achieve much fame during his life. Nevertheless, his teachings have been gospel in China for thousands of years thereafter, and have had an overwhelming influence on the cultural and educational direction of the nation. In this sense, it is perhaps his teachings more than the individual that has been deified.

Two examples of prophets that faced, and thwarted, attempts at deification during their lifetime were the Buddha and Muhammad. Huston Smith's comments on how this relates to the Buddha.

> Notwithstanding [the Buddha's] own objectivity toward himself, there was constant pressure during his lifetime to turn him into a god. This he rebuffed categorically, insisting that he was a human in every respect. He made no attempt to conceal his temptations and weaknesses.[4]

Similarly, because he was born into a cultural environment that believed in magic and miracles, Muhammad's followers were tempted to turn him into a god. But he was quick to insist that there was nothing divine or miraculous about him, and that he was simply God's messenger. He argued that people should direct all their reverence toward Allah rather than towards him. This is why it is still highly taboo to depict Muhammad directly in any form; he expressly forbade it as he did not want his followers to deify him for fear that they would worship him rather than God.

Finally, in Judaism and Taoism are examples of prophets described as immortal. In the Hebrew Bible, Enoch and Elijah are the only two human beings to never have died. They entered into the Kingdom of Heaven while still fully alive. And in Taoism, prophets such as Lao Tzu and Chuang Tzu are said to dwell in a heavenly realm among the Gods and other 'immortals'. They are seen as individuals who were so skilled at cultivating the Tao in their lifetime that they essentially achieved immortality, along with the ability to walk through fire, walk on clouds

---

[4]Huston Smith, *The Illustrated World's Religions* (New York: HarperCollins, 1995), 64.

and so forth. Sometimes, these prophets are said to be mythical creatures like dragons.

What we can take away, regardless of our interpretations of these birth narratives, is that the prophets were at the very least highly gifted individuals who provided us with inspiration and visions of a higher human potential through their lives and teachings. However, we should be aware of the potential for manipulation that arises from literal interpretations of these stories. If we believe that the prophets were brought into the world through divine intervention as manifestations of God, then their words become infallible and can be twisted and taken out of context by power-hungry modern-day leaders to make their followers think or do just about anything. These abuses are well chronicled and are important to be aware of.

17

Creation Myths

The creation myth was the essential bond that held the tribe together. It provided its believers with a unique identity, commanded their fidelity, strengthened order, vouchsafed law, encouraged valor and sacrifice, and offered meaning to the cycles of life and death. No tribe could long survive without the meaning of its existence defined by a creation story.[1]

—E.O. Wilson

One of the most ubiquitous types of narratives across religions are creation myths. Stories of the universe's creation determine the worldview of belief systems, and hence reveal a lot about the most fundamental principles of each religion. Most religions, for instance, describe and even define God as 'the creator'. And on a deeper level, these myths remind us that all living and non-living things—including humans—originate from a common source. Though creation myths often serve the function of uniting individual communities together (as noted by E.O. Wilson), they also help to bring all of humanity together if we interpret their meanings more broadly to see what is common across them. As author Wajihuddin Siddiqui observes,

[1]Edward O. Wilson, *The Social Conquest of Earth*, illustrated ebook edition (New York: W. W. Norton & Company, 2012).

'All of them describe the pre-creation cosmic state initially as that of darkness, chaos and of abundant water which then slowly starts taking shape and order.'[2]

Many of us probably have some familiarity with the creation myth from the biblical Book of Genesis, which is shared across the Abrahamic religions. 'In the beginning, God created the heavens and the earth. The earth was formless and empty. Darkness was on the surface of the deep and God's Spirit was hovering over the surface of the waters. God said, "Let there be light", and there was light. God saw the light, and saw that it was good. God divided the light from the darkness.'[3] God is said to have created all the planes of the universe and the creatures that dwell on them over the course of six days; the first man was created on the sixth day. 'Let's make man in our image, after our likeness. Let them have dominion over the fish of the sea, and over the birds of the sky, and over the livestock, and over all the earth, and over every creeping thing that creeps on the earth.'[4] It is sometimes said that the book of Genesis has two somewhat conflicting creation myths. The second one, of course, is the Garden of Eden story.

> No plant of the field was yet in the earth, and no herb of the field had yet sprung up; for Yahweh God had not caused it to rain on the earth. There was not a man to till the ground, but a mist went up from the earth, and watered the whole surface of the ground. Yahweh God formed man from the dust of the ground, and breathed into his nostrils the breath of life; and man became a living soul. Yahweh God planted a garden eastward, in Eden, and there he put the man whom he had formed.[5]

There are indeed a couple of inconsistencies here: the first story has plants and animals created before man and woman, whereas the second claims that one single man was created first (as opposed to all of humanity at once) and that this occurred before plants first appeared.

---

[2]Wajihuddin Siddiqui, *Commonalities and Similarities in World Religions* (Karachi: Royal Book Company, 2018), 88.

[3]Genesis 1:1-4 (World English Bible).

[4]Genesis 1:26 (World English Bible).

[5]Genesis 2:5-8 (World English Bible).

Storytelling, at the time when Genesis was written, had a particular style of its own; it didn't always demand complete consistency—and this is true of other cultures and other scriptures as well. In any case, as we will see, the basic features of this creation myth are shared across many religions.

Hinduism has many different creation myths. The Vedas, an early collection of Hindu scriptures, speak of the creator God, Purusha, as the primordial being preceding all of creation, similar to the Genesis account. As the story goes, humanity was also created out of parts of Purusha's body, corresponding to the different castes that structured Hindu society, for several millennia. The Vedas also describe Purusha as having hatched from a golden egg in the 'world egg' creation myth, where it is believed that the universe was 'hatched' from a cosmic egg. This is a common myth across religions and cultures, like Zoroastrianism, Greek mythology, Egyptian mythology, Chinese mythology, Finnish mythology and more. Purusha continues to appear in the later scriptures of the Upanishads, but is seen in more abstract, rather than anthropomorphic, terms.

Then there are the Puranas, another set of ancient Hindu texts, which tell a different creation story: one in which countless universes are born and wiped away through the inhalations and exhalations of Vishnu, all in a process of cyclical creation. Buddhists also believe in creation myths that involve cyclical creation, dissolution and the re-creation of universes.

Even Chinese creation myths (associated with Confucianism and Taoism) bear some resemblance to these other creation myths above. According to scholar Julia Ching, 'The Confucian Classics clearly enunciate a belief in God as the source and principle of all things, the giver of life and the protector of the human race.'[6] This belief in one God as the source and principle of all things is mythologized through various different stories in Chinese religions and wisdom traditions.

> The ancients said that the giant Pan-ku created the world when he separated the sky and earth with a great axe. The mountains and seas fell into their places; grass and trees sprouted from the ground, and the animals began to roam the earth. But there were

---

[6]Julia Ching, *Confucianism and Christianity: A Comparative Study* (Tokyo: Kodansha International, 1977), 118.

> no humans. Then the goddess Nü took yellow dirt, mixed it with water from the springs, and fashioned a small figure. When she put it on the ground, this little thing jumped and ran and made strange noises with its mouth. Its name is 'humanity'. The ancient Chinese saw life as a gift from heaven and recognized that we are made of the same material as the mountains, earth, plants, and animals.[7]

There are many striking resemblances to the Genesis narrative: the first stage of creation involves separating the universe into two halves (heaven and earth or sky and earth) after which arose the various terrains on earth as well the animals that populate them; finally, humanity was created in its own special process, which in both cases humans were moulded from the dirt of the ground. Furthermore, some versions of the Pan-ku story recount parts of the world being created from parts of Pan-ku's body—like the creation of the sun and moon from his eyes—quite similar to the Hindu Purusha stories.

These similar creation myths are getting at the same deeper meaning: that all of existence has a common origin, that human beings may be a special breed but ultimately, we were still made from the same basic material as the rest of the earth; we should, thus, make sure not to forget our fundamental interconnectedness with the rest of the world around us. We are different from other creatures, but not separate. As it is written in the Qur'an, 'And God has created every animal from water: of them there are some that creep on their bellies; some that walk on two legs; and some that walk on four. God creates what He wills; for verily God has power over all things.'[8] The diversity of life on earth can be traced to a common source.

Referring more broadly to creation of the rest of the world, the Qur'an references the basic Genesis narrative: 'Your guardian-Lord is God who created the heavens and the earth in six days and is firmly established on the throne (of authority): He draweth the night as a veil o'er the day each seeking the other in rapid succession: He created the sun the moon

[7]*Lieh-tzu: A Taoist Guide to Practical Living,* trans. Eva Wong (Boston: Shambhala, 2001), 24.

[8]Qur'an, 24:45 (Yusuf Ali).

and the stars (all) governed by laws under His command. Is it not His to create and to govern? Blessed be God the cherisher and sustainer of the worlds!'[9]

A similar theme regarding the origin of the many different parts of creation is delivered through the following formulation. It is taken from the basic Taoist cosmological creation myth, as presented by the Taoist sage Chuang Tzu.

> At the great Origin there was nothing, nothing, no name.
> The One arose from it; there was One without form.
> In taking different forms, it brought life, and became known as Virtue.
> Before any shape was given, their roles were assigned,
> varied and diverse but all linked to one another.
> This was their lot.[10]

This creation myth is a bit more abstract and succinct, attempting to directly get at the heart of the message. It claims that the various forms of living and non-living things share a unified core that underlie the exterior and visible diversity. Interpretations like these allow us to recognize our differences and to see them as a cause for celebration, instead of being read as a tool to incite fear and hatred of one another.

Therefore, we can think of creation myths not as closed books confined to a distant past, but as living narratives that are continually reminding us of truths which might otherwise be forgotten. Perhaps this is part of what the Baha'i leader 'Abdu'l-Bahá meant when he declared, 'The world of creation has had no beginning and will have no end, because it is the arena upon which the attributes and qualities of the spirit are being manifested. Can we limit God and his power? In the same manner we cannot limit his creations and attributes.'[11] The literal meaning of many of these creation myths is that all of existence was

[9]Qur'an 7:54 (Yusuf Ali).

[10]*The Book of Chuang Tzu*, trans. Martin Palmer, Penguin Classics edition (New York: Penguin Books, 2006), 97.

[11]'Abdu'l-Bahá, *'Abdu'l Baha on Divine Philosophy*, digital version (Boston, MA: The Tudor Press, 1918), 169. Baha'i Library Online, accessed 10 July 2022, http://bahai-library.com/abdulbaha_divine_philosophy&chapter=all.

created instantaneously in the past, but today we know that that isn't true. Life is constantly proliferating into new forms, terrain on earth is ever-changing and the universe is expanding and giving birth to new stars that live out their lives, die and are reborn as new stars yet again. Creation and destruction are intertwined.

The Hindu monk and guru Paramhansa Yogananda sums up this recurring characteristic of creation myths. 'Creation is ruled by the law of duality. For every up there is a down; for every plus there is a minus. Every pleasure is balanced by an equal displeasure; every joy, by an equal sorrow.'[12] Because these principles of duality complement one another, in Hindu philosophy it is often referred to as 'non-dualism'—that the dualities we perceive in life are in actuality just two sides of the same single coin. Creation myths are, therefore, an opportunity to illustrate this principle using the complementarity of creation and destruction to remind us that life's dualities, which may seem to us like contradictions, are in fact necessary pairs. We cannot have one without the other.

We might be tempted to think of this concept of complementary duality as something distinctly 'Eastern'. We can also cite another famous example of this as the yin-yang principle in Chinese religions. But this distinction is not necessarily true. The Jewish Hasidic leader Nachman of Breslov, for instance, writes, 'All creation is a rotating wheel, revolving and alternating. Everything goes in cycles. Man becomes angel, and angel, man. Head becomes foot, and foot head. All these things have a single root. All interchange, raising the low, lowering the high, spinning on the wheel of creation.'[13] There are many parallels to this in the religions of India and East Asia. Hinduism and Buddhism both describe the cycle of life and death as a rotating wheel; the principle of 'raising the low' and 'lowering the high' appears prominently in the teachings and writings of many Taoist sages, such as Lao Tzu's, Tao Te Ching. We are all part of this one cosmic dance of highs and lows and the many cyclical aspects of our universe. Realizing that we are all so many spokes on this single wheel

---

[12]Paramhansa Yogananda, c. ed. Swami Kriyananda, (Nevada: Crystal Clarity Publishers, 2013).

[13]Nachman of Breslov, 'Sichot HaRan' in *Tree of Souls: The Mythology of Judaism*, ed. Howard Schwartz (Oxford: Oxford University Press, 2007), 121.

should instill in us a sense of humility that ought to lessen any feelings of inferiority or superiority we may have.

Ultimately, there is and will likely remain a profound sense of mystery regarding the origin, purpose and fate of our universe. As our time on earth has led us to uncover new facts and discoveries, we have had to discard creation stories that simply lose their validity as a result of the shifting paradigms of human knowledge. This is also true of our conceptions of the current state of the cosmos. We have overcome the illusion that earth was the centre of the universe and that the sun was revolving around it. But there is still much that we do not understand.

Every religion is engaged in creation myths as yet another common meaning-making endeavour, and it makes sense that the stories share many similar elements given the similar conditions of early human development. Likewise, the more minor differences in creation myths can be easily explained by the minor variations in the development of different civilizations. In this sense, creation myths promote a sense of unity among all peoples and all forms of life. Hopefully, we can continue to cultivate this awareness in the years to come.

18

The Hero's Journey

We shall not cease from exploration
And the end of all our exploring
Will be to arrive where we started
And know the place for the first time.[1]

—T.S. Eliot

The narrative pattern of the 'the hero's journey' has been most famously described by Joseph Campbell in *The Hero with a Thousand Faces*. Campbell says that this is a cyclical journey that involves setting out from home to go on an adventure of truth-seeking and self-discovery, only to return where we started, but with greater knowledge to share with others. Campbell says, 'A hero ventures forth from the world of common day into a region of supernatural wonder: fabulous forces are there encountered and a decisive victory is won: the hero comes back from this mysterious adventure with the power to bestow boons on his fellow man.'[2] Wise individuals from across time and place in human history have similarly dwelt upon the paradox of

[1]T.S. Eliot, 'Little Gidding', *Four Quartets*. Columbia University, http://www.columbia.edu/itc/history/winter/w3206/edit/tseliotlittlegidding.html.

[2]Joseph Campbell, *The Hero with a Thousand Faces*, third edition (Novato: New World Library, 2008), 23.

the journey of life that resembles a path which ends where it started, and Campbell shows how this pattern is common across religions.

It has become a bit of a cliché to say that 'life is about the journey, not the destination', or simply, 'the journey is more important than the destination'. But like many clichés, it contains a lot of truth. After all, the destination of life is death, which is uncontrollable and unknowable, as is our birth and its circumstances. It is the part in between called life that we can wield some control over.

We all hope that our journeys in life will bring us closer to knowledge, but along the way, we make mistakes and confront our own defects; this is true even of the prophets. The Buddha, for instance, settled upon teaching the 'Middle Way', but only after he learned from his own personal experiences. He saw the folly of extreme hedonism on the one hand, and extreme asceticism on the other. The entire teachings of Hindu philosophy were brought to him at home, he being the son of a king. But he had to leave home to escape from a cultural system that he later felt was lacking in truth. Along the way, he suffered the trials of his ascetic and hedonistic phases, but it was because of those trials that he eventually managed to achieve enlightenment. Having undergone the hero's journey, he was able to put his insights into sermons and narratives that were relatable and universally understood by the audiences he taught. His lesson was also that enlightenment was less about 'gaining' something, and more about 'shedding' that which holds us back from understanding the knowledge that we all have within. Again, this is in line with the hero's journey as a cycle that involves making sacrifices—leaving home, giving up on socially conditioned values and beliefs, etc.

Similarly, Confucius went on a hero's journey in the midst of the violent and tumultuous Warring States era of Chinese history. He wished to see a unified and more peaceful China. To that end, he travelled from one state to the next, trying to share his thoughts and insights with various political and military rulers. He had to endure many trials, such as the repeated sting of rejections of his knowledge by these rulers, and it eventually forced him to give up and return home. But it was only once he returned that the Confucius we know really emerged—the one who taught lessons to his students which were codified as his famous Analects, and have formed the backbone of the Chinese education system for the past several millennia.

Another one of the great classics of religious literature, the Bhagavad Gita also tells the story of a great civil war. At the centre is the hero, Arjuna, who must be coaxed into fighting against his own relatives by Krishna. But the Bhagavad Gita is not a text that promotes violence. Rather, the scenario that Arjuna finds himself in is used as a parable to illustrate the arc of the hero's journey. The external conflict on the battlefield reflects the deeper, more important, internal conflict that Arjuna must learn to overcome. Hence, the actual teachings of the Bhagavad Gita are all about mental and spiritual conquest and the internal journey that such conquest involves.

Turning to the Abrahamic religions of the West, the prophets there had to go on their various heroes' journeys as well. Abraham had to endure a test of faith when he was asked to bring his only son to the top of a mountain to sacrifice him at God's command. Noah had to endure his time in the belly of a whale. Moses had to endure his time as a slave in Egypt, and subsequently lead his people out of exile, traversing an inhospitable desert on the way to the Promised Land. Jesus spent forty nights alone in the desert. Muhammad withdrew from society to meditate in caves, and so on. These heroes' journeys are reflected in the teachings of their respective scriptures.

Judaism itself can be seen as one grand journey. Journeying is the central motif driving the narrative of the canonical scriptures in the Hebrew Bible. The Israelites are constantly presented with hardships and obstacles on the way to God's Promised Land. Towards the end of their journey, Moses reminds his people, 'You shall remember all the way which Yahweh your God has led you these forty years in the wilderness, that he might humble you, to test you, to know what was in your heart, whether you would keep his commandments or not.'[3] The Jewish identity is heavily based around this sense of having one's faith tested by God—from the famous story of Abraham being asked to sacrifice his only son, to the more recent and horrific historic example of the Holocaust, and all the diasporic journeys and persecution in between.

---

[3]Deuteronomy 8:2 (World English Bible).

The Qur'an offers a similar message of being tested by God through the journey of individuals and humanity as a whole. 'To each among you have we prescribed a law and an open way. If God had so willed He would have made you a single people but (His plan is) to test you in what He hath given you: so strive as in a race in all virtues. The goal of you all is to God; it is He that will show you the truth of the matters in which ye dispute.'[4]

Stories in all the three Abrahamic religions are, in large part, about the grand goal of bringing disparate communities of humans together under the same God. Indeed, the goal is to understand that we all come from the same God, and are simply on a journey to return home. In the Qur'an, for instance, God asks, 'Did ye then think that we had created you in jest, and that ye would not be brought back to us (for account)?'[5] Similarly, in the Hebrew Bible, it is said, 'For then I will purify the lips of the peoples, that they may all call on Yahweh's name, to serve him shoulder to shoulder.'[6] This represents a reversal of the splitting up of humanity into separate linguistic communities, as told in the Hebrew Bible, through the story of the Tower of Babel. We were separated so that we might undergo the journey of reuniting with one another.

The popular British philosopher Alan Watts, who was friends with Joseph Campbell, encapsulated this common narrative of journeying to return to God by likening it to one big cosmic game of hide-and-seek.

> That's the drama. So, to be frank and sum up my metaphysics: there's the central self—you can call it God or whatever you like—and it's all of us. And it's playing all the parts of every single being throughout the universe, and it's playing the game of hide-and-seek with itself. It gets involved in far-out adventures, it gets lost, but in the end, it always wakes up and comes back to itself. And when you're ready to wake up, you're going to wake up. And if you're not ready to wake up yet, you'll keep pretending that you're just some 'poor little me'.[7]

---

[4]Qur'an, 5:48 (Yusuf Ali).

[5]Qur'an, 23:115 (Yusuf Ali).

[6]Zephaniah 3:9 (World English Bible).

[7]Alan Watts, *Out of Your Mind: Tricksters, Interdependence, and the Cosmic Game of Hide-and-Seek* (Boulder: Sounds True, 2017), 22.

Viewed this way, the narratives of journeys that we find in the scriptures of all religions are meant to apply to us individually as well. Read metaphorically, they are about the human journey. We feel like strangers in the world. It presents us with all sorts of mysteries and trials that we do not understand, and we yearn to live in a world that makes more sense. But what we discover is that the journey of life is more about waking up to our own world rather than travelling to a different one.

As novelist Gustav Meyrink notes, 'It is one thing to stay at home, and quite another to return home after one has been abroad for a great length of time.'[8] The Taoist sage Lieh Tzu must have had something similar in mind when reflecting upon life and death.

> Death helps the unscrupulous person to put an end to the misery of desire. Death, then, for everyone, is a kind of homecoming. That is why the ancient sages speak of a dying person as a person who is 'going home'. On the other hand, a living person is a traveling person. Normally, if a traveler fails to find home when his journeys are over, everyone will agree that this person has lost his way. However, in the journey of life, many travelers only know how to wander but do not know how to return home. And yet people do not see that these travelers have likewise lost their way.[9]

Surely, one of the great pitfalls we encounter along the journey of life is that of desire, of developing attachments to external and impermanent things. Lieh Tzu uses the analogy of travelling to, once again, make the point that life's journey must be undertaken to 'rediscover' home, to shed that which is extraneous and that which gets in the way of true knowledge and wisdom. In this case, it is desire.

The other important dimension to consider is that we are all on our own journeys, and we differ quite greatly in our starting points, circumstances and so forth. So much bigotry and religiously motivated conflict comes from this impulse to prove the value of our own paths by

---

[8]Meyrink, Gustav, *The Green Face*, trans. Mike Mitchell (Sawtry: Dedalus, 2004), 158.
[9]*Lieh-tzu: A Taoist Guide to Practical Living*, trans. Eva Wong (Boston: Shambhala, 2001), 40.

putting others down. But as Campbell writes, 'The whole sense of the ubiquitous myth of the hero's passage is that it shall serve as a general pattern for men and women, wherever they may stand along the scale. Therefore, it is formulated in the broadest terms.'[10]

Many religions emphasize that truth comes from within (indeed, there is a whole chapter in this book dedicated to that!), but there is also a general consensus that we each must come to this realization in our own ways by taking the journey of life. As Baha'i leader 'Abdu'l-Bahá notes:

> Briefly; the journey of the soul is necessary. The pathway of life is the road which leads to divine knowledge and attainment. Without training and guidance the soul could never progress beyond the conditions of its lower nature which is ignorant and defective.[11]

The stories and teachings of the prophets, written in the scriptures, across religions are meant to give us the training and guidance necessary for us to navigate our *own* hero's journeys, but because we are all different and we all make meaning in different ways, we will all benefit more from certain teachings over others. The various religious traditions are not at odds with one another. They are simply reflections of the diversity of our own species and the many different paths through which our lives unfold.

---

[10]Joseph Campbell, 'The Hero with a Thousand Faces' in *The Collected Works of Joseph Campbell* (Novato: New World Library, 2008), 101.

[11]'Abdu'l-Bahá, *The Promulgation of Universal Peace*, second edition (US: Bahá'í Publishing Trust: 1982), 296, Baha'i Reference Library. http://reference.bahai.org/en/t/ab/PUP/pup-97.html

19

Sacred Time

The equating of a single year in Paradise to one hundred of earthly existence is a motif well known to myth.[1]

—Joseph Campbell

Religions and other belief systems have been telling us for millennia that time, as we typically experience it, is an illusion. More recently, various branches of science have been providing empirical evidence and logical arguments to prove that time is an illusory human construct. Einstein famously wrote in a letter towards the end of his life, 'For people like us who believe in physics, the separation between past, present and future has only the importance of an admittedly tenacious illusion.'[2] And yet, despite this fact, most of us are unable to break free from this powerful illusion.

We can recognize some examples of time's relational dependence on events in our lives. As we get older, for instance, we feel as though time is passing faster—each year starts to feel shorter, and before we know it, we come to lament the loss of our youth. We also experience time as

---

[1]Joseph Campbell, *The Hero with a Thousand Faces*, The Collected Works of Joseph Campbell Series edition (Novato, CA: New World Library, 2008), 192.

[2]Albert Einstein, letter to the family of Michele Besso (March 1955), Christie's, https://www.christies.com/features/Einstein-letters-to-Michele-Besso-8422-1.aspx

moving more rapidly when we are enjoying ourselves.

Scriptures are filled with descriptions of alternative experiences of time, which we might call 'sacred time', or time as experienced by Gods and, to some extent, prophets and religious devotees. Descriptions of sacred time range from hyperbolically lengthy periods, to the ideal of living fully in the moment and experiencing life in a constant state of timelessness. Religious conceptions of time that are so hyperbolically grand serve to underscore both the relativity of time and the limitations of our own cognition, especially when we compare it to its cosmic scale. We are constrained by time and space, but God is outside of time and space.

The religions of India are known for describing the universe as progressing through incomprehensibly lengthy cycles of time. In the Vishnu Purana, for instance, it is said, 'Twelve thousand divine years constitute a period of the four Ages, and a thousand of the four Ages is called a day of Brahman, or an aeon (kalpa), in which there are fourteen Manus. At the end of the aeon there occurs the occasional dissolution brought about by Brahman.'[3] A 'day of Brahman', which signifies one life cycle of the world (after which the world is destroyed and reborn once more), is said to be 4.32 billion years. This happens to be strikingly close to our current conception of the earth's age— 4.54 billion years. A striking prescience when we consider that these are texts composed thousands of years ago! The Vishnu Purana also states that 'kala' (time) is one of the four forms of Vishnu. Indeed, in the Bhagavad Gita, Krishna tells the hero, Arjuna, 'I am time that has aged, who makes the world perish. I have come forth to destroy the worlds.'[4] Time, then, is a manifestation of God and the means whereby creation and destruction of the universe are cyclically performed.

When it comes to the Buddhist traditions, these same terms ('kalpa', 'manu', etc.) are preserved from Hinduism, but the Buddha preferred to describe these macro-units of time in terms of illustrations, rather than exact numbers. The Lotus Sutra is a Buddhist text that records some of

---

[3]*The Norton Anthology of World Religions: Vol. 1*, Ed. Jack Miles (New York: W.W. Norton & Company, 2015), 249.

[4]*The Bhagavad Gita*, trans. Laurie L. Patton (New York: Penguin, 2014), 11:32

these illustrations. In one example we are asked to imagine 'that someone took all the earth particles in the thousand-millionfold world and ground them to make ink powder, and as he passed through the thousand lands of the east, he dropped one grain of the ink powder no bigger in size than a speck of dust'.[5] The Buddha goes on to say that the time it would take for this person to deplete all of the ink powder if he carried on this way would be comparable to the time that has passed since the last Buddha appeared on earth. In other words, an unfathomably long period of time!

The lesson contained in these hyperbolic illustrations is twofold: (1) it is foolish and hubristic to try to put an exact number on a length of time so unfathomably large, and (2) it is incredibly rare to be born into a time so close to the life and teachings of a Buddha.

The Abrahamic traditions describe the vastness of God through vast scales of time. In the New Testament, it is said, 'One day is with the Lord as a thousand years, and a thousand years as one day.'[6] So omnipotent and ancient is God that the difference between a day and a thousand years—which seems like a huge gulf to us—is negligible for God. Similarly, in the Qur'an it is said that 'judgement day' will be experienced as, 'a day the measure whereof is (as) fifty thousand years'.[7]

The deeper meaning behind all this is a familiar message, one that underlies much of religious literature and ritual practice: in order to live a good life, we must strive towards dissolving our egoistic belief that the world revolves around us. Rather, time is constantly flowing, and so are we, moving along its stream. We are not the static creatures we feel we are, and from the perspective of the universe at large, our lives are not nearly as long or as consequential as we would like to believe. The Greek philosopher Heraclitus expressed this with his famous aphorism, 'We can never step in the same river twice.' The water in a river is constantly flowing, and each time we step into it, we will be stepping into a unique portion of that water that will exist where it is for only a moment, and then pass away to make room for the next flow. Even though the river

[5]Burton Watson, trans, *The Lotus Sutra* (New York: Columbia University Press, 1993), 117-18.

[6]2 Peter 3:8 (World English Bible).

[7]Qur'an, 70:2-4 (Yusuf Ali).

might look the same to us at each moment, it really is not the same. So, too, we are never the same, though we may not be aware of that. Our cells are constantly dying and being replaced by new ones, such that almost none of the cells that exist in our body at this moment existed seven or ten years ago. Thus, in deeply contemplating the passage of time, we can see that any sense of permanence we ascribe to things in our life—our egos, our possessions, our life itself—is merely an illusion. We are reminded of the many mysteries of life and told that we are not the masters of the universe; rather, we are the droplets of water in the river of time.

In this way, we are connected—not only with all of life, but indeed with all living and non-living things. All matter is composed of the same basic building blocks, and all matter is subject to the same mutability that is imposed by time, all particles constantly being exchanged and recombined with one another. And at this point in time, we are all simply in one of many infinite arrangements. There were many more before, and there will be many more to come. As the Baha'i leader 'Abdu'l-Bahá points out, 'The earth life lasts but a short time, even its benefits are transitory; that which is temporary does not deserve our heart's attachment.'[8] But rather than despairing over this realization, we can learn from it.

Much of what we stress over is really not all that serious. Life has its ups and downs, but if we do not identify so strongly with our individual egos, then we need not feel so high (or so low) with respect to the events that befall us.

And yet, once again, we need not despair over this. The constant flow of time does not rob the present moment of its beauty and magic. Indeed, much of contemplative practice is predicated upon the belief that the eternal can be found only in the present.

The Zen master Shunryu Suzuki taught that 'If you sit in the right manner, with the right understanding, you attain the freedom of your being, even though you are just a temporal existence.'[9] Similarly, the great Hindu teacher Swami Vivekananda maintained that 'The Vedanta

---

[8]'Abdu'l-Bahá, *'Abdu'l-Bahá on Divine Philosophy*, ed. Elizabeth Fraser Chamberlain (Boston: Tudor Press, 1918), 135, Baha'i Library Online, http://bahai-library.com/abdulbaha_divine_philosophy&chapter=3

[9]Shunryu Suzuki, *Zen Mind, Beginner's Mind* (Boston: Shambhala, 2011), 94.

teaches that Nirvana can be attained here and now, that we do not have to wait for death to reach it. Nirvana is the realization of the Self; and after having once known that, if only for an instant, never again can one be deluded by the mirage of personality.'[10]

A modern voice, Harvard-trained neuroscientist Jill Bolte Taylor reflects upon the life-altering event of suffering and recovering from a massive stroke: 'The present moment is a time when everything and everyone are connected together as one.'[11] By living in the present, we may not escape time's grasp or lose sight of the hold it has over us, but we come to a deeper and healthier understanding of time and of the world around us. We grasp the full weight of the reality that is the present, moment to moment. We realize it is futile and foolish to try to cling to the past or any one single moment in time, just as it is foolish to cling to our own individual selves, as if they were somehow more important than others. In our understanding, we finally develop a deep respect for each moment in time.

---

[10]Swami Vivekananda, *The Vedanta Philosophy: An Address Before the Graduate Philosophical Society of Harvard University,* 25 March 1896 (New York: Vedanta Society, 1901), 42.

[11]Jill Bolte Taylor, *My Stroke of Insight: A Brain Scientist's Personal Journey* (New York: Plume Books, 2009), 30.

20

Mantra and Recitation

It behoveth us one and all to recite day and night [...]to pray fervently and supplicate tearfully that we may be enabled to conduct ourselves in accordance with these divine counsels. These holy words have not been revealed to be heard but to be practised.[1]

—'Abdu'l-Bahá

The scriptures of all religions are full of stories, laws, prayers and so forth—all of which are important devotional guides. The fact is that much of this information is likely to not stick in our day-to-day lives. Our conscious minds are equipped to store only so much information at once, and even then, it takes a great deal of repetition to keep it there.

Recitation is the common religious practice. The most important parts of scripture are repeated and they become constant reminders for us, getting us through the day, functioning as a guide that can shape our attitudes and behaviours according to religious values. As the Baha'i prophet Baha'u'llah advised, 'Recite ye the verses of God every morn and

---

[1]Abdu'l-Bahá,'Deepening Our Knowledge and Understanding of the Faith, The Importance of,' in *Compilation of Compilations*, Vol. 1 (1991); Baha'i Library Online, http://bahai-library.com/compilation_importance_deepening#37

eventide.'[2] Recitation helps to bring the literary and theological aspects of religion into the world of daily practice.

Mantras are recitations that are especially easy to remember—attesting to their supreme importance—due to their brevity. The term 'mantra' originally comes from Hinduism, but it is also used colloquially by many to refer to short hymns, chants and other devotional phrases across religions, and even beyond religion, such as in areas like psychotherapy or dieting. Mantras are short phrases that help focus the mind on important goals or objects of contemplation.

The most famous, important and brief mantra is the single syllable, 'Om' or 'Aum', in the religions of India, including Hinduism, Buddhism and Jainism. It is a syllable that is believed to have created the entire universe, which is why its recitation is important. The sound itself is powerful, rather than just the written letters. 'Om' is also used as a part of various slightly longer mantras. In the Bhagavad Gita, it is written, 'Om Tat Sat: these three words represent Brahman, from which come priests and scriptures and sacrifice. Those who follow the Vedas, therefore, always repeat the word Om when offering sacrifices, performing spiritual disciplines, or giving gifts.'[3] Another important Hindu mantra is the Gayatri mantra, recited by pious Hindus every day at sunrise.

> oṃ bhūr bhuvaḥ svaḥ
> tat savitur vareṇyaṃ
> bhargo devasya dhīmahi
> dhiyo yo naḥ prachodayāt[4]

It translates as 'Let us meditate on this beloved light of the God who enlivens. May He inspire our thoughts.' These mantras are short enough to be easily remembered and recited on a daily basis, while still capturing the essence of the most important beliefs and scriptures.

Along similar lines, the Abrahamic traditions of the West have their

---

[2]Bahá'u'lláh, *The Kitáb-i-Aqdas* (Bahá'í World Centre: 1992), 73, Baha'i Reference Library,_http://reference.bahai.org/en/t/b/KA/ka-7.html

[3]*The Bhagavad Gita*, trans. Eknath Easwaran, Second Edition (Tomales: Nilgiri Press, 2007), 17:23-24.

[4]Wendy Doniger, *Hinduism, The Norton Anthology of World Religions: Vol. 1*, Ed. Jack Miles (New York: W.W. Norton & Company, 2015), 83.

own sacred phrases that are meant to be recited frequently. As author Philip Goldberg notes that, 'Many Christians intone one of these Latin phrases: Veni, Sancte Spiritus (Come, Holy Spirit) [and] Agnus Dei, qui tollis peccata mundi, miserere nobis (Lamb of God, who takes away the sins of the world, have mercy on us).'[5] There are, of course, many longer sacred phrases and prayers that are recited by Christians on a near-daily basis, but these are just two examples of particularly short ones.

Judaism and Islam attach great importance to the frequent recitation of short verses which serve as affirmations of God's oneness. In Judaism, this is known as 'shema' (which means to 'hear'): 'Sh'ma Yisrael Adonai Eloheinu Adonai Eḥad', or, 'Hear, Israel: Yahweh is our God. Yahweh is one.'[6] This is the most important Jewish prayer, and it is so important that not only is it meant to be recited multiple times per day, but many pious Jews even resolve to recite these words as their very last utterance before they die. The equivalent of this in Islam is the passage from the Qur'an known as the Surat al-Ikhlas.

1 Qul huwa l-lāhu 'aḥad(un)
2 'allāhu ṣ-ṣamad(u)
3 Lam yalid walam yūlad
4 Walam yaku n-lahū kufuwan 'aḥad(un)

This translates to, 'Say: He is God, The One and Only; God, the Eternal, Absolute; He begetteth not, Nor is He begotten; And there is none like unto Him.'[7] The importance of this phrase is underscored by the following historical exchange, reported by anthropologist Saba Mahmood. 'The Prophet said to Ali, if he recited Surat al-Ikhlas [a short chapter of the Quran comprising of four verses] three times before going to sleep, it was as if he had recited the whole Quran.'[8] In fact, many Muslims do memorize the entire Qur'an from an early age so that they *can* recite the entire thing. But this condensed statement is

---

[5]Philip Goldberg, *Spiritual Practice for Crazy Times: Powerful Tools to Cultivate Calm, Clarity, and Courage*, (New York: Hay House, 2020) 58.

[6]Deuteronomy 6:4 (World English Bible).

[7]Qur'an, 112:1-4 (Yusuf Ali).

[8]Saba Mahmood, *Politics of Piety: The Islamic Revival and the Feminist Subject* (New Jersey: Princeton University Press, 2004), 94.

especially important and can be recited many times every day.

I have been practising transcendental meditation for the last forty years. Initially, I was asked to share a few short names or words that I associate with either God or the general concept of goodness with my teachers. My answers were used to create and assign me with my own unique mantra. This mantra is supposed be the vehicle that enables travel to my deeper consciousness. I have been a big believer and a beneficiary of this meditation. Most Eastern meditative practices involve the use of some mantra; many involve sitting quietly and focusing on your natural breathing or on a word or phrase (mantra) that can be repeated silently. We are told to allow thoughts to come and go without judgement—and to turn our focus on the breathing, or the mantra. The basic idea is the same: the mantra helps us quieten the noise of our minds and puts us in touch with our deeper selves.

Devotees of many religions attest to the importance of recitations and mantras as it helps them to be more pious. This demonstrates the value that mantras can have in helping us shape our thoughts, attitudes and behaviour more broadly. They can help us to live more consciously, making us better people and infusing our lives with more meaning. There are examples of this in the ancient texts of Chinese religions as well. The Confucian scholar Zhu Xi taught the following:

> Choose what is good and firmly hold onto it. If we extend our knowledge and investigate the phenomena of things then this is choosing what is good. If we make our thoughts sincere, maintain an upright mind, and cultivate ourselves, this is firmly holding on. These two principles are all that we need.[9]

The conviction that just two principles can be all that we need to keep in mind closely parallels the aphorisms of ancient Greece, as well as the prayers of the Abrahamic religions.

The ubiquitous nature of mantras, across all the major religions of the world, is one manifestation of the importance of psychological observation and insight in religious traditions. Expounding on some of

---

[9]Chu Hsi, *The Su chin-ssu-lu*, 2:17, in *Further Reflections on Things at Hand: A Reader*, trans. Allen John Wittenborn (Lanham: University Press of America, 1991), 75.

the basic religious practices of Christianity, writer and theologian C.S. Lewis explains how they are meant to correspond to the natural flaws and limitations of our minds.

> That is why daily prayers and religious reading and church going are necessary parts of the Christian life. We have to be continually reminded of what we believe. Neither this belief nor any other will automatically remain alive in the mind. It must be fed.[10]

The reason that mantras and recitations are important is that we are constantly faced with distractions—both internal and external—and without constant reminders we may lose sight of what we hold to be most valuable in life. Mantras help us to tame our 'monkey mind'—the mind which is restless and which, just like a monkey, constantly jumps from one branch of a tree to another, or from one thought to another.

Zen master Shunryu Suzuki claims something similar in his description of the 'beginner's mind' and its role in Zen practices.

> In Japan we have the phrase shoshin, which means 'beginner's mind'. The goal of practice is always to keep our beginner's mind. Suppose you recite the Prajna Paramita Sutra only once. It might be a very good recitation. But what would happen to you if you recited it twice, three times, four times, or more? You might easily lose your original attitude towards it.[11]

Recitations, like any other ritual practice, can become mundane as they are so routine. But we should remember that it is not enough to just articulate the words and sounds, but to mean them as well. After all, the whole purpose of mantras and recitations is to bridge the gap between theory and practice, to value deeds over words.

Mantras and recitations not only help to cultivate a pious self, but also help to cultivate a kind of steadiness in our mind, or an improved ability to exert more conscious control over the more mercurial parts of our mind. Our moods change, our circumstances in life change, but if we train our minds to retain certain key principles, even in the midst

---

[10]C.S. Lewis, *The C.S. Lewis Signature Classics* (New York: HarperCollins, 2017), 117.
[11]Shunryu Suzuki, *Zen Mind, Beginner's Mind* (Boston: Shambhala, 2011), 1.

of all the internal and external chaos, then we can train our minds in other ways as well. This is just one religious practice among many that is ultimately about helping us overcome the non-rational and animalistic parts of our being that, left uncontrolled, can lead us towards selfishness and hate rather than empathy and love. There is incalculable value in this for all, regardless of our particular beliefs.

21

Prayer and Meditation

> *The purpose of spiritual exercises such as meditation and yoga is to open ourselves up to what is inside us and the ultimate goal is union—union with ourselves. There is an everyday self and a spiritual self, though most people go through their lives unaware of the latter.*[1]
>
> —Mike Mitchell

Since I was five, and till I was sixteen-years-old, I sat down every day in the temple within our home and offered prayers to Lord Krishna and observed silence with closed eyes. It is a common form of meditation. Of course I was just copying what my mother and father and most other Hindus did every day. There were also longer and more elaborate prayers on special occasions, like on family members' birthdays or any of the holy festivals. This practice is thought not just to be ceremonial, but also an important part of personal development. As the Bhagavad Gita puts it, 'The wise master their senses, mind, and intellect through meditation.'[2]

---

[1]Mike Mitchell, *Vivo: The Life of Gustav Meyrink* (Sawtry, UK: Dedalus, 2008), 211.
[2]*The Bhagavad Gita*, trans. Eknath Easwaran, Second Edition (Tomales: Nilgiri Press, 2007), 5:27-28.

Prayer and meditation are two of the most common and valuable contemplative practices that occupy a central role in any wisdom tradition. Prayer and meditation are two sides of the same coin. Essentially, the aim of both practices is and always has been the same: to penetrate into the divine residing within us and to bring this divine self (or soul) to the surface, creating a bridge between ourselves and whatever we consider holy—be it God, nature, deep consciousness, etc.

Each religion has a wide range of prayers and recitations for various occasions, but usually, there are one or two that stand out as most important. Every day at sunrise, for instance, devout Hindus recite the Gayatri Mantra (see Mantra and Recitation chapter).

Likewise, the Western monotheistic traditions have particularly important and oft-recited prayers for their daily worship. Jews recite the 'Shema': 'Hear, Israel: Yahweh is our God. Yahweh is one.'[3] Many Christians say the 'Lord's Prayer' every day.

> Our Father in heaven, may your name be kept holy.
> Let your Kingdom come.
> Let your will be done on earth as it is in heaven.
> Give us today our daily bread.
> Forgive us our debts,
> as we also forgive our debtors.
> Bring us not into temptation,
> but deliver us from the evil one.
> For yours is the Kingdom, the power, and the glory forever.
> Amen.[4]

And once a day at noon, those who follow the Baha'i faith recite the following prayer. 'I bear witness, O my God, that Thou has created me to know Thee and to worship Thee. I testify, at this moment, to my powerlessness and to Thy might, to my poverty and to Thy wealth. There is none other God but Thee, the help in peril, the self-subsisting.'[5]

---

[3]Deuteronomy 6:4 (World English Bible).

[4]Matthew 6:9-13 (World English Bible).

[5]Bahá'u'lláh, *Prayers and Meditations by Bahá'u'lláh,* pocket-size edition (US: Bahá'í Publishing Trust, 1987), 314, Baha'i Reference Library, https://reference.bahai.org/en/t/b/PM/pm-181.html.

Muslims say the following prayer five times a day, as it follows one of the Five Pillars of Islam (salat or namaz).

> In the name of God, Most Gracious, Most Merciful.
> Praise be to God,
> The Cherisher and Sustainer of the Worlds;
> Most Gracious, Most Merciful;
> Master of the Day of Judgement.
> Thee do we worship,
> And Thine aid we seek.
> Show us the straight way,
> The way of those on whom
> Thou hast bestowed Thy Grace,
> Those whose (portion)
> Is not wrath,
> And who go not astray.[6]

The anthropologist Saba Mahmood claims that prayer in Islam is arguably an inseparable feature of the Muslim identity itself.

> The performance of ritual prayer (singular: salat; plural: salawat [also known as namaz]) is considered so centrally important in Islam that the question of whether someone who does not pray regularly qualifies as a Muslim has been a subject of intense debate among theologians. The correct execution of salat depends on the following elements: (a) an intention to dedicate the prayer to God; (b) a prescribed sequence of gestures and words; (c) a physical condition of purity; and (d) proper attire.[7]

The importance of prayer is further underscored by criteria for *how* to pray, a list which includes both internal and external elements. Muslims are asked to look inward to establish the right kind of individual intention, as well as outward to see that—through a shared appearance—they are part of a larger community.

---

[6]Qur'an 1:1-7 (Yusuf Ali).

[7]Saba Mahmood, *Politics of Piety: The Islamic Revival and the Feminist Subject* (New Jersey: Princeton University Press, 2004), 123.

This element of intention is central to both prayer and meditation in other religions as well, including the other Abrahamic traditions. In the New Testament of Christianity, for instance, we are told, 'All things whatever you pray and ask for, believe that you have received them, and you shall have them.'[8] Even when our prayers are directed towards an external deity, they also require an inward focus to make them effective. This inward focus of intention keeps prayer—which is otherwise practised with the uniformity of any communal ritual—from becoming old and repetitive.

In popular imagination, meditation tends to be romanticized as something mysterious and exotic, something that only takes place in the forest or in the mountains by ascetics who have retreated fully from society in order to seek ultimate enlightenment. But there is plenty of religious precedent for seeing meditation as something very ordinary, something that simply demands a focused use of our excess psychic energy on a clear intention. The Confucian scholar Chu Hsi advised, 'Whenever you have to attend to your daily affairs, or undertake any matter, always spend some time in meditation and everything will be all right.'[9] Along similar lines, the early Taoist sage Chuang Tzu used the term 'zuowang' (sitting and forgetting) to describe meditation. 'I smash up my limbs and body, drive out perception and intellect, cast off form, do away with understanding, and make myself identical with the Great Thoroughfare. This is what I mean by sitting down and forgetting everything.'[10]

In his popular book *Zen Mind, Beginner's Mind*, Zen monk Shunryu Suzuki advocated against the idea of viewing meditation as a means towards some special goal. Instead, he argued that meditation and enlightenment are one and the same, emphasizing the accessibility of both. 'In this posture there is no need to talk about the right state of mind. You already have it. This is the conclusion of Buddhism.'[11] In this sense, enlightenment is more about realizing that the divine is not something

---

[8]Mark 11:24 (World English Bible).

[9]Chu Hsi, *The Su chin-ssu-lu, 4:25, in Further Reflections on Things at Hand: A Reader*, trans. Allen John Wittenborn (Lanham: University Press of America, 1991), 101.

[10]*Zhuangzi: Basic Writings*, trans. Burton Watson (New York: Columbia University Press, 2003), 87.

[11]Shunryu Suzuki, *Zen Mind, Beginner's Mind* (Boston: Shambhala, 2011), 11.

to be sought or obtained. Rather, through contemplative practices like meditation, we remind ourselves of the basic truth that our spiritual self—the Buddha nature—is and always has been present in each of us, even though we may fail to realize it. We are connecting with our deeper self, becoming fully aware. This is actually quite similar to the attitude towards prayer in the Abrahamic traditions and other theistic religions. We may pray to God, but we must remember that God exists within us as well. Otherwise, it would not be possible to communicate with God in the first place.

The meditative faculty is not exclusive to any particular religion, particular time period or culture. Rather, meditation is something that all people can benefit from, religious or not. As biologist E.O. Wilson points out, 'The idea of the mystical union is an authentic part of the human spirit. It has occupied humanity for millennia, and it raises questions of utmost seriousness for transcendentalists and scientists alike.'[12] Christian and Sufi mystics, as well as many Hindu saints, believe in a mystical union with God that is a result of prayer and meditation. But more broadly, we can just as well speak of the internal union of different parts of ourselves that can come together in prayer and meditation, making us healthier and more whole.

In even grander terms, the Baha'i leader 'Abdu'l-Bahá maintained that contemplative practice 'brings forth from the invisible plane the sciences and arts. Through the meditative faculty inventions are made possible, colossal undertakings are carried out; through it governments can run smoothly.'[13]

Numerous studies have proclaimed the benefits, in empirical terms, that regular meditation has on our health. Neuroscientists, for instance, have been studying how meditation affects the brain in particular. Deepak Chopra from Stanford University writes about one such study.

---

[12]E.O. Wilson, *Consilience: The Unity of Knowledge* (New York: Knopf Doubleday Publishing Group, 1998).

[13]'Abdu'l-Bahá, 'Address By 'Abdu'l-Bahá At The Friends' Meeting House, St Martin's Lane, London, W.C.' in *Paris Talks*, eleventh edition (UK: Bahá'í Publishing Trust, 1972), 173, Baha'i Reference Library: https://reference.bahai.org/en/t/ab/PT/pt-55.html

All mental activity has to have a physical correlation in the brain, and this aspect has been studied in relation to anxiety. Chronic worriers often display increased reactivity in the amygdala, the area of the brain associated with regulating emotions, including fear. Neuroscientists at Stanford University found that people who practiced mindfulness meditation for eight weeks were more able to turn down the reactivity of this area. Other researchers from Harvard found that mindfulness can physically reduce the number of neurons in this fear-triggering part of the brain.[14]

Chopra is alluding to the numerous studies that have been conducted by Stanford and Harvard to study the therapeutic effects of meditation in people who suffer from mental illness, ranging from anxiety disorders to PTSD and others. Harvard scientists have also 'found increased gray-matter density in the hippocampus, known to be important for learning and memory, and in structures associated with self-awareness, compassion, and introspection'. As Britta Hölzel, the primary author of a research paper, notes, 'It is fascinating to see the brain's plasticity and that, by practicing meditation, we can play an active role in changing the brain and can increase our well-being and quality of life.'[15]

Though the specific styles and philosophies behind these practices differ, all of them have proven to be effective means of shaping inner attitudes, mental patterns and ways of being and interacting in the world and with one another. Given their importance in many religious systems, we often think of prayer and meditation as special rituals with specific rules and spiritual goals. But in a broader sense, anybody who has ever sat in silence and taken a deep breath—even for a brief moment, just to collect their thoughts—has meditated. Anyone who has ever had a focused dialogue with themselves has prayed. The benefits of these practices go beyond religious devotion. Psychologist Mihaly Csikszentmihalyi, famous for his 'flow' theory, explains how '"flow"

[14]Deepak Chopra, 'How meditation can help anxiety', Stanford University Wu Tsai Neurosciences Institute, 14 September 2015, https://neuroscience.stanford.edu/news/how-meditation-can-help-anxiety.

[15]Sue McGreevey, 'Eight weeks to a better brain,' *Harvard Gazette*, 21 January 2011, https://news.harvard.edu/gazette/story/2011/01/eight-weeks-to-a-better-brain/

is the way people describe their state of mind when consciousness is harmoniously ordered, and they want to pursue whatever they are doing for its own sake.'[16] He has written at length about how people from all walks of life can tap into a higher human potential and sense of meaning when entering these flow states, which are often seen in those who engage in contemplative practices like meditation.

Practices such as prayer and meditation focus on drawing out what lies buries deep within us all, and we should pay attention to it rather than squabbling over the differences of their specific rules and guidelines, which will naturally vary from religion to religion due to different cultural developments.

---

[16]Mihaly Csikszentmihalyi, *Flow: The Psychology of Optimal Experience* (New York: Harper Collins, 1991), 6.

22

Rituals

From a narrowly rational or utilitarian point of view, ritual is a waste of time and money, yet it serves functions that nothing can replace [...] Ritual scripts our actions and directs our responses.[1]

—Huston Smith

Religion restores, at regular intervals and through rituals significantly connected with the important crises of the life cycle and the turning points of the yearly cycle, a new sense of wholeness, of things rebound.[2]

—Erik H. Erikson

When we think about what religion looks like we usually visualize a series of solemn-looking figures in special robes, chanting special incantations, cloaked in incense, bathed in candlelight. Wajihuddin Siddiqui explains:

> Rituals are the main lifeline of all societies; religious or secular. They serve as glue, a kind of strong binding cement, to keep

[1]Huston Smith, *The Illustrated World's Religions* (New York: HarperCollins, 1995), 196.
[2]Erik H. Erikson, *Identity: Youth and Crisis* (New York: W. W. Norton & Company, 1994), 83.

> the community well-knit, vibrant and healthy. Besides its spiritual input, rituals train people in the art of living together under a disciplined and organized system. They meet and satisfy so many pragmatic and aesthetic needs and urges of people that they have become a necessary component of human life regardless of the people's beliefs and traditions. Nothing is more common between different religions than the observance of the rituals enumerated below.[3]

All religions have their own permutations of sensorially rich practices that are full of symbolic imagery. They confer a sense of identity and community among worshippers in a deeply immersive setting. As scholar of psychology and religion Robert C. Fuller writes, 'Ritual sights, smells, and actions arrest our attention and lure us into seeking deeper connection with that causal presence or power that somehow lies "beyond" the physical universe.'[4]

But rituals have other functions as well. They attempt to bring about change at the level of individual consciousness. By participating in ritual practices, we may come to reform ourselves in ways that allow us to embody attitudes and behaviours that are more in line with the ideals of our belief systems. As Harvard University professor Michael Puett says, rituals transport us from the 'as is' world into the 'as if' world, or from the day-to-day world to a transcendent world. 'As humans, we tend to fall into sets of patterned responses to the world,' he writes. 'The goal of rituals—of "as if" spaces—is to break us out of these patterns.'[5]

From this perspective, it's not important which spirits or Gods we are imagining or trying to commune with, or which religious tradition our rituals fall into. The important thing about rituals is that they allow us to see past our normal socialized selves. The particular religion, spirit and

---

[3]Wajihuddin Siddiqui, *Commonalities and Similarities in World Religions* (Karachi: Royal Book Company, 2018), 105.

[4]Robert C. Fuller, *Wonder: From Emotion to Spirituality* (Chapel Hill: University of North Carolina Press, 2006), 67-68.

[5]Michael Puett, 'Ritual and Ritual Obligations: Perspectives on Normativity from Classical China,' *Brewminate*, 23 September 2018, https://brewminate.com/ritual-and-ritual-obligations-perspectives-on-normativity-from-classical-china/

God is only important insofar as it allows each of us to personally take the ritual seriously and believe in its power. But there are no rituals or Gods that are superior or inferior to any others. Rituals look different because we are different as a species. Hence, the 'as if' settings we each find most compelling will differ.

Puett is writing from the perspective of the ancient Chinese religions he studies and, undoubtedly, Confucianism is especially famous for its explicit emphasis on the importance of ritual. The backbone of this religious system is its adherence to prescribed rituals which, among other purposes, are meant to cultivate certain virtues of character, with the highest virtue being 'benevolence'—the capacity to behave generously and selflessly, recognizing the oneness of humanity. Confucius says as much in his Analects:

> If for one day you are able to restrain the self and return to the rites, this means that your capacity to be humane will open up to the world.[6]

Rituals typically involve temporarily and periodically occupying liminal spaces where we are compelled to play roles that differ from our regular social ones. Thus, we 'overcome' our normal ego-bound selves by putting ourselves in the shoes of others, realizing that our own way of being is just one among many, highlighting both the diversity and the unity of humanity.

The prescribed scripts of the rituals that are passed down generations also bring people together in shared practices. They offer opportunities for both personal reflection, as well as the experience of being part of a community of mutual interactions, making us capable of seeing the bigger picture beyond our ego-bound selves. Consider, for instance, some of the primary rituals of the Abrahamic religious traditions, as described by historian of religion Jeffrey Kripal. With regard to the Muslim ritual of praying (salat) while facing the holy city of Mecca, he writes, 'Islam displays a special brilliance in the employment of ritual and myth. Getting a billion people to bow down five times a day facing a small city in Saudi Arabia is an extraordinary ritual accomplishment, which unites

[6]Confucius, *The Analects*, trans. Annping Chin (New York: Penguin, 2014), 12:1.

peoples across radically different cultures and backgrounds.'[7] Moreover, the actual pilgrimage (hajj) to Mecca that all Muslims are encouraged to undertake, at least once in their lifetimes, unites people in an even more immediate way, bringing thousands, or even millions, of people together in one place at one time. This show of unity is all the more pronounced because of the clothing prescribed for this occasion. All Muslims on the hajj are meant to wear the same simple white garments, thus temporarily erasing any visual distinctions in social class, reminding everyone that we are all equal in the eyes of God. This ritual, therefore, serves the function of democratization: the rich and poor, rulers and commoners, all follow the same ritual because all are equal in God's eyes.

Just as these rituals in Islam are derived from historical events of the life of Prophet Muhammad, so too are the Jewish and Christian rituals tied to historical events as narrated in biblical stories. One of the most famous and evocative rituals in Judaism takes place during the springtime holiday of Passover. Jeffrey J. Kripal writes, 'At the center of the Passover rituals is the seder meal, during which Jewish families and communities remember, through a series of scripted questions, answers, prayers, and pious acts, their ancient ancestors' dramatic escape from Egypt.'[8] In addition to this, each food item during the meal is believed to be a symbolic reminder of the hardships and triumphs faced during this period of Jewish history, thus constituting an experience of solidarity between Jews in the present and their ancestors. Kripal goes on to say that 'eventually the Jewish Passover meal was transformed into the Christian Eucharist, which retold and re-enacted not the exodus from Egypt per se, but the death and resurrection of Jesus of Nazareth, now considered to be the Christ or Messiah'.[9] This important, and frequently performed, Christian ritual not only unites Christians with one another and with Christ, but also makes reference to Christ's Jewish identity, a subtle reminder that Christians should see Jews as their brothers and sisters rather than as enemies.

[7]Jeffrey J. Kripal, *Comparing Religions,* illustrated edition (West Sussex: John Wiley & Sons, 2014), 118.

[8]Jeffrey J. Kripal, *Comparing Religions,* illustrated edition (West Sussex: John Wiley & Sons, 2014), 118.

[9]Ibid.

Hinduism, meanwhile, has perhaps more rituals than any other religion, partly owing to the vast diversity of Hindu sects, all of which practise the religion differently from one another. Generally speaking, however, there are many common elements in day-to-day Hindu rituals. Many Hindus observe morning rituals at home (such as reciting passages from scriptures like the Bhagavad Gita, meditating, praying to images and icons of particular deities, making offerings of food). Also, as Siddiqui notes, 'Hindus observe numerous festivals. The popular ones are: Dasara, Holi and Divali. Dasara celebrates the victory of good against evil i.e. that of Rama against Ravan, the evil king; Deepavali is celebrated for the return of Rama and Sita to their Kingdom of Ayodhya; and Holi is celebrated in commemoration of slaying of demoness Holika by Lord Vishnu's devotee Prahlad.'[10]

These rituals foster a sense of community and equality among fellow human beings, and as acts of devotion and worship, they foster a personal connection with God as well. As anthropologist Saba Mahmood points out while referencing the rituals of Islam, these are not hollow performances, rather they serve as practices that actually instill practical and positive changes in one's character.

> [R]ituals [tuqus] and worship [ibadat] prepare for the creation of a type of person who thinks freely, is capable [mu'ahhal] of enlightened criticism on important daily issues, of distinguishing between form and essence, between means and ends, between secondary and basic issues.[11]

All the physical and sensory aspects of ritual, then, are truly aimed at eliciting psychological and cognitive changes in us—namely, allowing us to think critically about what matters most in life, and enabling us to distinguish between what society tells us on these matters and what we truly believe.

Furthermore, the emphasis on personal responsibility while

---

[10]Wajihuddin Siddiqui, *Commonalities and Similarities in World Religions* (Karachi: Royal Book Company, 2018), 117.

[11]Saba Mahmood, *Politics of Piety: The Islamic Revival and the Feminist Subject* (New Jersey: Princeton University Press, 2004), 132.

undertaking these rituals promotes reflection on the fact that we have control over how we want to live our lives and how we wish to shape our character. And these traits (self-reflection and personal responsibility) show up across religions. The prescribed rituals of religious traditions provide ready-made templates for us to step into, but it is equally important to understand the content and substance of the ritual itself as providing clear intentions and goals to strive for. The Buddhist monk and popular author Thich Nhat Hanh, for instance, suggests that we can derive value in this way even from very simple activities. 'From time to time, to remind ourselves to relax, to be peaceful, we may wish to set aside some time for a retreat, a day of mindfulness, when we can walk slowly, smile, drink tea with a friend, enjoy being together as if we are the happiest people on Earth.'[12]

For that reason, rituals are a means towards various ends. The rituals themselves can be quite meaningful and fulfilling for their own sake, but ultimately, they are not as important as the actual virtues of character that they are designed to promote. The Taoist sage Lao Tzu expresses this through a verse of poetry.

> Higher Ritual involves effort
> and should it meet with no response
> then it threatens and compels [...]
> ritual marks the waning of belief
> and the onset of confusion[13]

Among other things, Taoism was a response to Confucianism and its perceived overreliance on rituals. However, Taoism has always made ample use of rituals, just as in any other religion. There is no contradiction in this. They even describe many benefits to be derived from rituals. The important thing is to not let all the pomp and circumstance of ritual distract us from our ultimate goals. Similarly, in Buddhism there are several analogies used to illustrate this same point. Buddhist teachings and rituals act as a medicine for the sick,

---

[12]Thich Nhat Hanh, *Being Peace* (Berkeley: Parallax Press, 2005).

[13]Lao-Tzu, *Tao te ching*, trans. Red Pine (Port Townsend: Copper Canyon Press, 2009), Chapter 38, 76.

who, once cured, can toss aside the medicine. It is also like using a thorn to pick out another thorn—once the embedded thorn is removed, you can throw both away.

The challenge we face today is that many rituals that were powerful and appropriate for particular times and places in the past, which once played useful roles, have persisted into our day, even though much of their utility has been lost for many people. Look at how many people attend religious services in churches or synagogues or other houses of worship, just going through the motions of rituals they were taught to follow their whole lives, but which hold no real meaning for them. This is why many people understandably grow frustrated with religion and stop practising it. However, in doing so, we may be throwing out the baby with the bathwater. Religion still has an important role to play in our world today, and so do rituals. But in a rapidly changing world, what we need are new and updated rituals that are better suited for our time. Francis X. Clooney explains this well:

> [F]or this, we need to recover— and reinvent— public rituals of repentance, penance, and forgiveness [...] This is something Jews and Christians and Muslims, along with their Hindu and Buddhist sisters and brothers, might talk to one another about, creating rituals of confession, repentance, and forgiveness for today.[14]

Professor Clooney is also a Jesuit priest, and a few years ago I attended a Catholic mass at his church. I wanted to participate fully in the service out of respect for the tradition, even though I am not a Christian, so when everyone stood up and walked to the altar to receive communion from Father Clooney, I did the same. Later that day, he explained to me that he was technically not supposed to give me communion, as I am a non-Christian, but he did so anyway because he felt in his heart that it was the right thing to do. He did not let ancient rules get in the way of seeing the common humanity and goodness in me.

We do not need to give up on our rituals or religious identities, but

[14]Francis X. Clooney, 'Have We Forgotten How to Repent-and to Forgive?' *Harvard.edu blog*, 7 December 2017, https://projects.iq.harvard.edu/francisclooney/blog/have-we-forgotten-how-repent-and-forgive

nor should we feel compelled to go on practicing particular rituals which we have ceased to derive any benefits from. The beauty in the diversity that we see across religions is, as always, that we are provided with many different options for achieving the same goals. And this diversity will only be further deepened as more evolved forms of ritual practice arise from within, and from beyond, the confines of religious traditions.

23

Praxis

Great work requires great and persistent effort for a long time [...] Character has to be established through a thousand stumbles.[1]

—Swami Vivekananda

Praxis has been defined as 'the use of a theory or a belief in a practical way'.[2] We get so caught up noting the differences in belief systems that we forget the primary purpose of all religions—indeed all belief systems—is to translate those beliefs into practice. Mahatma Gandhi went so far as to proclaim, 'I have felt that the Gita teaches us that what cannot be followed out in day-to-day practice cannot be called religion.'[3] In praxis, as opposed to specific beliefs, we see much of the commonalities across religions. All religions agree that beliefs and doctrines ring hollow if we are unable to translate them into practice. However different these beliefs might seem across religions, the practical goals are strikingly consistent: praxis across religions is all about overcoming the self—or gaining self-control and discipline through repetition—thus transforming into

---

[1]Swami Vivekananda, *Personality Development* (India: Advaita Ashrama, 2015), 22.
[2]Oxford English Dictionary
[3]Mahatma Gandhi in Wendy Doniger, *Hinduism, The Norton Anthology of World Religions: Vol. 1*, ed. Jack Miles (New York: W.W. Norton & Company, 2015), 646.

more thoughtful, selfless and loving beings.

As Gandhi said, 'Be the change you want to see in the world.' And even though Gandhi was speaking from an Indian and Hindu perspective, the following quotes from the Christian New Testament are strikingly similar to Gandhi's teachings on the subject. 'But be doers of the word, and not only hearers, deluding your own selves'[4] and 'My little children, let's not love in word only, or with the tongue only, but in deed and truth.'[5] The most important form of praxis for Christians—following the teachings of Jesus—is to turn the principle of love for one's neighbour into tangible action. Writer and Christian theologian C.S. Lewis advises, 'Do not waste time bothering whether you "love" your neighbour; act as if you did. As soon as we do this we find one of the great secrets. When you are behaving as if you loved someone, you will presently come to love him.'[6] Echoing the sentiment, anthropologist Saba Mahmood's analysis of the devotional practices of Muslim women (like prayer and the wearing of head and face coverings) says, 'Instead of innate human desires eliciting outward forms of conduct, it is the sequence of practices and actions one is engaged in that determines one's desires and emotions.'[7] The point is that our actions not only affect the external conditions, such as when we give food to the poor, we help them; but they also affect our interior selves.

To put this another way, even if we intellectually agree with the great prophets when they laud the merits of modesty or command us to love our neighbours, that will not automatically lead to a lasting change in our character. D.C. Lau, in his translation of Confucius' Analects, explains this by drawing a distinction between 'learning' and 'studying'.

> We tend to 'learn' some things but 'study' others. For instance, a child learns to walk but an entomologist studies the behavior of ants. We learn something practical; we study something theoretical. In learning the focus is on the learner; in studying

---

[4]James 1:22 (World English Bible).

[5]1 John 3:18 (World English Bible).

[6]C.S. Lewis, *The C.S. Lewis Signature Classics* (New York: HarperCollins, 2017), 110-11.

[7]Saba Mahmood, *Politics of Piety: The Islamic Revival and the Feminist Subject* (New Jersey: Princeton University Press, 2004), 157.

> the focus is on the subject. In learning something new, a man improves himself. He either acquires a new skill or becomes more proficient in an old one. In studying, a man acquires new knowledge but this new knowledge need not make any difference to him as a practical man.[8]

We can study the Bible, the Qur'an or the Bhagavad Gita all we want, but if we fail to reflect upon how all those words relate to us in our own individual lives, especially in a way that galvanizes us to act differently, then we are not learning in any kind of practical manner.

Practices, like prayer, wearing a head-covering or showing random acts of kindness, should be done daily if possible. This is how we cultivate lasting change.

Essentially, developing these new habits through praxis is like fortifying them, keeping the virtues we wish to embody safe from the vicissitudes of the outside world. In fact, the Hebrew Bible employs such an analogy: 'Like a city that is broken down and without walls is a man whose spirit is without restraint.'[9] It takes a lot of resolve and willpower to sustain any new practice, and it takes a still mind to be able to focus on our resolve properly. Eva Wong, in her translation of the *Lieh-tzu*, notes how praxis requires a balanced focus on and control of both the mind and the body. 'If the mind is still but the body is not responsive, no intention can be communicated to the body. If the body is responsive and the mind is confused, the actions will come out confused.'[10] It is this philosophy that gave birth to and has continued to inform the ancient mind-body practices developed by Taoists, like tai chi, qi gong and various other forms of meditation and martial arts.

The religions of India are also quite famous for developing practices like meditation and yoga, which, likewise, seek to help us gain control over the mind and the body. In fact, the very term, 'yoga', is etymologically related to the English word for 'yoke', the mechanism

[8]D.C. Lau, "Introduction", Confucius, *The Analects*, trans. D.C. Lau, Penguin Classics edition (London: Penguin Books, 1971), 44.

[9]Proverbs 25:28 (World English Bible).

[10]*Lieh-tzu: A Taoist Guide to Practical Living*, trans. Eva Wong (Boston: Shambhala, 2001), 11.

which connects working animals to plows or carts. The symbolism of this image is twofold—one, yoga allows us to 'yoke' our mind and body together to act as one, and two, yoga puts us in the driver's seat, controlling our mind and body, rather than allowing us to be controlled by them. This is symbolized in the Bhagavad Gita, wherein Krishna, an incarnation of Vishnu, teaches the hero of the story, Arjuna, 'It is hard to renounce all action without engaging in action; the sage, wholehearted in the yoga of action, soon attains freedom.'[11] Krishna is talking about the ultimate spiritual goal for Hindus, i.e, moksha, or release from the karmic cycle of birth and death (which is known as samsara). This release from karma, and the actualizing of 'the self of all beings' comes through the intertwining of knowledge and action, which is what praxis is about.

In Hinduism, there are actually four paths to achieving this ultimate spiritual attainment: karma yoga, the path of action; bhakti yoga, the path of devotion; jnana yoga, the path of knowledge; and raja yoga, the path of meditation. There are different paths as every individual is different. What works for some of us, might not work for others. Thus, it is not uncommon for people to emphasize different paths to incorporate into their spiritual routine, though some people focus most of their energy on just one.

One simple, yet fascinating, suggestion about how we can develop self-control in our lives, which anyone can put into practice, comes from the Buddhist monk and popular author Thich Nhat Hanh:

> During walking meditation, during kitchen and garden work, during sitting meditation, all day long, we can practice smiling. At first you may find it difficult to smile, and we have to think about why. Smiling means that we are ourselves, that we have sovereignty over ourselves, that we are not drowned in forgetfulness. This kind of smile can be seen on the faces of Buddhas and bodhisattvas.[12]

We do not need to engage in any specific religious practices to follow the general guidance of this common religious thread of praxis. As Thich Nhat Hanh points out, we can and should find ways to bring

[11] *The Bhagavad Gita*, trans. Stephen Mitchell (New York: Harmony Books, 2000), 5:7.
[12] Thich Nhat Hanh, *Being Peace* (Berkeley, California: Parallax Press, 2005).

this kind of focus and consistency into parts of our ordinary lives as well, like cooking or gardening. The content of the act—in this case, smiling—is not as important as the purpose of the act—that is, to develop the capacity for self-control. So we can do other things as well, such as reminding ourselves to frequently take slow deep breaths throughout the day, or we can make a conscious effort to eat more slowly, focus more on our footsteps, etc. It really can be anything, depending on what suits you.

The point is to be able to control your own mind and body, and this starts with deliberate conscious actions. That is what praxis is all about. The common religious theme of developing praxis reminds us that lasting change requires conscious and sustained efforts. If we want to become better, more loving and live more meaningful lives, we must start with doing little things that enhance our ability to think and act more consciously. Furthermore, as specific practices are not as important as the purpose and goal, we can see how there really is no conflict between different religions on this subject. All the religious systems offer different suggestions on how to live a certain way, but that way of life itself is very consistent across all religions.

24

Fasting and Diet

> *From a comparativist perspective, the truth is that it does not matter what the dietary rules are, as long as there are dietary rules. Put a bit differently, what the dietary codes are about is not the content of the codes themselves, but their functions [...] They help make a world.*[1]
>
> —Jeffrey J. Kripal

When I was younger, my mother fasted for my sake every Friday, for a whole year, appealing to the Goddess Mother Santoshi, so that I could gain admission into IIT—one of the most prestigious and coveted undergraduate institutions in the world. Contrary to my own expectations, I actually got in! I'll never know if my mother's fasting had anything to do with it, but her dedication and faith in the power of devotional activities has stuck with me as a reminder of how important such practices are for many people.

Human civilizations have constantly inquired and explored different techniques about preparing and eating foods. Which dishes are good to eat? Which are bad? How much should we eat? How often? How do

[1]Jeffrey J. Kripal, *Comparing Religions*, illustrated edition (West Sussex: John Wiley & Sons, 2014), 150.

our eating practices affect the multitudinous other forms of life living alongside us? Religions have played a big role in helping human cultures grapple with these questions, and this influences the many dietary rules that religious adherents continue to follow.

Most practising Jews try to abide by some of the dietary restrictions set by their traditional law. The three most common and most well-known among these are the requirements to abstain from pork products and shellfish and making sure to not have meat and dairy as part of the same meal. But there are many other, more specific, restrictions—such as which types of meat products can be eaten—according to the notoriously lengthy and specific list laid out in the Book of Leviticus. Various explanations have been proposed for these laws, ranging from the practical to the symbolic, but the fact remains that all but the most orthodox of Jews adhere rather loosely to many of these restrictions.

Islam is another religion that forbids the consumption of pork, as well as dictates additional restrictions, like the consumption of alcohol. But even in the Qur'an, there is room for flexibility.

> He hath only forbidden you dead meat and blood and the flesh of swine and that on which any other name hath been invoked besides that of God but if one is forced by necessity without wilful disobedience nor transgressing due limits then is he guiltless. For God is oft-forgiving, most merciful.[2]

The common insight revealed through this Islamic passage and the practices of most Jews today is that what matters most is intention. It can be difficult to remember all the nuances of dietary restrictions, and impractical to adhere to all of them all of the time. But as long as a conscious effort is made to live by as many of these guidelines as possible, then the main goal—showing devotion to God and to the ancestors of the tradition—is still being honoured.

Other religions take a stronger stance and forbid the consumption of all meat products, as in accordance with certain theological beliefs. This is especially true of some of the religions of India, where belief in reincarnation is one of their main principles. The following Buddhist

[2]Qur'an 2:173 (Yusuf Ali).

scriptural passage demonstrates why vegetarianism is a rational response to this belief:

> There is not a single being, wandering in the chain of lives in endless and beginning less samsara, that has not been your mother or your sister. An individual, born as a dog, may afterward become your father. Each and every being is like an actor playing on the stage of life. One's flesh and the flesh of others is the same flesh. Therefore the Enlightened Ones eat no meat.[3]

The main reason for abstaining from meat is an ethical position to affirm that all life is one, and that meat-eating is incompatible with the core Buddhist practice of compassion.

The injunction not to eat meat can even be traced as far back as the laws of Manu, attributed to the legendary first man—like Adam from the Abrahamic traditions—in Hinduism.

> One can never obtain meat without causing injury to living beings, and killing living beings is an impediment to heaven; he should, therefore, abstain from meat.[4]

Again, the consumption of meat is said to be unethical, as well as damaging to progress towards moksha ('enlightenment') in accordance with karmic law. However, to complicate this picture, as in the cases of Judaism and Islam, not all Hindus or Buddhists abstain completely from meat: some interpret this commandment more loosely. Even the Buddha himself, as legend has it, ate meat because he felt it was improper to deny the generosity of people who offered him whatever food they could spare. Once again, the most important aspect is intention—the Buddha advocated for the importance of compassion, and there are many ways to express compassion. One way would be, of course, to abstain from eating meat when possible, so as to minimize the harm that is done to other sentient creatures to make this meat

---

[3]'Aṅgulimālīya Sūtra' in *Shabkar Food of Bodhisattvas: Buddhist Teachings on Abstaining from Meat,* trans. Padmakara Translation Group (Boston: Shambhala Publications, 2004), 64.

[4]*The Law Code of Manu,* 5.48-49, trans. Patrick Olivelle (New York: Oxford University Press, 2004), 88.

available. But there are still differing opinions over whether this must be done without exception.

Religious texts from across traditions tend to lay out laws prohibiting certain behaviours, like the consumption of meat. Many religious followers thus feel that it is important to adhere closely to these laws, but it is also important to guard against allowing this strict adherence to lead us down the path of dogma and uncritical positions. We are seeing an increasing trend towards vegetarianism and veganism in the world, driven by health and ethical issues, along with advancements in medical knowledge, which affirm the concerns behind most religions. Eating beef leads to increased risk of diseases and release of significant amounts of greenhouse gases such as CO2, methane and nitrous oxide which is damaging to the environment and contributes to global warming.

Prophets and scriptures across many religions teach us to avoid letting our strict adherence to any one rule violate the spirit of religious traditions in general. As is written in the New Testament of Christianity, 'food will not commend us to God. For neither, if we don't eat, are we the worse; nor, if we eat, are we the better.'[5] Above all, our attitudes and intentions bring us towards God. The rules and practices are, therefore, means toward cultivating these inner virtues. They may be expedient means, but that does not mean they should take priority over the greater goals. Today, there are an increasing number of people turning into vegetarians and vegans. These trends are driven by health and environmental consciousness.

Another dietary practice that has been advocated across religions for millennia is fasting. Modern science has revealed that periods of fasting can be good for our physical health. Ancient religious leaders likely had some sense of this and sought to promote the health of their people by explaining the benefits of fasting in a different language, one that corresponded more with religious mythology and belief. But religions also promote fasting as a good way to cultivate inner health and values, like proper character and intention. But this, too, comes with qualifications. For instance, the Baha'i prophet Baha'u'llah proclaims, 'Verily, I say, fasting is the supreme remedy and the greatest healing for

[5]1 Corinthians 8:8 (World English Bible).

the disease of self and passion.'[6] His successor 'Abdu'l-Bahá reminds us that 'Exaggerated fasting destroys the divine forces'.[7] Our practices are meant to be conducive to promoting positive internal change, but when they achieve the opposite of this intention, then it is only sensible to stop.

In the Abrahamic traditions, periods of fasting like Yom Kippur, Lent and Ramadan are important, and they abide by this very principle of ordering people to fast, not just for the sake of fasting, but in order to promote reflection on the importance and value of self-restraint. There is an aphorism in the Hebrew Bible that captures one part of this: 'A full soul loathes a honeycomb; but to a hungry soul, every bitter thing is sweet.'[8] If we are forced to train ourselves to regularly and temporarily give up certain necessities, we come to a greater appreciation of things we otherwise take for granted; and it also acts as a reminder to ourselves to not overindulge. The Christian observance of Lent is one clear example of this. Lent is a yearly occasion for Christians to reflect upon the life and sacrifices of Jesus Christ, focusing specifically on the forty days he spent in the wilderness, abstaining from food and resisting the temptations of Satan. During Lent, Christians are called upon to emulate Christ by giving up certain luxuries for a forty-day period. Traditionally, Christians have given up meat, animal products and wine during this time, but customs now vary. The point is that Christians should sacrifice something that is difficult for them to give up so that they can experience, in some small way, the hardships and sacrifice of Jesus.

Similarly, the Muslim observance of Ramadan involves a month-long period of fasting each day, between dawn and sunset, as well as giving up other lustful or sinful behaviours. The practice of fasting can therefore be seen to apply well beyond the specific realm of food. Anthropologist Saba Mahmood explains this in the context of Islam:

---

[6]Bahá'u'lláh, 'The Importance of Obligatory Prayer and Fasting,' A Compilation Prepared by the Research Department of the Universal House of Justice (May 2000).
[7]'Abdu'l-Bahá, *'Abdu'l-Bahá on Divine Philosophy,'* ed. Elizabeth Fraser Chamberlain (Boston: Tudor Press, 1918), 98, Baha'i Library Online, http://bahai-library.com/abdulbaha_divine_philosophy&chapter=2
[8]Proverbs 27:7 (World English Bible).

'Fasting is not simply abstaining from food, but it is a condition through which a Muslim comes to train herself in the virtues [fada'il] of patience [sabr], trust in God [tawakkul], asceticism from worldly pleasures [zuhd], etc.'[9]

Prescribed religious practices can act as great guides as they are based on the wisdom and achievements of prophets, gurus and other religious leaders of the past. But ultimately, these practices are means toward certain ends and should not be mistaken as the ends in themselves. When misunderstood in this way, they become 'folkloric customs'; they might retain their historical significance, but they lose their practical significance.

Likewise, Gandhi notes, 'Fasting can help to curb animal passion, only if it is undertaken with a view to self-restraint [...] That is to say, fasting is futile unless it is accompanied by an incessant longing for self-restraint.'[10] As such, fasting usually is not mandatory for Hindus, and different sects observe different optional fasting routines and ceremonies depending on their customs. However, one fast that most Hindus observe is a day-long fast on the day Krishna was born. A large number of Hindus also fast on a selected day every week, depending on the God or Goddess they worship. Thus, those who worship Hanuman (Rama's superhuman monkey) observe fasts on Tuesdays. In any case, having a fast focused around a particular deity helps to foster a more personal connection, helping to make it more intentional.

Similarly, the Taoist sage Chuang Tzu illustrates how fasting by choice is different from thoughtlessly fasting due to necessity:

> The goal of fasting is inner unity. This means hearing, but not with the ear; hearing, but not with the understanding; hearing with the spirit, with your whole being. [...] Hence it demands the emptiness of all the faculties. And when the faculties are empty, then the whole being listens. There is then a direct grasp of what is right there before you that can never be heard with

---

[9]Saba Mahmood, *Politics of Piety: The Islamic Revival and the Feminist Subject* (New Jersey: Princeton University Press, 2004), 50.

[10]M.K. Gandhi, *An Autobiography, Or, The Story of My Experiments with Truth: A Table of Concordance,* (Prabhat Prakashan, 2008).

> the ear or understood with the mind. Fasting of the heart empties the faculties, frees you from limitation and from preoccupation. Fasting of the heart begets unity and freedom.[11]

What matters is not how extreme your fast is, but how thoughtful and intentional it is. In the Analects, for instance, there are several mentions of Confucius's austerity practices. 'When fasting, he thought it necessary to have his clothes brightly clean and made of linen cloth. When fasting, he thought it necessary to change his food, and also to change the place where he commonly sat in the apartment.'[12] These modifications might not be particularly difficult or impressive, but they are deliberate and conducive towards cultivating the kinds of virtues that fasting practices are designed for.

One example of how the capacity for even small acts of sacrifice and delayed gratification may have surprisingly great effects is the famous Stanford marshmallow experiment of 1972, where children were offered a choice between receiving one marshmallow now or two marshmallows if they waited a little longer. What the researchers found when they followed up with the same test subjects years later is that the ones who were able to wait for the two-marshmallow reward seemed to have achieved more success in life (as measured by things like test scores and physical well-being). This does seem to support the claims of many religious traditions, regarding some of the reasoning behind regular fasting. Nowadays, there is a trend in wanting everything *now.* We want new cars, or rush to buy the latest gadgets as soon as they hit the market. At the level of political and global leadership, there is too much focus on short-termism, which threatens the future security of our species and our planet. Our world indeed can benefit from a return to valuing more long-term views and delayed gratification.

We are each free to make our own decisions with respect to our dieting and fasting practices. However, these various religious guidelines provide us with tools for how we might think more deeply about these

---

[11]*The Way of Chuang Tzu,* trans. Thomas Merton (New York: New Directions, 2010), 52-53.

[12]'Analects' in *Confucian Analects, The Great Learning, The Doctrine of the Mean,* trans. James Legge (Pantianos Classics, 2017), 10:7.

decisions. They provide us with different perspectives on what to eat and when, and they all agree that following any of these guidelines is pointless if it is not driven by an inner sense of conviction in the rationality of the practices and their value. They can help us achieve greater self-control over the whims and desires of the mind and body. While the prescriptions and proscriptions surrounding food may be different in different cultural settings, the fact is that all religions emphasize some set of rules.

25

Sacrifice

The process of offering is Brahman; that which is offered is Brahman. Brahman offers the sacrifice in the fire of Brahman. Brahman is attained by those who see Brahman in every action.[1]

—Bhagavad Gita

There are many different ways to engage in the common religious practice of sacrifice. Sometimes, it involves the literal sacrifice of animals, or even humans, though these practices are now far less common across the world than they once were. Sometimes, sacrifice takes place in the form of simple offerings to the Gods by leaving portions of food and harvested crops, or various other objects, on an altar dedicated to a particular deity. Sometimes, there may be no physical act involved at all, and sacrifice is embodied in spirit as a particular attitude or orientation towards life.

In each of these cases, the common theme involves relinquishing something thought to be valuable. In addition to sacrifice as a way to supplicate the Gods, religions also encourage sacrifice as a practice that teaches us to loosen our attachments to material things, thus loosening our sense of attachment to our impermanent physical bodies and the transient physical world. In doing so, we can also live more selfless,

[1]*The Bhagavad Gita*, trans. Eknath Easwaran, Classics of Indian Spirituality, 2nd ed (Tomales, California: The Blue Mountain Center of Meditation, 2007), 4:24.

magnanimous and joyful lives; we can learn, through these practices, to not be dominated by greed, jealousy or the fear of losing our possessions, including our lives.

One famous example of a story of sacrifice, which has been the subject of contemplation, debate and fascination, especially throughout Western civilization, is that of Abraham and Isaac in the Hebrew Bible. As a test of faith, Abraham is called upon by God to take his only son to the top of a mountain and sacrifice him. God sends an angel to stop Abraham at the last minute, allowing him to replace his son for a goat. It is this event that is seen as foundational in Abraham's role as the founding father of God's chosen people.

> Yahweh's angel called to Abraham a second time out of the sky, and said, 'I have sworn by myself,' says Yahweh, 'because you have done this thing, and have not withheld your son, your only son, that I will bless you greatly, and I will multiply your offspring greatly like the stars of the heavens, and like the sand which is on the seashore. Your offspring will possess the gate of his enemies. All the nations of the earth will be blessed by your offspring, because you have obeyed my voice.'[2]

For centuries, theologians and philosophers have grappled with the ethical implications of this story. Devotion to God is one thing, but should we really be teaching our children to be prepared to kill on God's behalf?

Human and animal sacrifices are surely some of the most troubling religious rituals from a modern-day perspective. Even several thousands of years ago, the ancient Taoist sage Lieh Tzu grappled with some of these ethical questions, ultimately deciding that 'All these customs are established traditions in the countries where they are practiced. They are observed by all the people and there is nothing strange about them. We call them barbaric and are shocked by them only because we have different customs.'[3] Similarly, the Qur'an teaches us to respect the

---

[2]Genesis 22:15-18 (World English Bible).

[3]*Lieh-tzu: A Taoist Guide to Practical Living,* trans. Eva Wong (Boston: Shambhala, 2001), 138.

customs of others, as all customs are ultimately derived from the same God who prescribes different rituals and sacrifices for different groups of people. 'To every people did we appoint rites (of sacrifice), that they might celebrate the name of God over the sustenance He gave them from animals (fit for food). But your God is one God. Submit then your wills to Him (in Islam): and give thou the good news to those who humble themselves.'[4] It is necessary to think twice before judging others by our own cultural standards, but how do we reconcile the messages of love and compassion we see across religions with rituals that involve killing living creatures?

The story of Abraham and Isaac has been analysed, interpreted and re-interpreted in countless different ways, but one way to read it is to see it as a moment of departure *away* from real sacrifice and towards more symbolic forms of sacrifice. The following commandment indicates this: 'Sanctify to me all the firstborn, whatever opens the womb among the children of Israel, both of man and of animal. It is mine.'[5] The point is not to physically kill in God's name, but rather, to reflect upon the fact that we should offer God our gratitude for what we hold as our most valuable possessions.

Similarly, in the Bhagavad Gita, Hindus are urged to make offerings to God (Krishna or Vishnu, in this case), but the list of offerings encompasses much more than humans or animals. 'Any offering—a leaf, a flower or fruit, a cup of water—I will accept it if given with a loving heart. Whatever you do, Arjuna, do it as an offering to me—whatever you say or eat or pray or enjoy or suffer.'[6] What matters, then, is not *what* is being offered or sacrificed, but *how* and *why*. If we look at the deeper meaning and purpose behind what a sacrifice represents, rather than the specifics of what is being sacrificed, we can see similarities across the sacrificial practices of different religions much more clearly.

Remarking on the importance of sacrifice during the time of Confucius in China, scholar Ruth H. Chang offers a broad explanation

---

[4]Qur'an, 22:34 (Yusuf Ali).

[5]Exodus 13:2 (World English Bible).

[6]*The Bhagavad Gita*, trans. Stephen Mitchell (New York: Harmony Books, 2000), 9:26-27.

of the purposes of sacrifice that could apply to many religious traditions throughout human history. 'People believed that spirits and ancestors could affect human destinies; therefore, sacrifices could bring good fortune or avert disaster. Offering sacrifices was a major responsibility.'[7] But this is just one aspect among many to explain why sacrifices are performed. We can see clearly that sacrifices are more than direct transactions, as anthropologist Pascal Boyer points out: '[W]hatever the ritual guarantee, farmers and hunters never dispense with any empirical measures that increase their likelihood of success. You may give a goat to the Gods but you still plow your fields to the best of your abilities. The ways in which the Gods actually confer benefits are not really described or even thought about.'[8]

In other words, even those who perform actual ritual sacrifices do not interpret them as actual payments, made in full faith that the Gods will take care of all their needs. There is, thus, more to religious sacrifice than simply whatever effects it is thought to bring about.

In fact, scriptures from across religions make it clear that the whole point of sacrifice is that we are not to expect anything in return. In the Bhagavad Gita, for instance, Krishna proclaims that religious activities like sacrifices, and, 'Even the most praiseworthy acts should be done with complete nonattachment and with no concern for results.'[9] And in the Tao Te Ching, Lao Tzu notes that we should 'reduce self-interest and limit desires'.[10] To go along with this, the Indian spiritual teacher and translator Eknath Easwaran further explains the relationship between knowledge and selfless action in Hindu scriptures:

> The universe is founded on two principles, they discovered. One is rita, law, order, or regularity. Without it no scientific discovery would be possible; more importantly, no moral discovery would

---

[7]Ruth H. Chang, 'Understanding Di and Tian: Deity and Heaven from Shang to Tang Dynasties,' *Sino-Platonic Papers*, no. 108 (September 2000), 3.

[8]Pascal Boyer, *Religion Explained: The Evolutionary Origins of Religious Thought* (New York: Basic Books, 2001), 242.

[9]*The Bhagavad Gita*, trans. Stephen Mitchell (New York: Harmony Books, 2000), 18:6.

[10]Lao-Tzu, *Tao te ching*, trans. Red Pine (Washington: Copper Canyon Press, 2009), Chapter 19, 38.

> be possible. Human experience would have no meaning, for we would have no way to learn from our experiences. The second principle is yajna, sacrifice. The universe, they tell us, runs on renunciation. The most significant human action is the sacrifice of personal gain for the sake of something higher and holier. If rita is the moral law, yajna is the human response to live in accordance with that law, taking nothing from life for oneself but everywhere seeking to give of oneself to life.[11]

Similarly, Swami Adiswarananda writes, 'Self-knowledge is the consummation of all desires. According to Vedanta scriptures, one should give up individual self-interest for the sake of the family, the family for the sake of the country, the country for the sake of the world, and eventually everything for the sake of self-knowledge.'[12]

Christianity is another religion that clearly illustrates the selfless nature of sacrifice. In fact, the central belief uniting all Christians is the belief in Jesus as the son of God who came to earth and eventually sacrificed his own life for the benefit of all humanity. This is precisely what the great medieval saint Teresa of Avila had in mind.

> Forget your own good for their sakes no matter how much resistance your nature puts up; and, when the occasion arises, strive to accept work yourself so as to relieve your neighbor of it. Don't think that it won't cost you anything or that you will find everything done for you. Look at what our Spouse's love for us cost Him; in order to free us from death, He died that most painful death on the cross.[13]

Echoing this, in the New Testament, we are told, 'But don't forget to be doing good and sharing, for with such sacrifices God is well

---

[11]Eknath Easwaran in *The Upanishads*, trans. Eknath Easwaran (Tomales: Nilgiri Press, July 2007), 121.

[12]Swami Adiswarananda, *The Vedanta Way to Peace and Happiness* (Woodstock: SkyLight Paths Publishing, 2007), 22.

[13]Teresa of Avila, *The Interior Castle*, trans. Kieran Kavanaugh and Otilio Rodriguez (New Jersey: Paulist Press, 1979), 102.

pleased.'[14] Religious sacrifice, therefore, need not be thought of as the performance of specific rituals that must take place in a special setting and with special materials. We can perform sacrifice on a day-to-day basis, as a kind of attitude that manifests itself in all kinds of actions, whether big or small, flashy or simple.

Helping the needy and distancing ourselves from material attachments are worthwhile goals, regardless of our belief in any particular God or Gods. The Dalai Lama, for instance, describes the rationale behind voluntary sacrifice for Buddhists in nontheistic terms:

> Some people get the impression that Buddhism talks too much about suffering. In order to become prosperous, a person must initially work very hard, so he or she has to sacrifice a lot of leisure time. Similarly, the Buddhist is willing to sacrifice immediate comfort so that he or she can achieve lasting happiness.[15]

Our sacrifices obviously should be undertaken, first and foremost, for the welfare of others, but it is true that they also yield benefits for the performer.

---

[14]Hebrews 13:16 (World English Bible).

[15]Dalai Lama, 'Oprah Talks to The Dalai Lama,' O, *The Oprah Magazine,* August 2001, https://www.oprah.com/omagazine/oprah-interviews-the-dalai-lama/all

26

Clothing

As one abandons worn-out clothes and acquires new ones, so when the body is worn out a new one is acquired by the Self, who lives within.[1]

—Bhagavad Gita

Rightly or wrongly, the way we dress is often one of the first things that others notice about us. As such, clothing plays an important role in building group and individual identities. This is true with respect to religious identities as well. Buddhists can be identified by their robes, Sikhs by their turbans and silver bracelets, Jains by their face masks, Jews by their kippot (their small caps), Hindu swamis and sadhus by their saffron clothes, and so on. Growing up in Old Delhi, one of the most religiously pluralistic communities in the world, these diverse clothing styles were all regular sights to me. As a young boy, I used to be fascinated by the richness I observed in people's outfits in my city.

Sometimes, the privilege of wearing such clothing must even be earned—by clergymen and other religious leaders, for instance—marking them special sub-identities. In Catholicism, members of the

---

[1]*The Bhagavad Gita*, trans. Eknath Easwaran, Second Edition (Tomales: Nilgiri Press, 2007), 2:22.

clergy—ranging from monks and priests, to higher-ups, like bishops and cardinals—wear black 'cassocks' publicly, with different colour markings on them to designate their position in the hierarchy. In this way, they carry their identity with them wherever they go. The Pope, of course, wears his famous white garments. In the actual church setting, depending on the ceremony, these clergy members will wear different types of ceremonial robes, called 'vestments'.

But the function of clothing in religion is not just an external one of marking someone, it is, more importantly, a means of cultivating an inner attitude. Generally speaking, religions advocate attitudes of modesty and humility, which can be cultivated inwardly in conjunction with their outward expression of simple clothing. In this way, we come to learn not to attach too much importance to material goods. We should not rely on flashy clothing to make us feel good or garner respect from others. Rather, our intentions and our actions should determine who we are as people. This is why religious and holy individuals like monks and saints choose to wear the same very simple clothing each day.

Notably, during hajj, the Muslim pilgrimage to the holy city of Mecca, everyone wears the same simple white garb, to show that all are equal before God and that status symbols are only an artificial human construct. Similarly, most Hindus, even the rich, wear the simplest of clothes when they visit temples. In India, where non-Muslims are allowed to visit mosques, they too have to be dressed in a certain way to gain entry.

The clothing we wear communicates a lot of information, both to ourselves and others. Religious leaders and devotees have taken advantage of this principle to further their own spiritual missions. Mahatma Gandhi, for instance, is known as the Father of the Nation in India for leading the country towards independence and away from British rule. One practice he advocated was 'swadeshi'—he ceased to wear Western clothing in favour of indigenous hand-spun simple clothes, and he encouraged others to do the same. The famous images of Gandhi in his simple white loincloth has become a symbol of Indian identity, but they are also symbolic of Gandhi's solidarity with and compassion for the poor. Gandhi went from the traditional Western dress, befitting him as an educated lawyer, to the much simpler garb of a spiritual ascetic.

Another famous spiritual leader who led by example by the way he dressed was Confucius, the paragon of Chinese wisdom. While by no means a complete ascetic, Confucius believed in moderation and is reported in his Analects as having said, 'There is no point in talking to a man with professional aspirations [shi] who sets his heart on the Way but who is ashamed of poor clothing and poor food.'[2] Modesty is perhaps the most important common principle behind the requirement to don certain items across religious traditions. Another example to illustrate this comes from Chang Tzu, one of the founding figures of the other native Chinese religion, Taoism. He wrote that, 'a nobleman can follow the Tao without having to dress the part. Indeed, he might wear the dress but not understand the Tao at all!'[3] In other words, just because you wear the right clothes does not mean that you are holy or enlightened, just as an absence of the right clothes does not indicate that you are *not* holy or enlightened. Clothes don't change who we are deep within.

Of course, we do not need to relinquish our ties to the social world completely in order to live modestly. But if we see clothing as a status symbol, we will be unable to focus on what truly matters in life. This is what is meant by the passage in the New Testament of Christianity, which says, 'Let your beauty be not just the outward adorning of braiding the hair, and of wearing jewels of gold, or of putting on fine clothing.'[4] Religions seek to cultivate the beauty of what lies within, or the authentic self within each of us, that reflects the divine and tends towards compassion and unity, rather than artificial class distinctions.

The Buddha meant something similar when he said, 'Those who put on the saffron robe without purifying the mind, who lack truthfulness and self-control, are not fit to wear the saffron robe.'[5] The yellow (or orange) robe is a symbol of someone's choice to live by Buddhist principles. But if a person is not in control of their own thoughts and continues to live selfishly, then how can they embody any kind of religious life? The prescribed clothing of religions often functions as a symbol of

---

[2]Confucius, *The Analects*, trans. Annping Chin (New York: Penguin, 2014), 4:9.

[3]*The Book of Chuang Tzu*, trans. Martin Palmer (New York: Penguin Classics, 2006), 181.

[4]1 Peter 3:3 (World English Bible).

[5]*The Dhammapada*, trans. Eknath Easwaran, Second Edition (Tomales: Nilgiri Press, 2007), 106.

commitment to a particular system of practices and beliefs, as well as a reminder to the wearer to hold firm to that commitment.

In Judaism, for instance, men and women are urged not only to dress modestly by covering their bodies up sufficiently, but also to wear certain accessories. In the Hebrew Bible, Jews are commanded by God: 'You shall make yourselves fringes on the four corners of your cloak with which you cover yourself.'[6] These tassels, known as 'tzitzit' or 'tallit', are still worn by Jews, especially in the orthodox community, as reminders to do good deeds and maintain faith in God. Jews are also supposed to wear head coverings: small round caps known as 'kippahs' for men, and shawls, called 'tichel' for married women.

Several other religions make use of head coverings as well. In Sikhism, similar to the kippah in Judaism, the turban is a head covering that serves as a reminder to oneself and others of a person's devotion to the faith and good deeds. Devout Sikhs are, in fact, required to keep on their person five items at all times: uncut hair and beard ('kesh'), a wooden comb ('kangha'), an iron bracelet ('kara'), a simple cotton undergarment ('kachera'), and an iron dagger ('kirpan'). These items are visible symbols of the faith commitments of a Sikh, as well as reminders of what those commitments are; the uncut hair, for instance, is an acknowledgement that God's creation is perfect and does not need to be shaped or styled by us, while the dagger is a reminder (as well as a means) to protect innocent people.

Muslim men also wear turbans to emulate Muhammad, and Muslim women adhere to various interpretations of head-covering requirements, differing over whether to cover the face as well ('niqab') or not ('hijab'). Anthropologist Saba Mahmood explains that the wearing of a face veil is often taken on voluntarily by women, even if it is not strictly imposed upon them. Women claim that 'the veil is a necessary component of the virtue of modesty because the veil both expresses "true modesty" and is the means through which the virtue of modesty is both created and expressed'.[7] This echoes the voices of all the other religions we have

---

[6]Deuteronomy 22:12 (World English Bible).

[7]Saba Mahmood, *Politics of Piety: The Islamic Revival and the Feminist Subject* (New Jersey: Princeton University Press, 2004), 23.

discussed—from Gandhi's intention to put his beliefs into action and lead by example, to the robes of Buddhism and the tassels of Judaism to symbolize commitment not just to a set of beliefs, but to selfless acts and lifestyles as well. The head-coverings for Muslim women have, of course, been the subject of many controversies. From a Western perspective, it may seem like a symbol of oppression, but as the above comments suggest, many women see it as quite the opposite: they derive great strength from the head-coverings and feel incomplete without it. Recently proposed laws in France that threaten to restrict the choice of Muslim women (when it comes to wearing their head-coverings in the workplace and other public settings) have elicited many passionate pleas from women in defence of their right to continue wearing what is called a sacred garment. One such woman describes the trials she endured in her adolescence due to prejudices against Muslims and their clothes, even before there was an actual law prohibiting it.

> The local Muslim groups and the mosque told me to remove my scarf, but I refused. To me, it felt like asking me to strip. I felt violated by the demand to undress. I'm naturally a very modest person anyway. I was 14 years old and had to educate myself at home through remote learning. I ended up very isolated.[8]

Regardless of our own feelings about such laws, we should have the compassion and empathy to understand why some people are so distraught at the prospect of having their rights to wear sacred garments taken away.

Generally speaking, the Qur'an does advise both men and women to dress in ways that are conducive to practising modesty. This passage demonstrates it: 'Say to the believing men that they should lower their gaze and guard their modesty: that will make for greater purity for them: and God is well acquainted with all that they do.'[9] This is especially true while entering mosques. All visitors, Muslim or not, are asked to remove

---

[8]Myriam François, 'I felt violated by the demand to undress: three Muslim women on France's hostility to the hijab', *The Guardian,* 27 July 2021, https://www.theguardian.com/world/2021/jul/27/i-felt-violated-by-the-demand-to-undress-three-muslim-women-on-frances-hostility-to-the-hijab

[9]Qur'an, 24:30 (Yusuf Ali).

their shoes and to wear clothing that is not too revealing, and women also must cover their hair. In limiting the extent to which we are showing our clothes and/or bodies, we remind ourselves that these things, which we view as personal possessions, are only temporary.

To take another example, Hindus believe that the body is external, a cloth for the eternal soul which, when worn out, results in death, and this subsequently leads to reincarnation in a different body. It is just like putting on a new pair of clothes (see opening quote of this chapter from the Bhagavad Gita).

The scriptures of many religions provide followers with broad guidelines. Even prophets recognize that fashions and customs change across time and place and affirm that modesty and selflessness can still be achieved by those who accord with local customs of clothing.

In very simple terms, the Taoist sage Lieh Tzu observes, 'People in southern countries cut their hair and go naked; people in northern countries wear turbans and leather garments; people in temperate countries wear hats and clothing of fabric.'[10] From a more modern perspective, Christian theologian and author C.S. Lewis urges Christians to consider that standards of modest clothing are temporally and geographically relative, and that we should not judge the character of people too harshly by their external appearance.

> A girl in the Pacific islands wearing hardly any clothes and a Victorian lady completely covered in clothes might both be equally 'modest', proper, or decent, according to the standards of their own societies: and both, for all we could tell by their dress, might be equally chaste (or equally unchaste).[11]

If we look at the fashion trends and customs of other cultures through the lens of our own, then we might feel shocked and even offended by what we perceive as improper. It is only when we look at others with a more open mind that we can appreciate the beauty of unfamiliar clothing on its own terms and as a unique expression of human imagination and creativity.

---

[10]Lieh Tzu, *The Book of Master Lie*, trans. Thomas Cleary, (2009), 1083.

[11]C.S. Lewis, *The C.S. Lewis Signature Classics* (New York: HarperCollins, 2017), 83.

27

Music

Communication, entertainment, and psychological healing of the community occur through aesthetic means, at the deeply embodied level of rhythm and movement.[1]

—Michelle Voss Roberts

Without a doubt, music is one of the greatest human creations. It is non-verbal form of communication that helps establish a connection to the authentic spiritual self within us, while also evoking unspoken bonds between souls. People in vastly different parts of the world, and across different eras of history, can still intuitively understand and appreciate the music of others because music is an expression of our cognitive faculties and emotions. Music can be shared across our species.

A musical mind is a meaning-making mind. Given our shared cognitive structures, we are all predisposed to seek out meaning and order in the world around us. This is why we also all have an innate appreciation for, and enjoyment of, music. Music harmonizes various sounds and rhythms into a singular whole and satisfies our cravings for order, rhythm and beauty. As anthropologist Pascal Boyer writes,

[1]Michelle Voss Roberts, *Tastes of the Divine* (New York: Fordham University Press, 2014), 145.

'[H]umans are predisposed to detect, produce, remember and enjoy music. This is a human universal. There is no human society without some musical tradition. Although the traditions are very different, some principles can be found everywhere.'[2] Neuroscientists have established that a part of the brain is designed only to appreciate music. Furthermore, a Harvard University study from 2018 showed that people from widely different places across the world could identify a song's genre/purpose—lullaby song, dancing song, healing song—just from listening to it for 14 seconds.[3] This suggests that music can be understood and appreciated almost universally, regardless of its cultural context and origins: music transcends cultural boundaries.

Every culture and religion, throughout human history, has not only produced its own music, but has also placed very high value on music as an art. As biologist E.O. Wilson puts it, 'In almost all living societies, from hunter-gatherer to civilized-urban, there exists an intimate relation between music and religion.'[4] Furthermore, in every culture, we see the same broad categories of musical instruments—percussion, strings and wind instruments—although the complexity and exact design of these instruments vary across different cultures.

The use of devotional music as an integral part of worship ceremonies and rituals is common across religions. Music echoes through the halls of churches, cathedrals, synagogues and temples of all kinds. Music engages both the mind and the body in ways that reinforce the intended sensory and emotional impacts of religious settings. Music is used for healing in India and in Tibet. Hazrat Inayat Khan, the founder of the Sufi Islam order in the Western world, describes the evocative capacity of music.

---

[2]Pascal Boyer, *Religion Explained: The Evolutionary Origins of Religious Thought* (New York: Basic Books, 2001), 132.

[3]Peter Reuell, "Songs in the key of humanity", *The Harvard Gazette*, 26 January 2018, accessed on 14 July 2022, https://news.harvard.edu/gazette/story/2018/01/music-may-transcend-cultural-boundaries-to-become-universally-human/.

[4]Edward O. Wilson, *The Meaning of Human Existence* (New York: Liveright Publishing, 2014).

A person does not hear sound only through the ears;
he hears sound through every pore of his body.
It permeates the entire being,
and according to its particular influence either slows
or quickens the rhythm of the blood circulation;
it either wakens or soothes the nervous system.
It arouses a person to greater passions
or it calms him by bringing him peace.
According to the sound and its influence
a certain effect is produced.[5]

Music exerts great power and influence over us and it can impact a variety of other religious activities—like prayer, meditation, scripture, ritual—and make it sink into our bones. This finds further support in the words of Baha'i leader Shoghi Effendi who writes that, 'It is the music which assists us to affect the human spirit; it is an important means which helps us to communicate with the soul.'[6] Confucius, whose fondness for music is clearly evident throughout the Analects, urges his students, 'The Odes are to stimulate [our mind and spirit]. The rites are to steady us. Music is the final lesson.'[7]

In scriptures from the Abrahamic traditions, we see an additional image of music as something that not only affects us but is also appreciated by God. The New Testament urges 'speaking to one another in psalms, hymns, and spiritual songs; singing and making melody in your heart to the Lord.'[8] Similarly, the Old Testament encourages abundant use of devotional music:

Praise God in his sanctuary!
Praise him in his heavens for his acts of power!

---

[5]Hazrat Inayat Khan, *The Sufi Message Volume 2: The Mysticism of Music, Sound and Word* (Delhi: Motilal Banarsidass, 2009), 112.
[6]Shoghi Effendi, *Bahá'í News*, no. 71 (West Englewood, New Jersey: The National Spiritual Assembly of the Bahá'ís of the United States and Canada, February 1933), 2, accessed via Baha'i Works, accessed on 10 July 2022, https://bahai.works/Baha%27i_News/Issue_71/Text.
[7]Confucius, *The Analects*, trans. Annping Chin (New York: Penguin, 2014), 8:8.
[8]Ephesians 5:19 (World English Bible).

Praise him for his mighty acts!
Praise him according to his excellent greatness!
Praise him with the sounding of the trumpet!
Praise him with harp and lyre!
Praise him with tambourine and dancing!
Praise him with stringed instruments and flute!
Praise him with loud cymbals!
Praise him with resounding cymbals!
Let everything that has breath praise Yah![9]

Music is also special in its ability to help us articulate what is otherwise difficult to articulate. For this reason, music has also been particularly admired by great artists and literary figures. The well-known British author and philosopher Aldous Huxley once remarked, 'After silence, that which comes nearest to expressing the inexpressible is music.'[10] Echoing this very closely, the famous French poet and novelist Victor Hugo asserted, 'Music expresses that which cannot be said, and which cannot be suppressed.'[11] And German philosopher Arthur Schopenhauer wrote, 'The composer reveals the innermost nature of the world, and expresses the profoundest wisdom in a language that his reasoning faculty does not understand.'[12] These enigmatic statements get to the heart of one of the great mysteries of music. Music is both loud and unmistakable, but also helps to stir within us those parts of ourselves that remain otherwise submerged and silent. This capacity to evoke emotion, express silence and the inexpressible within, is very important to all religions, as religious practices are designed to delve into our interior being and to allow us to engage with the deep part of us that is most closely connected with the divine.

---

[9]Psalm 150:1-6 (World English Bible).

[10]Aldous Huxley, 'The Rest is Silence' in *Music at Night and Other Essays* (London: Chatto and Windus, 1957), 19.

[11]Victor Hugo, *William Shakespeare*, trans. Melville B. Anderson (Chicago: A.C. McClurg and Co., 1891), 92.

[12]Arthur Schopenhauer, *The World as Will and Representation*: *Volume 1*, trans. E. F. J. Payne (New York: Dover Publications, 1969), 260.

It is worth pointing out that the Bhagavad Gita, one of India's most cherished scriptural texts, translates to 'Song of God'. Perhaps this is why the Hindu monk Swami Vivekananda even went so far as to say that 'Drama and music are by themselves religion; any song, love song or any song, never mind; if one's whole soul is in that song, he attains salvation, just by that.'[13] Given that music has the power to focus our minds and our bodies into a state of full absorption, we can understand why Vivekananda acknowledges it as one of the most powerful acts towards spiritual attainment.

In Hermann Hesse's famous novel *Siddhartha*, the eponymous character—who represents a fictionalized version of the Buddha—eventually comes to have this exact insight, describing it as the 'music of life'. 'It was all one, it was all interwoven and knotted together, interconnected in a thousand ways. And all of this together, all the voices, all the goals, all the longing, all the suffering, all the pleasure, all the good and evil, all of this together was the world. All of this together was the river of events, the music of life.'[14] Music, in bringing together a variety of disparate sounds into a harmonious whole, expresses one of the primary goals that religious scriptures and practices across traditions strive for, i.e., the establishment of a similar harmony in the mind. Music allows us to perceive the true wholeness and interconnectedness of what we usually perceive as a chaotic and discordant world.

Religions not only praise the literal value of music, but they also turn to music as a useful metaphor of unity, particularly the unity of all religions. Early on in this book we mentioned a very powerful line from the Rig Veda, *'Ekam sat vipra bahuda vadanti'* (truth is one, but called differently by many).[15] The famous scholar of comparative mythology and religion Joseph Campbell evokes this sentence to draw on the metaphor of religious diversity to liken it to a single human choir of many voices.

---

[13]Swami Vivekananda, *Complete Works of Swami Vivekananda*, Digitally published by Partha Sinha, 27 November 2019, 1449.

[14]Hermann Hesse, *Siddhartha*, trans. Stanley Appelbaum, Dover Thrift edition (New York: Dover Publications, 1999), 73.

[15]Rig Veda (I.164.46)

> A single song is being inflected through all the colorations of the human choir [...] The way to become human is to learn to recognize the lineaments of God in all of the wonderful modulations of the face of man.[16]

Similarly, the Kangxi emperor, Chinese emperor of the Qing dynasty, stated, 'Different religions have different customs; singing and crying are not done the same. If we mix them up and use them, some hear crying and are pleased; others listen to singing and become sad. But their feelings of grief and joy are the same.'[17]

Expressed in a musical metaphor, one of my guiding principles in life is to recognize that we are all part of an orchestra and not solo players. And unless we each play our parts perfectly, the music will not have its desired harmonious effect.

These are very beautiful ways of expressing the central idea in this book, which is that we are all one species, regardless of where we are born or what our belief systems might be. We all experience the same basic emotions, we are all captivated by the same looming questions and we are all on the same quest, towards truth and making out of the world around us, all in our own unique ways. As Campbell points out, we all become fuller as humans if we plumb the value of religious diversity, synthesizing as many perspectives as possible, just like a well-harmonized choir.

The music of world religions—especially those which have spread to vastly different places and cultures across the globe, like Judaism, Christianity, Islam, Baha'i and Buddhism—varies widely even within the given religious tradition, reflecting the diversity of people across the world. But as scholar of religion and psychology Robert C. Fuller notes, 'there has been considerable research in the field of "music and the emotions", and there is compelling evidence in support of the view that people discern very similar emotional expressions while listening to the same piece of

[16]Joseph Campbell, *The Hero with a Thousand Faces,* The Collected Works of Joseph Campbell Series edition (Novato: New World Library, 2008), 335-36.
[17]Hsi K'ang, *Philosophy and Argumentation in Third-Century China: The Essays of Hsi K'ang,* trans. Robert G. Henricks (New Jersey: Princeton University Press, 1983), 74-75.

music.'[18] As a universal human language, music breaks down barriers of all kinds, be it those of race, religion, culture, history, etc.

I have had the good fortune to participate in ritual worships of multiple religions and have witnessed the all-consuming enchanting effect music can have. I grew up in Chandni Chowk, a densely populated area in Old Delhi, India, which was a true cultural melting pot where people of multiple faiths co-existed harmoniously in close quarters. Our neighbourhood was surrounded by temples of all faiths. I recall waking up to the soul-stirring azan (call for prayers for Muslims) from a nearby mosque. On my way to school, I often met a group of devout Sikhs doing their early rounds of prabhat-feri and joined them in singing hymns until I had to part ways to head for my school but the beautiful shabads kept echoing all the way. I occasionally accompanied my dad to attend Urs Sharif at Khwaja Nizamuddin Aulia's shrine and rocked back and forth to the beats of naat and qawwalis. My dad and I both favoured Sufi music and dad would often hum the newly learned verses at home. During my middle school summer holidays, my mom would ask me to accompany her to late night satsang (religious meetings) in a nearby park. Although at that age toys and games were more enticing, I willingly joined my mom to listen to Mukund Hari Baba, a religious sage who had an amazing flair to tell the famous stories of prominent devotees using simple harmonium which created music that felt ethereal even to me despite my young age. During holidays, my dad and mom used to take us to various pilgrimage places. They later told me stories of how I used to skilfully dance and copy rhythmic gyrations of the ISKCON temple devotees in Vrindavan. I recall enjoying the kirtan and the upbeat music but have no recollection of me dancing, perhaps due to a self-imposed amnesia to suppress embarrassment. What I do vividly recall is watching a religious performance of whirling dervish and feeling an unfamiliar but trance-like state of peace.

After coming to Stanford University, I got exposed to many other religions from around the world through friends. When I was living in Newport Beach, I was dating a girl named Emily, who was a devout

---

[18]Robert C. Fuller, *Wonder: From Emotion to Spirituality* (Chapel Hill: University of North Carolina Press, 2006), 118.

Christian. I accompanied her to the church many times and used to recite some biblical passages during these services but remained silent when I heard other passages that I did not believe in. But when the music played, I would get totally immersed in the holy energy of the church. Such was the power of music!

I respect all religions, but I do not consider myself very religious. Still, even though I questioned the merits of many rituals, the music helped evoke the amalgamation of strong feelings of joy, peace, calm, and tranquillity at a cellular level and left a lasting imprint on my mind.

28

Sacred Spaces and Objects

Among the common features of ritual in vastly different cultural environments, we find an obsession with marking boundaries—for instance, marking off some part of the ceremonial space as special.[1]

—Pascal Boyer

Much of religion is aimed at transcending the material world, either by outwardly reaching towards God or inwardly seeking to uncover the mysteries of the mind. Often, the material world we are in can serve as a catalyst for the sought-after effects of spiritual and contemplative practices. There are many commonalities among the objects used by different religions in devotional environments, such as incense, candles, prayer beads as well as the environments themselves. All religions identify special places that are particularly conducive to their practices: temples, churches, mosques, monasteries, synagogues, monuments to mark special events, and pilgrimage sites to pay homage.

The use of sacred spaces as gathering spots obviously helps to serve the community-building aspect of religion, and historically, these spaces and objects have functioned to allow all community members—not just

[1]Pascal Boyer, *Religion Explained: The Evolutionary Origins of Religious Thought* (New York: Basic Books, 2001), 237.

priests and other spiritual leaders—to be active participants. Historian of religion Jeffrey Kripal explains why this is so important:

> It is an often forgotten fact that the vast majority of people in human history were illiterate. They could not read their own sacred scriptures. The situation was often more dramatic still, for in many traditional religious systems people (especially women) were not allowed to read the sacred scriptures. Religious institutions, then, had to turn to other means to instruct and edify their members. One of the most common means of doing this has been what we call material religion—all those physical objects or 'things', from miniature statues and posters to holy cards and amulets, that enable people to imagine their religious worlds into being on a daily basis.[2]

Even though literacy and access to scriptures have become more widespread, 'material religion' continues to serve a vital role across all belief systems.

One commonality is that the sites of birth and death of many major prophets are considered holy in their respective traditions. As Joseph Campbell has remarked, 'Wherever a hero has been born, has wrought, or has passed back into the void, the place is marked and sanctified.'[3] This can be said of Jesus, Muhammad, Confucius, the Buddha, Krishna and many others.

The Buddha, for instance, is also associated with two additional sacred spaces: the site of the Bodhi Tree, where he attained enlightenment and where now stands the Mahabodhi Temple, and the Deer Park at Sarnath, the site of his first sermon. More broadly, some of the most prevalent and important sacred spaces are those which are historically tied to prophets and founding figures of religions. The city of Jerusalem, for instance, is famously revered as holy by Jews, Christians and Muslims alike. Jews can be seen praying at the western wall, the last standing wall of the ancient

---

[2]Jeffrey J. Kripal, *Comparing Religions*, illustrated edition (West Sussex: John Wiley & Sons, 2014), 219.

[3]Joseph Campbell, *The Hero with a Thousand Faces*, The Collected Works of Joseph Campbell Series edition (Novato, CA: New World Library, 2008), 35.

holy temple. Christians visit the sites of Jesus's crucifixion as well as his empty tomb at the Church of the Holy Sepulchre. And Muslims visit the shrine known as the Dome of the Rock, the site of Muhammad's famous night-time journey to heaven, which is also believed to be the same spot where God created Adam, the first human, and where Abraham was asked to sacrifice his only son.

The sites of Jesus's birth and death/resurrection are both considered holy, and today there stands a church in each of these locations. These churches (the Church of Nativity and the Church of the Holy Sepulchre, respectively) have become sites of pilgrimage for devout Christians. When Jesus was born in Bethlehem, his mother Mary, 'gave birth to her firstborn son. She wrapped him in bands of cloth, and laid him in a feeding trough, because there was no room for them in the inn.'[4] This is a story that underscores the humble beginnings of Jesus. Thematically, it seems to give rise to the love and compassion he showed towards the poor and needy later in life. Later in the Bible he was sentenced to death by crucifixion, and Jesus 'went out, bearing his cross, to the place called "The Place of a Skull", which is called in Hebrew, "Golgotha"'.[5] This is why the cross is the symbol of Christianity, its most sacred object and a reminder to all that Christ suffered for us and continues to suffer with us, and that he is with us when we too must 'bear our own cross' in life.

Somewhat similarly, Mount Sinai represents the site where a foundational revelation was shared with the Jewish community. The ten commandments, which Moses received from God, were delivered here. 'When he finished speaking with him on Mount Sinai, he gave Moses the two tablets of the covenant, stone tablets, written with God's finger.'[6] Scholar of religion Huston Smith notes the special prominence in Judaism of not just important historical sites, but historically significant sacred objects as well:

> In sinking the roots of their lives deep into the past, Jews draw nourishment from events in which God's acts were clearly visible. The Sabbath eve with its candles and cup of sanctification, the

---

[4]Luke 2:7 (World English Bible).

[5]John 19:17 (World English Bible).

[6]Exodus 31:18, (World English Bible).

> Passover feast with its many symbols, the austere solemnity of the Day of Atonement, the ram's horn sounding the New Year, the scroll of the Torah adorned with breastplate and crown.[7]

These sacred objects have both actual and symbolic meanings in Jewish history and theology. The ram horn, for instance, refers to the ram that Abraham was commanded to sacrifice. Since this event is seen as the culmination of a test of faith, whose result was the initial covenant made by God with his people, the ram horn also serves as a symbol for ushering in the new year as it harks back to the legendary historical beginning of Western monotheism.

The physical aspect of these sacred spaces and objects, thus, derive their importance largely from history and tradition. But the deeper, practical impact they have on religious devotees comes through a confluence of history and the symbolic meanings associated with them. Confucius notes, 'Surely when one says "The rites, the rites", it is not enough merely to mean presents of jade and silk. Surely when one says "Music, music", it is not enough merely to mean bells and drums.'[8] In both cases, it is not enough merely to be in the presence of certain objects. It is necessary to dwell upon what those objects represent, why they are considered sacred and how they function. In this manner they can be made to point towards something beyond our immediate material world.

Following up on this, Hindus place more emphasis on intention when it comes to rituals rather than the precise nature of the objects used. For example, there are many different materials used to make japa mala, the string of 108 prayer beads used by many Hindus. Beads made from the rudraksha tree, the sandalwood tree, and holy basil are thought to be especially effective medicinally and spiritually, but it is just as permissible to use beads made from any other material. Many other religions make use of prayer beads: Catholics use rosary beads to say Hail Mary and Muslims use prayer beads to keep track of the 99 names of Allah; and Sikhs and Baha'is use prayer beads when reciting scriptural verses. But these beads themselves are not the main point—they are simply tools

---

[7]Huston Smith, *The Illustrated World's Religions* (New York: HarperCollins, 1995), 196.
[8]Confucius, *The Analects*, trans. D.C. Lau, Penguin Classics edition (London: Penguin Books, 1971), 17:11.

used to help devotees maintain focus while worshipping.

This same lesson about sacred objects applies equally to sacred spaces. The Dalai Lama expresses this as well:

> We, Buddhists, believe that merit is accumulated when you take part in something religious, with discipline and faith, because in doing so you shape a proper attitude within. With the right attitude, any journey to a sacred place becomes a pilgrimage.[9]

The Dalai Lama highlights the importance of proper attitude and intention, both of which are important Buddhist virtues. Whether you travel internationally to visit the Buddha's birthplace, or simply walk down the street to visit a local temple, you are expressing an intention to undertake a pilgrimage of sorts. From this perspective, the length of the pilgrimage is not what is most important, nor is the exact location. What is important is reflecting upon the commitment to undertake such a journey. Intention shapes us deeply as it makes us commit to a certain set of teachings, beliefs, attitudes, and/or behaviours that can be expressed throughout our daily lives.

One interesting illustration of the role of intention when engaging with sacred spaces is that of the Ka'ba in Islam, which the Qur'an describes as, 'the Sacred House, an asylum of security for [humankind]'[10], and 'The first House (of worship) appointed for [humankind]'.[11] The Ka'ba is considered the most sacred site in Islam, the focal point of the pilgrimage to Mecca that all Muslims are encouraged to undertake at least once in their lives. It is also the direction towards which all Muslims face when they pray, meaning that even when they are thousands of miles away, and praying while in different continents, all Muslims are engaging with this same sacred space in mind and spirit. Another significant element of the Ka'ba as a shared focal point of prayer and worship is that it showcases how sacred spaces can bring people of different sub-sects and communities together. The Ka'ba is considered holy by Sunnis and Shia

---

[9]Dalai Lama, 'The Dalai Lama on the Value of Pilgrimages,' *Newsweek*, 20 April 2007, https://www.newsweek.com/dalai-lama-value-pilgrimages-97425.

[10]Qur'an, 5:97 (Yusuf Ali).

[11]Qur'an 3:96 (Yusuf Ali)

alike, as well as Muslims of all races and nationalities.

In other religions, too, sacred spaces offer an opportunity for unifying different communities of worship. In Hinduism, the parallel to the hajj is the visiting of the four dhams (holy places), corresponding to the four points of the compass, which are sites where the great teacher Shankara set up special centres. Millions of Hindus visit these sites every year. Hindu temples contain elaborate statues from the pantheon of Gods and even the Ganges River has been imbued with a divine energy by people. Jeffrey Kripal observes, 'Many of the Hindu temples, for example, display in striking form a most remarkable comparative practice: numerous Gods and Goddesses share the same sacred space, as each is understood to be a part of a larger cosmic vision or sacred whole.'[12] This can be seen as part of a broader conception of what sacred places represent across religions. They form places that bridge and dissolve boundaries. Thus, across religions, sacred spaces are seen as sites that facilitate unification, both cosmologically and socially. Expressing this capacity to dissolve social boundaries, the Baha'i leader 'Abdu'l-Bahá has written, 'In brief, the original purpose of temples and houses of worship is simply that of unity—places of meeting where various peoples, different races and souls of every capacity may come together in order that love and agreement should be manifest between them.'[13] In Hinduism, the Ganges river in India is considered especially holy, and every twelve years, a mass gathering of tens of millions of Hindus is held, known as the Kumbh Mela. Considering the enormously large number of devotees that take part in the ritual of taking a dip in the sacred river, the Kumbh Mela is arguably the largest peaceful religious gathering in the world.

Similarly, the sacred spaces of religions from China are thought to be the sites of 'crossing over'. They are often found on mountains as they are the points on earth that most closely approach heaven, thereby allowing humans to cross between these planes. In Taoism, for instance, there are four sacred mountains that hold special significance. This raises an

---

[12]Jeffrey J. Kripal, *Comparing Religions*, illustrated edition (West Sussex: John Wiley & Sons, 2014), 34.

[13]'Abdu'l-Bahá, *The Promulgation of Universal Peace*, second edition (US: Bahá'í Publishing Trust: 1982), 65, Baha'i Reference Library, http://reference.bahai.org/en/t/ab/PUP/pup-27.html

interesting observation: all ancient places of worship across all religions reach upwards, vertically—tall church steeples, for instance—as if they are trying to touch the sky. Furthermore, the major spaces of worship across religions are famously ornate, and are some of the most impressive and beautiful examples of human architecture. This attention to beauty and detail is a display of enormous love and devotion to God. Through their unique aesthetic senses, they are displays of the beauty to be gleaned from the rich diversity of humanity.

Sacred spaces and objects are thought to be effective in allowing us to witness or experience the transcendent through material means. They allow us to concretize abstract concepts to help direct our focus towards that which is beyond our normal everyday awareness in the material realm. Material religion allows us to experience the divine through touch and feel, rather than just as words of a text.

29

Holy Water

To understand water is to understand the cosmos, the marvels of nature, and life itself.[1]

—Masaru Emoto

Modern science has taught us a lot of surprising and marvellous things about water. Our bodies are 60–70 per cent water, and 70 per cent of the earth's surface is water. We know that all life began in water, from the simplest single-celled organisms to more complex microorganisms, to fish and amphibians, then land mammals, and then us. All life traces its roots back to water and all life continues to depend on water.

Anthropologically speaking, human civilization can be traced back to water as well. It is widely accepted that the first major human civilizations began in Mesopotamia, by the Tigris and Euphrates rivers, and then, in Egypt along the Nile River. Since then, the most powerful civilizations and most important cities have owed their primacy to their proximity to major bodies of water, which conferred advantages for agriculture, trade and more.

The Hindu God Vishnu, incarnated on earth many times according to Hindu mythology, and the sequence of forms he took closely mirrors

[1]Masaru Emoto, *The Hidden Messages in Water* (New York: Simon and Schuster, 2011), 19.

that of our own evolutionary trajectory: he first appeared as a fish, then a tortoise, then a boar, then a half-lion/half-man, then in various human forms. In the biblical creation story of Genesis, all life was created in seven days. The first animals created by God are said to be those of the sea, which is consistent with scientific evidence—albeit in a much different scale of time. And in the Qur'an, it is said, 'Allah has created every animal from water: of them there are some that creep on their bellies; some that walk on two legs; and some that walk on four.'[2]

As much as the world's religions may seem to be different, we all share the same earth with one another. Human beings have been making observations and hypotheses about this same earth for tens of thousands of years. Perhaps it shouldn't be too surprising that all religions have focused on water as particularly important and foundational to life, as all religions have been part of the same human meaning-making process.

Even the ritual and practical dimensions of religions echo one another with respect to the way that water is used and understood. Across many religions, worshippers must cleanse themselves with water before entering a holy space—this is true in the case of Shinto shrines, mosques, and Hindu temples, to name just a few.

In Christianity, Jesus is said to have performed several miracles through water, like turning water into wine, walking on water, helping frustrated fishermen catch fish. But, of course, most notably in Christianity is the sacrament of baptism. The Bible records Jesus himself as being baptized by John the Baptist. Christians, from nearly all denominations, practise baptism, usually baptizing infants within the first few weeks of birth by pouring holy water over them or immersing them in this water. This is meant to symbolically replicate the moment of Jesus's baptism, when he was blessed by the Holy Spirit. In Judaism, there is a similar sacrament, known as 'mikveh', where a person is immersed in water to achieve spiritual purity. In fact, because Jesus himself was a Jew, it is generally believed that these early 'baptisms' in the New Testament were, in fact, instances of 'mikveh'.

Jesus also invokes water as a path to salvation, which he himself represents. As he says in the Bible, 'Everyone who drinks of this water

[2]Qur'an, 24:45 (Yusuf Ali).

will thirst again, but whoever drinks of the water that I will give him will never thirst again; but the water that I will give him will become in him a well of water springing up to eternal life.'[3] The meaning behind this is beautifully expressed by the Baha'i leader 'Abdu'l-Bahá, who explained, 'Water is the cause of life, and when Christ speaks of water, He is symbolizing that which is the cause of Everlasting Life. This life-giving water of which He speaks is like unto fire, for it is none other than the Love of God, and this love means life to our souls.'[4]

Water has similar connotations in Hinduism, and the rituals are often centred around water. As scholar Deepa Joshi writes, 'The Rig Veda identifies the Waters as the first residence or ayana of Nara, the Eternal Being and therefore water is said to be pratishtha, the underlying principle, or the very foundation of this universe.'[5] The most important body of water, the river Ganges is still believed to be an incarnation of a Goddess in the Hindu pantheon. This is why water is regarded with such supreme importance and holiness in Hinduism. In fact, water is used in Hindu temples to 'bathe' the deities. This water—known as theertha—is not simply discarded, but is instead collected to be doled out to those worshipping at the temple. When I was a child, I remember queuing up to get a few drops of the theertha myself.

This holy water is believed to cleanse and purify the body and also protect against sickness. This is not without some scientific merit. The holy water is generally kept in copper or silver pots, thereby infusing the water with these essential trace elements which are vital nutrients for the body and help with absorption of other essential minerals/nutrients. At times, tulsi (holy basil), cardamom, edible camphor, cloves, or other items are added to the holy water, thereby increasing its medicinal impact.

Hindus understand certain rivers—most notably the Ganges—as containing healing and purification powers that may help individuals

---

[3]John, 4:13-14 (World English Bible).

[4]'Abdu'l-Bahá, *Paris Talks*, eleventh edition (UK: Bahá'í Publishing Trust, 1972), 82, Baha'i Reference Library, http://reference.bahai.org/en/t/ab/PT/pt-31.html.

[5]Deepa Joshi and Ben Fawcett, 'Water, Hindu Mythology and an Unequal Social Order in India', Second Conference of the International Water History Association (Bergen, August 2001), 2.

attain better circumstances in their next life. This belief is illustrated through the following passage from the Kurma Purana, which speaks of Varanasi, a holy city along the Ganges:

> The city of Varanasi is my place of utmost mystery, said Shiva, which conveys all creatures across the ocean of existence [...] My devotees who go there enter into me. There gifts, prayers, offerings, oblations, tapas and all other acts, meditation, Vedic study and knowledge become indestructible. All the evil accumulated in a thousand previous lives is destroyed for one who enters Avimukta.[6]

Due to strong religious belief that taking a ritual dip in the sacred river during the month-long festival of the Kumbh Mela will help get rid of the sins and facilitate attainment of moksha, it is estimated that more than 9 million people thronged the shores of the Ganges River in 2021 despite the COVID warnings from health care professionals.

As Wendy Doniger, a leading scholar of Hinduism, writes, 'Hindus hope to die in Varanasi, and the river's banks are crowded with corpses waiting to be consigned to its waters.'[7] In Hinduism, death is not the end. Life and death are believed to be part of a cyclical process. Like most religions, Hinduism acknowledges that all life comes from water. And because a person's soul is carried over into a new life after death, it makes sense for life to end in water as well.

The Hindu poet Ramprasad Sen has written about this:

> You end, brother,
> Where you began, a reflection
> Rising in water, mixing with water,
> Finally one with water.[8]

The concept of the soul in Hinduism is called atman, which is understood to be the deeper self that resides in every individual and is actually a manifestation of God, or brahman. The relationship

---

[6]Wendy Doniger, *Hinduism, The Norton Anthology of World Religions: Vol. 1*, ed. Jack Miles (New York: W.W. Norton & Company, 2015), 271.

[7]Ibid, 271.

[8]Ibid, 532.

between atman and brahman is explained through various parables and metaphors in Hindu literature, many of which involve water. One of the most famous is from the Upanishads, involving an exchange between a father and his son named Svetaketu.

> 'Put this chunk of salt in a container of water and come back tomorrow.' The son did as he was told, and the father said to him: 'The chunk of salt you put in the water last evening—bring it here.' He groped for it but could not find it, as it had dissolved completely.
>
> 'Now, take a sip from this corner,' said the father. 'How does it taste?'
>
> 'Salty.'
>
> 'Take a sip from the centre.—How does it taste?'
>
> 'Salty.'
>
> 'Take a sip from that corner.—How does it taste?'
>
> 'Salty.'
>
> 'Sir, teach me more.'
>
> 'Very well, son.
>
> 'Throw it out and come back later.' He did as he was told and found that the salt was always there. The father told him: 'You, of course, did not see it there, son; yet it was always right there.
>
> 'The finest essence here—that constitutes the self of this whole world; that is the truth; that is the self (atman). And that's how you are, Svetaketu.'[9]

There are similar stories and concepts in Buddhism. Look how similar the themes are in the following excerpt from the Zen Buddhist monk, Shunryu Suzuki.

> After we are separated by birth from this oneness, as the water falling from the waterfall is separated from the rocks, then we have feeling [...] When you do not realize that you are one with the river, or one with the universe, you have fear. Whether it is separated into drops or not, water is water.[10]

---

[9]'Chandogya Upanishad' in *Upanisads,* trans. Patrick Olivelle, Oxford World's Classics (London: Oxford University Press, 1996), 6:12-13.

[10]Shunryu Suzuki, *Zen Mind, Beginner's Mind* (Boston: Shambhala, 2011), 83.

In both cases, the underlying idea is the same: we experience ourselves as separate individuals in life, and to some extent, we are. But we are also like droplets of water. We might go through life with feelings of separation, but really, we are all one, interconnected like a single body of water. One of the common spiritual goals of religions is the attainment of a state of consciousness that recognizes that profound oneness and interconnectedness.

The cultivation of consciousness is at the heart of spiritual practice for all religions. Water is frequently used as a metaphor in scriptures across religions while dealing with the topics of consciousness and enlightenment because it naturally represents things, like stillness and clarity. For instance, the Taoist sage Chuang Tzu pointed out, 'People don't look at a flowing river for a mirror, they look at still waters, because only what is still stills things and holds them still.'[11] Similarly, the Book of Proverbs in the Hebrew Bible is home to many such metaphors, including, 'Like water reflects a face, so a man's heart reflects the man,'[12] and 'Counsel in the heart of man is like deep water, but a man of understanding will draw it out.'[13] Interestingly, the name of one of the most important prophets across Judaism, Christianity, Islam and Baha'i, translates as 'to draw out of': 'The child grew, and she brought him to Pharaoh's daughter, and he became her son. She named him Moses, and said, "Because I drew him out of the water."'[14] Moses was pulled out of the Nile by a servant of the Pharaoh's daughter. This story is metaphorically connected with the other verses from Proverbs, since Moses, as a Prophet of God, does indeed become a vessel for God's counsel and guidance of the Hebrew people.

There is one more common metaphorical use of water across religious scriptures and spiritual leaders that is worth pointing out. It has to do with the recognition of the common wisdom underlying religious diversity and pluralism. One particularly clear expression of this metaphor comes from the Baha'i leader 'Abdu'l-Bahá:

---

[11]Chuang Tzu, *The Book of Chuang Tzu*, Penguin Classics edition, trans. Martin Palmer (New York: Penguin Books, 2006), 39.

[12]Proverbs, 27:19 (World English Bible).

[13]Proverbs, 20:5 (World English Bible).

[14]Exodus, 2:10 (World English Bible).

> God's grace is like the rain that cometh down from heaven: the water is not bounded by the limitations of form, yet on whatever place it poureth down, it taketh on limitations—dimensions, appearance, shape—according to the characteristics of that place. In a square pool, the water, previously unconfined, becometh a square; in a six-sided pool it becometh a hexagon, in an eight-sided pool an octagon, and so forth. The rain itself hath no geometry, no limits, no form, but it taketh on one form or another, according to the restrictions of its vessel. In the same way, the Holy Essence of the Lord God is boundless, immeasurable, but His graces and splendours become finite in the creatures, because of their limitations.[15]

There are many examples of water metaphors used to illustrate this important and fundamental idea, like the following from the Hindu saint Sri Ramakrishna:

> Truth is one; only It is called by different names. All people are seeking the same Truth; the variance is due to climate, temperament, and name. A lake has many ghats [paths leading down to a river]. From one ghat the Hindus take water in jars and call it 'jal'. From another ghat the Mussalmāns take water in leather bags and call it 'pāni'. From a third the Christians take the same thing and call it 'water'. Suppose someone says that the thing is not 'jal' but 'pāni', or that it is not 'pāni' but 'water', or that it is not 'water' but 'jal', it would indeed be ridiculous. But this very thing is at the root of the friction among sects, their misunderstandings and quarrels. This is why people injure and kill one another, and shed blood, in the name of religion. But this is not good. Everyone is going toward God. They will all realize Him if they have sincerity and longing of heart.[16]

---

[15]'Abdu'l-Bahá, *Selections From the Writings of 'Abdu'l-Bahá* (Bahá'í World Centre: 1982), 162, Baha'I Reference Library, http://reference.bahai.org/en/t/ab/SAB/sab-145.html.

[16]Sri Ramakrishna, *The Gospel of Sri Ramakrishna*, trans. Swami Nikhilananda (New York: Ramakrishna-Vivekananda Center, 1942), 191.

Just as water that has been taken from any source and been called by any name is still water, so too is God the same, regardless of each religion's particular expressions. Hazrat Inayat Khan, an important figure in modern Sufism, has explained this idea further: 'To a Sufi, revelation is the inherent property of every soul. There is an unceasing flow of the divine stream, which has neither beginning nor end.'[17]

Similarly, in the foundational Taoist text, Tao Te Ching, Lao Tzu writes:

> To picture the Tao in the world
> Imagine a stream and the sea[18]

In Taoism, the 'Tao' translates roughly as the 'path' or 'way', as in, the way of the universe or the ways of life. In Taoism it is believed that the key to a peaceful and fulfilling life is to study, understand and live in accordance with the natural patterns and rhythms of the world around us. The 'Tao' is often likened to running waters, such as streams, as it follows a fixed course that nothing can change. That is why Lao Tzu also writes:

> Nothing in the world is weaker than water
> But against the hard and strong
> Nothing outdoes it
> For nothing can change it.[19]

Just as a stream will empty out into the ocean—no matter what—if we imagine ourselves as all caught up in that same stream of life, we can accept that path, and either go with it, or struggle against it. Either way, we are all part of the same stream and will all end up in the same ocean.

There are many more examples of water metaphors we could point to, but let's end with one more powerful example from modern literature.

[17]Hazrat Inayat Khan, *The Sufi Message Volume 1: The Way of Illumination* (Delhi: Motilal Banarsidass, 2011), 56.

[18]Lao-Tzu, *Tao te ching*, trans. Red Pine (Port Townsend: Copper Canyon Press, 2009), Chapter 32, 64.

[19]Lao-Tzu, *Tao te ching*, trans. Red Pine (Port Townsend: Copper Canyon Press, 2009), Chapter 78, 156.

In his famous novel *Siddhartha*, Hermann Hesse fictionalizes the life of the Buddha. Towards the end, he beautifully describes a moment of enlightenment that Siddhartha undergoes while resting by a river:

> It was all one, it was all interwoven and knotted together, interconnected in a thousand ways. And all of this together, all the voices, all the goals, all the longing, all the suffering, all the pleasure, all the good and evil, all of this together was the world. All of this together was the river of events, the music of life. And whenever Siddhartha listened attentively to that river, that song of a thousand voices, when he listened neither to the sorrow nor the laughter, when he tied his soul not to any individual voice, entering into it with his self, but instead hearing them all, perceiving the totality, the oneness, then the great song of a thousand voices consisted of a single word, which was om, the absolute.[20]

[20]Hermann Hesse, *Siddhartha*, trans. Stanley Appelbaum, Dover Thrift edition (New York: Dover Publications, 1999), 73.

30

Golden Rule

The good which every man who pursues virtue aims at for himself he will also desire for the rest of mankind, and all the more as he acquires a greater knowledge of God.[1]

—Baruch Spinoza

Few religious threads are as simple and universal as the golden rule. It is thrilling to see how closely aligned all religions are on this principle, and all cultures seem to have stumbled upon it independently, through their respective wisdom traditions. The prophets and scriptures of every major religious system contain nearly identical formulations of this succinct mantra. More pertinently, all religions agree on the supreme importance of the golden rule, and in many cases they go as far as to say that it contains the entirety of an otherwise complex and detailed system of moral beliefs and practices.

I was taught the golden rule before I knew it by that name. Whenever I used to do mischievous things to my older sister as a young boy, my mother would pull me aside and ask me, 'Would you like it if she did those things to you? No? Then don't do them to her.' I found that logic to be very persuasive, even as a child, and in retrospect it's very impressive

[1]Baruch Spinoza, *The Essential Spinoza: Ethics and Related Writings* (Cambridge, Massachusetts: Hackett Publishing, 2006), 120.

how effective my mother was at modifying my behavior with such a simple concept. I was also taught to extend that principle to others, as my mother explained that God appears in different masks, even as beggars and other destitute people, to test you to see whether you were kind to every person you met or not, whether you treated them as you wish to be treated.

The golden rule advises us, in the words of the Baha'i prophet Baha'u'llah, to 'Choose thou for thy neighbor that which thou choosest for thyself'.[2] Most of us are taught this principle at such an early age that it may seem completely banal. Yet, how many of us can claim to truly put this into practice on a daily basis? It is not easy. However, as conscious and self-aware beings, we are able to recognize the facets of our interconnectedness, and as such, we are able to step back and see that more of our needs and desires can be met by working together as a collective, rather than by competing against one another. The golden rule is just a simple expression of this principle: it states that if I help you, and you help me, then we will benefit mutually from our interactions, enabling each of us to flourish more fully.

There is a famous story from the Babylonian Talmud to illustrate this. It is told through the wise figure of Rabbi Hillel.

> Once there was a gentile who came before Shammai, and said to him: 'Convert me on the condition that you teach me the whole Torah while I stand on one foot.' Shammai pushed him aside with the measuring stick he was holding. The same fellow came before Hillel, and Hillel converted him, saying: 'That which is despicable to you, do not do to your fellow, this is the whole Torah, and the rest is commentary, go and learn it.'[3]

Quite similarly, in the New Testament we are told, 'Therefore, whatever you desire for men to do to you, you shall also do to them; for this

---

[2]Baha'u'llah, *Tablets of Baha'u'llah Revealed after the Kitab-i-Aqdas* (Haifa: Baha'i World Centre, 1978), 64.

[3]Hillel the Elder, Babylonian Talmud, Shabbat 31a, Jewish Virtual Library, https://www.jewishvirtuallibrary.org/rabbi-hillel-quotes-on-judaism-and-israel, accessed on 14 July 2022.

is the law and the prophets.'[4] Confucius, when asked if there was a single word to sum up his teachings on proper conduct, replied, 'It is perhaps the word "shu". Do not impose on others what you yourself do not desire.'[5] The similarities of these statements speak for themselves. No matter how different these religious traditions might be from one another in their metaphysical beliefs and practices of worship, they all ultimately give the same simple advice when it comes to how we should live our lives.

There are, of course, nuances that can and have been added to the basic formulation of the golden rule. Some religious traditions stress on the importance of empathy, i.e., not in terms of treating others as you would want to be treated, but also, specifically wanting other people to have what you want. For instance, Prophet Muhammad told his followers, 'None of you [truly] believes until he loves for his brother that which he loves for himself.'[6] In loving for others what we love for ourselves, we come to realize that we share in the joy and misery of others. Consider the following examples from the Taoist sage Lao Tzu and the Hindu scripture Bhagavad Gita respectively.

> Regard your neighbour's gain as your own gain, and your neighbour's loss as your own loss.[7]

> One who everywhere sees equality, through likeness with oneself,
> whether pleasure or pain, is thought to be the highest practitioner
> of yoga.[8]

The golden rule can be logically deduced in the Upanishads. Since the soul (or the true self of every living being) is identical with that of the universe (expressed through the mantra 'tat tvam asi' which translates as 'That art thou'), it follows that one must identify his

[4]Matthew 7:12 (World English Bible).

[5]Confucius, *The Analects*, trans. D.C. Lau, Penguin Classics edition (London: Penguin Books, 1971), 15:24.

[6]Al-Bukhari, Hadith 13.

[7]Laozi Taiqing, *T'ai Shang Kan Ying P'ien*, trans. Daisetz Teitaro Suzuki and Dr Paul Carus (1906), 6.

[8]Laurie L. Patton, trans, *The Bhagavad Gita* (New York: Penguin, 2014), 6:32.

own self with all other selves. Hence, the golden rule sets forward the well-being of all.

The golden rule is not put forward to minimize interpersonal conflict, but also enables us to maximize our feelings of unity and interconnectedness, urging us to really allow ourselves to engage with others' feelings and to realize that the happiness of each of us is dependent on the happiness of all.

In light of this, it is logical to conclude that the golden rule must be applied universally. It is not enough to wish well for our friends and neighbours, but we must extend this to our enemies and outsiders as well. The Qur'an tells us, 'Nor can Goodness and Evil be equal. Repel (Evil) with what is better: Then will he between whom and thee was hatred become as it were thy friend and intimate!'[9] While the Hebrew Bible reminds the people of Israel: 'He who sacrifices to any God, except to Yahweh only, shall be utterly destroyed.'[10] Similarly, in the Buddhist scriptural text, Udanavarga, we are advised, 'Hurt not others with what pains yourself.' [11] In the Hindu epic, the Mahabharata, we are once again told that 'One should never do that to another which one regards as injurious to one's own self. This, in brief, is the rule of Righteousness.'[12]

It is a hard but important lesson to learn. Nothing good comes from fighting violence with violence or responding to malicious acts with maliciousness of our own.

Simply put, the golden rule is a conscious decision to always put yourself in the shoes of another person before conducting yourself in a way that will have a direct effect upon them. And as neurobiologist Donald W. Pfaff posits, 'If it's really true that all religions have this ethical principle, across continents and across centuries, then it is more likely to have a hardwired scientific basis than if it was just a neighborhood

---

[9]Qur'an 41:34 (Yusuf Ali)

[10]Exodus 22:20 (World English Bible).

[11]*Udanavarga,* trans. William Woodville Rockhill, 5:18 (London, England: Psychology Press, 2000), 27.

[12]Kisari Mohan Ganguli, trans, *Mahabharata*, Anusasana Parva 113.8, Sacred Texts, accessed on 14 July 2022, https://www.sacred-texts.com/hin/m13/m13b078.htm#fn_255.

custom.'[13] We should look at the golden rule not just as something that was invented by humans, but as something that is unchangeably fundamental to who we *are* biologically. As a single species, we are all making meaning in similar ways to transcend time and place. The golden rule is the common mantra, shared across all religions, that can turn the elusive dream of a utopian society—where every human being can flourish—into a reality.

---

[13]Donald W. Pfaff, 'The Neuroscience of Fair Play: Why We (Usually) Follow the Golden Rule' (Dana Press, 2007) in Brains Are Hardwired To Act According To The Golden Rule, *Science Daily*, 23 March 2008, https://www.sciencedaily.com/releases/2008/03/080321131055.htm.

31

Forgiveness

Father, forgive them, for they do not know what they are doing.[1]

—New Testament

Great is repentance, for it brings healing to the world [...] When an individual repents, s/he is forgiven, and the entire world with him.[2]

—Babylonian Talmud

The essential message of all major world religions has always been love and compassion. It is often the most difficult to show love and compassion to our enemies, and to ourselves. To be able to love, we must forgive—after all, nobody is perfect. And so, forgiveness is an important command of all wisdom traditions.

If we expect to live in a peaceful world, forgiveness is indispensable. Without it, we will be trapped in an endless series of senseless and violent feuds with others. Forgiveness is a two-way street, and it follows the golden rule: if we wish for others to forgive us, we must be ready to forgive others. If we desire to use religious wisdom to help heal our

[1]Luke 23:34 (World English Bible).

[2]Babylonian Talmud, Yoma 86b *in* Rabbi John Rosove, 'The Central Personal Challenge of the High Holiday Season', *Jewish Journal*, 27 September 2017, https://jewishjournal.com/commentary/blogs/224988/central-challenge-high-holiday-season/

divided world, then such an attitude is necessary. The past cannot be changed, but the future can. If we want to have a better future, we need to be ready to move past our own mistakes and the misdeeds of others, and forgiveness is one of the primary ways we can move on.

The Western monotheistic religions point to God as the ultimate source of forgiveness in the world. For example, the Baha'i prophet Bahá'u'lláh has said, 'Verily, the breezes of forgiveness have been wafted from the direction of your Lord, the God of Mercy; whoso turneth thereunto shall be cleansed of his sins, and of all pain and sickness.'[3] God's forgiving nature is also seen as an example for people to model their own behaviour. In the New Testament, we are told that 'bearing with one another, and forgiving each other, if any man has a complaint against any; even as Christ forgave you, so you also do'.[4] Similarly, the Qur'an urges, 'Let not those among you who are endured with grace and amplitude of means resolve by oath against helping their kinsmen, those in want, and those who have left their homes on God's cause: let them forgive and overlook, do you not wish that God should forgive you? For God is oft-forgiving, most merciful.'[5] Just as God forgives us for our bad behaviour—as we are all likely to slip up from time to time—so too are we instructed to forgive those who have wronged us. This will enable us to recognize that we all are flawed creatures, we all make mistakes and we are all deserving of compassion and forgiveness.

Hindus point to forgiveness (kshama) as one of the six cardinal virtues. In Book 3 of the Hindu epic the Mahabharata, it has been said, 'Forgiveness is virtue; forgiveness is sacrifice; forgiveness is the Vedas [...] forgiveness is holiness; and by forgiveness is it that the universe is held together.'[6] In order to forgive we must overcome our baser animal instincts—the reactionary, emotional response of anger and the impulse to retaliate using physical force. It takes strength to cultivate mental control and composure that is necessary if we want to see the bigger

---

[3]Bahá'u'lláh, *The Summons of the Lord of Hosts* (Bahá'í World Centre: 2002), 68, Baha'i Reference Library. http://reference.bahai.org/en/t/b/SLH/slh-6.html.

[4]Colossians 3:13 (World English Bible).

[5]Qur'an 24:22 (Yusuf Ali).

[6]*The Mahabharata of Krishna-Dwaipayana Vyasa Translated Into English Prose: Virata parva,* trans. Kisari Mohan Ganguli,(Calcutta, India: Bhārata Press, 1884), 84.

picture, even when we are wronged. The truth is that violence only begets more violence, and by harming others, we are harming ourselves.

In the ancient Taoist scriptures we are similarly taught to reorient our perspective about strength and weakness—those we normally see as weak-willed, in fact, outlast the stronger, like blades of grass that are flexible and low enough to the ground to survive strong winds that are capable of toppling trees and even houses. This is illustrated through the example of a baby, a being who is flexible enough to forget and innocent enough to forgive. In the Tao Te Ching, Lao Tzu writes, 'Can you make your breath as soft as a baby's/Can you wipe your dark mirror free of dust?'[7] The baby represents innocence, but also inner strength. Nothing external to the baby can disrupt her internal calmness and purity. Forgiveness is the ability to erase negative memories from our minds; it requires us to give up our hold on negative emotions like anger and contempt.

The Dalai Lama maintains that we must forgive a person while retaining full awareness of the infraction itself. 'Forgiveness doesn't mean forget what happened [...] If something is serious and it is necessary to take counter-measures, you have to take counter-measures.'[8] Forgiveness is important if we are to cleanse ourselves of negative attitudes towards other people. However, it would be foolish to not take preventative actions to avoid being wronged or harmed again in the future. A professor at Harvard Tyler J. VanderWeele notes, 'Forgiveness, understood as the replacing of ill-will with good-will towards the offender, does not imply condoning the action or not demanding justice. Forgiving simply means desiring the ultimate good of the offender, and this can be done without excusing the wrongful action and while still pursuing a just outcome.'[9]

Just as forgiveness achieves its fullness through clear recognition of

---

[7]Lao-Tzu, *Tao te ching*, Trans. Red Pine (Port Townsend, Washington: Copper Canyon Press, 2009), Chapter 10, 20.

[8]Dalai Lama, 'Dalai Lama suggests Osama bin Laden's death was justified', Mitchell Landsberg, *The Los Angeles Times*, 4 May 2011, https://www.latimes.com/local/la-xpm-2011-may-04-la-me-0504-dalai-lama-20110504-story.html

[9]Tyler J. VanderWeele, 'Forgiveness: An Important Aspect of Flourishing', *Psychology Today*, 27 June 2019, https://www.psychologytoday.com/us/blog/human-flourishing/201906/forgiveness-important-aspect-flourishing.

another's wrongs alongside active steps to avoid falling victim to these wrongs again in the future, so too does repentance involve the willingness to directly confront your own mistakes, acknowledge and accept them for what they are, and vow to learn from them. As Confucius wisely remarked, 'Not to mend one's ways when one has erred is to err indeed.'[10] C.S. Lewis has also expounded upon this principle in Christian terms:

> A live body is not one that never gets hurt, but one that can to some extent repair itself. In the same way a Christian is not a man who never goes wrong, but a man who is enabled to repent and pick himself up and begin over again after each stumble—because the Christ-life is inside him, repairing him all the time, enabling him to repeat (in some degree) the kind of voluntary death which Christ Himself carried out.[11]

To forgive others we must recognize that human beings are inherently flawed creatures who make mistakes from time to time. Repentance, in the same vein, is the act of applying this reasoning to ourselves as well.

There are instances across many religions of repentance being ritualized, in order to provide us with constant reminders of the value of this attitude and practice. Catholics, for instance, place high value on confessional booths where individuals can go to confidentially confess their sins to a priest in the presence of God. The priest may grant the person forgiveness and/or offer them advice on how to properly repent. Repentance also plays a big role in Judaism. One of the most important holidays in the Jewish calendar is Yom Kippur, or the day of atonement. It is addressed in the Hebrew Bible: 'This shall be an everlasting statute for you, to make atonement for the children of Israel once in the year because of all their sins.'[12] Thus, there is an important communal aspect to repentance in the Jewish tradition. Communities heal best together. This is true on all scales—whether familial or global.

In the Uttaradhyayana Sutra which is considered to be one of the

---

[10]Confucius, *The Analects*, trans. D.C. Lau, Penguin Classics edition (London, England: Penguin Books, 1971), 15:30.
[11]C.S. Lewis, *The C.S. Lewis Signature Classics* (New York: HarperCollins, 2017), 59.
[12]Leviticus 16:34 (World English Bible).

most important sacred books of Jainism, the prophet Mahavira also explains the importance of repentance and seeking forgiveness: 'By begging forgiveness he obtains happiness of mind; thereby he acquires a kind disposition towards all kinds of living being; by this kind disposition he obtains purity of character and freedom from fear.' [13] Forgiveness and repentance are therefore pathways not only to outward peace, but inner peace as well.

There are many different circumstances that might call for acts of forgiveness or repentance. These acts and attitudes are indispensable. They help keep our perceptions of ourselves and others broad, unmarred by negative feelings or grudges. They help us move forward with our lives, and make us beings who are always striving to improve ourselves and our relationships with others.

Compelling empirical evidence emerging on the positive effects of forgiveness on our well-being can also be found. VanderWeele has done research on the subject:

> [O]ur research indicates that forgiveness reduces subsequent depression and anxiety by about 15-20%, when controlling for other variables, and suggests that forgiveness is a freeing and healing alternative to maladaptive responses like rumination and suppression.[14]

And according to the results of another major study that he was involved in, 'All forgiveness measures were positively associated with all psychosocial well-being outcomes, and inversely associated with depressive and anxiety symptoms.'[15]

---

[13] *Uttarādhyayana Sūtra,* trans. Hermann Jacobi, 29:17, Wisdom Library, accessed on 14 July 2022, https://www.wisdomlib.org/jainism/book/uttaradhyayana-sutra/d/doc424239.html.

[14] Tyler J. VanderWeele, 'Forgiveness: An Important Aspect of Flourishing', *Psychology Today*, 27 June 2019, https://www.psychologytoday.com/us/blog/human-flourishing/201906/forgiveness-important-aspect-flourishing.

[15] Ying Chen, Sion Kim Harris, Everett L Worthington Jr, and Tyler J VanderWeele, 'Religiously or Spiritually-Motivated Forgiveness and Subsequent Health and Well-Being among Young Adults: An Outcome-Wide Analysis', *Journal of Positive Psychology*, 14 (5): 649-658, *PubMed,* 13 September 2018, https://pubmed.ncbi.nlm.nih.gov/31360213/

If forgiveness can be so beneficial to those combating some of the most debilitating mental-health symptoms, then there's a high likelihood that it can benefit all of us as well! The paradoxical thing about forgiveness is that it is less about the one being forgiven and more about liberating oneself.

32

Peace and Non-violence

[Non-violence] is the truest radicalism, destabilizing to societies built on transaction and domination because it inverts their workings, lays bare their weaknesses, dissolves their core ethic.[1]

—Ezra Klein

All major religions have words and phrases in their native languages to express a message of peace: Jews say 'shalom', Christians and Muslims say 'amen' and 'ameen', respectively, at the end of prayers and recitations of scripture. Even the very term 'Islam' is based on the root word 'salaam', which means peace and is used as a common greeting among Muslims and other Arabs, just as shalom is used among Jews. Hindus say 'Om', and every major discourse by a Hindu monk ends with 'om shanti, shanti, shanti', meaning, 'peace, peace, peace'. This is true of other religions as well, including indigenous and tribal religions. The author David Price offers the following as examples:

> Some Native American tribes call it the 'Beauty Path'. The Hopi call it 'The Hopi Way'. Christians call it 'agape' and psychologists

[1]Ezra Klein, 'Imagining the nonviolent state', *Vox*, 17 June 2020, https://www.vox.com/2020/6/17/21279950/nonviolence-king-gandhi-protesters-rioters-george-floyd.

> refer to it as 'unconditional love for all'. To Buddhists it is the 'Middle Way'. Africans call it 'ubuntu'. Hawaiians call it 'Aloha'. To Jamaicans and reggae fans worldwide, it is known as 'One Love'. It is the path of striving to offer love, compassion and forgiveness to everyone, in every situation, no matter what the circumstances.[2]

Though religion is sometimes attacked for its potential to incite violence, the truth is that all religions, on the contrary, teach non-violence and peace above all else. Those who commit violence in the name of religion—whichever religion that might be—are not being faithful to the teachings of their tradition. They may draw upon, distort, or even directly quote particular scriptural passages out of context, but in so doing they lose sight of the bigger picture, which is always peace. Religious individuals and institutions surely err from time to time, but peace is the goal behind all religions.

Non-violence is such a universal thread across religions that Gandhi—one of history's great paragons of peace—once described it as a 'master key' for understanding the unity among religions.

> That master-key is that of truth and non-violence. When I unlock the chest of a religion with this master-key, I do not find it difficult to discover its likeness with other religions.[3]

The term used for non-violence across the religious traditions of India, Gandhi's native land, is 'ahimsa', which is founded on a universal respect for all life. It is one of the three principal tenets of living life, according to the ancient Jain tradition. In the Bhagavad Gita, we are told, 'Realize the truth of the scriptures; learn to be detached and to take joy in renunciation. Do not get angry or harm any living creature, but be compassionate and gentle; show good will to all.'[4] We can interpret this as applying to the scriptures of *all* religions, echoing Gandhi's point

---

[2]David Price, 'The Birth of Peace', *Medium*, 19 November 2021, https://davidprice-26453.medium.com/the-birth-of-peace-a6175676d62b

[3]K. L. Seshagiri Rao, *Mahatma Gandhi and Comparative Religion* (Delhi: Motilal Banarsidass, 1990), 61.

[4]*The Bhagavad Gita*, trans. Eknath Easwaran, Second Edition (Tomales: Nilgiri Press, July 2007), 16:1-2.

about non-violence being a master key to unlock religion's mysteries.

A further point about ahimsa is that it is undertaken not just as an attitude, but as a lived practice. In fact, followers of Jainism are urged to wear face coverings and carry around small brooms to avoid accidentally inhaling or stepping on creatures that are too small to be visible to the naked eye. This underscores the fact that religions recognize that total commitment to non-violence requires a great deal of effort. In the New Testament, for instance, it is said that we should 'Follow after peace with all men, and the sanctification without which no man will see the Lord.'[5] Jesus explains that non-violence applies to our enemies as well, famously advising us to 'turn the other cheek'.

> You have heard that it was said, 'An eye for an eye, and a tooth for a tooth.' But I tell you, don't resist him who is evil; but whoever strikes you on your right cheek, turn to him the other also. [...] You have heard that it was said, 'You shall love your neighbor and hate your enemy.' But I tell you, love your enemies, bless those who curse you, do good to those who hate you, and pray for those who mistreat you and persecute you, that you may be children of your Father who is in heaven.[6]

Similarly, the Qur'an teaches us to respond to violence with non-violence. 'If thou dost stretch thy hand against me to slay me it is not for me to stretch my hand against thee to slay thee: for I do fear God the Cherisher of the worlds.'[7] On occasions when self-defence is necessary, the Qur'an teaches to 'Fight in the cause of God those who fight you but do not transgress limits; for God loveth not transgressors'.[8]

If the core message behind all religions is one of peace, then why have we seen so much religiously-motivated violence throughout human history?

It is true that there are scriptural passages which make exceptions for violence, but there are important contextual components to these

---

[5]Hebrews 12:14 (World English Bible).

[6]Matthew 5:38-48 (World English Bible).

[7]Qur'an 5:28 (Yusuf Ali).

[8]Qur'an, 2:190 (Yusuf Ali).

that, when misunderstood, become perverted and corrupted into false justifications for violence. The Qur'an, for instance, contains passages like this:

> To those against whom war is made, permission is given (to fight), because they are wronged; and verily, God is most powerful for their aid; (they are) those who have been expelled from their homes in defiance of right, (for no cause) except that they say, 'Our Lord Is God'.[9]

When new religions emerge, as in the case of Islam in its infancy, their followers almost always face heavy and violent persecution. The scriptural passages that condone violence are doing so in the name of self-defence, without glorifying violence itself. For instance, in the Hebrew Bible it is written, 'When you draw near to a city to fight against it, then proclaim peace to it.'[10] Violence for the self-preservation of a group of innocent and otherwise peaceful people who are being wrongfully persecuted may be allowed according to scripture, but the overarching commandment is to do everything possible to prevent the need for violence at all. This is also the attitude of the Taoist sage Lao Tzu.

> Weapons are not auspicious tools
> [The ruler] wields them when he has no choice [...]
> When you kill another
>
> Honor him with your tears
> When the battle is won
> Treat it as a wake.[11]

If, for some reason, violence is unavoidable, reverence for life and a desire for peace and non-violence can always be maintained.

Returning to the Islamic and Jewish scriptures, the allowances made for self-defence are always balanced out by reminders of the severe

---

[9]Qur'an, 22:39-40 (Yusuf Ali).

[10]Deuteronomy 20:10 (World English Bible).

[11]Lao-Tzu. *Tao te ching*, trans. Red Pine (Port Townsend: Copper Canyon Press, 2009), Chapter 31, 62.

consequences of committing violence against the innocent. The Qur'an notes, 'On that account: We ordained for the Children of Israel that if anyone slew a person unless it be for murder or for spreading mischief in the land it would be as if he slew the whole people: and if anyone saved a life it would be as if he saved the life of the whole people.'[12] Similarly, a passage from the Talmud says, 'Man was created alone in order to teach you that if anyone causes a single soul to perish from Israel, Scripture imputes to him the destruction of the entire world; and if anyone saves alive a single soul in Israel, Scripture imputes to him the saving alive of the entire world.'[13] This echoes the attitude of ahimsa—that all life is precious, and to kill one innocent creature is a serious attack on the sanctity of life itself.

These examples from the Abrahamic religions also are somewhat analogous to the idea of karma in the religions of India. It is believed that there is a cosmic law of cause and effect through which all of our actions have lasting consequences in these religious systems. In the Dhammapada, a collection of sermons and teachings from the Buddha, there is an illustration of how karma relates to non-violence: 'If you have no wound on your hand, you can touch poison without being harmed. No harm comes to those who do no harm. If you harm a pure and innocent person, you harm yourself, as dust thrown against the wind comes back to the thrower.'[14] Thus, both in religions from the East and the West we see a bird's-eye view of how violence can have rippling effects. In the Abrahamic scriptures, we are taught that even one instance of an innocent person being killed harms the entire species; the Buddha, in teaching the principle of karma, notes that acts of violence harm not only the victim, but the perpetrator as well.

The advice given by spiritual leaders, like the Dalai Lama, claims that preventing violence in the physical world starts by eliminating the root causes of violence, which ultimately begin in the mind.

---

[12]Qur'an, 5:32 (Yusuf Ali).

[13]Babylonian Talmud, Sanhedrin, 38a in Hayyim Nahman Bialik and Yehoshua Ḥana Rawnitzki, *The Book of Legends: Sefer Ha-Aggadah,* trans. William Gordon Braude (New York: Schocken Books, 1992), 14.

[14]*The Dhammapada,* trans. Eknath Easwaran, Second Edition (Tomales: Nilgiri Press, 2007), 124-25.

> Genuine non-violence will come only after the inner disarmament of our mind. Only with inner disarmament, we can bring outer disarmament. Lots of problems in this world are created out of ignorance and greed. With our minds full of fear and hatred, it is impossible to achieve non-violence.[15]

This line of reasoning led Ashoka, the Indian emperor, to convert to Buddhism, having realized, first-hand, that greed and violence had to be eliminated through peace and compassion. As author Robert Wright explains, 'Ashoka renounced conquest, horrified by the event that had preceded and triggered his conversion to Buddhism—his own bloody conquest of a neighbouring region. "The most important conquest", he announced, is "moral conquest".'[16]

The ancient founders of the religions of China came to similar conclusions and offered the same advice to the statesmen of their day. They too were asked to lead by example and overcome violence through non-violence. Confucius reasoned, 'In administering your government, what need is there for you to kill? Just desire the good yourself and the common people will be good.'[17] And in the Tao Te Ching, Lao Tzu writes:

> The best are like water
> Bringing help to all
> Without competing
> [...] governing with peace
> Working with skill
> And moving with time
> And because they don't compete
> They aren't maligned

---

[15]Dalai Lama, 'The Dalai Lama receives Mahatma Gandhi International Award in Bodh Gaya,' *Dalailama.com*, 4 January 2012, https://www.dalailama.com/news/2012/homepage-news-the-dalai-lama-receives-mahatma-gandhi-international-award-in-bodh-gaya-the-dalai-lama-receives-mahatma-gandhi-international-award-in-bodh-gaya/amp

[16]Robert Wright, *The Evolution of God*, (New York: Little, Brown and Company, 2009).

[17]Confucius, *The Analects*, trans. D.C. Lau, Penguin Classics edition (London: Penguin Books, 1971), 12:19.

To the famous question posed by Machiavelli—whether it is better for a ruler to be feared or loved—Confucius and Lao Tzu (along with Ashoka and the Dalai Lama) replied that love is the answer. Leaders that care about the needs of their people do not have to govern with force or fear because they will be happy and satisfied with their conditions.

We are agreed upon the urgent necessity of peace and the end and prevention of evils like violence and killing. But it is equally important to point out the reasons to desire peace and to explain what peace can allow us to achieve, beyond just reducing hostilities. The Baha'i Universal House of Justice, drawing upon the words of the Baha'i prophet Bahá'u'lláh provides us with one such vision:

> Beyond the initial armistice forced upon the world by the fear of nuclear holocaust, beyond the political peace reluctantly entered into by suspicious rival nations, beyond pragmatic arrangements for security and coexistence, beyond even the many experiments in co-operation which these steps will make possible lies the crowning goal: the unification of all the peoples of the world in one universal family.[18]

We still have a long way to go, especially as a species, towards enacting world peace, but for now, we can hold on to the conviction that we are unavoidably interconnected; we are, at the deepest level, one unified family.

[18]Universal House of Justice, *The Promise of World Peace* (Haifa, Israel: Bahá'í World Centre, October 1985), Baha'i Reference Library, http://reference.bahai.org/en/t/uhj/PWP/pwp-5.html

33

Pluralism

Every religion mixes universal principles with local peculiarities. The former, when lifted out and made clear, speak to what is generically human in us all.[1]

—Huston Smith

Pluralism is a state of coexistence among multiple groups. In the context of this book, this principle extends to cultural and religious groups. Throughout human history, we have made great strides towards making this a global reality. What began as a species of disparate and dislocated tribes, has now evolved over thousands of years into a global community. Today we have no choice but to coexist and cooperate in order to secure the ongoing welfare of the species and the planet. As rabbi and philosopher Jonathan Sacks notes, religions have played a major role both in the facilitation of pluralism as well as the challenges associated with it.

> Faiths, as we know, unite and divide. They unite by dividing: by identifying an 'us' as opposed to 'them'. Hence both the good and harm they do come hand-in-hand. We are the children of the light; they are the children of the darkness. That generates light

[1]Huston Smith, *The Illustrated World's Religions* (New York: HarperCollins, 1995), 234-236.

> but also darkness. There is only one non-utopian way of creating the good without the harm, and that is to create programmes of what in Hebrew is called chessed, in Latin caritas, or in English, loving kindness, across boundaries.[2]

The ancient prophets and scriptures of the great world religions recognized the importance of pluralism, as well as the need to remind people of its value so as to ward off the darkness of division.

Many people are familiar with the injunction in the Qur'an to respect the 'people of the book'—intending to mean Jews and Christians, with whom Muslims share many of the same prophets and stories. The Sufi tradition of Islam—considered the third major branch, in addition to Sunni and Shia—takes this ideal even further, arguing that all religions should be seen as alternative and equally valid paths to the same God. The Qur'an teaches, 'To God belong the East and the West; whithersoever ye turn there is the presence of God. For God is All-Pervading All-Knowing.'[3] The Prophet Muhammad himself said that, 'The number of paths (ṭuruq, pl. of ṭarīqah) to God is equal to the number of children of Adam',[4] and that 'At the beginning of every century Allah will send to this ummah [community] someone who will renew its religious understanding'.[5] In other words, the Prophet Muhammad assured his people that God had sent, and would continue to send, other messengers just like himself to communities all over the world. For that reason, he urged his followers to recognize and respect members of foreign faiths, for they too were following the same God.

This respect for other religions is, however, not exclusive to Islam. India, for instance, is one of the most religiously pluralistic places on earth, and it has been so for millennia. The words from the Rig Veda, *'Ekam sat vipra bahuda vadanti'*, translates as 'truth is one but called differently by many', has served as a guiding mantra of my spiritual upbringing in

---

[2]Jonathan Sacks, *The Home We Build Together*, 180, The Office of Rabbi Sacks, accessed on 12 July 2022, https://rabbisacks.org/quotes/acts-kindness-chessed-3/.

[3]Qur'an 2:115 (Yusuf Ali).

[4]Seyyed Hossein Nasr, 'The Integration of the Soul', in *Psychology and the Perennial Philosophy: Studies in Comparative Religion*, ed. Samuel Bendeck Sotillos (Bloomington, Indiana: World Wisdom, 2013), 168.

[5]Sunan Abi Dawud, Hadith 4291.

a Hindu family. In Hinduism, there is plenty of scriptural support to foreground respect for the various religions of the world. There is also an eagerness to actively explore other faiths, a view championed by famous Hindu figures such as Mahatma Gandhi, Ramakrishna and Swami Vivekananda. God is thought of by Hindus to be too mysterious and all-encompassing to be accurately depicted by a single representation. That is why even just within Hinduism, there is a staggering amount of pluralism in religious belief and expression.

Hindus depict God in the form of a vast pantheon of beings (as Gods) with both human-like and animal-like qualities that each represent different ways in which God is manifested throughout the universe. This allows each Hindu to form their own personal connection to God, based on each person's subjective preference for one or more of these representations over others. Devdutt Pattnaik, an Indian mythologist and author, writes, 'The idea of 330 million Hindu deities is a metaphor for the countless forms by which the divine makes itself accessible to the human mind.'[6] Because we are all different, we all imagine God in different ways, and Hindus are very conscious of this in their worship. The particular conception of God that each person chooses to implement in pursuing this shared goal (of seeking connection with God) is akin to one liking the colour yellow while another prefers green. The God or Goddess you choose to focus on, like a colour, is simply a personal choice; it doesn't indicate any kind of superiority or inferiority in belief or worship. Others will not judge or hate you based on such differences. What matters is the intention and practice itself. Picking one particular deity can help you deepen your intention in worship, but it doesn't make your God or Goddess 'better' than anyone else's.

Another Indian religious tradition, Sikhism, provides a good illustration of respect for various religions. Its founder, Guru Nanak, famously proclaimed, 'There is no Hindu, there is no Muslim.' He meant to say that we are all one human species, worshipping the same God in different ways.

Another Indian spiritual figure worth mentioning is the third century BCE Indian emperor Ashoka, who purportedly converted to

---

[6]Devdutt Pattanaik, *Myth = Mithya: Decoding Hindu Mythology* (UK: Penguin, 2008).

Buddhism after being horrified by the violence of warfare, which he was witness to and complicit in. But Ashoka did not simply try to declare Buddhism to be the only valid religious path. Rather, he proclaimed that 'all sects may dwell in all places, for all seek self-control and purity of mind',[7] and that, 'concord is meritorious, (i.e.) that [different religions] should both hear and obey each other's morals. For this is the desire of Devanampriya, (viz.) that all sects should be both full of learning and pure in doctrine.'[8] Support for such plurality can be found in writing from the Buddha himself, 'If a person has faith, Bhāradvāja, he preserves truth when he says: "My faith is thus"; but he does not yet come to the definite conclusion: "Only this is true, anything else is wrong."'[9]

Even in Christianity, a tradition which is often critiqued for its rigid dogma, we can find statements to illustrate such an ideal. The Scottish Anglican theologian John Macquarrie wrote that, 'I do not deny for a moment that the truth of God has reached others through other channels indeed, I hope and pray that it has. So while I have a special attachment to one mediator, I have respect for them all.'[10] More institutional support for pluralism in Christianity can be found as well. For instance, one of the official 'Articles of Faith' of the Church of Jesus Christ of Latter-Day Saints, reads: 'We claim the privilege of worshipping Almighty God according to the dictates of our own conscience, and allow all men the same privilege, let them worship how, where, or what they may.'[11] Further, and more strikingly, a document released by the Vatican and endorsed by Pope Paul VI in 1965, titled 'Nostra Aetate' (In Our Time), shares this ideal. It is a beautiful statement of support for pluralism by the Catholic Church, encapsulated well by the following excerpt:

---

[7]Romila Thapar, *Asoka and the Decline of the Mauryas* (Delhi: Oxford University Press, 1997), 8.

[8]Ibid, 8.

[9]Bhikkhu Bodhi, *In the Buddha's Words: An Anthology of Discourses from the Pali Canon* (Somerville: Wisdom Publications, 2005), 99.

[10]John Macquarrie, *Mediators between Human and Divine* (New York: Continuum, 1996), 12.

[11]*Articles of Faith,* Article 11, The Church of Jesus Christ of Latter-day Saints, accessed on 12 July 2022, https://www.churchofjesuschrist.org/study/manual/gospel-topics/articles-of-faith?lang=eng,.a

> In our time, when day by day mankind is being drawn closer together, and the ties between different peoples are becoming stronger, the Church examines more closely her relationship to non-Christian religions. In her task of promoting unity and love among men, indeed among nations, she considers above all in this declaration what men have in common and what draws them to fellowship [...] Likewise, other religions found everywhere try to counter the restlessness of the human heart, each in its own manner, by proposing 'ways', comprising teachings, rules of life, and sacred rites. The Catholic Church rejects nothing that is true and holy in these religions. She regards with sincere reverence those ways of conduct and of life, those precepts and teachings which, though differing in many aspects from the ones she holds and sets forth, nonetheless often reflect a ray of that Truth which enlightens all.[12]

It is also important to recognize that pluralism is not just an *acceptance* of difference, but a full celebratory *embrace* of diversity. The Baha'i International Community describes this:

> Unity in diversity stands in contrast to uniformity. It cherishes the natural diversity of temperament and talents among individuals as well as humanity's variegated experiences, cultures and viewpoints, inasmuch as they contribute to the human family's progress and well-being. Much like the role played by the gene pool in the biological life of humankind and its environment, the immense wealth of cultural diversity achieved over thousands of years is vital to the development of the human race.[13]

The first part of this statement is important. Pluralism seeks to *highlight* differences rather than to erase or ignore them. In the mid-twentieth century, psychologist Erich Fromm lamented that 'Equality today

---

[12]Pope Paul VI, 'Nostra Aetate', In Our Time, *Vatican Archives,* 1965, https://www.vatican.va/archive/hist_councils/ii_vatican_council/documents/vat-ii_decl_19651028_nostra-aetate_en.html.

[13]Bahá'í International Community, 'Valuing Spirituality in Development,' paper presented at the World Faiths and Development Dialogue, at Lambeth Palace, London, UK: February 18, 1998, Baha'i International Community, accessed on 12 July 2022, https://www.bic.org/statements/valuing-spirituality-development#I.

means "sameness", rather than "oneness"'.[14] We now know that we share 99.9 per cent of our DNA with each other. This is what makes us a species of equals. But that 0.1 percent is also what saves us from sameness and drives human progress and evolution. Imagine if everyone was just like you or me—life would be so boring!

Diversity is a necessary and beautiful part of all biological life. Evolution depends on, and is driven by, variations preserved through natural selection. Populations and communities of animals without diverse gene pools do not last long, as organisms are more well-suited for survival if they have a mix of genes that perform different functions. This is why inbreeding results in so many problems in the offspring. Human society functions along similar lines: a society composed entirely of farmers or lawyers or any other single profession would not last long. Many key features of society would be amiss. When we let people make choices freely about their professions, their religious beliefs and so on, it results in a degree of diversity that promotes healthy community, just as free choices across generations promote healthy natural selection in biological communities. Pluralism, freedom and collective health all go hand-in-hand.

Every being, human or not, has its own role to play in preserving the health of any pluralistic community. Various religions have tried to capture and express this idea in their scriptures. In the Jewish Talmud, one passage argues, 'Even those creatures that you may look upon as superfluous in the world, such as flies, fleas, or gnats—they too are part of the entirety of creation. The Holy One affects His purpose through all creatures, even through a frog or a flea.'[15] Similarly, the Taoist sage Lieh Tzu writes, 'All things have their place in the universe, whether it is active or passive, moving or not moving. They fulfill their function in the world simply by being what they are. Everything plays a part in the process of creating, nourishing, transforming, and destroying.'[16]

---

[14]Erich Fromm, *The Art of Loving*, Fiftieth Anniversary edition (New York: HarperCollins, 2006), 14.

[15]Genesis Rabbah, 10:7 in Hayyim Nahman Bialik and Yehoshua Ḥana Rawnitzki, *The Book of Legends: Sefer Ha-Aggadah*, trans. William Gordon Braude (New York: Schocken Books, 1992), 12.

[16]*Lieh-tzu: A Taoist Guide to Practical Living*, trans. Eva Wong (Boston: Shambhala, 2001), 26-27.

From a more modern perspective, Rabbi Jonathan Sacks argues, 'We should feel enlarged by the people who are different.'[17] All human progress—scientific, social and otherwise—has come through cooperation between diverse individuals. Everyone is born into different circumstances, and we all pursue different courses in life. These determine what we experience, what we learn and the unique insights we are able to share with others. Humans had been gazing at stars for millennia, but none before Galileo had access to the unique combination of past technological and theoretical advancements; this allowed him to glean certain truths about celestial bodies and physics. Similarly, humans had seen apples falling from trees for millennia, but only Newton—so the tale goes—gleaned from this common occurrence a theory about gravity, drawing upon what he had learned from Galileo and others before him, adding his own unique set of genes and life circumstances, to change the world.

We should see diversity not as a source of conflict and division but as necessary for evolution. It is also an expression of human love, with its diverse manifestations in temples, churches, other religious sites and in universities (our greatest temples of human knowledge) all over the world. The Buddhist monk Shantideva encapsulated this beautifully in a poetic verse.

> The hand and other limbs are many and distinct,
> But all are one—the body to be kept and guarded.
> Likewise, different beings, in their joys and sorrows,
> Are, like me, all one in wanting happiness.[18]

This expression of love is where the true value of religion is to be gleaned. The fact is that we are incomplete, and we may achieve our fullness only by loving others.

Pluralism does not mean an elimination of our differences. It means that we engage with one another, learn from one another, and build a better future together where we can all fully flourish.

---

[17]Jonathan Sacks, 'Archive: Quotes,' The Office of Rabbi Sacks, accessed on 12 July 2022, https://rabbisacks.org/quotes/.

[18]Shantideva, *The Way of the Bodhisattva* (Shambhala Classics: Boston, 2006), 8:91.

34

Service and Justice

Injustice anywhere is a threat to justice everywhere. We are caught in an inescapable network of mutuality, tied in a single garment of destiny. Whatever affects one directly, affects all indirectly.[1]

—Martin Luther King Jr.

We are all aware of how many times young children say 'it is not fair!' They have an innate sense of justice. Not surprisingly, one of the most popular courses for undergraduates at Harvard University is a course on Justice taught by Michael Sandel, who weaves in the teachings from different religions and philosophers. This course also has the distinction of being the first Harvard University course to be offered for free to the public online.

Performing deeds in service of the welfare of others, especially those who are vulnerable and needy, is one of the most important activities of any religious person. Indeed, the New Testament goes so far as to basically define religion itself as this kind of service: 'Pure religion and undefiled before our God and Father is this: to visit the fatherless and widows in

[1]1 Martin Luther King, Jr., "Letter from Birmingham, Alabama jail", 16 April 1963, African Studies Center—University of Pennsylvania, accessed on 12 July 2022, https://www.africa.upenn.edu/Articles_Gen/Letter_Birmingham.html.

their affliction, and to keep oneself unstained by the world.'[2] Similarly, the Baha'i leader 'Abdu'l-Bahá states that 'Service in love for mankind is unity with God'.[3] Love for humanity can be translated into action through selfless intentions, and this itself can be seen as an expression of the interconnectedness in the world. Even in the Bhagavad Gita, Krishna says, 'Every selfless act, Arjuna, is born from Brahman, the eternal, infinite Godhead. Brahman is present in every act of service.'[4] Thus, the most authoritative sources of wisdom from three seemingly disparate religions all agree on the supreme importance of selfless and loving service for humankind. The scholar of religion Huston Smith equally argues, 'The Buddha's entire life was powered by a strong sense of mission. Immediately after his enlightenment, he saw in his mind's eye the whole of humanity—people milling and lost, desperately in need of help and guidance.'[5]

Religious scriptures urge devotees to take the supreme importance of service seriously. It draws a connection between the service we have done in life and our fate in our afterlives. In Indian religions, like Buddhism and Hinduism, selfless deeds allow a person to accrue good karma and erase bad karma—and the total karmic actions in the current life carry over into and determine the conditions of our next lives. The Buddha described this in one of his sermons:

> Those who are selfish suffer in this life and in the next. They suffer seeing the results of the evil they have done, and more suffering awaits them in the next life. But those who are selfless rejoice in this life and in the next. They rejoice seeing the good that they have done, and more joy awaits them in the next life.[6]

In Sikhism, too, 'seva' (selfless service) is one of the key tenets and is considered an act of worship. Serving other people is considered to be an

---

[2]James 1:27 (World English Bible).

[3]'Abdu'l-Baha, *The Promulgation of Universal Peace*, Second edition (Illinois: Baha'i Publishing Trust, 1982), 186.

[4]*The Bhagavad Gita*, trans. Eknath Easwaran, Second Edition (Tomales: Nilgiri Press, 2007), 3:15.

[5]Huston Smith, *The Illustrated World's Religions* (New York: HarperCollins, 1995), 64.

[6]*The Dhammapada*, trans. Eknath Easwaran, Classics of Indian Spirituality Edition (California: The Blue Mountain Center of Meditation, 2007), 17-18.

essential devotional practice of indirectly serving God: by serving God's creation, we are serving the divine essence residing in all human beings.

Beyond this goal of reincarnation, the long-term goal of both practioners of Buddhism and Hinduism is to accrue enough good karma to be able to escape entirely from the cycle of birth and death (samsara), achieving the state of release known in Buddhism as 'nirvana', and in Hinduism as 'moksha'. In the Bhagavad Gita, we are told that devoted service for others is one of the most expedient paths toward this ultimate goal. 'Strive constantly to serve the welfare of the world; by devotion to selfless work one attains the supreme goal of life. Do your work with the welfare of others always in mind.'[7]

In the Abrahamic religions, the logic is rather similar: good deeds equal good merit. In the Hebrew Bible, we are commanded to 'Defend the weak, the poor, and the fatherless. Maintain the rights of the poor and oppressed. Rescue the weak and needy. Deliver them out of the hand of the wicked.'[8] Echoing this, a Talmudic passage explains, '[The prophet] Elijah said: I call heaven and earth to witness that whether it be Jew or Gentile, man or woman, manservant or maidservant, the holy spirit will suffuse each in proportion to the deeds he or she performs.'[9] Ultimately, human beings should help other human beings. The value and importance of good deeds thus transcends artificial identity divisions like religion, gender and social class. It is also argued in the Qur'an:

> O ye who believe! Stand out firmly for justice as witnesses to God even as against yourselves or your parents or your kin and whether it be (against) rich or poor: for God can best protect both. Follow not the lusts (of your hearts) lest ye swerve and if ye distort (justice) or decline to do justice verily God is well-acquainted with all that ye do.[10]

---

[7]*The Bhagavad Gita*, trans. Eknath Easwaran, Second Edition (Tomales: Nilgiri Press, 2007), 3:19-20.

[8]Psalm 82:3-4 (World English Bible).

[9]Seder Eliyyahu Rabbah, 48 in Hayyim Nahman Bialik and Yehoshua Ḥana Rawnitzki, *The Book of Legends: Sefer Ha-Aggadah*, trans. William Gordon Braude (New York: Schocken Books, 1992), 354.

[10]Qur'an, 4:135 (Yusuf Ali).

Justice, as the saying goes, is meant to be blind. If different groups of people are treated according to different sets of rules, then that is not justice. Zakah, or charity, is the third pillar in Islam—only the affirmation of Allah as the one God and daily prayer is more important that zakah. It is said in the Qur'an, 'And be steadfast in prayer and regular in charity: and whatever good ye send forth for your souls before you ye shall find it with God; for God sees well all that ye do.'[11] Elsewhere in the Qur'an, believers are commanded to give 2.5 percent of their total wealth to the poor and hungry, although many Muslims interpret zakah more loosely as a general command to give however much is reasonably possible. This is very similar to the concept of tithes in Christianity, which traditionally was set at 10 per cent of one's wealth being shared with the poor, although most Christians (as with Muslims) interpret this more broadly as simply sharing what you can. The equivalent of this in Judaism is tzedakah, which differs slightly from its Muslim and Christian counterparts in that it is technically required of everybody—even those who are poor themselves.

The Qur'an calls sharing wealth with others a 'beautiful loan to God', and this loan will be returned on the day of judgement. In Arab traditions, charity is also associated with the notion of 'muruwwah', a term used to describe a righteous person who demonstrates attributes such as generosity, honesty, standing up against injustice. These are essentially the same qualities that are associated with the analogous 'mensch' in Judaism, a Yiddish term derived from the German. In the Christian tradition, Jesus Christ is the great exemplar of what service to humanity looks like. His efforts culminate in his act of self-sacrifice on the cross. 'Defend the weak, the poor, and the fatherless. Maintain the rights of the poor and oppressed. Rescue the weak and needy. Deliver them out of the hand of the wicked.'[12] Thus, we are likewise encouraged to 'contributing to the needs of the saints; given to hospitality'.[13]

Charity, as an act of service in the interest of social justice, demonstrates empathy and compassion for those of lesser means; it

---

[11]Qur'an, 2:110 (Yusuf Ali).

[12]Mark 10:45 (World English Bible).

[13]Romans 12:13 (World English Bible).

is a recognition of our common humanity, our interconnectedness and the fact that it is not justice to allow others to suffer the travails of poverty if we have a reasonable amount of wealth to spare. The Baha'i leader 'Abdu'l-Bahá taught, 'Be ye loving fathers to the orphan, and a refuge to the helpless, and a treasury for the poor, and a cure for the ailing. Be ye the helpers of every victim of oppression, the patrons of the disadvantaged. Think ye at all times of rendering some service to every member of the human race.'[14] Across religions there is an emphasis on selfless acts of service and justice, especially charity, and a command to remember those who are less fortunate than us and whose plight might otherwise be all too easy to ignore.

It is no surprise, then, that some of the loudest cries in the midst of social justice battles have come from religious and spiritual leaders, both in the present and in the past. For instance, Episcopal Bishop Mariann Edgar Budde noted, amidst recent protests for social justice in the United States, 'Scripture is clear: Justice, which is the societal expression of love, matters most to God.'[15] This closely echoes the justice defined by Dr Martin Luther King Jr., who wrote that, 'Power at its best is love implementing the demands of justice, and justice at its best is love correcting everything that stands against love.'[16]

When we arrive at the knowledge of our fundamental interconnectedness, how can we not be galvanized into taking up selfless and loving acts for fellow human beings? If the universe is understood in this way, it is only logical that we must live our life with service as a guiding principle. This close relationship between love and justice has been championed by religious individuals. Here is an example: a statement from Andrew Harvey, a scholar of religion and founder of the Institute for Sacred Activism:

---

[14]'Abdu'l-Bahá, *Selections From the Writings of 'Abdu'l-Bahá* (Bahá'í World Centre, 1982), 3, Baha'i Reference Library, http://reference.bahai.org/en/t/ab/SAB/sab-2.html

[15]Mariann Edgar Budde, 'Trump's Visit to St. John's Church Outraged Me,' *The New York Times*, 4 June 2020, https://www.nytimes.com/2020/06/04/opinion/trump-st-johns-church-protests.html.

[16]Dr. Martin Luther King Jr., *Where Do We Go from Here: Chaos or Community?* (Boston: Beacon Press, 2010).

> The beauty of Sacred Activism is that it brings together what is best in both the mystic and the activist: the mystic's fiery passion for God, and the activist's fiery passion for justice. What is born from the fusion of those two great ennobling fires is a third fire that is love and wisdom in action.[17]

Harvey, who was born in India and has closely studied both Hinduism and Buddhism, certainly speaks here of a religious type of activism that is found not just in Christianity and other Western religions, but also in the religions of India and East Asia.

Service is the main path through which religions practise what they preach. As author Wajihuddin Siddiqui observes, 'All religious or reform movements have been started by individuals of high moral character [...] All religions have emerged primarily as reform movements to correct the course of religious or secular societies that had degenerated and succumbed to pleasure and undesirable practices such as injustice to human beings.'[18] Activities, like charity and activism, should be undertaken to advocate for the downtrodden and destitute according to various belief systems. This shows that individuals are meant to take the messages of love and interconnectedness found in scriptures and the words of prophets seriously. We are to look at those in need and apply the golden rule: 'If I was in such a position, how would I want people to treat me?' Life has its ups and downs, and we never know when we might be in a position where we too will need help. These acts of service unite us all in a common quest for human flourishing.

[17]Andrew Harvey, *Radical Passion: Sacred Love and Wisdom in Action* (Berkeley: North Atlantic Books, 2012), 290.

[18]Wajihuddin Siddiqui, *Commonalities and Similarities in World Religions* (Karachi: Royal Book Company, 2018), 59.

35

Primacy of Intention

Your actions produce reactions that follow you like shadows. Just as a tall person's shadow is tall and a short person's shadow is short, ugly words will produce ugly echoes, and good intentions will produce good reactions. For every action there is a reaction, and for every cause there is an effect.[1]

—Lieh-tzu

We all have some innate sense of the primacy of intention; we know that a purposeful transgression against ourselves or others is different from an accidental one. While we can observe the behaviour of others, we cannot directly know their intentions. Nevertheless, we tend to judge people by the intentions we impute to their behaviour rather than by their behaviour itself. We have evolved to make judgements about perceived intentions, because failing to do so could be fatal. If, in our infancy, we waited to see what a potential predator's behaviour would be, it would be too late! Instead, our ancestors had to predict what other animals' intentions were based on particular cues. Today, we do the same with other people: we develop and use mental models that relate behaviour to

[1]Lieh-tzu, *Lieh-tzu: A Taoist Guide to Practical Living*, Trans. Eva Wong (Boston: Shambhala, 2001), 211.

intention, but these models are not perfect. Different people have different ways of expressing and/or hiding their intentions based on cultural, historical and individual differences, and we constantly run the risk of misunderstanding people. Still, if we see the common humanity in everyone and wish to extend universal love and empathy, we can choose to give others the benefit of the doubt and trust that what is bad behaviour in our judgement is not necessarily motivated by bad intentions.

As fallible creatures, we all make mistakes. Sometimes, we end up causing harm, even though our intentions are good. Or we misunderstand things and come to believe in falsehoods. But as Saint Augustine writes:

> [N]ot every one who says a false thing lies, if he believes or opines that to be true which he says [...] Now whoever utters that which he holds in his mind either as belief or as opinion, even though it be false, he lies not. For this he owes to the faith of his utterance, that he thereby produce that which he holds in his mind, and has in that way in which he produces it.[2]

In other words, Augustine applies intent as a criterion. If you don't know what you're talking about, you speak falsely, but you're not necessarily a liar.

Religions highlight the importance of intention by attributing cosmic significance to it. As scholar of religion Todd Tremlin writes, 'Around the world, Gods are consistently represented as concerned with the morally relevant aspects of social interaction, attentive to people's inner attitudes and outward behaviors.'[3] One of the hallmark features of God (as described in the Abrahamic traditions), is that God is always watching us, ever-aware not only of what we do but also of what we think and what we intend. The New Testament argues that, 'the word of God is living and active, and sharper than any two-edged sword, piercing even to the dividing of soul and spirit, of both joints and marrow, and is able to

---

[2]St. Augustine of Hippo, 'On Lying, Retractations: Book I,' in *Moral Treatises of St. Augustine*, trans. Rev. H. Browne (Germany: JazzyBee Verlag, 2012).
[3]Todd Tremlin, *Minds and Gods: The Cognitive Foundations of Religion* (Oxford: Oxford University Press, 2006), 117.

discern the thoughts and intentions of the heart.'[4]

One of the major implications is that we believe that God can tell the difference between people whose actions are motivated by genuine faith, and between those who merely subscribe to religious practices unconsciously and for show. It is written in the Hebrew Bible that 'these people draw near with their mouth and honor me with their lips, but they have removed their heart far from me, and their fear of me is a commandment of men which has been taught'.[5] Intention is of supreme importance with regard to religious devotion.

But sometimes, we fail to act in accordance with our intentions, for one reason or another.

Various passages in Islamic literature demonstrate a recognition of this failing, once again pointing to the supremacy of intention over action. In Islam, the word for intention is 'niyyah', and niyyah matters above everything else in action, including worship. God will see through our intentions in every action and prayer and judge us accordingly. As one Hadith has put it, 'The deeds are considered by the intentions, and a person will get the reward according to his intention.'[6] And in the Qur'an, it is said, 'God will not call you to account for thoughtlessness in your oaths but for the intention in your hearts; and He is oft-forgiving most forbearing.'[7] Illustrating this is another example: 'He hath only forbidden you dead meat and blood and the flesh of swine and that on which any other name hath been invoked besides that of God but if one is forced by necessity without wilful disobedience nor transgressing due limits then is he guiltless. For God is Oft-Forgiving Most Merciful.'[8]

Hinduism is another religion that provides very straightforward statements on the supremacy of intention, such as in the Chandogya Upanishad.

> Intention is clearly greater than the mind, for it is only after a man has formed an intention that he makes up his mind; after that,

[4]Hebrews 4:12 (World English Bible).

[5]Isaiah 29:13 (World English Bible).

[6]Riyad as-Salihin, Hadith 1, Bukhari & Muslim.

[7]Qur'an, 2:225 (Yusuf Ali).

[8]Qur'an, 2:173 (Yusuf Ali).

> he vocalizes his speech—and he vocalizes it to articulate a name. The vedic formulas are contained in the name, and rites, in vedic formulas. Now, intention (samkalpa) is the point of convergence of all these things; intention is their essence (atman); and on intention they are based.[9]

Intention, thus, has an escalating effect on our thoughts, as well as the words and actions arising from these thoughts. Intent influences religions of India, like Hinduism and Buddhism through 'karma', the cosmic principle of cause and effect, by which the actions of our prior incarnations determine the circumstances of our current and future reincarnations. As scholar of religion Yuki Miyamoto writes, 'Karma dictates certain conditions over which we have no control—when and where we are born, for instance—but within that situation we are presented with choices.'[10] The intentions we cultivate, determine the choices we make, which in turn, impact our karmic ties—and this impact reverberates across our circumstances in life and even in our future reincarnations.

The causal relationship between our intentions, on the one hand, and our thoughts and actions on the other, has a ripple effect on our lives. Among the most important of these effects relates to how our intentions affect our perceptions of others and, consequently, how we treat them. The Baha'i leader 'Abdu'l-Bahá explains how the intention to see the good in others is a necessary precondition for universal love and respect.

> One must see in every human being only that which is worthy of praise. When this is done, one can be a friend to the whole human race. If, however, we look at the people from the standpoint of their faults, then being a friend to them is a formidable task [...] Thus it is incumbent upon us, when we direct our gaze toward other people, to see where they excel, not where they fail.[11]

---

[9]'Chandogya Upanisad' in *Upanisads,* trans. Patrick Olivelle, Oxford World's Classics (London: Oxford University Press, 1996), 7.4:1-2.

[10]Yuki Miyamoto, *Beyond the Mushroom Cloud: Commemoration, Religion, and Responsibility After Hiroshima* (New York: Fordham University Press, 2012), 103.

[11]'Abdu'l-Bahá, *Selections From the Writings of 'Abdu'l-Bahá* (Bahá'í World Centre: 1982), 169, Baha'I Reference Library: http://reference.bahai.org/en/t/ab/SAB/sab-145.html

This general principle has been affirmed not only across religions, but also among the modern scientific community, particularly among scientists working in the neurosciences. For instance, Harvard-trained neuroanatomist Jill Bolte Taylor writes, 'Our minds are highly sophisticated "seek and ye shall find" instruments. We are designed to focus in on whatever we are looking for. If I seek red in the world then I will find it everywhere.'[12]

This tendency is known as 'confirmation bias': 'if we are not careful, then all the new information we collect out in the world will seemingly 'confirm' what we already believe, making us inflexible to questioning our beliefs and forming new ones when necessary. Applied to the realm of interpersonal relations, confirmation bias can lead us to see the best in people, or the worst in people. To illustrate this, Lieh Tzu offers a short parable:

> A man who lost his axe suspected his neighbor's son—'Look at the way he walks—he's stolen the axe! The expression on his face—he's stolen the axe! The way he talks—he's stolen the axe!' Every act, every attitude, indicated that he'd stolen the axe. One day the man found the axe as he was digging in the valley. The next time he saw his neighbor's son, he wasn't acting like he'd stolen the axe.[13]

Confirmation bias may lead us to falsely accuse an innocent person. Furthermore, this bias is also why prejudice against and stereotyping of particular groups is so pernicious. Without realizing it, the preconceptions of certain groups, which have little or no basis in reality, may come to dominate our attitudes and behaviours towards individuals belonging to those groups, simply because our minds tend to selectively reinforce such preconceptions.

The only real way to alleviate such conditions is by being aware, conscious, and intentional. We should look for the good in others and not judge others before we get to know them. As Buddhist monk Thich Nhat Hanh writes, 'The most precious gift we can offer anyone is our

---

[12]Jill Bolte Taylor, *My Stroke of Insight: A Brain Scientist's Personal Journey* (New York: Plume Books, 2009), 146.

[13]*The Book of Master Lie*, trans. Thomas Cleary, (2009), 1985-99.

attention. When mindfulness embraces those we love, they will bloom like flowers.'[14]

Intention and attention are closely related. We cannot fully control our intentions until we have mastered the art of attention. Physicist and writer Arthur Zajonc explains this in the context of contemplative practices like meditation:

> It is clear within all traditions, Eastern or Western, that initially our thoughts are not under our direction. Early on and throughout our practice it is, therefore, essential to school our thinking to come more and more under our control. The first exercise is aimed at the mastery of thinking and particularly of voluntary attention. Specifically, it is both revealing and helpful to concentrate on an extremely simple object such as a pin, paper clip, or pencil. The more insignificant the object, the better it serves the purposes of the exercise. Since the object lacks inherent interest, the attention we give it is entirely the result of our decision and effort.[15]

There are many ways in which we can practice cultivating our attention and intention, but the important lesson is that it requires focused practice of some kind.

It is not always easy to form new habits and overcome old and deeply-rooted ones, like the habit of confirmation bias. It takes practice to learn how to see things as they truly are, whether it's with regard to a pencil or a person. Still, by consciously directing our intentions, we can change the way that our brains present reality to us, and thereby, we can change reality itself (hopefully for the better). Former US President George W. Bush underscored and lamented the harsh way we currently perceive one another, urging us to see the best in everyone.

> At times, it can seem like the forces pulling us apart are stronger than the forces binding us together. Argument turns too easily into animosity. Disagreement escalates into dehumanization.

---

[14]Thich Nhat Hanh, *Living Buddha, Living Christ: 20th Anniversary Edition* (New York: Penguin, 2007), 20.

[15]Arthur Zajonc, *Meditation as Contemplative Inquiry: When Knowing Becomes Love* (Massachusetts: Lindisfarne Books, 2009), 70.

> Too often, we judge other groups by their worst examples while judging ourselves by our best intentions—forgetting the image of God we should see in each other.[16]

If we continue to focus on the differences between us, then our animosity towards those who are different will continue to determine the shape of our world. If we, however, choose to see what is lovable in others, we will find it easier to love. We are limited in our ability to love everyone, but we are not limited in our intention and imagination to love everyone.

[16]George W. Bush, 'The most memorable passage in George W. Bush's speech rebuking Trumpism,' *The Washington Post,* 20 October 2017, https://www.washingtonpost.com/news/on-leadership/wp/2017/10/20/the-most-memorable-passage-in-george-w-bushs-speech-rebuking-trumpism/

36

Grace and Surrender

Only when you discard completely, through understanding, the whole structure of the self, can that which is eternal, timeless, immeasurable, come into being. You cannot go to it; it comes to you.[1]

—Jiddu Krishnamurti

As we have seen, religions may differ in specific aspects of their beliefs and devotional practices, but the core meaning and purpose underlying these practices is very consistent. They all agree that there is a higher power permeating the universe, however we might describe it, and we can be more in tune with this power if we can put our own egos and desires aside to follow this cosmic will. This is what the pioneering psychologist William James meant when he announced, 'There is a state of mind, known to religious men, but to no others, in which the will to assert ourselves and hold our own has been displaced by a willingness to close our mouths and be as nothing in the floods and waterspouts of God.'[2] In the Western monotheistic traditions, this state of mind has been called 'grace', and it is closely related to the concept of faith. It can simply be called an

[1]Jiddu Krishnamurti, *The First and Last Freedom* (New York: HarperCollins, 1975), 119.
[2]James, William, *The Varieties of Religious Experience* (Cambridge, MA: Harvard University Press, 1985), 46.

act of 'surrender', as in surrendering the lower animalistic self so that the higher self within us can shine through.

The main idea here is that if we wish to achieve spiritual progress or union with the divine, we cannot do so directly. As the Christian saint Teresa of Avila puts it, 'However great the effort we make to do so, we cannot enter. His Majesty must place us there and enter Himself into the center of our soul.'[3] All we can do is clear out the cobwebs, so to speak, removing any selfish desires or negative mental patterns that hinder the divine will from acting through us. Similarly, in the Bhagavad Gita, the process of spiritual surrender is described as a process of cleansing ourselves of our vanity. 'Seek refuge in the attitude of detachment and you will amass the wealth of spiritual awareness.'[4] In Hinduism, one of the three spiritual paths is bhakti, or devotion, where one surrenders to the will of God and accepts whatever comes. Believers follow spiritual practices designed towards unifying the many layers of consciousness, and they do so without attachment to the results of these practices—as such attachments keep them tied to the lower ego states of consciousness.

Modern-day rabbi and author Shoni Labowitz likewise describes grace as something to be found within us at a level of consciousness displayed in action.

> You are born with grace. There is nothing for you to do to deserve grace; it is an ordained state of generosity, goodness, and purity that already resides in your consciousness. When you are gracious to another, grace emanates through you and serves humanity and the earth.[5]

Thus, the concepts of grace and surrender in Western and Eastern traditions are not so different after all. Perhaps the main difference is in the language used. The Western monotheisms describe grace as something that comes from God, and therefore, is driven by faith. In

---

[3]Teresa of Avila, *The Interior Castle*, trans. Kieran Kavanaugh and Otilio Rodriguez (New Jersey: Paulist Press, 1979), 91.

[4]*The Bhagavad Gita*, trans. Eknath Easwaran, Second Edition (Tomales: Nilgiri Press, 2007), 2:49.

[5]Shoni Labowitz, *Miraculous Living: A Guided Journey in Kabbalah Through the Ten Gates of the Tree of Life* (New York: Simon and Schuster, 1998), 128.

the Qur'an, for instance, it is said, 'It is He who sent down tranquillity into the hearts of the believers, that they may add faith to their faith; for to God the forces of heavens and the earth; and God is full of knowledge and wisdom.'[6] And in the New Testament we are told, 'For by grace you have been saved through faith, and that not of yourselves; it is the gift of God, not of works, that no one would boast.'[7] The Baha'i leader 'Abdu'l-Bahá adds to this God-based perspective on grace quite poetically: 'The grace of God is beating down upon mankind [...] Wherefore, let us put our hopes in whatever the strong arm of the Beloved can bring about.'[8]

To underscore the similarities between these religious traditions, Christian theologian and author Marcus J. Borg writes:

> The image of following 'the way' is common in Judaism, and 'the way' involves a new heart, a new self-centreed in God. One of the meanings of the word 'Islam' is 'surrender': to surrender one's life to God by radically centering in God. And Muhammad is reported to have said, 'Die before you die.' Die spiritually before you die physically, die metaphorically (and really) before you die literally. At the heart of the Buddhist path is 'letting go'—the same internal path as dying to an old way of being and being born into a new. According to the Tao te Ching, a foundational text for both Taoism and Zen Buddhism, Lao Tzu said: 'If you want to become full, let yourself be empty; if you want to be reborn, let yourself die.' This process of personal spiritual transformation—what we as Christians call being born again, dying and rising with Christ, life in the Spirit—is thus central to the world's religions.[9]

It is indeed true that 'Islam' itself means surrender. Concepts of 'grace' and 'surrender' are quite central to the religion, in the same way that faith in Jesus Christ—his divine life and sacrificial death—is the most

---

[6]Qur'an, 48:4 (Yusuf Ali).

[7]Ephesians 2:8-9 (World English Bible).

[8]'Abdu'l-Bahá, *Selections From the Writings of 'Abdu'l-Bahá* (Bahá'í World Centre, 1982), 277, Baha'i Reference Library, http://reference.bahai.org/en/t/ab/SAB/sab-222.html

[9]Marcus J. Borg, *The Heart of Christianity: Rediscovering a Life of Faith* (New York: HarperCollins, 2003), 119.

important concept in Christianity. In the Buddhist and Taoist traditions, true wisdom is said to come through a kind of 'unlearning', or a letting-go of all the preconceptions and prejudices instilled in us through socialization in a particular culture. By letting go, we can experience life more freely and selflessly, recognizing the interconnectedness of everything. One of the central ideas in Taoist thought is that humanity has essentially gotten in its own way. Too often, in thinking that we can control everything in our lives, we simply create more problems for ourselves, and generate unnecessary suffering. The Taoist sage Chuang Tzu writes:

> Life stops and starts, is born and dies, grows and declines, and there is nothing which can be done about this. People think the ruler of all this is humanity. Forget that, forget Heaven and be known as one of those who forgot self. The person who forgets self can be known as the one who enters Heaven.[10]

Chuang Tzu is speaking of the concept of 'wu wei', often translated as 'effortless action' or 'actionless action', which can be seen as the Taoist equivalent of 'grace'. Further elaborating on this, Tzu references his predecessor, Lao Tzu. 'To practice the [Tao] requires daily diminishment. Diminish again and yet again, until you reach non doing, doing nothing and yet leaving nothing undone.'[11] Life provides us with many opportunities, and if we are patient and perceptive enough, we can realize it. Much of Taoism is based on observing and trying to be more in tune with nature. Practitioners argue that animals are not anxious in the way that we are, and perhaps our instincts and consciousness are better guides for us than our socialized egotistic selves. 'Wu wei' can also be understood as a form of radical acceptance and an affirmation of nature and instinct—in the same way that grace represents a radical faith in God's will.

In the Talmudic writings of Judaism, it is said, 'No man bruises his

---

[10] *The Book of Chuang Tzu,* trans. Martin Palmer, Penguin Classics edition (New York: Penguin Books, 2006), 98.

[11] *Zhuangzi: The Essential Writings,* trans. Brook Ziporyn (Indianapolis: Hackett Publishing, 2009), 85-86.

finger on earth unless it is decreed in heaven.'[12] With this simultaneity in mind, Jewish philosopher Martin Buber (who thought highly of the Taoist classics and concept of wu wei) wrote:

> This is the activity of the human being who has become whole: it has been called not-doing, for nothing particular, nothing partial is at work in man and thus nothing of him intrudes into the world. It is the whole human being, closed in its wholeness, at rest in its wholeness, that is active here, as the human being has become an active whole. When one has achieved steadfastness in this state, one is able to venture forth toward the supreme encounter.[13]

Buber's account not only echoes the Taoist attitude of wu wei, but also harks back to the goals of unifying consciousness and loosening attachments that we saw in Hinduism and Buddhism. These goals are also aimed at attaining wholeness. Attachments keep us from wholeness; our desires and attention are fixated on particular individual things. With a wandering mind and a not-unified consciousness, we are thus lost.

The loosening of attachments is also advocated in the ancient Greek philosophical school of stoicism. Historian of philosophy, Pierre Hadot, compares stoicism to the theology of the early Christian monk, Dorotheus of Gaza:

> [Spiritual perfection] is the transformation of the will so that it becomes identified with the Divine Will: He who has no will of his own always does what he wishes. For since he has no will of his own, everything that happens satisfies him.[14]

As with Chuang Tzu's descriptions of wu wei, the line of reasoning here is that much of our suffering in life comes from the staunch effort we make by trying to control things that are ultimately beyond our control. What is within our control is how we respond to the events and

[12]Babylonian Talmud (Ḥul. 7b), Jewish Virtual Library, accessed on 12 July 2022, https://www.jewishvirtuallibrary.org/providence.

[13]Martin Buber, *I and Thou* (New York: Simon and Schuster, 1996), 125.

[14]Pierre Hadot, *Philosophy as a Way of Life*, ed. Arnold I. Davidson, trans. Michael Chase (Massachusetts: Blackwell, 1995), 136.

challenges of life—and in this case, we are given the advice to respond to everything with an attitude of radical acceptance by surrendering. Ultimately, we must give up our patterns of limited thought and the misplaced will of the ego-driven self. Somewhat similar in spirit to this is the famous Serenity Prayer, which was coined by the Christian theologian Reinhold Niebuhr.

> God, grant me the serenity to accept the things I cannot change,
> courage to change the things I can,
> and wisdom to know the difference.[15]

In this sense, acceptance is surrendering to forces larger than ourselves. There are causes that we do not understand, nor can we presume to be able to predict them.

Of course, much of this advice has been given in very abstract and even paradoxical terms, with the term 'actionless action' being a perfect example of such abstraction. The point of such enigmatic and counterintuitive phrases is to force us to think differently, and to go beyond our ordinary sense of logical reasoning. Still, wouldn't it be nice to have more straightforward practical advice on how we could achieve this surrendering of the self? Perhaps the point being made is that even such a desire for directness is a desire that must be surrendered, and that we must look for answers within ourselves to determine what we each—specifically and particularly—must do to get rid of our own particular limitations.

Religions certainly do offer prescribed practices of self-transformation (as we have seen in previous chapters). One example that is interesting in its simplicity is the practice of bowing, which Zen master Shunryu Suzuki has recommended:

> Bowing helps to eliminate our self-centered ideas. This is not so easy. It is difficult to get rid of these ideas, and bowing is a very valuable practice. The result is not the point; it is the effort to improve ourselves that is valuable.[16]

---

[15]"The Serenity Prayer", attributed to Reinhold Niebuhr.

[16]Shunryu Suzuki, *Zen Mind, Beginner's Mind* (Boston: Shambhala, 2011), 30.

Bowing is a simple, easy and physically actionable form of self-surrender. But even this description is a bit paradoxical. Bowing is said to be valuable for its self-transformative capacity, but we are told that the result is not important. Isn't transformation a result? Mahatma Gandhi, commenting on the Bhagavad Gita, offers one suggestion of how to resolve this paradox.

> This is the unmistakable teaching of the Gita. He who gives up action falls. He who gives up only the reward rises. But renunciation of fruit in no way means indifference to the result. In regard to every action one must know the result that is expected to follow, the means thereto, and the capacity for it.[17]

Gandhi draws a distinction between the reward (or 'fruit') and the result. Applying this to Suzuki's practice of bowing, self-transformation can be consciously viewed as a result (and a worthwhile reason for undertaking the practice) without being viewed as a reward.

Seeing something as a reward implies self-gratification, which fuels our attachments and desires. When we focus on the rewards of a spiritual practice, we think too much about what we *want* to achieve, and we are likely to become frustrated and give up on the practice if we fail to attain that reward within a short period of time. Focusing only on a result, however, is more conducive to 'grace' and 'surrender'. We can continue to practice something because we have full faith in the value to be derived from it, regardless of whether or not we are consciously aware of the results as they are taking place. This may seem like a subtle distinction, but it is an important one that is worth dwelling on. It represents a difference of attitude that can be applied to all arenas of life, not just religion.

Having too much attachment to any particular belief or practice keeps us locked in our own separate silos. When we loosen these attachments, we can see the value of all religions and their respective practices of self-transformation.

---

[17]Mahatma Gandhi in Wendy Doniger, *Hinduism, The Norton Anthology of World Religions: Vol. 1*, Ed. Jack Miles (New York: W.W. Norton & Company, 2015), 645.

37

Moderation

Whoever takes delight in the golden mean, safely avoids the squalor of a shabby house, and, soberly, avoids the regal palace that incites envy.[1]

—Horace

The Buddha referred to the balance between practical matters, material concerns and spiritual practices as the 'middle way' (or 'path'), but various other phrases affirm the principle of moderation. The Buddha practised extreme asceticism and extreme worldly pursuits before, ultimately rejecting both as misguided and not conducive toward attaining enlightenment. He explains this in one of his sermons:

> Monks, these two extremes should not be followed by one who has gone forth into homelessness. What two? The pursuit of sensual happiness in sensual pleasures, which is low, vulgar, the way of worldlings, ignoble, unbeneficial; and the pursuit of self-mortification, which is painful, ignoble, unbeneficial. Without

[1]Horace, 'The Odes,' *Book II: X*, trans. A.S. Kline, 2003, Poetry in Translation, https://www.poetryintranslation.com/PITBR/Latin/HoraceOdesBkII.php#anchor_Toc39742784.

> veering toward either of these extremes, the Tathāgata has awakened to the middle way, which gives rise to vision, which gives rise to knowledge, and leads to peace, to direct knowledge, to enlightenment, to Nibbāna.[2]

Following the middle way requires us to follow spiritual pursuits over worldly ones, while still recognizing and respecting our nature as material beings, taking care of physical needs and family and social obligations. Elsewhere, he uses the following analogy to demonstrate this aspect.

> Just as a bird, wherever it goes, flies with its wings as its only burden, so too, the bhikkhu becomes content with robes to protect his body and with alms food to maintain his stomach, and wherever he goes he sets out taking only these with him. Possessing this aggregate of noble virtue, he experiences within himself a bliss that is blameless.[3]

The spiritual goal of enlightenment can be arrived at through clarity and alertness of the mind, but the mind cannot remain clear and alert if it is burdened by an unhealthy body that is crying out for its basic needs to be met. At the same time, the necessary resources to meet this requirement are few: some food for sustenance, some clothing for warmth and protection, and not much more.

I learnt moderation from my father. Like the Buddha himself, my father took spirituality and asceticism to the extreme and began to neglect family and other important material aspects of life. However, around the age of sixty, he realized his folly and became much happier and fulfilled once he sought a proper balance. He lived a great life until the age of ninety, finding a comfortable mean between spiritual and material life, and he left us with a great model to follow.

The medieval Jewish philosopher Maimonides argued, '[A man] should have the intent that his body be whole and strong, in order

---

[2]Bhikkhu Bodhi, *In the Buddha's Words: An Anthology of Discourses from the Pali Canon* (Massachuset:Somerville: Wisdom Publications, 2005), 75.

[3]*Majjhima Nikaya (Middle Length Discourses)*, Sutta 51, Verse 15, trans. B. Nanamoli and B. Bodhi (Somerville: Wisdom Publications, 1995), 450

for his inner soul to be upright so that [it will be able] to know God. For it is impossible to understand and become knowledgeable in the wisdoms when one is starving or sick, or when one of his limbs pains him.'[4] Humans have multiple instincts and multiple drives, and rarely are these in harmony. We should strive for balance in life and never give in so completely to any one impulse to the point where we lose control. As one Hindu proverb puts it, 'Even nectar is poison if taken to excess.' The same thing can be said even of medicine: too much of it can be poisonous.

In religions as different from one another, as Buddhism from Islam and from Taoism, variations of this phrase—'the middle way'—appear in the translations of the most important scriptures. One passage from the Qur'an, for instance, reads 'Neither speak thy prayer aloud, nor speak it in a low tone, but seek a middle course between'.[5] And the Taoist sage Chuang Tzu writes, 'Our life has a boundary but there is no boundary to knowledge. To use what has a boundary to pursue what is limitless is dangerous [...] Follow the Middle Course, for this is the way to keep yourself together, to sustain your life, to care for your parents and to live for many years.'[6]

Most of these examples share a particular and recurring motif on the common thread of moderation: steering away from extreme fanaticism in religious practice. In the case of the Buddha, there is caution against ascetic practices of self-mortification. The Qur'an cautions us against praying too loudly too or quietly. If it is too loud, then the prayer exceeds the boundary of modesty and slips into pride and boasts; too quiet, and the prayer may signal a lack of conviction and commitment in the act of worship. And Chuang Tzu cautions us to dedicate enough time to care for our boundary-bound lives and those of our loved ones before plunging into the rabbit hole of pursuing knowledge.

The Hebrew Bible provides a similar cautionary message: 'It is not good to eat too much honey, nor is it honorable to search out matters

---

[4] Rabbi Moshe ben Maimon, *De'ot: The Laws of Personal Development*, 3:3, trans. Eliyahu Touge, Chabad, accessed on 12 July 2022, https://www.chabad.org/library/article_cdo/aid/910343/jewish/Deot-Chapter-Three.htm.

[5] *The Qur'an*, 17:110 (Yusuf Ali).

[6] *The Book of Chuang Tzu*, trans. Martin Palmer, Penguin Classics edition (New York: Penguin Books, 2006), 22.

that are too deep.'[7] Serious devotion to religious studies and practices is a noble pursuit, but even the great religious prophets and scriptures make it clear that our devotion to the divine should not be cause for us to neglect our responsibilities in the profane and material world. As a famous passage from the New Testament puts it, 'For everything there is a season, and a time for every purpose under heaven.'[8] Even as the lines between what's good and what's bad become blurred, this passage reminds us that context is important in evaluating whether to abstain from something or not.

In Western antiquity, the term used for moderation (here too seen as a guiding principle) was the 'golden mean'. Socrates advised 'to choose the mean and avoid the extremes on either side, as far as possible' in Plato's *Republic*.[9] 'Nothing in excess', was carved on the door to the temple of Delphi. Of course, even in the famous Greek myth of Icarus, the angel crashes to the ground when he fails to heed his father's warning to not fly too close to the sun. Expounding further on the theme of moderation in ancient Greece, political scientist Aurelian Crăiuțu shares the following insights and observations:

> Tacitus called it, in fact, 'the most difficult lesson of wisdom', while Horace linked moderation to the golden mean and balance, all good things in his view, but difficult to achieve in practice. Plato highlighted both the importance and difficulty of moderation in *The Republic*.[10]

We tend to think that more of a good thing is always better, but everything has its limits—even religious devotion. When scripture tells us to avoid an excess of worldly pursuits and pleasures, we must remind ourselves that the implication is that we should also avoid an excess of abstinence from these very things. The famous quip 'everything in

---

[7]Proverbs 25:27 (NIV).

[8]Ecclesiastes 3:1-8 (World English Bible).

[9]Plato, *The Republic of Plato,* trans. Benjamin Jowett (Oxford: Clarendon Press, 1881), 324.

[10]Sam Haselby, 'Moderation May Be The Most Challenging and Rewarding Virtue,' *Aeon*, 17 July 2017, https://aeon.co/ideas/moderation-may-be-the-most-challenging-and-rewarding-virtue

moderation, including moderation',[11] is a good principle to apply, and it is a common religious theme. Even something like the principle of moderation, if adhered to in a strict fanatical manner, may lead us astray in certain situations.

Religious scripture provides us with guidance, but there is wisdom in trusting our own knowledge and instincts as well, even when it contradicts the words of a particular scripture. We must always have the flexibility of mind to exercise our own judgement in specific situations. The Baha'i leader Shoghi Effendi underscores this point, emphasizing that what is most important is preserving the essential spirit of a religious system, rather than selectively following interpretations of isolated sentences and phrases; these interpretations might tip us over into one extreme or the other. In a letter, he writes:

> We believe in balance in all things; we believe in moderation in all things—we must not be too emotional, nor cut and dried and lacking in feeling, we must not be so liberal as to cease to preserve the character and unity of our Bahá'í system, nor fanatical and dogmatic.[12]

This echoes the writings of the founding prophet Bahá'u'lláh, 'Whatsoever passeth beyond the limits of moderation will cease to exert a beneficial influence.'[13]

Reminiscent of this point of moderation in a person's emotional expression is a description of Confucius by one of his students, as recorded in the Analects.

> My master spoke only when it was the right time for him to speak, and so others were not tired of him speaking. He laughed when he was happy, and so others were not tired of him laughing. He

[11]Variously attributed to Oscar Wilde, Mark Twain and others.

[12]Shoghi Effendi, Letter from 5 July 1947 to an individual believer, in "Science and Technology", compiled by Research Department of the Universal House of Justice; Baha'i Library Online: https://bahai-library.com/compilation_science_technology

[13]Bahá'u'lláh, *Gleanings From the Writings of Bahá'u'lláh* (US Bahá'í Publishing Trust, 1990), 216, Baha'i Reference Library: http://reference.bahai.org/en/t/b/GWB/gwb-110.html.

> only took when it was right for him to take, and so others were not upset about his taking. [14]

Throughout the Analects, Confucius is described as good company—sociable and likeable—and the principle of moderation seems to be guiding his conduct. Similarly, Lao Tzu lauds the wisdom in knowing when one has acquired enough and knowing when to stop.

> Instead of pouring in more
> better stop while you can
> making it sharper won't help it last longer.[15]

Moderation is not just a religious commandment to be followed for the sake of obedience. Confucius and Lao Tzu explain the logic of moderation in more secular and practical terms. Confucius reasons that behaviours that tend towards the excessive can damage our reputation among our peers, while Lao Tzu reasons that excessive work yields only an inefficient expenditure of effort and an excess of wealth, which can cause problems in our lives. In Hinduism too, the Bhagavad Gita also argues for moderation on the basis of the adversity and suffering it serves to prevent. 'He who eats too much food or too little, who is always drowsy or restless, will never succeed in the yoga of meditation. For the man who is moderate in food and pleasure, moderate in action, moderate in sleep and waking, yoga destroys all sorrow.'[16]

Moderation is not just a guiding principle for the religious, but it is also applicable in many other spheres of life. In politics, moderation is essential as it allows us to arrive at compromises on divisive issues. The principle of moderation is also built into modern economics, i.e., the demand curve is based on diminishing marginal utility—as we consume something, the utility for the next unit of consumption goes down, and there is always an optimum level of any activity to maximize the utility function. We know this to be true of the functioning of our minds as well.

---

[14]Confucius, *The Analects,* trans. Annping Chin (New York: Penguin, 2014), 14:13.
[15]Lao-Tzu, *Tao te ching,* trans. Red Pine (Port Townsend: Copper Canyon Press, 2009), Chapter 9, 18.
[16]*The Bhagavad Gita,* trans. Stephen Mitchell (New York: Harmony Books, 2000), 6:16-17.

Carlin Flora from 'Psychology Today' writes, citing a study conducted by Harvard University:

> [R]esearchers asked people to translate sentences into a new made-up language. Subjects who practiced the language moderately beforehand made fewer errors than those who practiced extensively or not at all. High levels of knowledge can make people too attached to traditional ways of viewing problems across fields—the arts, sciences, and politics. High complexity in a job role exacerbates stress, burnout, and dissatisfaction. High conscientiousness is related to lower job performance, especially in simple jobs where it doesn't pay to be a perfectionist.[17]

Diminishing returns impact even the amount we study and work, and more is not always better! But the reason why we mistakenly think it is because, as Flora goes on to say, 'We've evolved to see things in black and white, rather than shades of gray. If you have to make life-or-death decisions about others in a split second, blunt categories are useful [...] Nuanced assessments are mentally taxing, extreme labels are quick and easy to apply.'[18]

There are evolutionary reasons for why our brains have evolved to prefer extremism over moderation. This is why it can sometimes seem helpful, or even necessary, to turn to the wisdom found in religious scriptures and other belief systems to find inspiration and advice. Practices like mindfulness and meditation allow us to transcend this cognitive proclivity and embrace more moderation in our lives and all the benefits that come from it.

---

[17]Carlin Flora, 'Moderation Is the Key to Life,' *Psychology Today*, 4 July 2017, https://www.psychologytoday.com/us/articles/201707/moderation-is-the-key-life.
[18]Ibid.

38

Simplicity

The greatest ideas are the simplest.[1]

—William Golding

In 2015, William C. Campbell received the Nobel Prize in medicine for co-discovering the drug Ivermectin. Ivermectin is a drug that has been enormously helpful in treating roundworm infections as well as infections caused through hosting other parasites. He titled his acceptance speech 'Ivermectin: A Reflection on Simplicity', proclaiming that, 'To a very large extent the drug Ivermectin was brought about by simple science. It was not conventional science; it was not obvious science; but it was simple science.'[2] Some of humanity's greatest problems and mysteries have been solved through very simple methods and insights.

For all the complex theories about life and the world around us, religious prophets and sages have often based their philosophies with an underlying sense of simplicity. In most religious systems, truth and meaning in life are simple matters. However, the simplicity of this

---

[1]William Golding, *Lord of the Flies* (New York: Penguin, 1954), 181.

[2]William C. Campbell, 'Ivermectin Nobel Prize speech—Ivermectin: A Refection on Simplicity Nobel Lecture,' 7 December 2015, https://www.nobelprize.org/prizes/medicine/2015/campbell/lecture/

wisdom is occluded by many layers of socialization, biases, prejudices and baser impulses. If we could remove these artificial layers, we too would arrive at a state of simplicity and, through that, contentment and happiness. As the Harvard philosopher Roberto Unger writes, 'Simplicity is the disposition to renounce the material and immaterial bric-a-brac of ordinary experience for the sake of focus on what matters.'[3]

One religion that values simplicity as one of its core values is Taoism. It is based around the belief that human beings have lost their innate nature and that our goal in life should be to seek a return to this originary pure state by striving for minimalism and simplicity. As Taoist sage Chuang Tzu explains:

> Fishes are born in water
> Man is born in Tao.
> If fishes, born in water,
> Seek the deep shadow
> Of pond and pool,
> All their needs
> Are satisfied.
> If man, born in Tao,
> Sinks into the deep shadow
> Of non-action
> To forget aggression and concern, He lacks nothing
> His life is secure.[4]

The Tao is essentially understood as the governing force in the universe and the natural order towards which all things tend. Arriving at a state of simplicity, therefore, we allow ourselves to be effortlessly guided by the Tao, satisfied with the setting and circumstances in which we find ourselves—just like a fish in water. When we cultivate this inner state of simplicity, or so the Taoist creed goes, we arrive at a state of 'wu wei', or 'actionless action', wherein we can live simply and be free of worry. Similarly, in the Bhagavad Gita, Krishna teaches, 'He

---

[3]Unger, Roberto Mangabeira, *The Religion of the Future* (Cambridge: Harvard University Press, 2014), 379.

[4]*The Way of Chuang Tzu,* trans. Thomas Merton (New York: New Directions, 2010), 65.

who can see inaction in the midst of action, and action in the midst of inaction, is wise and can act in the spirit of yoga.'[5] Both perspectives derive from the ideal that if we reduce our desires and simplify our egotistic involvement in things, proper actions will flow more naturally.

In the Abrahamic traditions, it is God who acts as a conscious governing force in the universe. However, a philosophy similar to Taoism applies here as well: contentment is found when we place our trust in God. As the Christian Apostle Paul declares in the New Testament, 'Charge those who are rich in this present world that they not be arrogant, nor have their hope set on the uncertainty of riches, but on the living God, who richly provides us with everything to enjoy.'[6] As humans, we like to think we have full control over our own success and happiness, but wealth can come and go and it rarely ever provides lasting happiness. Instead, as the famous passage from Psalms in the Hebrew Bible puts it, 'But the humble shall inherit the land, and shall delight themselves in the abundance of peace.'[7] Religion teaches us to recognize that we are not the masters of the universe; we are better off if we can accept this truth fully and place our trust in some higher power, whatever that might be.

Religions also agree that the pursuit of material wealth is dangerous, and not only because the satisfaction it brings is fleeting and illusory, but also because material desires turn people against one another. Consider the following words of the Baha'i leader Abdu'l-Baha:

> Observe how darkness has overspread the world. In every corner of the earth there is strife, discord and warfare of some kind. Mankind is submerged in the sea of materialism and occupied with the affairs of this world.[8]

Of course, material wealth itself is not the problem—it is our relationship to it that is unhealthy. As the British economist and statistician Ernest Friedrich Schumacher wrote in his essay, 'Buddhist Economics', 'It

[5]*The Bhagavad Gita*, trans. Stephen Mitchell (New York: Harmony Books, 2000), 4:18.
[6]1 Timothy 6:17 (World English Bible).
[7]Psalm 37:11 (World English Bible).
[8]Abdu'l-Baha, *The Promulgation of Universal Peace*, Second Edition (US Bahá'í Publishing Trust: 1982), 335, Baha'i Reference Library, https://reference.bahai.org/en/t/ab/PUP/pup-106.html.

is not wealth that stands in the way of liberation but the attachment to wealth; not the enjoyment of pleasurable things but the craving for them. The keynote of Buddhist economics, therefore, is simplicity and non-violence.'[9] Indeed, the essence of the Buddha's teaching is that worldly suffering comes from unhealthy desires and attachments. And when we relinquish these attachments, there is no need for violence. The Hindu attitude is similar. In the Ishavasya Upanishad, it is said, '(Know that) all this, whatever moves in this moving world, is enveloped by God. Therefore, find your enjoyment in renunciation; do not covet what belongs to others.'[10] The simpler our lives, the more wealth and resources there are to go around for others who are in desperate need for basic life-sustaining support.

In keeping with an attitude of non-attachment, many spiritual leaders and scriptures also emphasize simplicity in our relationship to religion and spirituality itself. Lao Tzu wrote that:

> Without going out your door
> you can know the whole world
> without looking out your window
> you can know the Way of Heaven.[11]

If we focus on our need for specific things, even with respect to religious practice—temples, gurus, specific practices, books and so on—we stray away from the essence of religion: looking within to find what really matters and efforts towards becoming a more loving and peaceful person. As Confucius noted, we should focus more on specific character traits to cultivate rather than any particular system of knowledge. As he said, 'The firm, the enduring, the simple, and the modest are near to virtue.'[12]

---

[9]Ernest Friedrich Schumacher, 'Buddhist Economics,' Schumacher Center for a new economics, accessed on 12 July 2022, https://centerforneweconomics.org/publications/buddhist-economics/.

[10]Ishavasya Upanishad, trans. Sri Radakrishnan, *The Principal Unpanisads* (London: George Allen and Unwin Ltd., 1955), 567.

[11]Lao-Tzu, *Taoteching*, trans, Red Pine (Port Townsend: Copper Canyon Press, 2009), Chapter 47, 94.

[12]*Confucian Analects, The Great Learning, The Doctrine of the Mean*, trans. James Legge (Pantianos Classics, 2017), 13:27.

Religions also advise against attachments to excessive knowledge-seeking and over-gratifying the desires of the intellect. In the Old Testament, for instance, there is a psalm that expresses this idea:

> Yahweh, my heart isn't arrogant, nor my eyes lofty;
> nor do I concern myself with great matters,
> or things too wonderful for me.
> Surely I have stilled and quieted my soul,
> like a weaned child with his mother,
> like a weaned child is my soul within me.[13]

The above statement is a profession of faith in God, and an acknowledgement that it is not our job, as humans, to find definitive answers to all the mysteries of our existence and the universe. The larger point being made here is that if we pursue intellectual gratification too far, it can be a sign of unhealthy attachment and desire. Furthermore, as the Indian guru Swami Sri Yukteswar Giri notes, 'Continual intellectual study results in vanity and the false satisfaction of an undigested knowledge.'[14] Being overambitious in the pursuit of knowledge can be counterproductive. We think the amount of output when it comes to knowledge acquisition will always match the effort, but beyond a certain point, this is no longer the case.

The famed British novelist and philosopher Aldous Huxley once wrote, 'The course of every intellectual, if he pursues his journey long and unflinchingly enough, ends in the obvious, from which the non-intellectuals have never stirred.'[15] This is a profound idea, and one that has been backed by evidence. Many prominent writers, artists, philosophers and scientists have espoused the idea that simplicity of ideas is the highest state of achievement. In conclusion I offer a few examples.

---

[13]Psalm 131:1-2 (World English Bible).

[14]Swami Sri Yukteswar Giri in Paramahansa Yogananda, *The Autobiography of a Yogi: The classic story of one of India's greatest spiritual thinkers* (London, UK: Arcturus Publishing, 2016), ebook. https://books.google.com/books?id=KQseDQAAQBAJ&printsec=frontcover&output=html_text&source=gbs_ge_summary_r&cad=0.

[15]Aldous Huxley, *Point Counter Point* (Champaign, Illinois: Dalkey Archive Press, 2009), 317-18.

Mark Twain the novelist has said, 'Plain question and plain answer make the shortest road out of most perplexities.'[16] Similarly, the poet Khalil Gibran mentioned, 'The obvious is that which is never seen until someone expresses it simply.'[17] Hans Hofmann, the painter, also argues, 'The ability to simplify means to eliminate the unnecessary so that the necessary may speak.'[18]

Simplicity is not just a mark of intellectual or spiritual achievement, but it is also, more broadly, the key to lasting happiness. Albert Einstein once said, 'The trite objects of human efforts—possessions, outward success, luxury—have always seemed to me contemptible.'[19] Einstein himself did not write from the perspective of any particular religious tradition, but his words actually resonate quite well with similar statements made by religious prophets and scriptures. We don't need fancy possessions, titles or socially constructed markers of success to make us happy. The truth of happiness is much simpler: simply engage in our three deepest longings—loving, learning and playing.

---

[16]Mark Twain, *Life on the Mississippi* (New York: Harper & Brothers, 1883), 262.

[17]Kahlil Gibran, *Sand and Foam: A Book of Aphorisms* (New York: Alfred A. Knopf. 1959), 54.

[18]Hans Hofmann, *Search for the Real: And Other Essays,* ed. Sara T. Weeks, Bartlett H. Hayes (Cambridge: MIT Press, 1967).

[19]Albert Einstein, 'What Life Means to Einstein: An Interview by George Sylvester Viereck,' *The Saturday Evening Post,* October 26, 1929.

39

Money

Wealth and high station are what men desire but unless I got them the right way I would not remain in them. Poverty and low station are what men dislike, but even if I did not get them in the right way I would not try to escape from them.[1]

—Confucius

Humble living is a well-known and common trope across religions. Most of the founding figures and saints of various religions were wandering ascetics of some sort or another; they all turned their backs on wealth and material possessions. There is nothing inherently wrong with money. It is simply our attachment to money that becomes corrupting.

In Hindu scriptures, earning money is one of the four pursuits of life. There are four stages known as the four ashramas: Brahmacharya (the student), Grihastha (caretaker of the household), Vanaprastha (the forest-walker/forest-dweller), and the Sannyasa (the renunciate). As a householder in the Grihastha stage we have a duty to earn money, as we are responsible for ourselves and our family members as well. In the later phases, believers are called upon to seek knowledge and eventually

[1]Confucius, *The Analects*, trans. D.C. Lau, Penguin Classics edition (London: Penguin Books, 1971), 4:5.

renounce the worldly life in preparation of the next life to come. In some religions, however, the attitude towards acquiring money is a bit stricter. As Jesus told his disciples, 'It is easier for a camel to go through a needle's eye than for a rich man to enter into God's Kingdom.'[2] The ideal Christian, therefore, should seek to live with as little money as possible throughout life, rather than embracing a stage like the Hindu grihastha at any point in life.

Religious prophets and scriptures specifically react against the pursuit of money which, when taken to an extreme, corrupts people and leads to selfishness. When they advise against the pursuit of money, they do not mean to celebrate taking up a life of poverty for its own sake; instead, they try to make people understand that money can corrupt people and lead them unwittingly into self-inflicted harm. One of the most famous expressions of such a sentiment comes from the apostle Paul in the New Testament: 'For the love of money is a root of all kinds of evil. Some have been led astray from the faith in their greed, and have pierced themselves through with many sorrows.'[3] Similarly, in the Qur'an it is said, 'O ye who believe! There are indeed many among the priests and anchorites, who in falsehood devour the substance of men and hinder (them) from the way of God. And there are those who bury gold and silver and spend it not in the way of God: announce unto them a most grievous penalty.'[4] Thus, there is concern that the allure of money has the capacity to lead astray even the most religiously committed individuals—rabbis and monks, for instance—from their spiritual pursuits and obligations to God.

Religions command us to share our wealth, and when we instead hoard wealth, we forsake this duty and become dangerously devoted to money instead. This is what Jesus had in mind when he said, 'No one can serve two masters, for either he will hate the one and love the other, or else he will be devoted to one and despise the other. You can't serve both God and Mammon.'[5] Indeed, there are people who become so captivated by money that they come to worship it as though it were God! In a speech delivered

[2]Matthew, 19:24 (World English Bible).

[3]1 Timothy 6:10 (World English Bible).

[4]Qur'an, 9:34 (Yusuf Ali).

[5]Matthew 6:24 (World English Bible).

at Kenyon College, novelist David Foster Wallace spoke about this:

> There is no such thing as not worshipping. Everybody worships. The only choice we get is what to worship. If you worship money and things, if they are where you tap real meaning in life, then you will never have enough, never feel you have enough. It's the truth.[6]

We are incomplete creatures. We are pulled in different directions and are confused about how we should live our lives. Hence, as suggested above, we are inclined to choose something to worship or follow as a guiding principle, as such a commitment eases our existential anxiety about the lack of an apparent meaning. The beauty that God represents is expansive and infinite: such as beauty found in love or knowledge. But money is different, and this sentiment is shared in the Hebrew Bible: 'He who loves silver shall not be satisfied with silver; nor he who loves abundance, with increase: this also is vanity.'[7]

Of course, this idea is not exclusive to Judaism or the other two Abrahamic religions. We see different expressions of this principle expressed in the religious traditions of east Asia and India. The Buddha taught that all suffering in the world is fundamentally caused by desire, and this certainly includes the desire for money. As recorded in the Dhammapada, he explained, 'Even a shower of gold cannot quench the passions. They are wise who know that passions are passing and bring pain in their wake. Even celestial pleasures cannot quench the passions. They are true followers of the Buddha who rejoice in the conquest of desires.'[8] The Buddha argues that people who are stricken by the desire for things like money are deeply lost; unknowingly, they are the agents of their own suffering. He has taught that such people deserve our compassion and are in need of guidance and wisdom to help them see the error of their ways.

However, the Buddha did not teach that there was anything

---

[6]David Foster Wallace, Commencement Speech at Kenyon College (Gambier, Ohio, 2005), Kenyon College Archive, accessed on 8 July 2022, http://bulletin-archive.kenyon.edu/x4280.html.

[7]Ecclesiastes 5:10 (World English Bible).

[8]*The Dhammapada,* trans. Eknath Easwaran, Second Edition (Tomales: Nilgiri Press, 2007). 186-87,

intrinsically wrong with money, especially when laypersons acquire money (as opposed to monks, who take stricter vows). He acknowledged that when earned and used properly, wealth can actually be a source of genuine happiness for people. 'When he thinks, "I have wealth earned through my efforts & enterprise, amassed through the strength of my arm, and piled up through the sweat of my brow, righteous wealth righteously gained", he experiences bliss, he experiences joy.'[9] The great prophets and religious scriptures do not denounce money entirely. They understand its necessity in society and simply urge us to approach money with the proper attitude. For example, money must be earned, rather than stolen; it must be given and not hoarded and so on. This is exemplified, for instance, by the Hindu principle of 'artha', which acknowledges that acquiring money through proper means should be encouraged as an essential part of life.

Confucius also acknowledged that money has its proper place in our lives, arguing that we should remain guided by the principle of moderation, avoiding both extreme poverty and extreme wealth. As recorded in the Analects, he notes that, 'It is a shameful matter to be poor and humble when the Way prevails in the state. Equally, it is a shameful matter to be rich and noble when the Way falls into disuse in the state.'[10] In other words, when the community we live in is prospering and there is wealth to go around, it is foolish to deliberately surrender our own wealth simply for the sake of appearing poor and humble. On the other hand, if those around us are in dire straits and we have wealth to spare, it is deplorable to turn a blind eye and hoard it all for ourselves. He goes on to say, 'If in your action you think only of profit, then you will incur much unhappiness [with yourself and with the world].'[11] This is echoed by Chuang Tzu's advice; 'Value life. If you value life then you will put profit into perspective.'[12]

---

[9]'Aṅguttara Nikāya', trans. Thanissaro Bhikkhu, 4:62, *Dhamma Talks*, accessed on 14 July 2022, https://www.dhammatalks.org/suttas/AN/AN4_62.html.

[10]Confucius, *The Analects*, trans. D.C. Lau, Penguin Classics edition (London: Penguin Books, 1971), 8:12-13.

[11]Confucius, *The Analects*, trans. Annping Chin (New York: Penguin, 2014), 4:12.

[12]*The Book of Chuang Tzu*, trans. Martin Palmer (New York: Penguin Classics, 2006), 256.

All of this is perhaps best summed up by the medieval Islamic theologian Ibn Qayyim Al-Jawziyyah who had said, 'When there is money in your hand and not in your heart, it will not harm you even if it is a lot; and when it is in your heart, it will harm you even if there is none in your hands.'[13] We all end up making different amounts of money throughout our lives, and we do so according to the conditions of our birth, our differing levels of education, our work ethic, our particular career paths and a variety of other factors beyond our control. What is always within control, however, is the attitude we can cultivate towards wealth and how we make use of it. This has a great impact on our happiness and our flourishing, regardless of how much money we have or what religion we belong to. Our attitude toward wealth also has a great impact on others, as our willingness to give to those in need largely depends on how tightly we hold on to, or how attached we are, to money in our hearts. Money is an extrinsic object—something outside of who we are that distracts us from the intrinsic.

Money is meant as a means to a legitimate end. What religions are against is pursuing money as the ultimate goal. Unfortunately, this is the reality in our capitalistic world. The profit-driven pursuit of money is increasingly preferred to the pursuit of more important goals, like lasting happiness, well-being and flourishing, goals which admittedly are harder to quantify.

The message from our organization, UEF, is: 'Make enough money so that money is not a constraint in your life. But *never* let money become a value in your lives. Don't judge yourself or others by how much money you or they have.' As I see it, the most worthwhile pursuits in our lives, the ones that do lead to lasting happiness and flourishing, are the pursuits of our three deepest longings i.e., loving, learning and playing, and engaging in all our day-to-day practices with these three things as a guiding mindset.

---

[13]Ibn Qayyim al-Jawziyyah, 'The Sayings of Ibn Qayyim al-Jawziyyah,' trans. Ikram Hawramani, 2017, *Ikram Hawramani*, accessed on 12 July 2022, https://hawramani.com/the-sayings-of-ibn-qayyim-al-jawziyyah/.

40

Family and Community

A family is a nation in miniature. Simply enlarge the circle of the household, and you have the nation. Enlarge the circle of nations, and you have all humanity.[1]

—'Abdu'l-Bahá

In the fifty years since I left my home, my parents and I were not able to spend much time together. In their old age, I accepted my duty to take care of them, especially during the COVID-19 pandemic. In our quiet interludes, we reminisced over fond childhood memories. On reflection, I realize my happiest days were when I was a child growing up with my parents, my four siblings, my grandmother, and my aunt, living on approximately one hundred dollars a month. We were a close-knit family who loved and cared for each other. My father's four cousins and their twenty children were our neighbours, living in one haveli (compound). We played together a lot and we read a lot. I missed that community life enormously when I had to leave home to go for my undergraduate studies at IIT.

Community is an important part of any religious tradition. Family—

---

[1]'Abdu'l-Bahá, *The Promulgation of Universal Peace*, second edition (US: Bahá'í Publishing Trust, 1982), 157, Baha'i Reference Library, http://reference.bahai.org/en/t/ab/PUP/pup-58.html

the first micro-community we learn to inhabit—serves as a model for broader community systems. The family unit is where we first learn what it means to love and to be loved. Our childhood plays such a huge role in laying the groundwork for the rest of our lives. Without a nurturing family environment in our early life, it is difficult to learn to love and develop healthy relationships later. Hence, the health of a community depends a lot on the health of its family dynamics. If we do not learn how to love and be loved by our closest family members, it is doubtful that we will be able to love our neighbours, much less those who look and think very differently from us. The ultimate expression of love is to see the entire world as your family and to treat the most remote stranger as your closest kin.

The supreme importance of community has been attested by faith leaders across religious traditions. The great rabbi and scholar Hillel the Elder succinctly advised, 'Do not separate yourself from the community.'[2] In Buddhism, the community (known as 'sangha') is one of the 'three jewels' that devotees are taught to take refuge in. The Buddha explains, 'Admirable friendship, admirable companionship, admirable camaraderie is actually the whole of the holy life. When a monk has admirable people as friends, companions, and comrades, he can be expected to develop and pursue the Noble Eightfold Path.'[3] From a more contemporary perspective, Buddhist monk Thich Nhat Hanh explains, 'The sangha is a community where there should be harmony and peace and understanding. That is something created by our daily life together. If love is there in the community, if we've been nourished by the harmony in the community, then we will never move away from love.'[4] Buddhists are taught to extend love and compassion towards all living beings. Thus, it is important to be a part of a community—whether formally through the sangha, or informally through a circle of friends—in order to practise giving and receiving love. Indeed, building loving communities can be said to be an important purpose of all religious communities.

---

[2]Hillel the Elder

[3]'Samyutta Nikāya', trans. Thanissaro Bhikkhu, 45:2, *Dhamma Talks,* accessed on 14 July 2022, https://www.dhammatalks.org/suttas/SN/SN45_2.html.

[4]Thich Nhat Hanh, 'Building a Community of Love: bell hooks and Thich Nhat Hanh', *Lion's Roar*, 24 March 2017, https://www.lionsroar.com/bell-hooks-and-thich-nhat-hanh-on-building-a-community-of-love/.

Confucius also placed great emphasis on the importance of friends and friendship, along with his more well-known emphasis on family roles, especially filial piety. As recorded in his Analects, he explained, 'If a person in a ruling position [junzi] is generous toward his family and kin, the common people will be inspired to act humanely. If he does not forget old friends and acquaintances, the common people will not be uncharitable.'[5] Here too, the idea is that friendships provide an opportunity for practising good conduct towards others. Furthermore, the way we treat our friends creates a model not just for ourselves, but for others to follow in their dealings. Similarly, the love we show our parents, through both words and actions, echoes across our other relationships in life.

As such, the scriptures of just about every religion contains explicit statements of the importance of filial piety. In the Hebrew Bible, we are told, 'Honor your father and your mother, that your days may be long in the land which Yahweh your God gives you.'[6] And the New Testament of Christianity warns us, 'But if anyone doesn't provide for his own, and especially his own household, he has denied the faith, and is worse than an unbeliever.'[7] The whole purpose of a family, after all, is so that everyone has at least a few close compatriots in their lives that they can depend on for support and unconditional love. Just as we find nourishment from our relatives—especially our parents—so too is it important to reciprocate this care. This sentiment is also made clear in the Qur'an:

> Thy Lord hath decreed that ye worship none but Him, and that ye be kind to parents. Whether one or both of them attain old age in thy life, say not to them a word of contempt, nor repel them, but address them in terms of honour. And, out of kindness, lower to them the wing of humility, and say: 'My Lord! Bestow on them thy mercy even as they cherished me in childhood.' Your Lord knoweth best what is in your hearts: if ye do deeds of righteousness, verily He is most forgiving to those who turn to Him again and again (in true penitence).[8]

---

[5]Confucius, *The Analects*, trans. Annping Chin (New York: Penguin, 2014), 8:2.
[6]Exodus 20:12 (World English Bible).
[7]1 Timothy 5:8 (World English Bible).
[8]Qur'an, 17:23-25 (Yusuf Ali).

We are completely dependent on our parents when we are children, and once they reach a certain old age, they become similarly dependent on the children they raised—emotionally, financially and physically.

It should come as no surprise that religions place just as much emphasis on the importance of childrearing as they do on the principle of filial piety. These are truly the two sides of the same coin. For instance, the Baha'i leader 'Abdu'l-Bahá declares, 'The education and training of children is among the most meritorious acts of humankind.'[9] Indeed, one of the main goals of the Baha'i faith is to provide proper education to children across the globe. Our species, as a whole, can only improve if an educational foundation has been laid down for its youth. Judaism, too, is a religion known for its emphasis on education, and the Hebrew Bible advises, 'Train up a child in the way he should go, and when he is old he will not depart from it.'[10]

The Chinese religions, Confucianism and Taoism, also closely echo this idea of laying good foundations for the children. The scriptures also expound on the consequences that this has for them in later life. As Confucius notes in one of the very first passages of the Analects:

> The gentleman devotes his efforts to the roots, for once the roots are established, the Way will grow therefrom. Being good as a son and obedient as a young man is, perhaps, the root of a man's character.[11]

The importance of filial piety is expressed, but this time from the perspective of how teaching children obedience will benefit them later in life. The Taoist sage Lao Tzu in the Tao Te Ching, idealized the thought of planting strong roots as a way to cultivate virtues that will echo across the many spheres of communities we inhabit.

[9]'Abdu'l-Bahá, *Selections From the Writings of 'Abdu'l-Bahá* (Bahá'í World Centre, 1982), 129-30; Baha'i Reference Library, http://reference.bahai.org/en/t/ab/SAB/sab-104.html

[10]Proverbs 22:6 (World English Bible).

[11]Confucius, *The Analects*, trans. D.C. Lau, Penguin Classics edition (London: Penguin Books, 1971), 1:2.

Thus view others through yourself
View families through your family
View villages through your village
View states through your state
View other worlds through your world[12]

Lao Tzu describes the process of expanding our circle of love, applying the love we learn from our parents and other familial relationships to ever-broadening levels of community, from family to the village to the state to the entire world.

This same line of reasoning can be found across religions. One of the common messages is the reminder that the community of humankind should be seen as a single family. As 'Abdu'l-Bahá reasons, 'Mankind has been created from one single origin, has branched off from one family. Thus in reality all mankind represents one family. God has not created any difference. He has created all as one that thus this family might live in perfect happiness and well-being.'[13] Similarly, the Maha Upanishad, a Hindu scripture, invokes the phrase, 'Vasudhaiva Kutumbakam', which means, 'the world is one family'. This phrase is held in high esteem in the Hindu consciousness and is engraved in the Indian parliamentary building. The Maha Upanishad also advises, 'Only small men discriminate saying: One is a relative; the other is a stranger. For those who live magnanimously the entire world constitutes but a family.'[14] In Japan, particularly in the prefecture of Okinawa, the phrase 'ichariba chode' is a close analogue to the Hindu, 'Vasudhaiva Kutumbakam'. It is used to express the sentiment towards one another that, 'once we meet, we become brothers and sisters.'[15] Finally, in the Analects, Confucius

[12]Lao-Tzu, *Tao te ching*, trans. Red Pine (Port Townsend: Copper Canyon Press, 2009), Chapter 54, 108.

[13]'Abdu'l-Bahá, *Foundations of World Unity*, sixth printing (US: Bahá'í Publishing Trust, 1979), 38, Baha'i Reference Library, http://reference.bahai.org/en/t/c/FWU/fwu-10.html

[14]A. G. Krishna Warrier, trans, *Maha Upanishad* (Chennai,: The Theosophical Publishing House), Vedanta Shastras Library, accessed on 12 July 2022, https://www.shastras.com/upanishads-sama-veda/maha-upanishad/.

[15]Okinawa Prefectural Government, 'Japan's Okinawa Uploads Welcome Movie, Featuring "Ichariba-Chode" Hospitality,' 6 January 2014, PR Newswire, accessed on

reassures one of his students who feels lonely for having no brothers by saying, 'All within the Four Seas are his brothers.'[16]

We can all learn from these various perspectives to see the family as foundational to becoming a community member and citizen of the world. This perspective is especially needed in the United States today, as Dr Francie Hart Broghammer, a psychiatry resident at UC Irvine, explains: 'Historically, family has been the first society, where children gain social identity and security. But our homes are becoming less stable, less intimate, and, consequently, less formative than ever before.'[17] This reminds me of a passage from the Bhagavad Gita, in which we are told, 'When a family declines, ancient traditions are destroyed. [...] It disrupts the process of spiritual evolution begun by our ancestors'.[18]

The pattern of care that is determined by our nuclear families—where parents caring for children, who later come to care for their parents in their old age—reminds us more broadly to extend our care to other relationships as well. We should take care of others when we are in position to do so, and we should reciprocate the care that we receive from others. In this way, we can all live like a single family, seeing everyone as our brothers and sisters.

---

12 July 2022, https://www.prnewswire.com/news-releases/japans-okinawa-uploads-welcome-movie-featuring-ichariba-chode-hospitality-238820761.html#.

[16]Confucius, *The Analects*, trans. D.C. Lau, Penguin Classics edition (London: Penguin Books, 1971), 12:5.

[17]Francie Hart Broghammer, 'Death By Loneliness,' *Real Clear Policy*, 6 May 2019, https://www.realclearpolicy.com/articles/2019/05/06/death_by_loneliness_111185.html

[18]*The Bhagavad Gita*, trans. Eknath Easwaran, Second Edition (Tomales: Nilgiri Press, 2007), 1:40.

41

Conversion and Proselytizing

Although proselytizing is not in itself necessarily intolerant, it does close the open-ended door of pluralism.[1]

—Wendy Doniger

In the introduction to his wonderful book *Commonalities and Similarities in World Religions*, author Wajihuddin Siddiqui describes a disconcerting experience from his youth that he had with an elderly stranger. The elder was somewhat aggressive in his attempts to convert the author to Christianity. Siddiqui, a Muslim, was told by this man that he would burn in hell if he did not seek salvation through Jesus Christ. He describes the impact this made on his worldview.

> I was overwhelmingly shocked [...] Back at home, I had been told and which I had also firmly believed that all non-Muslims would have a fate in the next world like to what he was predicting for non-Christians. So, for the first time in my life I had a direct experience of knowing that there were billions of non-Muslims in this world who thought that we Muslims were the misguided

[1]Wendy Doniger, *The Hindus: An Alternative History* (Oxford: Oxford University Press, 2010), 513.

people while they were the true believers. I started wondering as to what the un-adulterated, unvarnished truth was! And how could one decide as to who is right and who is wrong?[2]

Despite the uncomfortable nature of this exchange, Siddiqui describes how it galvanized him into studying other religions, learning about the common themes they all share, and writing his book on the subject. This is very similar to my own journey and mission with this book!

The act of seeking out new converts is laid out as an explicit command in the scriptures of some of the major world religions, including Christianity and Islam, and it is therefore seen as a holy duty or mission by its adherents. Given the grandiose nature of religious revelations, it makes perfect sense for people to want to share their own divine insights with the rest of the world. In this sense, proselytizing can be a very benevolent gesture. It has the intention of improving other people's lives. After all, if someone truly believes—as both Siddiqui and the elderly stranger did—that their God is the only true God, and their truth is the only truth, why wouldn't you want to share that with others, whether it is laid out as an explicit command or not? Unfortunately, history shows there is a fine line between sincere proselytizing born out of the goodness of one's heart, and outright coercion and even violence. But if we look closer at the words from the scriptures and prophets across religions, we see that they too had a keen awareness of this problem and made a point to expressly caution followers against the kind of religious zeal and fundamentalism that leads to violence. Instead, they taught peaceful means of teaching that were meant only to improve humanity.

Unsurprisingly, the world's two most populous religions—Christianity (with 2.3 billion followers) and Islam (with 1.9 billion followers)—both place great emphasis on teaching and spreading their faith to other parts of the world, and both have been fairly successful at this throughout history. One Hadith in the Islamic literature reads that, 'It is reported on the authority of Abu Huraira that he heard the Messenger of Allah say: I have been commanded to fight against people, till they

[2]Wajihuddin Siddiqui, *Commonalities and Similarities in World Religions* (Karachi: Royal Book Company, 2018), 8.

testify to the fact that there is no God but Allah, and believe in me (that) I am the messenger (from the Lord) and in all that I have brought.'[3] In the New Testament, Christians are very clearly told to, 'Go and make disciples of all nations, baptizing them in the name of the Father and of the Son and of the Holy Spirit.'[4] Missionary activity is an important part of the Christian faith as Christians believe that salvation only comes through the acceptance of the Holy Trinity, and most importantly, the saviour Jesus. Thus, by converting others, Christians are doing a good deed because they are facilitating the salvation of others. Christian missionary activity has done a lot of good throughout the world. They have brought education and essential resources (like clean water) to impoverished areas. But these missions have also been met with criticism for sometimes being too forceful and stripping cultures of their native identities.

So too has the proselytizing element of Islam been met with criticism for its forceful nature, most notably due to the so-called 'sword verse' of the Qur'an which, taken out of context, seems to promote violence against all who oppose the spread of Islam. 'But when the forbidden months are past, then fight and slay The Pagans wherever ye find them, And seize them, beleaguer them, and lie in wait for them in every stratagem (of war).'[5] Violent groups of Islamic extremists have been known to cite this verse as justifications for their actions, and to recruit others to their cause, but they omit the context where the Qur'an makes clear that this verse refers to those who were persecuting Muslims in the early days of the faith. The Qur'an, therefore, contains passages that condone acts of violence *only* in the case of self-defence and in response to wrongful acts of violence against innocent people who are trying to peacefully practise their faith.

Incidentally, a close friend and colleague of mine works to deradicalize young people who are being recruited by Islamic extremists. He listens to the young people and hears them quote the Qur'anic verses that justify violence. In response, he quotes back to them the passages in the Qur'an

---

[3]Abu Huraira, Sahih Muslim 1:31.

[4]Matthew 28:19 (World English Bible).

[5]Qur'an 9:5 (Yusuf Ali).

which provide more context and give a very different message—one of love and peace. The common reaction he hears is, 'But we were never told about this sura!' He has an 80 per cent success rate in deradicalizing or preventing radicalization.

The Qur'an furthermore instructs Muslims to 'Invite (all) to the way of thy Lord with wisdom and beautiful preaching; and argue with them in ways that are best and most gracious: for thy Lord knoweth best, who have strayed from His path, and who receive guidance.'[6] This attitude is encapsulated by the term for proselytizing in Islam—'Da'wah'—which means 'invitation' in Arabic. Muslims are encouraged to help spread their faith to others, but only through peaceful means, such as openly and honestly explaining the tenets of the faith and allowing people to convert voluntarily, bearing in mind the Qur'anic principle of: 'Let there be no compulsion in religion.'[7]

These passages from the Qur'an illustrate a general principle that appears across many religions of the world: that there is an important difference between 'good' and 'bad' proselytizing, such that some religions even choose to forgo the term proselytizing altogether. For instance, the Baha'i Universal House of Justice describes the proper spread of their faith simply as 'teaching'.

> It is true that Bahá'u'lláh lays on every Bahá'í the duty to teach His Faith. At the same time, however, we are forbidden to proselytize, so it is important for all believers to understand the difference between teaching and proselytizing. It is a significant difference and, in some countries where teaching a religion is permitted, but proselytizing is forbidden, the distinction is made in the law of the land. Proselytizing implies bringing undue pressure to bear upon someone to change his Faith. It is also usually understood to imply the making of threats or the offering of material benefits as an inducement to conversion. In some countries mission schools or hospitals, for all the good they do, are regarded with suspicion and even aversion by the local authorities because they are considered to be

[6]Qur'an 16:125 (Yusuf Ali).
[7]Qur'an 2:256 (Yusuf Ali).

material inducements to conversion and hence instruments of proselytization.[8]

The Baha'i faith places a great deal of emphasis on the importance of education, and teaching the faith is seen as an extension and reflection of this. However, recognizing that 'education' is sometimes used as part of a more forceful proselytizing programme, Baha'is are encouraged to be conscious of this fine line, to recognize the difference between these sides and strive to avoid any kind of coercion. As such, the Baha'i faith makes up a relatively small portion of the world population, but it has also managed to spread to every major continent.

The religious traditions of Asia also provide good examples of affirming the value in peacefully teaching and seeking out only voluntary conversion. Dogen, the founder of the Soto Zen branch of Buddhism in Japan, reportedly once said, 'When you say something to someone, he may not accept it, but do not try to make him understand it intellectually. Do not argue with him; just listen to his objections until he himself finds something wrong with them.'[9] Buddhism, similar to Christianity, seeks to teach the message of a certain kind of salvation. But even though this message is thought to be supremely important for the good of humanity, the faith argues that one should remain gentle and patient in transmitting this message. Buddhists additionally also believe that the pursuit of enlightenment is a process which takes place across many lifetimes. Everyone has their own path and purpose to follow in this current lifetime, even if that's a different religion for now. Trying to coerce them into converting to Buddhism when they're not ready would only do a disservice to them with regard to their overarching spiritual quest across lifetimes. This is why Buddhists have not been aggressive in proselytizing throughout the religion's history. Similarly, Hindus do not proselytize, as they see all religions as different paths toward the same God. Buddhism and Hinduism are, despite this, two of the most populous religions in the world.

[8]The Universal House of Justice: Department of The Secretariat, 'Letter to an Individual', 3 January 1982, https://www.bahai.org/library/authoritative-texts/the-universal-house-of-justice/messages/19820103_001/1#003634893

[9]Shunryu Suzuki, *Zen Mind, Beginner's Mind* (Boston: Shambhala, 2011), 80.

Another reason why certain religious traditions and/or individuals may choose not to proselytize is the belief that good ideas should speak for themselves. If they have to be conveyed through force, there's a good chance they might not be so good after all. The Taoist sage Chuang Tzu gets at something similar when he writes, 'The great man shows his greatness by combining all the common aspects of humanity. So, when ideas come to him from outside, he can receive them but does not cling to them. Likewise, when he brings forth some idea from within himself, they are like guides to those around but they do not seek to dominate.'[10] What need is there to try and force others to accept your ideas if you have full confidence in their value? It should be enough to simply demonstrate the value of your ideas by example.

There is a similar case of this in the Hebrew Bible, when Moses advises his people, 'Behold, I have taught you statutes and ordinances, even as Yahweh my God commanded me, that you should do so in the middle of the land where you go in to possess it. Keep therefore and do them; for this is your wisdom and your understanding in the sight of the peoples who shall hear all these statutes and say, "Surely this great nation is a wise and understanding people."'[11] Judaism is a non-proselytizing religion: it does not actively seek converts and, in fact, makes it quite difficult for people to undergo a full conversion. Part of this is because Jews see themselves as a lineage of God's chosen people, and they believe this lineage is sacred and should be preserved. However, the Jewish community is not entirely unwelcoming to new converts and some Talmudic passages suggest that converts should be seen as the most devout members of the community.

> [T]he Holy One said: Much did I have to labor for Israel: I brought them out of Egypt, lit the way for them, sent down manna for them, swept in quail for them, made the well gush up for them, and encompassed them with clouds of glory before they were willing to accept My Torah. But this one came on his own. He is therefore deemed by Me the equal of an Israelite, even of a Levite.[12]

---

[10] *The Book of Chuang Tzu,* trans. Martin Palmer (New York: Penguin Classics, 2006), 231.

[11] Deuteronomy 4:5-6 (World English Bible).

[12] Numbers Rabbah, 8:2 in Hayyim Nahman Bialik and Yehoshua Ḥana Rawnitzki, *The Book of Legends: Sefer Ha-Aggadah,* trans. William Gordon Braude (New York: Schocken Books, 1992), 350-51.

The reason conversion to Judaism is such a lengthy process is that the process serves as a test of commitment—that only those who deeply understand and value the faith will be accepted into the community. Thus, the conversion rate is low, and Judaism remains a relatively small religion in terms of the global population.

As a further explanation for the philosophy behind having a lengthy and difficult conversion process, consider C.S. Lewis's musings on the difference between nominal conversion and practical conversion:

> If conversion to Christianity makes no improvement in a man's outward actions—if he continues to be just as snobbish or spiteful or envious or ambitious as he was before—then I think we must suspect that his 'conversion' was largely imaginary.[13]

Lewis raises the question of whether we should judge people by what they say or what they do. He answers it himself by saying that it is our behaviour that defines our faith.

In closing, the particular faith we each subscribe to—Christianity, Islam, Hinduism, Buddhism, etc.—matters less than the degree to which we take that faith seriously and truly try to live up to its examples. Consider the messages of the following three paragons of devotion to both God and humanity:

> Yes, I do convert. I convert you to be a better Hindu, a better Christian, a better Catholic, a better Sikh, a better Muslim. When you have found God, it's up to you to do with him what you want.[14]
>
> I do not want you to become a Hindu. But I do want you to become a better Christian by absorbing all that may be good in Hinduism and that you may not find in the same measure or not at all in the Christian teaching.[15]

---

[13]C.S. Lewis, *The C.S. Lewis Signature Classics* (New York: HarperCollins, 2017), 164.
[14]Navin B. Chawla, 'I convert you to be a better Hindu, a better Christian, a better Muslim', *The Economic Times India*, 5 September 2016, https://economictimes.indiatimes.com/blogs/et-commentary/73995/.
[15]J.T.F. Jordens, *Gandhi's Religion: A Homespun Shawl* (New York: St. Martin's press, 1998), 153.

> I don't want to convert people to Buddhism—all major religions, when understood properly, have the same potential for good.
>
> Fundamentalism is terrifying because it is based purely on emotion, rather than intelligence. It prevents followers from thinking as individuals and about the good of the world.[16]

Though these individuals—Mother Teresa, Mahatma Gandhi and the Dalai Lama, respectively—are all regarded as important spiritual leaders of particular religious traditions, none of them seem to be interested in converting others to their own native faith. Their missions, instead, were to help people become more loving and compassionate human beings, and they all agreed that different religions are allies in this project. We only deepen our own faith by exploring the ideas and beliefs of other faiths.

[16]Alice Thompson, 'Westerners are too self-absorbed,' *The Telegraph,* 1 April 2006, https://www.telegraph.co.uk/news/worldnews/asia/burmamyanmar/1514537/Westerners-are-too-self-absorbed.html

42

Prophets and Priests

For the priest's lips should keep knowledge, and they should seek the law at his mouth; for he is the messenger of Yahweh of Armies.[1]

—Hebrew Bible

Does it really matter if someone is recognized as a sage or not? If you are truly honest, sincere, and upright in everything you do, do you need others to acknowledge your virtues to make you virtuous?[2]

—Lieh-Tzu

The problems of religious conflict and exclusivism in the world are not to be blamed on scriptures or prophets of the great world religions themselves. Across religions, prophets have always sought to share their wisdom as widely as possible, spreading above all the message of love and hoping to unite rather than divide people.

The problematic aspects of religion and religiously motivated conflict have risen because of the events that have unfolded after the death of

[1]Malachi 2:7 (World English Bible).

[2]Lieh-tzu, *Lieh-tzu: A Taoist Guide to Practical Living*, trans. Eva Wong (Boston: Shambhala, 2001), 111.

the founding prophets. Almost all major religions have a priestly class of religious leaders who act as spiritual authorities on earth. As with any profession, there are some who handle the power that comes with such authority responsibly while and who do not. In other words, there are good priests and bad priests.

Good priests are those who understand and faithfully uphold the original intentions of the prophets, seeing themselves as humble servants of a higher cause. Bad priests, on the other hand, are those who distort and manipulate the words of the prophets and the meaning of scriptures for selfish purposes, seeing the congregants that trust them as their own servants. They remain in power by fuelling exclusivist attitudes of (us versus them) that damage their own religion and, ultimately, humanity itself.

Understanding the difference between prophets and priests, and the proper roles and responsibilities of priests today, is an essential part of the kind of religious literacy that will make the world a better, more peaceful and cooperative place for all. When we understand the difference between prophets and priests, we are less likely to be exploited by the latter and more likely to embrace and embody the compassion, warmth and love for humanity of the former. In addition, we need not let the misdeeds of priests negatively colour our impressions of those respective religious traditions: such misdeeds are not reflections of the original prophets and their teachings, but rather result from improper interpretations or intentions on the part of priests.

There are many commonalities amongst all the major prophets, such as the fact that all sought to reform the cultural and/or religious systems where they lived, or that they had to embark on personal quests to make themselves into proper vessels who could receive such knowledge, and they all endured trials and hardships along the way. The Buddha left home in search of truth, unsatisfied with his lavish royal life. He tried both asceticism and hedonism before settling on the middle way and, while meditating, he had to resist the temptations of the demon, Mara, in order to achieve enlightenment. Confucius wished to bring peace to a divided China and had to wander, trying to get various rulers to enact his philosophy, and he only found higher wisdom worth sharing with more eager students back at home. The Baha'i prophet Bahá'u'lláh was imprisoned for over two years. Muhammad, who was raised as a travelling merchant, persevered in prayer, asceticism and solitude in caves. He was eventually visited by the angel Gabriel taken on his famous night journey through heaven and was hence chosen as a human vessel to receive the words of the Qur'an from God, which enabled him to unite the many disparate Arabian tribes. Even Jesus, whom Christians believe to be a manifestation of God himself, had to endure his trials and self-mortification while fasting and praying in the inhospitable desert for forty days.

Above all, the prophets across religions all preached peace, love and compassion for all. The last thing they would have wanted is for the people of different religions to fight with each other over minor differences with respect to belief. This is why the Sikh founding prophet Guru Nanak taught people to see beyond religious identity markers like 'Hindu' and 'Muslim'. And in fact, many religions share prophets. Baha'is believe that the prophets of all major religions received their revelations from the same God. Hindus revere the Buddha as a deity in the pantheon. And all three Abrahamic religions—Christianity, Judaism, Islam—share many prophets in common, such as Abraham, Moses and Elijah. In fact, some interpretations of Islam maintain that Allah revealed teachings to as many as 124,000 prophets, even though only twenty-five are mentioned by name in the Qur'an. The vast majority of these prophets, then, presumably belong to non-Islamic religions and cultures, since Allah is said to have sent forth prophets to all parts of the world at different points in history. According to such thought, any commonalities across religious prophets or texts are believed to not just be coincidences, but rather serve as evidence that all are descended from the same one God.

All prophets exhibited great humility in their lives, wanting people to understand that it was their teachings that were more important than them as people. Even Jesus and Krishna, who were supposedly manifestations of God, willingly lived in humble circumstances. They attached significance not to themselves, but to the teachings they transmitted. One prophet who exemplifies this image of humility is Muhammad, the founder of Islam, who is described by scholar of religion Huston Smith:

> In an age charged with supernaturalism, when miracles were accepted as the stock-in-trade of the most ordinary saint, Muhammad refused to pander to human credulity. Allah, he

> insisted, had not sent him to work wonders. If signs be sought, let them not be of Muhammad's greatness but of God's, and for these one need only open one's eyes to the wonders of nature. The only miracle that Muhammad claimed was that of the [Qur'an] itself. That he with his own resources could have produced such truth—this was the one naturalistic hypothesis he could not accept.[3]

Muhammad never claimed to be anything more than human. Indeed, the Qur'an itself says, 'Muhammad is no more than an Apostle: many were the Apostles that passed away before him. If he died or were slain will ye then turn back on your heels? If any did turn back on his heels not the least harm will he do to God; but God (on the other hand) will swiftly reward those who (serve him) with gratitude.'[4] Muhammad was not the only prophet sent by God. He was merely an ordinary man selected to serve a particular purpose. He was an uneducated man, in the modern sense of the word, making his act of writing the words of the Qur'an a miraculous act of God. The significant reason Muslims are heavily discouraged from depicting Muhammad through images is because he himself did not want believers to divert the focus of their worship towards him and away from where it really belongs: Allah. Priests and other people in power have distorted the original intention of this rule to depict Muhammad into excuses for violence against non-Muslims.

The prophets shared an equivocal attitude towards seeking truth as equals. One example of this is Confucius.

> Confucius was undoubtedly one of the world's greatest teachers. Prepared to instruct in virtually all the disciplines of his day, he was a one-man university. His method of teaching was Socratic [...] Not for a moment assuming that he was himself a sage—sagehood being for him a matter of comportment, not a stock of knowledge—he presented himself to his students as their fellow learner.[5]

---

[3]Huston Smith, *The Illustrated World's Religions* (New York: HarperCollins, 1995), 151.
[4]Qur'an 3:144 (Yusuf Ali).
[5]Huston Smith, *The Illustrated World's Religions* (New York: HarperCollins, 1995), 101-02.

Like any prophet, Confucius had access to a great deal of knowledge and wisdom that most others did not possess. And yet, all of this knowledge only reinforced a sense of humility about what he did not know and strengthened his conviction with regard to the essence of his teachings: that everyone has something to teach the other, and that this was the key to revitalizing society. He saw our relationships with one another as opportunities for constantly reforming and perfecting ourselves.

In the above description, Smith describes Confucius as a Socratic teacher, which is indeed an apt comparison. This is illustrated further through the following description of Socrates by the historian of philosophy, Pierre Hadot:

> Socrates had no system to teach. Throughout, his philosophy was a spiritual exercise, an invitation to a new way of life, active reflection, and living consciousness. Perhaps the Socratic formula: 'I know that I know nothing' ought to be given a deeper meaning. We are thus brought back to our starting point: Socrates knows that he is not a sage. As an individual, his conscience was aroused and spurred on by this feeling of imperfection and incompleteness.[6]

Both Confucius and Socrates sought to demonstrate (through dialogue) that the highest wisdom is: 'I know that I know nothing.'

When the Buddha started to wander around India, shortly after his enlightenment, he had a notable exchange with a curious man who inquired about his identity.

> When asked, 'Are you a deva?' you answer, 'No, brahman, I am not a deva.' When asked, 'Are you a gandhabba?' you answer, 'No, brahman, I am not a gandhabba.' When asked, 'Are you a yakkha?' you answer, 'No, brahman, I am not a yakkha.' When asked, 'Are you a human being?' you answer, 'No, brahman, I am not a human being.' 'Then what sort of being are you?' [...]
>
> 'Just like a red, blue, or white lotus—born in the water, grown in the water, rising up above the water—stands unsmeared by the water, in the same way I—born in the world, grown in the

[6]Pierre Hadot, *Philosophy as a Way of Life*, ed. Arnold I. Davidson, trans. Michael Chase (Massachusetts: Blackwell, 1995), 157.

world, having overcome the world—live unsmeared by the world. Remember me, brahman, as "awakened".[7]

There is a similar episode recorded in the New Testament about John the Baptist, who was sent as a messenger by God to anticipate and facilitate the teachings of Jesus:

> Now this was John's testimony when the Jewish leaders in Jerusalem sent priests and Levites to ask him who he was. He did not fail to confess, but confessed freely, 'I am not the Messiah.' They asked him, 'Then who are you? Are you Elijah?' He said, 'I am not.' 'Are you the Prophet?'
>
> He answered, 'No.'[8]

Again, one of the main hallmarks of the great prophets was their insistence on the authority of knowledge and revelation itself over any particular vessel of it. The Buddha and John both refused to claim divine status, but they both affirmed that they were the bearers of profound truths that must be shared with humanity.

This leads us back to the subject of priests, whose purpose is just that: the transmission of higher wisdom and truths as revealed by the prophets in order to ensure that this knowledge can continue to thrive across time and place. As the Hebrew Bible explains, 'For the priest's lips should keep knowledge, and they should seek the law at his mouth; for he is the messenger of [God].'[9] Priests have played an essential role in the histories of all living religions and continue to have a purpose today. But as the Baha'i prophet Bahá'u'lláh cautioned his followers, 'Fear thou God, but not the priest.'[10]

Baha'i, a very young religion that is scarcely two-hundred-years-old, takes this attitude of equality with respect to religion so seriously

---

[7]*Doṇa Sutta (AN 4:36),* trans. Thanissaro Bhikkhu, *Dhamma Talks,* accessed on 12 July 2022, https://www.dhammatalks.org/suttas/AN/AN4_36.html.

[8]John: 1:19-21 (World English Bible).

[9]Malachi 2:7, (World English Bible).

[10]Bahá'u'lláh, *Trustworthiness: A Cardinal Bahá'í Virtue* (Universal House of Justice Research Department) August 1990, https://www.bahai.org/library/authoritative-texts/compilations/trustworthiness/trustworthiness.pdf?4fda74d6

that there is no formal clergy or priesthood. Bahá'u'lláh is recognized as a founding prophet, and the prophets of all other major religions are recognized as genuine messengers of the same God, but modern-day priests are thought to be unnecessary and even unhealthy. Here is how Baha'i writer Moojan Momen describes it:

> Bahá'u'lláh asserted that priests and other religious professionals had their role in former times when the majority of people were illiterate and needed guidance. Today, however, humanity has the ability to bring education and literacy to all. Therefore it is possible for all to read the scriptures themselves and come to their own understanding of them. Bahá'u'lláh has therefore abolished the priesthood and the professional religious class.[11]

Several thousands of years ago, during the time of the prophets of the major world religions, literacy rates were extremely low. Even if the prophets knew everything, they were limited in what they could share. Primitive means of transportation and lack of mass communication technologies, like the radio and internet, meant that the prophets were limited to teaching small local communities. A lineage of disciples and priests was necessary for the continuation and codification of the more complex revelations so that they may reach audiences over time and across geographies.

Today, however, the role of priests should be more about fostering social harmony among their communities and helping others to extract meaning from religion by showing people how to find their own truths. The Hindu monk Swami Vivekananda once lamented that people 'have made themselves helpless and dependent on others. We are so lazy, we do not want to do anything ourselves. We want a Personal God, a Savior or a Prophet to do everything for us.'[12]

The dangers of religion emerge from those who seek to capitalize on the human inclination to seek guidance. Such people have the potential

---

[11]Moojan Momen, 'The Baha'i Community' in *A Short Introduction to The Bahá'í Faith* (Oxford: Oneworld, 1997), Baha'i Library Online, http://bahai-library.com/books/introduction/intro5.html

[12]Sister Gayatriprana, *Swami Vivekananda's History of Universal Religion and Its Potential for Global Reconciliation* (Illinois: Cook Communications, 2020), 221.

to exploit the masses. Examples of such abuses are abundant across religions: the Catholic Church selling indulgences, extorting people for money with promises of salvation; Islamic extremists who brainwash children with distorted interpretations of the Qur'an in order to turn them into weapons of war; plantation owners in the United States taking biblical verses out of context to justify the institution of slavery; Brahmins in India upholding the caste system, keeping large portions of the population destitute and subservient. The list goes on.

In my own life I have seen both the good and bad when it comes to priests exercising their authority. Many rituals in India require people to provide offerings to Brahmins. On the anniversary of someone's death, you are supposed to feed Brahmins, believing that one's ancestors are fed through such offerings. My father performed this ritual religiously for his father, but he prohibited me from doing it for his own death anniversaries, as he understood that there were no true Brahmins in spirit and that the Brahmin class was exploiting the beliefs of people by demanding material goods from them to perform rituals. A gift to a Brahmin was always meant to be completely voluntary, but Brahmins themselves have gotten people to believe in the stories that justify such rituals in the first place! Instead, my father asked that we feed poor people on his death anniversary, which is what we have started doing.

However, one of the most positive influences in my early life was our family guru, a Muslim saint, whom my father first met during a time of hardship. We all believed that God had sent this saint to save us! And whether or not that was true, his kind presence and supportive role in our own spiritual pursuits was incredibly valuable for us all.

We are all capable of making meaning on our own and finding truth within ourselves. The founding prophets certainly did not envision a world in which a select class of priests and prophets would have a monopoly over wisdom and truth. Rather, they stood by the conviction that truth comes from within and believed that we can all become our own greatest teachers. Prophets like Jesus, Muhammad and the Buddha believed that their teachings were applicable to all human beings. If they had access to the same technologies we have today, they would have no reason to limit their messages to one particular region of the world. They surely would have shared their wisdom with audiences far beyond their own geographical and cultural communities. As spiritual humanist, Jay Lakhani writes, 'The reason why we have such vastly varying religions is not because these prophets had different experiences, but because they came up with different interpretations to their experiences.'[13] In other words, priests and other institutional forces might look very different across different religions, but if we go back to the root source—the prophets and their revelations—then their common foundation is more apparent.

There are many priests and spiritual leaders in our present moment who recognize this. The Dalai Lama and Pope Francis, for instance, tour the entire world and make an effort to spend time with people who may look and think very differently from them. In doing so, they make attempts to translate the teachings of their respective traditions into terms that are adapted for a variety of different cultures. Spiritual wisdom is not the property of any one community of people, and is a treasure to be shared amongst all of humanity. But they are not actively trying to convert—they simply strive to make the teachings accessible to those who may find them helpful. This is true not only on a linguistic level, but on a visual level as well. As Archbishop of Canterbury Justin Welby explains, when you walk into a church 'you see a Black Jesus, or Chinese Jesus, or a Middle Eastern Jesus—which is of course the most accurate. You see a Fijian Jesus—you see Jesus portrayed in as many ways as there are cultures, languages and understandings', which serves as a 'reminder of the universality of the God who became fully human'.[14]

If we are religiously informed and understand religion as a meaning-making process, we can realize that no single person or single group has access to the full truth. Therefore, we need not fall for the lies of those who seek to exploit with exclusivist messages. This is what we want the readers of this book to realize. We all have the capacity to make meaning on our own, albeit in different ways, and religious scriptures and leaders are simply tools that can help us along.

---

[13]Jay Lakhani, 'Science and Spirituality,' *Wellbeing Foundation*, 2009, accessed on 12 July 2022, https://wellbeing-foundation.co.uk/spiritual%20humanism.html.

[14]Justin Welby, BBC Radio interview, Quoted in Henry McDonald, 'C of E should rethink portrayal of Jesus as white, Welby says,' *The Guardian*, 26 June 2020, accessed on 12 July 2022, https://www.theguardian.com/uk-news/2020/jun/26/church-of-england-justin-welby-white-jesus-black-lives-matter.

43

Sacred Books

What you learn or find in a book will not be the real. But you can experience it, you can watch yourself in action, watch yourself thinking, see how you think, how rapidly you are naming the feeling as it arises—and watching the whole process frees the mind from its centre. Then the mind, being quiet, can receive that which is eternal.[1]

—Jiddu Krishnamurti

Books and other texts have become powerful means of passing on wisdom and information across generations and geographical locations since the dawn of literacy and print. Books allow us to share in the process of meaning-making and truth-seeking, transcending barriers of time and space. It is remarkable that the sacred texts of religions have maintained their degree of importance and popularity for so many thousands of years. We can attribute this to the fact that these texts seem to clearly speak to some deep universal part of the human psyche. They were also composed to be highly accessible. As author Wajihuddin Siddiqui notes, 'A common feature of all religious texts is that they are either in the form of poetry or rhymed prose. This made their remembering and recitation easier. Further, reading

[1]Jiddu Krishnamurti, *The First and Last Freedom* (New York: HarperCollins, 1975), 254.

texts in this form inspires and creates ecstasy.'[2] Scriptures are beautiful and highly important features of religions for a variety of reasons. They codify major beliefs, stories and guidelines for conduct and give a clear structure to each tradition. They shape the identity of entire communities while still providing individuals with the opportunity to personalize meaning for themselves.

Jews hold the Hebrew Bible as their collection of sacred texts. These texts are also foundational spiritual material for Christians and Muslims, whose main sacred texts are the New Testament and the Holy Qur'an, respectively. The Guru Granth Sahib is the foundational text of Sikhs, Buddhist texts are split into three main 'baskets', collectively known as the Tripitaka, and in the Hindu tradition, sacred texts are divided into two broad groupings: smriti (that which is remembered), texts attributed to particular authors which were transmitted through writing; and srutis (that which is heard), which are considered to be more direct revelations, transmitted orally, but not originally composed, by human beings. Smriti include the two great Hindu Epics (the Mahabharata and Ramayana), The Puranas, and other scriptures corresponding to various schools of Hindu philosophy. The srutis are deemed to be more foundational and authoritative for all Hindu sects, most notably the Vedas and Upanishads. Finally, the Chinese religions of Confucianism and Taoism hold Confucius's Analects and Lao Tzu's Tao Te Ching as their foundational texts.

Like all books, a major function of scripture is pedagogic, teaching believers more about their traditions as well as imbibing wisdom that will hopefully be conducive to better living. Confucius, for instance, advised his students, 'Be stimulated by the Odes, take your stand on the rites and be perfected by music,'[3] and both, the 'odes' and 'rites', are two of the 'five classics' in Confucian literature. As explained in the New Testament, 'For whatever things were written before were written for our learning, that through perseverance and through encouragement of

[2]Wajihuddin Siddiqui, *Commonalities and Similarities in World Religions* (Karachi: Royal Book Company, 2018), 210.

[3] Confucius, *The Analects*, trans. D.C. Lau, Penguin Classics edition (London: Penguin Books, 1971), 8:8.

the Scriptures we might have hope.'[4] Indeed, hope and endurance are two character traits that Christians aspire to, following the example of Jesus who endured persecution while on earth.

What most clearly separates religious scriptures from other books is not necessarily the content or subject matter, but the perceived holiness of the source. Again, in the New Testament it is said that, 'Every scripture is God-breathed and profitable for teaching, for reproof, for correction, and for instruction in righteousness.'[5] The way we understand religious scriptures depends, in part, on how we understand God and religion. If we see all religions as worshipping a different God, then naturally, we will assume that the messages contained within scriptures across religions are entirely different and that every religion believes only in its own truth claims. But, in reality, that is not what the scriptures or the prophets convey.

For instance, Muslims believe in progressive revelation, which is to say that they recognize one God as having sent many prophets down to earth throughout history to transmit versions of the same essential religious teachings that reflect changing cultural and historical contexts of human civilizations. This is reflected in Allah's own words in the Qur'an:

> To thee we sent the scripture in truth confirming the scripture that came before it and guarding it in safety; so judge between them by what God hath revealed and follow not their vain desires diverging from the truth that hath come to thee. To each among you have we prescribed a law and an open way.[6]

Specifically, this makes reference to the Hebrew Bible of Judaism and the New Testament of Christianity, both books which Muslims believe to have been revealed by the same God (Allah). Muslims therefore also recognize biblical prophets, like Moses and Jesus, as messengers of God, though believers will not go so far as to adopt the Christian claim that Jesus was more than human.

Going even further than this, the religion of Baha'i—which emerged

[4]Romans 15:4 (World English Bible).
[5]2 Timothy 3:16 (World English Bible).
[6]Qur'an 5:48 (Yusuf Ali).

in nineteenth-century Persia—adds figures as Krishna and the Buddha to their own list of authentic messengers of the one God. What the Baha'i leader 'Abdu'l-Bahá has to say about the scriptures of various religions reveals a highly inclusive attitude towards them.

> The Heavenly Books, the Bible, the Qur'an, and the other Holy Writings have been given by God as guides into the paths of Divine virtue, love, justice and peace. Therefore I say unto you that ye should strive to follow the counsels of these Blessed Books, and so order your lives that ye may, following the examples set before you, become yourselves the saints of the Most High![7]

Thus, Baha'i followers read the texts of other religions just as devoutly as they read the texts of their own prophet, Baha'u'llah, who is simply seen as the latest in a long line of prophets. Members of the Baha'i religion, in fact, believe it is quite important to read the scriptures of other religions, as each text offers a different glimpse of God.

Though the religions of Islam and Baha'i provide particularly clear examples of recognizing the value in a plurality of scriptures, they are not the only examples. The Taoist sage Chuang Tzu, while referencing the Chinese classics, notes, 'Their principles are scattered throughout the world', and goes on to lament the folly of exclusivist attitudes, 'Many in the world congratulate themselves complacently for their insight into some single aspect of it. [...] How sad! The various schools go forth without returning, making it impossible for them to ever come together.'[8] Sense of authorship of the scriptures in east Asian religions like Taoism is also presumed to be looser. Scripture in Taoism—as well as some other religions—is recognized as having been composed entirely by human beings rather than being transmitted by God. Accordingly, the content itself is prioritized over the source to the point where the actual identity of the author becomes unimportant. Here's how translator Martin Palmer explains it:

---

[7]'Abdu'l-Bahá, *Paris Talks*, eleventh edition (UK: Bahá'í Publishing Trust, 1972), 61-62, Baha'i Reference Library: http://reference.bahai.org/en/t/ab/PT/pt-18.html

[8]*Zhuangzi: The Essential Writings*, trans. Brook Ziporyn (Indianapolis: Hackett Publishing, 2009), 118-19.

> The custom in many cultures of the past was to ascribe a book to a great figure from the past. By doing so you were not necessarily trying to claim that they had written every word. [...] Thus, for example, the five books of the Torah (Genesis to Deuteronomy) were ascribed to Moses, despite the fact that they record his death![9]

The way we think about the authorship of sacred books has changed over time. New historical findings reveal to us that the legendary authors to whom we attribute the writing of certain texts could not have possibly written all of those texts, and in some cases, perhaps did not exist at all. But this need not have any effect on the value we attribute to the content.

Ultimately, scriptures were written by human beings like us. Even if their contents had been revealed by God or some other divine source, the fact is that one or more human beings had to translate such revelations into written language. We cannot ignore the importance of the human hand in this process. I used to believe, as my mother still does, that God incarnated on earth as Lord Krishna to deliver sermons, which we can read today in the form of texts like the Bhagavad Gita. But the Gita was, of course, written over a period of time by *multiple* human authors, just as the Bible and the Qur'an were. Even the sayings of the Buddha and Confucius had to be memorized and recited for many years until they were written down by their followers. All these texts, even if they were inspired by revelations from God, were mediated by fallible human minds, mouths and hands.

New Testament scholar Marcus J. Borg notes how this is relevant to the modern-day sensibilities of Christians who want to hold on to their belief in the holiness of scripture without ignoring the obvious historical facts relating to their authorship.

> Like the earlier paradigm, the emerging paradigm sees the Bible as sacred scripture. But unlike the earlier paradigm, the emerging paradigm sees the Bible's status as sacred, as 'Holy Bible', as the

---

[9]Martin Palmer, 'Introduction' in *The Book of Chuang Tzu,* trans. Martin Palmer, Penguin Classics edition (New York: Penguin Books, 2006), xvii-iii.

> result of a historical process, not as the consequence of its divine origin. The process is known as canonization. The documents that now make up the Bible were not sacred when they were written, but over time were declared to be sacred by ancient Israel and early Christianity.[10]

Taking a step back, it is nothing short of miraculous that these scriptures have remained relevant to people of many different backgrounds, and for thousands of years. In order to achieve this impressive literary feat, the authors of sacred books had to resort to indirect methods of teaching their messages, such as storytelling. The only way scriptures have endured for so long is because they contain stories that invite a near-infinite number of possible interpretations, so much so that a person in ancient Rome and another in present-day Africa could derive an equal depth of meaning from the same words.

Religious traditions are living traditions, and in order to survive over time, their textual traditions must not be allowed to stagnate. Texts must be constantly reinterpreted in light of new scientific evidence, historical discoveries and new ways of life. Often, this can even necessitate the authoring of new sacred texts. As historian of religion Jeffrey Kripal writes, 'This is especially evident in a tradition like Judaism, where the process of midrash—scriptural interpretation—is itself seen as an ongoing revelation and the ancient collections of midrash, called Talmud, are treated as authoritative.'[11] Famed Jewish philosopher and historian of religion Gershom Scholem explains this even further in the context of mysticism: 'To the mystic, the original act of Revelation to the community—the, as it were, public revelation of Mount Sinai, to take one instance—appears as something whose true meaning has yet to unfold itself; the secret revelation is to him the real and decisive one.'[12] For some individuals, the literal words of a sacred text might be meaningful

---

[10]Marcus J. Borg, *The Heart of Christianity: Rediscovering a Life of Faith* (New York: HarperCollins, September 2003), 46-47.

[11]Jeffrey J. Kripal, *Comparing Religions*, illustrated edition (West Sussex: John Wiley & Sons, 2014), 309.

[12]Gershom Scholem, *Major Trends in Jewish Mysticism*, reissue edition (New York: Schocken Books, 2011), 9.

enough, but many of us crave deeper meaning that can only be unlocked through more analytical and metaphorical interpretations which enable the reader to craft their own individual meanings.

Similarly, the Hindu monk Swami Vivekananda argued that the Vedanta school of Hindu philosophy understands scripture through multiplicity. 'First, [Vedanta] does not believe in a book—that is the difficulty to start with. It denies the authority of any book over any other book. It denies emphatically that any one book can contain all the truths about God, soul, the ultimate reality.'[13] Clearly, people have taken different attitudes towards sacred books across time and religious traditions. As we move along these two vectors, there is a broad approach to the perceived 'sacredness' of the books (differing between whether they are written indirectly through God, and even the rigidity of the words or the degree to which a steady stream of new interpretations is encouraged).

We must always remember to reflect upon the words of the scriptures, discuss them, reinterpret them and see how they apply to the broader goals of religion, i.e., helping us make meaning of the world around us, and helping us to be more loving and compassionate towards others. This is why the selective readings of religious fundamentalists cannot be seen as faithful to their own traditions as specific passages are removed from their larger context and made to justify violent and non-religious actions, often against those who they deem to be inferior or evil simply for having different belief systems. The value of scriptures can be enhanced if we distinguish between what is eternal and what is circumstantial, what is literal and what is metaphorical.

[13]Swami Vivekananda, 'Is Vedanta The Future Religion?', 8 April 1900, https://www.ramakrishnavivekananda.info/vivekananda/volume_8/lectures_and_discourses/is_vedanta_the_future.htm

44

Sectarianism and Politics

I am the thread that runs through all these pearls, and each pearl is a religion or even a sect thereof. These are the different pearls, and the Lord is the thread that runs through all of them; most people, only the majority of mankind, are entirely unconscious of it.[1]

—Swami Vivekananda

I learned a lot about Christianity through my Christian friends. At first, I could not believe that there were so many denominations within Christianity! It made me pay more attention to the different sects within all other religions as well: Sunnis, Shias, and Sufis in Islam; Theravada, Mahayana and many others in Buddhism (especially if you look at the Chinese and Japanese variants). Not to mention Hinduism, wherein there are too many sects to count—one analyst puts the number of Hindu Gods and Goddess in the hundreds of thousands! For a while, my curiosity as to why these splits existed at all was suspended, as I was pursuing the course of my professional life. But since retirement, I have had the luxury to study and think more about this. It is evident that the existence of different sects is

[1]Swami Vivekananda, *Vivekananda, World Teacher: His Teachings on the Spiritual Unity of Humankind*, ed. Swami Adiswarananda (Woodstock: SkyLight Paths Publishing, 2006), 53.

a common theme across religions, though the reasons for these splits are different in each religion.

Just about all religions have inevitably split into different sects throughout their history. As author Wajihuddin Siddiqui writes, 'There is a set pattern under which new religions crop up, develop and then split up into two or three, mostly two, major sects due to different interpretations of the original sacred text or because of periodical reform movements.'[2] There are many factors that contribute to such splits. Sometimes sectarian divides occur for purely theological reasons—that is, differences in belief system—but often, politics becomes the true catalyst. As twentieth-century British rabbi Jonathan Sacks notes, 'Most conflicts and wars have nothing to do with religion. They are about power, territory, and glory, things that are secular, even profane. But if religion can be enlisted, it will be.'[3] It is important to point out that religions do not inherently promote violence. However, religion has often been one of the most expedient tools for justifying warfare, since the emotional and moral compasses of many people are so heavily influenced by their religious leaders.

The words of the foundational scriptures and prophets of religious traditions consistently anticipated the dangers of religious schisms and presented clear warnings against these divisions. For instance, the Qur'an addressed the matter: 'And hold fast all together by the rope which God (stretches out for you) and be not divided among yourselves; and remember with gratitude God's favour on you; for ye were enemies and He joined your hearts in love so that by His grace ye became brethren; and ye were on the brink of the pit of fire and He saved you from it. Thus doth God make his signs clear to you: that ye may be guided.'[4] The early days of Islam were characterized by an impressively rapid spread that—while admittedly not completely free of violence—resulted in the unification of geographically and culturally diverse tribes of people that had previously been in conflict with one another. This passage of the Qur'an thus appeals to Muslims by reminding them of this sense of

---

[2]Wajihuddin Siddiqui, *Commonalities and Similarities in World Religions* (Karachi: Royal Book Company, 2018), 43.

[3]Jonathan Sacks, *Not in God's Name: Confronting Religious Violence* (New York: Schocken Books, 2017), 39.

[4]Qur'an, 3:103 (Yusuf Ali).

brotherhood and unification, cautioning them to not slip back into the old ways of tribal divisions and conflicts. It is a reminder that peace is difficult to preserve in the wake of religious schism.

Nevertheless, it was not long after its founding that Islam did fracture into its two major sects, the Sunnis and the Shias. As with all such splits, there was likely a complex set of factors involved, but the main precipitating reason that is often cited is a dispute over the rightful successor of the founding Prophet Muhammad following his death. The Sunnis, who today account for over 80 per cent of all Muslims worldwide, believed that Muhammad's successor should be elected by members of the community, whereas the Shia believed that such human decision-making would inevitably be flawed and argued that Muhammad's cousin and son-in-law, Ali, should be the first rightful successor in what should continue to be a hereditary lineage. During his own life Muhammad tried to discourage sectarian divisions, following the commands of God as laid down in the Qur'an: 'As for those who divide their religion and break up into sects thou hast no part in them in the least: their affair is with God: He will in the end tell them the truth of all that they did.'[5] Nevertheless, the Prophet was unable to prevent this from happening to his own people and, tragically, the political nature of this split continues to echo today in the ongoing bloodshed between Sunnis and Shia in the tumultuous political landscape of the Middle East.

In the New Testament, the apostle Paul lays out a similar command, hoping to prevent sectarian divides amongst the Christian community:

> [S]hun foolish questionings, genealogies, strife, and disputes about the law; for they are unprofitable and vain. Avoid a factious man after a first and second warning, knowing that such a one is perverted and sins, being self-condemned.[6]

Today, Christianity is split into a variety of different sects. Indeed, many of the differences in belief and practice are relatively minor, but there are still some who continue to see their fellow Christians of other denominations as enemies. While wars and large-scale conflicts

[5]Qur'an, 6:159 (Yusuf Ali).

[6]Titus 3:9-11 (World English Bible).

between Christian sects are rarer today, historically, the emergence of sectarian divides has corresponded with some of the lengthiest and bloodiest wars of premodern and early modern European history. The first split in Christianity took place in 1054. Now known as the Great Schism, this event marked the division between Roman Catholicism and Eastern Orthodoxy. But serious intra-religious warfare between Christians did not erupt until many more years later, with the Reformation sparked by Martin Luther in 1517, which saw the rise of Protestantism as yet another split from the Catholic Church. Luther was reacting against the corruption in the Catholic Church with respect to the selling of 'indulgences' as tickets to salvation, as well as other such ostentatious practices. Overall, his belief was that people should not have to perform specific prescribed actions and deeds to achieve salvation. The movement was further facilitated by translations of the Bible that could be read more widely. In any case, what followed was a series of wars that lasted for over a hundred years, destroying millions of lives across the European continent, until the Peace of Westphalia in 1648 ended most of the violence. Though it began due to religious differences, it is generally agreed today that the warring was mostly a reaction to political power struggles, where religion was merely used as an identity-marker to draw divisions along these political lines. Francis Fukuyama, the famous author and currently a political scientist at Stanford University, explains:

> While Europe's religious wars were driven by economic and social factors, they derived their ferocity from the fact that the warring parties represented different Christian sects that wanted to impose their particular interpretation of religious doctrine on their populations.[7]

Considering the devastation of such wars, it is not surprising that voices of religious leaders since then have, by and large, decried the senselessness of sectarian conflicts. The Dalai Lama, for instance, very clearly stated, 'Sectarian feelings and criticism of other teachings or

[7]Francis Fukuyama, 'Liberalism and Its Discontents', *American Purpose,* 5 October 2020, https://www.americanpurpose.com/articles/liberalism-and-its-discontent/.

other sects is very bad, poisonous, and should be avoided.'[8] And the Baha'i leader 'Abdu'l-Bahá declared to his people:

> A new religious principle is that prejudice and fanaticism—whether sectarian, denominational, patriotic or political—are destructive to the foundation of human solidarity; therefore, man should release himself from such bonds in order that the oneness of the world of humanity may become manifest.[9]

Fukuyama explains how the European religious wars of the sixteenth and seventeenth centuries were the spark that led to the codification of the principles of political liberalism, as 'simply a pragmatic tool for resolving conflicts in diverse societies'.[10] There is no real reason why sectarian differences must boil over into violence and conflict, since we are all one species and there are common goals and values we all hold dear.

The problem is not the existence of sects per se, but our attitudes about the relationship between different intra-religious sects. When different sects coexist peacefully, they add a lot of value and richness to their respective religious tradition just as the diversity of different religions adds value to the overall shared human quest of meaning-making. The great Hindu monk, Swami Vivekananda, referencing the words of Krishna in the Bhagavad Gita, writes, 'The varieties of religious belief are an advantage, since all faiths are good, so far as they encourage us to lead a religious life. The more sects there are, the more opportunities there are for making a successful appeal to the divine instinct in all of us.'[11] Religions share the basic goal of transforming people's lives into a religious one where they are more loving towards others and constantly searching for the truth. But not everyone can meet these goals through

---

[8]Dalai Lama, *Dalai Lama: A Policy of Kindness*, ed. Sidney Piburn (Delhi: Motilal Banarsidass, 2002), 87.

[9]'Abdu'l-Bahá, *The Promulgation of Universal Peace*, Second Edition (US: Bahá'í Publishing Trust: 1982), 445, https://reference.bahai.org/en/t/ab/PUP/pup-134.html.

[10]Francis Fukuyama, 'Liberalism and Its Discontents,' *American Purpose*, 5 October 2020, https://www.americanpurpose.com/articles/liberalism-and-its-discontent/.

[11]Swami Vivekananda, *Complete Works of Swami Vivekananda*, Digitally published by Partha Sinha 27 November 2019, 1257.

the same path as we are all different and we all make meaning differently.

India has always been one of the most religiously pluralistic nations on earth. There are far too many sects of Hinduism to count, hundreds of thousands of Gods and Goddesses that people worship. Generally there are three main sects of Hinduism: (1) Vaishnavism, where the God Vishnu is worshipped through meditation, devotional practices and reading scriptures that recount the lives of Vishnu's incarnations on earth; (2) Shaivism, where the God Shiva is worshipped through extreme forms of asceticism (including yoga) to manifest the God within; (3) Shaktism, where several different Goddesses are worshipped as embodiments of 'shakti', the cosmic animating energy in the universe, cultivated through Tantric rituals. These divisions are not seen as competing or antagonistic, since all Hindus recognize the truth in all these deities and the validity of each other's different paths up the same mountain.

Similarly, Buddhism is split up into three main sects which, while disagreeing on certain issues, still share a lot in common and respect each other. They are (1) Theravada, the branch of Buddhism that focuses on the original teachings of the Buddha, and which today exists primarily in Sri Lanka and Southeast Asia; (2) Mahayana, which is a branch with a focus on teachings that emphasized the importance of helping others to achieve enlightenment, perceiving Theravada as concentrated on personal enlightenment alone. Mahayana is primarily found in east Asia and has therefore been infused with some influence from other east Asian religions like Taoism, Confucianism, Shintoism, etc.; and (3) Vajrayana Buddhism, with a big presence in Tibet and some parts of east Asia, is similar to the Shaktism branch of Hinduism as it emphasizes tantric rituals of cultivating cosmic energies and achieving enlightenment through the material world. These splits do not amount to total differences and are rarely a source of violence.

My own upbringing in India's pluralistic society illustrated this truth and gave me the space to participate in the religious and spiritual lives of others, treating every such interaction as an opportunity—to explore and learn from a spectrum of religions and sub-sects. I feel a shared spirit of generosity and intention whenever interacting with those who are different from me, and each interaction has led to something new and exciting in my life. I hope I can encourage others to pursue such opportunities.

We can still have debates and disagreements, but even these should be viewed as opportunities for mutual learning and growth. After all, we can only really have intelligent debates if both sides understand each other. This is what the Taoist sage Chuang Tzu is getting at in the following passage from his book:

> When the Way relies on little accomplishments and words rely on vain show, then we have the rights and wrongs of the Confucians and the Mohists. What one calls right the other calls wrong; what one calls wrong the other calls right.[12]

All too often we are bogged down by minute details and end up entirely dismissing the value of other beliefs. Luckily, though Taoism has manifested itself in many different sects and remains split into two main branches today, there is rarely any sectarian conflict or even much practical difference between them.

Even beyond the realm of religion itself, this problem of dismissing the value of certain wisdom systems and disciplines of knowledge remains a prevalent one. The Baha'i Universal House of Justice explains the severity of consequences that can arise from such a siloed approach to knowledge.

> The sundering of science and religion is but one example of the tendency of the human mind (which is necessarily limited in its capacity) to concentrate on one virtue, one aspect of truth, one goal, to the exclusion of others. This leads, in extreme cases, to fanaticism and the utter distortion of truth, and in all cases to some degree of imbalance and inaccuracy.[13]

The fanatical championing of one ideology over all others was a major theme behind the unprecedented violence throughout the twentieth century, and more human beings were killed by other humans in this

---

[12]*Zhuangzi: Basic Writings,* trans. Burton Watson (New York: Columbia University Press, 2003), 34.

[13]Baha'i Universal House of Justice, 'Scholarship, Bahá'í: Statements from the World Centre,' *Bahá'í Studies Review, Vol. 3, No. 2* (London: Association for Baha'i Studies of English-Speaking Europe, 1993), https://bahai-library.com/compilation_scholarship_bsr.

one century than all previous centuries put together. Most of this strife was not specifically motivated by religion, but propagated by extreme ideologies revolving around one 'virtue' or nationalistic or racial identity to the exclusion of others. The two world wars, the Holocaust, the gulags, the Armenian genocide, and the Indo-Pakistan conflicts are just a few examples of this. More recently, we have seen a proliferation of terrorist attacks and mass shootings that are motivated by religious and political extremism, fear and hatred of the 'other'. The antidote is to seek what connects us rather than what divides us—to see beyond divisions across race, religion, nation, class, gender, politics and so forth. As Confucius once said, 'By nature, men are nearly alike; by practice, they get to be wide apart.'[14] We all possess so many different facets of identity that it is wrong to divide humanity along any particular lines. We are all unique, and there is still so much that binds us as one human family. The Dalai Lama argues:

> From the moment of birth every human being wants happiness and does not want suffering. Neither social conditioning, nor education, nor ideology affect this. From the very core of our being, we simply desire contentment.[15]

Given our diversity as a species, it is inevitable that our opinions and beliefs would differ on all sorts of issues. The real tragedy is when those differences are hijacked and taken advantage of by those in positions of power. These people seek to promote discord for their own gain. Much damage has been caused within various religions by such individuals, but this damage can be undone if we remember that every sect of a given religious tradition is ultimately following the teachings of the same prophets, and that all sects of all religions are worshipping the same God, though in different ways. If we recognize this, then we will be on our way towards loving and learning more from one another.

---

[14] *Confucian Analects, The Great Learning, The Doctrine of the Mean*, trans. James Legge (Pantianos Classics, 2017), 17:2.

[15] His Holiness the Dalai Lama, *The Compassionate Life* (Boston: Wisdom Publications, 2003), 7.

45

Wholeness

Civilization is harmony and completeness. Reason, feeling, instinct, the life of the body.[1]

—Aldous Huxley

Religions are holistic systems that provide us with comprehensive worldviews and corresponding codes of conduct for how best to live in accordance with such views. As anthropologist Pascal Boyer writes, 'The particular panoply of techniques used varies a lot from one group to another, but there is generally no religion that is confined to one and only one kind of experience.'[2] It is not surprising that religions stress the importance of wholeness. Indeed, as scholar of religion Huston Smith notes, 'Seeing ourselves as belonging to the whole is what religion—religio, rebinding—is. It is mankind's fundamental thrust at unification.'[3] Understood in this way, it is no surprise that wholeness is truly a common theme across religions. We have learned through millennia of human observation, research, knowledge and wisdom—whether through science, religion or other

[1]Aldous Huxley, *Point Counter Point* (Champaign: Dalkey Archive Press, 1996), 103.
[2]Pascal Boyer, *Religion Explained: The Evolutionary Origins of Religious Thought* (New York: Basic Books, 2001), 317.
[3]Huston Smith, *The Illustrated World's Religions* (New York: HarperCollins, 1995), 248.

disciplines—that the natural state of the world is one of profound unity and interconnectedness. We simply have forgotten this in many ways and have severed some of our connections. Restoring wholeness is imperative in our world today. This goal is achievable if we work together, respecting each other's unique insights.

Towards this end, the great prophets and spiritual leaders across religions preach the importance of cultivating internal harmony. In contemporary language, we might refer to this as the mind-body-spirit connection. It is an ancient piece of wisdom that has been expressed in varying terms across traditions. In Christianity, for instance, the Holy Trinity corresponds to this trinity of human components: God, the father, who is the mind from which all creation was born; Jesus, the son, who is the bodily form of God on earth; and the Holy Ghost, who is the spirit of God dwelling in the hearts of the faithful. And in the Taoist Book of Lieh Tzu, a piece of literature from a very different tradition, the sage Kang-sen-tzu says:

> My body merges with mind, mind merges with energy, energy merges with spirit, spirit merges with nothingness. Whatever comes to me, the slightest existent, the faintest sound, be it far beyond the eight infinities, or as close as between eyebrow and eyelash, I invariably cognize it. But I don't know if this is the awareness of my seven apertures and four limbs, or the cognition of my heart, gut, and internal organs; it's just spontaneous knowing, that's all.[4]

This brings us to another common element within the theme of wholeness across religions: that we should bring every dimension of ourselves and all of our resources into everything that we do. This is common even in the honorific title given to Prophet Muhammad in the Muslim faith: 'al-Insān al-Kāmil', meaning the 'perfect' or 'complete' person. The notion of a 'complete' person also appears in the Analects of Confucius, who proposes, 'If he is mindful of what is right when he sees profit, is ready to lay down his life when faced with danger, and does not forget what he said as a youth about promises made

---

[4]*The Book of Master Lie*, trans. Thomas Cleary (2009), 792.

long ago, he can well be a complete man.'[5]

Confucius also placed great emphasis on learning as a key to completeness. He was particularly convinced that there is something to learn from everyone we meet. In the Jewish tradition, the rabbinic sage Ben Zoma remarked, 'Who is wise? He who learns from everyone.'[6]

There is, of course, a limit to what we can learn through solitary practices like reading and watching videos. Experiential learning is what makes us truly whole and is only possible through interactions with others. Poetically, astrophysicist Enrico Ramirez-Ruiz offers another cultural perspective on this all-important truth in life:

> I would like to end my talk by sharing a myth that is very close to my heart. A myth from the Chichimeca culture, which is a very powerful Mesoamerican culture. And the Chichimecas believe that our essence was assembled in the heavens. And on its journey towards us, it actually fragmented into tons of different pieces. So my abuelo used to say, 'One of the reasons you feel incomplete is because you are missing your pieces.' But don't be fooled by that. You've been given an incredible opportunity of growth. Why? Because it's not like those pieces were scattered on earth and you have to go and pick them up. No, those pieces fell into other people. And only by sharing them you will become more complete. Yes, during your life, there's going to be individuals that have these huge pieces that make you feel whole. But in your quest of being complete, you have to treasure and share every single one of those pieces.[7]

This is such a beautiful myth because it encourages us to look at each other as integral parts of our own selves and affirm that our interactions with others are the key to wholeness and contentment in life.

---

[5]Confucius, *The Analects*, trans. Annping Chin (New York: Penguin, 2014), 14:12.

[6]Rabbi Ben Zoma, 'Pirkei Avot,' 4:1, *My Jewish Learning*, accessed on 12 July 2022, https://www.myjewishlearning.com/article/pirkei-avot-ethics-of-the-fathers-chapter-4/.

[7]Enrico, Ramirez-Ruiz, 'Your Body Was Forged in the Spectacular Death of Stars,' *TED Talk*, November 2019, https://www.ted.com/talks/enrico_ramirez_ruiz_your_body_was_forged_in_the_spectacular_death_of_stars?language=en#t-40721.

In fact, there are many religious texts that invite us to view all of humanity as a single body. For instance, the Prophet Muhammad is purported to have said, 'The Muslims are like a single man. If the eye is afflicted, then the whole body is afflicted. If the head is afflicted, then the whole body is afflicted.'[8] Similarly, in the New Testament it is written, 'For even as we have many members in one body, and all the members don't have the same function, so we, who are many, are one body in Christ, and individually members of one another.'[9] Not only is the basic welfare of a community dependent on that of each individual, but—as with Ramirez-Ruiz's Mesoamerican myth—each member is viewed as serving its own unique and integral function. The Taoist sage Chuang Tzu remarks, 'The sage gets through to the intertwining of things, so that everything forms a single body around him, but without knowing it to be "right". For this is his inborn nature.'[10] The ultimate sign of respecting diversity is not just a tolerance of difference, but rather an integration of different perspectives into a larger whole, bound by a common human essence, that everyone can take part in and benefit from.

One more example of this 'one body' metaphor comes from the Baha'i Prophet Bahá'u'lláh, who wrote to his followers: 'Be ye as the fingers of one hand, the members of one body.'[11] His son 'Abdu'l-Bahá, pleaded that humanity, 'must bring to an end the benighted prejudices of all nations and religions and must make known to every member of the human race that all are the leaves of one branch, the fruits of one bough.'[12] This latter imagery is reminiscent of the Hindu notion that each individual is like 'a drop of water' or 'the crest of a wave in the ocean of Brahman'. Though we experience ourselves as entirely separate from one another, we are in fact unified at a much deeper level. Furthermore, the implication of this

---

[8]Ṣaḥīḥ Muslim, Hadith 2586.

[9]Romans, 12:4-5 (World English Bible).

[10]*Zhuangzi: The Essential Writings,* trans. Brook Ziporyn (Indianapolis: Hackett Publishing, 2009), 108.

[11] Bahá'u'lláh, *Proclamation of Bahá'u'lláh* (US: Bahá'í Publishing Trust, 1978 reprint), 118, Baha'i Reference Library. https://reference.bahai.org/en/t/b/PB/pb-62.html.

[12]'Abdu'l-Bahá, *Selections From the Writings of 'Abdu'l-Bahá* (Bahá'í World Centre, 1982), 277, Baha'i Reference Library, http://reference.bahai.org/en/t/ab/SAB/sab-145.html.

Hindu belief is that wholeness lies within, as the composition of each droplet of water is roughly identical to the ocean as a whole. So too do we all share the same fundamental essence: atman. The following allegory from the Upanishads attempts to further illustrate this.

> Now, take the bees, son. They prepare the honey by gathering nectar from a variety of trees and by reducing that nectar to a homogenous whole. In that state the nectar from each different tree is not able to differentiate: 'I am the nectar of that tree', and 'I am the nectar of this tree'. In exactly the same way, son, when all these creatures merge into the existent, they are not aware that 'We are merging into the existent'. No matter what they are in this world—whether it is a tiger, a lion, a wolf, a boar, a worm, a moth, a gnat, or a mosquito—they all merge into that. The finest essence here—that constitutes the self of this whole world; that is the truth; that is the self (atman). And that's how you are, Svetaketu.[13]

The divisions that we draw between ourselves and others may therefore be much more arbitrary than we assume them to be. We are truly part of an integrated whole, a single body. As Deepak Chopra writes:

> You cannot make yourself whole, because you are already whole. You are merged into the stream of life, and everything that happens in collective consciousness includes you. This is why it is important to identify with a higher consciousness, in order to realize that there is a field of infinite possibilities from which you draw life, love, imagination, creativity, and personal growth. In wholeness you are constantly renewed, because the field of infinite possibilities has something new to offer you every day, if you are open, alert, and ready to receive.[14]

---

[13]'Chandogya Upanisad' 6.9:1-4 in *Upanisads*, trans. Patrick Olivelle, Oxford World's Classics edition (London: Oxford University Press, 1996).

[14]Deepak Chopra, 'How To Experience Renewal,' 5 April 2021, *DeepakChopra*, https://www.deepakchopra.com/articles/how-to-experience-renewal/

46

Focus on the World Within

Reality exists in the human mind, and nowhere else.[1]

—George Orwell

Whether we are praying, meditating, or simply dwelling on life's greatest mysteries, much of our spiritual lives take place in solitude. Some of our greatest mysteries begin in solitude; we ask, why are we conscious and self-aware, and even, what is consciousness? Do we have souls that persist beyond death? Religions have much to say about such questions on a philosophical and theological level. But religions also speak on a practical level about how the state of our inner world affects our worldview and behaviour. They provide us with resources to exert control over our minds, to clear out the cobwebs within that prevent us from flourishing.

Many religions point towards the presence of God within us, as a living presence. It defines our relationship with God. In the New Testament, it is repeatedly made clear that, 'Don't you know that you are a temple of God, and that God's Spirit lives in you?' [2] and that it would be foolish to say, '"Look, here!" or, "Look, there!" for behold, God's

[1]George Orwell, *1984* (Kowloon: Enrich Spot, 2016), 283.

[2]1 Corinthians 3:16 (World English Bible).

Kingdom is within you.'[3] The sense of awe we feel when apprehending the beauty of nature, our intuitive sense that there must be some purpose for our existence, the compulsion we feel to love one another and treat each other well—all of these things can be interpreted as the influence of the God within us.

Philosophers and theologians from many other religions have similar feelings about locating God within us. Hindus refer to this concept as 'Paramatman', the supreme part of our innermost self that contains the ultimate reality. Hence, the well-known phrase, 'Namaste', is a greeting that means, 'I bow to the God inside you'. The great Hindu monk and philosopher Swami Vivekananda said something similar: 'All that is real in me is He; all that is real in Him is I. The gulf between God and man is thus bridged. Thus we find how, by knowing God, we find the kingdom of heaven within us.'[4] Likewise, the mystic poet Kabir—whose writings are celebrated by Hindus, Muslims and Sikhs alike—composed a couplet expressing this same idea:

> Not in temple, nor in mosque, not in Kaaba,
> nor Kailas, but here right within you am I.[5]

In other words, we do not need to go to a physical location, like a temple or a mosque, in order to find God because God is always within us. Such locations might help to facilitate the inner exploration that is needed to establish a relationship with God, but their material walls do not hold God.

It is often said, across religions, that the nature of God is love. For God to be within us means that love, too, is an inherent capacity we all possess. We are naturally inclined towards love, even if we don't always see that to be the case in the world.

In order to get in touch with our true nature, we must learn to be alone with ourselves, we must truly listen to the truth within us rather than the truths we have simply inherited from society. According to

---

[3]Luke 17:21 (World English Bible).

[4]Swami Vivekananda, *Complete Works of Swami Vivekananda*, e-book (digitally published by Partha Sinha, 27 November 2019), 179,

[5]Kabir in Eknath Easwaran, *The Bhagavad Gita for Daily Living: A Verse-by-Verse Commentary: Vols 1–3* (Tomales: Nilgiri Press, 2020).

social psychologist Erich Fromm, this is how we cleanse ourselves of the barriers to love.

> The most important step in learning concentration is to learn to be alone with oneself without reading, listening to the radio, smoking or drinking. Indeed, to be able to concentrate means to be able to be alone with oneself—and this ability is precisely a condition for the ability to love.[6]

The technological advancements of our modern world are impressive displays of human ingenuity, and there is nothing inherently wrong with taking some time to indulge in entertaining ourselves. But many of us today spend so much of our time absorbed in escapist activities that we have lost the ability to be content without these things. It can be surprisingly difficult to meditate for even five minutes, for instance, but without this capacity for fixed and focused attention, it is impossible to truly love ourselves and others. Meditation is necessary if we want to stop the chattering of our minds and allow travel within.

The ability to find contentment in the solitude of our own inner worlds is also instrumental to flourishing and achieving fulfillment in our lives. Some of the wisest prophets, philosophers and sages throughout history have consistently made this the backbone of their teachings. Buddhism, for instance, teaches us that the root cause of our suffering is our many desires, which is why the Dalai Lama has said that, 'Human happiness and human satisfaction must ultimately come from within oneself. It is wrong to expect some final satisfaction to come from money or from a computer.'[7] Similarly, the ancient Greek school of philosophy, Stoicism was centreed around finding contentment in what *is* rather than how we think things should be. One of the most famous Stoic philosophers, Seneca, expressed this by saying, 'The greatest blessings of mankind are within us and within our reach. A wise man is content with his lot, whatever it may be, without wishing

---

[6]Erich Fromm, *The Art of Loving*, Fiftieth Anniversary Edition (New York: HarperCollins, 2006), 103.

[7]His Holiness the Dalai Lama, 'Feb 2,' *The Path to Tranquility: Daily Wisdom*, ed. Renuka Singh (New York: Penguin, 2002), 38.

for what he has not.'[8] Even in the Chinese religious tradition of Taoism, one of the foundational guiding principles is an emphasis on simplicity in life. The Taoist sage Chuang Tzu wrote, 'One who understands the great completeness seeks nothing, loses nothing, abandons nothing, never letting mere beings alter who he is. He returns only to his own self, yet he finds it inexhaustible.'[9]

From these examples, it seems as though religion has been consistent on this theme across time and place. Religions have attempted to help guide people towards finding contentment in life from within. Thus, the Buddha declared that, 'Avoid all evil, cultivate the good, purify your mind: this sums up the teaching of the Buddhas.'[10]

Eastern religions have always touted the benefits of contemplative practices, like meditation, which can help us understand and exert more control over our minds, thus allowing us to reach the authentic self within. The Bhagavad Gita, for instance, narrates the benefits of meditation.

> Renouncing wholeheartedly all selfish desires and expectations, use your will to control the senses. Little by little, through patience and repeated effort, the mind will become stilled in the Self. Wherever the mind wanders, restless and diffuse in its search for satisfaction without, lead it within; train it to rest in the Self. Abiding joy comes to those who till the mind. Freeing themselves from the taint of self-will, with their consciousness unified, they become one with Brahman.[11]

Meditation helps us discern and diminish the inflated influence that our socialized egotistic selves have over our thoughts and behaviours, thereby allowing us to see the world more inclusively, i.e., allowing us to see beyond the illusion of being a separate individual among other separate individuals.

---

[8]Lucius Annaeus Seneca, *Seneca's Morals of a Happy Life, Benefits, Anger And Clemency,* trans. Sir Roger L'estrange (Chicago: Belford, Clarke & Co., 1882), 126.

[9]*Zhuangzi: The Essential Writings,* trans. Brook Ziporyn (Indianapolis: Hackett Publishing, 2009), 105.

[10]*The Dhammapada,* trans. Eknath Easwaran, Second Edition (Tomales: Nilgiri Press, 2007),183.

[11]*The Bhagavad Gita,* trans. Eknath Easwaran, Second Edition (Tomales: Nilgiri Press, 2007), 6:24-27.

The saints, mystics and monks of India have passed down these insights for thousands of years, asking and answering questions about the nature of reality and our minds. As Indian author and translator Eknath Easwaran explains,

> Since consciousness is the field of all human activity, outward as well as inner—experience, action, imagination, knowledge, love—a science of consciousness holds out the promise of central principles that unify all of life. 'By knowing one piece of gold,' the Upanishads observed, 'all things made out of gold are known: they differ only in name and form, while the stuff of which all are made is gold.' And they asked, 'What is that one by knowing which we can know the nature of everything else?' They found the answer in consciousness. Its study was called brahmavidya, which means both 'the supreme science' and 'the science of the Supreme'.[12]

As we get more in touch with the depths of our inner world, we come to perceive the profound interconnectedness of the world outside us. In fact, because our lives are so interdependent on one another, we can learn a lot about our interior worlds from our external interactions with others, which is why Confucius advised, 'When we see men of worth, we should think of equaling them; when we see men of a contrary character, we should turn inwards and examine ourselves.'[13] Swami Vivekananda also stressed the supremacy of inward knowledge acquisition, noting that, 'the infinite library of the universe is in your own mind. The external world is simply the suggestion, the occasion, which sets you to studying your own mind; but the object of your study is always your own mind.'[14] According to this reasoning, when you imagine or consider an idea, you are actually searching within yourself, almost like tapping into a database that holds all the knowledge about

---

[12]Eknath Easwaran, 'Introduction' in *The Upanishads*, trans. Eknath Easwaran (Berkeley: Nilgiri Press, 2007), 25-26.

[13]*Confucian Analects, The Great Learning, The Doctrine of the Mean*, trans. James Jegge (Pantianos Classics, 2017), 4:17.

[14]Swami Vivekananda, *Karma-Yoga and Bhakti-Yoga*, Revised edition (New York: Ramakrishna-Vivekananda Center, 1955), 3.

the universe. The time we spend studying our minds through more solitary practices allow us to strengthen the neurological structures that increase access to this knowledge. We all have the same potential for accessing knowledge, but we differ when it comes to how we actualize this potential and which parts of this database we access; this is why different individuals and religions make meaning differently.

That all knowledge, and even the entire universe, could be stored in the mind is a bold claim! However, this claim has been echoed across many religions, and even supported by secular thinkers, like psychologists, scientists and philosophers. As one example, Zen Buddhist master Shunryu Suzuki went so far as to say that this concept is the heart of religion itself: 'That everything is included within your mind is the essence of mind. To experience this is to have religious feeling. [...] Big mind and small mind are one.'[15] The religious emphasis on inner focus is not about escaping from the outside world—on the contrary, it is about fostering a deeper connection between the two to see how our perceived boundaries between them are actually more fluid than we think. This is what it means for a 'big' and a 'small' mind to be one.

Another religious thinker who spoke of the all-encompassing nature of the mind is the Baha'i leader 'Abdu'l-Bahá, who pointed towards humanity's scientific achievements as evidence of how special and full of potential our inner world is.

> This other and inner reality is called the heavenly body, the ethereal form which corresponds to this body. This is the conscious reality which discovers the inner meaning of things, for the outer body of man does not discover anything. The inner ethereal reality grasps the mysteries of existence, discovers scientific truths and indicates their technical application.[16]

From the perspective of a modern-day scientist, the biologist E.O. Wilson elaborates on the significance and the implications of the mind as the source of all knowledge:

---

[15]Shunryu Suzuki, *Zen Mind, Beginner's Mind* (Boston: Shambhala, 2011), 19.

[16]'Abdu'l-Bahá, *Foundations of World Unity*, sixth printing (US Bahá'í Publishing Trust, 1979), 109; Baha'i Reference Library: http://reference.bahai.org/en/t/c/FWU/fwu-29.html

> All that is or could ever be known is experience, and all experience is known in the form of mind. Therefore, to know the nature or ultimate reality of anything that is known, it is first necessary to know the nature of mind. Genes make the brain, minds make reality. Until the mind knows its own essential nature, it cannot be sure that anything it knows or experiences is absolutely true rather than simply a reflection of its own limitations. Everything that we know and can ever know about existence is created there (in the mind).[17]

Neuroscience has certainly been helping us learn a lot about the roles of our brains and consciousness when it comes to how we perceive and experience the world around us. The main lesson from the science is that we do not experience external reality itself, only our own nervous system along with whatever cultural biases we inherited. As cognitive anthropologist Pascal Boyer writes:

> Our minds are prepared because natural selection gave us particular mental predispositions. Being prepared for some concepts, human minds are also prepared for certain variations of these concepts.[18]

Neuroscience, therefore, sheds some light both on why religions share so many common themes as well as why they exhibit so many variations within these themes. As a single species, we share the same structure of our minds and hence we are all hardwired to ask certain questions and find the same kinds of questions compelling and important, but each culture does so in its own way.

All cultures and religions provide resources for thinking about the mind and focusing on the world within, but it is important to remember that even these ideas are filtered through the individual and collective parts of the mind. We should each practice whatever form of self-inquiry makes the most sense for us, but we should also recognize that others might have very different methods of self-inquiry based on their own

---

[17]E.O. Wilson, *Consilience: The Unity of Knowledge* (Knopf Doubleday Publishing Group), 105.

[18]Pascal Boyer, *Religion Explained: The Evolutionary Origins of Religious Thought* (New York: Basic Books, 2001), 3.

conceptions of how the mind works. As the famous line from John Milton's *Paradise Lost* goes, 'The mind is its own place, and in itself can make a heaven of hell, a hell of heaven.'[19]

[19]John Milton, *Paradise Lost* (London: Oxford University Press, 2005), 24.

47

Life's Illusions

If speech is sweet, the echo will be sweet; if speech is harsh, the echo will be harsh. If the body is long, the shadow will be long; if the body is short, the shadow will be short.[1]

—Lieh Tzu

It is a scientific fact that our lives are defined by illusions of all sorts. Some stem from our limited cognitive capacities, which are simply not designed to allow us to grasp the fullness of reality. On one end of the spectrum, Newtonian physics suggests that 99.9999999 per cent of what we experience as solid matter is actually empty space. On the other end, astronomers have estimated that there could be up to an estimated 10^{24} stars in the universe! The scales of these numbers are completely unfathomable to us; not to mention the fact that our naked eyes can only see stars as tiny little glimmers of light, despite the fact that some of them can be more than 1500 times the size of our sun. And the sun itself is large enough to contain one million earth-sized objects! Even time and space themselves are illusions, at least in the way that we experience them. Truly, our entire experience of the world can be said to be one big illusion, filtered through the relatively narrow limits of our brains.

[1] *Taoist Teachings*, trans. Lionel Giles, (Ashland, Ohio: Library of Alexandria, 2009), 81.

But perhaps the most insidious human illusion that we seem cognitively predisposed towards is the illusion we each grow up with (and hopefully eventually grow out of): that we are the centre of the universe rather than just a single node on a deeply interconnected web. As psychologist Rick Hanson describes, 'The effort to maintain separations is at odds with the myriad ways you're actually connected with the world and dependent upon it. As a result, you may feel subtly isolated, alienated, overwhelmed, or as if you're in a struggle with the world.'[2] Religious teachers and scriptures have, therefore, taken this illusion seriously not just because it promotes obvious selfishness—greed at the individual level and xenophobia at the collective level—but also because it can be personally distressing and a major source of unnecessary suffering.

Religions claim that most of us go through life enshrouded by an illusory veil of which we are blissfully unaware. One of the clearest and most well-known illustrations of this is the Hindu concept of 'maya', which is described by scholar of religion Huston Smith:

> Maya comes from the same root as magic. In saying the world is maya, non-dual Hinduism is saying that there is something tricky about it. The trick lies in the way the world's materiality and multiplicity pass themselves off as being independently real—real apart from the stance from which we see them—whereas in fact reality is undifferentiated Brahman throughout, in the way a rope lying in the dust remains a rope while being mistaken for a snake.[3]

Often, people unfamiliar with this concept have a hard time making sense of it. Across religions, statements about the illusory nature of the world are misinterpreted and taken to mean that the universe itself is entirely unreal and does not exist. But as Smith points out, there is a real world—in his analogy, like a rope. The world is real, just as the rope is real, but we experience it as something other than what it truly is, just as we might mistake a rope for a snake if it is obscured by a layer of dust. This is a result of our brain's evolutionary natural

---

[2]Rick Hanson, *Buddha's Brain: The Practical Neuroscience of Happiness, Love, and Wisdom* (Oakland, California: New Harbinger Publications, 2009), 47.

[3]Huston Smith, *The Illustrated World's Religions* (New York: HarperCollins, 1995), 53.

inclination to make quick judgements, like taking the cautious approach of assuming the rope to be a snake surely is a good adaptation for survival! And this is just one very small example. The world around us is infinitely complex and our brains have developed to translate that complexity into simplified models that are easier to process efficiently.

In Judaism, there is a parallel concept to maya in the form of the 'olam', which can simply mean the 'world', but it is etymologically also related to the words 'hidden' or 'hide'. Theologically, this has been interpreted to mean that the world itself is like a veil behind which God dwells, hidden from us, in much the same way that Hindus believe that Brahman—the ultimate reality, or God—is hidden behind the veil of maya, the sensory material world.[4] Related to this is the idea of 'tikkun olam', which represents the duty of repairing or re-establishing the world in a way that is more reflective of God's will and laws, which includes facilitating social justice and making sure that the well-being of other individuals and society as a whole is taken care of. It also necessitates turning away from idolatry, or resisting the distractions and temptations of worshipping worldly things like money and fame rather than worshipping God. In this sense, the veil of illusion is one that is strengthened primarily through selfishness.

Collectively, as a species, we have managed to overcome the illusion that the earth is the centre of the universe and that the sun and all other planets revolve around it. In Christianity, Jesus's teachings are heavily focused on helping people overcome the illusion of selfishness. James, one of his first disciples, urges people to consider such questions as 'Where do wars and fightings among you come from? Don't they come from your pleasures that war in your members?'[5] and 'Whereas you don't know what your life will be like tomorrow. For what is your life? For you are a vapor that appears for a little time, and then vanishes away.'[6] We tend to go through each day under the illusion that we are enduring creatures and we will not die; we believe that somehow the world itself

[4]'Olam', *The Jewish Chronicle*, 24 November 2016, https://www.thejc.com/judaism/jewish-words/olam-1.8049.

[5]James 4:1 (World English Bible).

[6]James 4:14 (World English Bible).

will forever remain suspended in our current period of history because we are the main characters in the story of our world. But of course, we all do die and the world goes on without us afterwards.

Indeed, one of the root causes of our illusory perception of the world that all religions point towards is our inability to accept that the very nature of existence is change. As Zen master Shunryu Suzuki writes:

> The basic teaching of Buddhism is the teaching of transiency, or change. [...] This teaching is also understood as the teaching of selflessness. Because each existence is in constant change, there is no abiding self. In fact, the self-nature of each existence is nothing but change itself, the self-nature of all existence.[7]

Buddhism certainly represents the most extreme expression of this principle. Buddhists believe that existence is so fundamentally characterized by change that not only is there no abiding self, but there is no abiding anything, and no eternal unchanging core of reality. This concept is one of the main ways that Buddhism differentiated its beliefs from Hinduism, which teaches that 'beyond this unmanifest nature is another unmanifest state, a primal existence that is not destroyed when all things dissolve'.[8]

Interestingly, even Jesus may have taught something similar, as is suggested by the Gospel of Thomas, a non-canonical ancient Christian text recently uncovered in the 1940s as part of the Nag Hammadi Library. As scholar Elaine H. Pagels described, this Gospel teaches, 'Everything that is experienced physically and through sense perception, everything in this world that you can perceive in this way is nothing. It is, at best, chaos and, at worst, it doesn't even exist in reality. The only thing that really exists is your divine spirit or your divine soul, which is identical in its quality with God himself.'[9]

Not all religions go so far as to reject the existence of all that we experience, but all religions do agree that retaining a warped understanding of the nature of self or the nature of reality is bound to

---

[7]Shunryu Suzuki, *Zen Mind, Beginner's Mind* (Boston: Shambhala, 2011), 91.

[8]*The Bhagavad Gita,* trans. Stephen Mitchell (New York: Harmony Books, 2000), 8:20.

[9]Elaine H. Pagels, 'The Gospel of Thomas,' *PBS Frontline*, April 1998, https://www.pbs.org/wgbh/pages/frontline/shows/religion/story/thomas.html.

prevent us from finding happiness and flourishing in our lives. In the Qur'an, for instance, we are taught that, 'Know ye (all), that the life of this world is but play and amusement, pomp and mutual boasting and multiplying, (in rivalry) among yourselves, riches and children [...] and what is the life of this world, but goods and chattels of deception?'[10] Even if we are unable to fully perceive the true ultimate reality, we can see that the social world we exist in, one that is driven by material pursuits, is an artificial one and can offer us no lasting fulfilment. Often what we think will bring us happiness turns out to feel hollow once it is attained, just as the Baha'i Prophet Bahá'u'lláh points out:

> [T]he world is like the vapor in a desert, which the thirsty dreameth to be water and striveth after it with all his might, until when he cometh unto it, he findeth it to be mere illusion.[11]

The great prophets and scriptures across religions urge us to reflect upon examples from our own lives where we have experienced the feeling of grasping at an illusion. Once we admit to and understand the veil that hangs before us, we can start to lift it away.

Religions and other wisdom traditions therefore define wisdom not by the amount of knowledge someone has accumulated, but by how perceptive they are of their own illusions, biases and ignorance. Socrates, for instance, is hailed as the father of all Western philosophy and even Western civilization itself, and yet he himself claimed he knew nothing and had nothing to teach. His wisdom becomes apparent, however, in how skilfully he was able to guide others towards recognizing their own ignorance and identifying as illusions what were previously taken to be facts. The essence of this principle was captured poetically by William Shakespeare, who wrote, 'The fool doth think he is wise, but the wise man knows himself to be a fool.'[12] There are close parallels to this in the

---

[10]Qur'an, 57:20 (Yusuf Ali).

[11]Bahá'u'lláh, *Gleanings From the Writings of Bahá'u'lláh* (US: Bahá'í Publishing Trust, 1990), 328, Baha'i Reference Library, http://reference.bahai.org/en/t/b/GWB/gwb-110.html.

[12]William Shakespeare, *As You Like It*, ed. Samuel Thurber, Jr. and Louise Wetherbee (Boston: Allyn and Bacon, 1922), *Shakespeare Online*, 10 August 2010, http://www.shakespeare-online.com/plays/asu_5_1.html.

religious traditions of very different cultures as well. In Chinese religious history, for instance, Confucius taught, 'To say you know when you know, and to say you do not when you do not, that is knowledge,'[13] and the Taoist sage Chuang Tzu wrote, 'The one who knows he is stupid is not that stupid; the one who knows he is confused is not that confused.'[14] The Confucian classics have functioned as the bedrock of the Chinese educational system for thousands of years, and the model for the Western university system is similarly based on the Socratic method of teaching and learning through dialogue.

Through investing their excess psychic energy into contemplative exercises like meditation and prayer, prophets and other spiritual teachers claim to have transcended the biases of the mind, allowing them to experience the world through a purer state of consciousness, free of prejudice. Neuroscientists and others who study the brain and mind through a more secular lens have come to similar conclusions: that overcoming illusions that arise from within involves a constant state of vigilance. For instance, psychologist Mihaly Csikszentmihaly writes that, 'One must painstakingly match one's preconceptions against actual, ongoing experience to begin separating truth from illusion [...] These distortions are "inside" each one of us—no human being is immune to the illusions they foster.'[15] Fields like psychology and neuroscience have uncovered many different biases and illusions, which our brains are prone to fall for. Two common cognitive biases, for instance, are confirmation bias, the tendency for us to filter our experience of the world through the lens of things we already believe in, ignoring information that contradicts those preconceptions, and recency bias, the tendency to interpret our experiences disproportionately in relation to the most recently acquired knowledge and events in our lives.

Similarly, there are many different kinds of illusions that reveal the limits and flaws in all dimensions of our sensory capacities. The Müller-

---

[13]Confucius, *The Analects*, trans. D.C. Lau, Penguin Classics edition (London, England: Penguin Books, 1971), 2:17.

[14]*The Book of Chuang Tzu*, trans. Martin Palmer, Penguin Classics edition (New York: Penguin Books, 2006), 103.

[15]Mihaly Csikszentmihaly, *The Evolving Self: a Psychology For the Third Millennium* (New York: Harper Perennial, 1994), 63.

Lyer illusion is the well-known optical illusion in which two lines of equal length appear unequal because they are each capped at the ends by arrows pointing in different directions. The one with outward-pointing arrows appears longer, even though the lines themselves are of the same length. But there are also cognitive illusions tied to other senses, like the phantom-limb phenomenon, where most amputees report that they can still 'feel' their missing limb, sometimes for as long as several years after its removal!

All religions recognize that we are psychologically, and even physically prone, to many biases and illusions, but they want us to still see life as meaningful. The reason religious scriptures, prophets and other features of wisdom traditions have left such an indelible mark on human history is because their approaches to knowledge and wisdom have proven to be effective in helping others overcome illusions. It is all too easy for us to go through life under the spell of the illusion that our way of experiencing the world is the only and true way. But when we do this, we often are unable to respect and love those who differ from us as equals. What the great sages and prophets throughout history and across religions have always done is to call into question many of the assumptions of their respective cultures, and have shown others the illusory nature of these assumptions.

48

Dreams

The whole life is a succession of dreams. My ambition is to be a conscious dreamer, that is all.[1]

—Swami Vivekananda

Dream is the personalized myth, myth the depersonalized dream; both myth and dream are symbolic in the same general way of the dynamics of the psyche. But in the dream the forms are quirked by the peculiar troubles of the dreamer, whereas in myth the problems and solutions shown are directly valid for all mankind.[2]

—Joseph Campbell

In the scriptures of the Abrahamic traditions, there are many instances of God communicating to people on earth by way of messages encoded in the dreams of prophets. This is expressed in the Hebrew Bible: 'Now hear my words. If there is a prophet among you, I, Yahweh, will make myself known to him in a vision. I will

[1]Swami Vivekananda, 'Epistles,' in *Complete Works of Swami Vivekananda*, Digitally published by Partha Sinha, 27 November 2019, 1140.

[2]Joseph Campbell, *The Hero with a Thousand Faces*, 3rd edition, The Collected Works of Joseph Campbell Series edition (Novato, CA: New World Library, 2008), 14.

speak with him in a dream.'[3] Probably the most famous and extensive instance of this in the Hebrew Bible comes to Joseph, the simple shepherd whose interpretation of dreams proves to be so prophetic that the Egyptian Pharaoh eventually grants him enormous power over his kingdom: 'Pharaoh said to Joseph, "Because God has shown you all of this, there is no one so discreet and wise as you. You shall be over my house. All my people will be ruled according to your word. Only in the throne I will be greater than you."'[4] This fulfils the symbol-laden predictions from Joseph's own dreams that his brothers would one day come to bow down to him. Joseph's God-endowed gift to interpret dreams not only saved him from being enslaved in Egypt, but also enabled him to save the Egyptian people from several years of impending famine. In the New Testament, meanwhile, God imparts dreams to prophets in order to spread the message of spiritual salvation: 'A vision appeared to Paul in the night. There was a man of Macedonia standing, begging him, and saying, 'Come over into Macedonia and help us.' When he had seen the vision, immediately we sought to go out to Macedonia, concluding that the Lord had called us to preach the Good News to them.'[5] In the Abrahamic traditions at least, dreams are God's way of transmitting knowledge and giving commands that are usually meant to help people in some way.

One question this raises, however, is how to know which dreams are actually from God. The Baha'i prophet 'Abdu'l-Bahá wrote, 'As to truthful dreams: I beg of God that thy inner eye (insight) may be so opened that thou mayest thyself differentiate between truthful and untruthful dreams.'[6] And the Islamic Hadith records report several statements from the Prophet Muhammad on the subject; for instance, 'A good vision (ru'ya) is from Allāh and a bad dream (hulm) is from Satan; so if one of you sees anything (in a dream which he dislikes), he should spit on his left side thrice and seek refuge with Allāh from its evil, and then it will

[3]Numbers, 12:6 (World English Bible).

[4]Genesis, 41:39-40 (World English Bible).

[5]Acts 16:9-10 (World English Bible).

[6]'Abdu'l-Bahá, *Tablets of Abdul-Baha Abbas* (Bahá'í Publishing Committee, 1909 edition), 196, Baha'i Reference Library, https://reference.bahai.org/en/t/ab/TAB/tab-240.html., 6

never harm him,'[7] and 'Whoever sees me (in a dream) then he indeed has seen the truth, as Satan cannot appear in my shape.'[8] These may not be perfect criteria for evaluation, as they still leave some room for subjective judgement and interpretation, but the general point for our purposes is that these quotes demonstrate awareness of a very important question that runs through the dreams across religions: how real are our dreams and how can we know when to trust them?

This aspect of assessing the reality of dreams is not confined simply to the question of whether or not dreams come from God, nor is it confined to the Western Abrahamic traditions. In the Shribhashya, a Hindu text, the focus is on picking apart the elements of dreams to show that dreams are partly real and partly unreal: 'For it is not true that the perceptions in a dream are unreal. It is only the objects that are contradicted (by the perceptions of the waking state), not the perceptions.'[9] The difference between the particular objects of dreams and the subjective experience of perceiving these objects—the former may be completely nonsensical and therefore not real, but the perception itself surely is. Scholar of religion Huston Smith puts this into its context in the Hindu belief system:

> If we ask if dreams are real, our answer must be qualified. They are real in that we have them, but most of their images do not exist in the real—i.e., waking—world. Strictly speaking, a dream is a psychological construct, a mental fabrication. The Hindus have something like this in mind when they characterize the world as maya.[10]

In other words, the larger and more interesting question is not just, 'how real are dreams', but rather, 'how real is the waking world?' After all, isn't our experience of the world around us psychologically mediated? How do we know that the human way of perceiving the world corresponds to the way the world really is?

Many other scriptures and sages across religions have called into

---

[7]Sahih al-Bukhari, Hadith 3118.

[8]Sahih al-Bukhari, Hadith 6997.

[9]Wendy Doniger, *Hinduism, The Norton Anthology of World Religions: Vol. 1*, Ed. Jack Miles (New York: W.W. Norton & Company, 2015), 300.

[10]Huston Smith, *The Illustrated World's Religions* (New York: HarperCollins, 1995), 53.

question this assumption most of us have that the waking world as we experience it is the *real* world. The Taoist sages Lieh Tzu and Chuang Tzu, for instance, explain how blurry the lines could be between dreaming and waking life, and they even urge us to consider the possibility that the dreaming world may in fact be closer to reality than the waking world!

> Are events in our waking life more real than dreams? To people who sleep all the time, dreams are more real than waking life. However, to those who divide their time equally between waking and sleeping, experiences in their waking life are real, and events in dreams are unreal [...] What then is the difference between waking and dreaming?[11]

Chuang Tzu illustrates this existential question through a now-famous concrete and humorous anecdote.

> Once Zhuang Zhou dreamt he was a butterfly, a butterfly fluttering around, happy with himself and doing as he pleased. He didn't know he was Zhuang Zhou. Suddenly he woke up and there he was, solid and unmistakable Zhuang Zhou. But he didn't know if he was Zhuang Zhou who had dreamt he was a butterfly, or a butterfly dreaming he was Zhuang Zhou.[12]

Most of us can probably relate quite directly to this characterization of the experience of dreaming and the profound sense of mystery therein. Few of us in the waking world would entertain the idea that we could be something other than our familiar selves, but then again, few of us dream lucidly enough to be aware in the dreaming world of our waking selves. What conclusions are we to draw from this? Chuang Tzu leaves this as an open question and invites us to dwell in the mystery and not rush into a final answer merely based on our socialized assumptions.

There is a very similar story in Indian literature about the Hindu king

---

[11]*Lieh-tzu: A Taoist Guide to Practical Living,* trans. Eva Wong (Boston: Shambhala, 2001), 92.

[12]*Zhuangzi: Basic Writings,* trans. Burton Watson (New York: Columbia University Press, 2003), 44.

Janaka, who had a dream that he was a beggar and came to question, 'Am I a beggar dreaming myself to be a king or Am I a king dreaming myself to be a beggar? What is real? This or that?' The Vedic sage Ashtavakra explains to him, 'Neither this is real nor that, O king. The self that illumines both, alone is real. The one that remains awake, and is witness to both, your dream and your wakefulness, is real.'[13] The legend goes that Janaka became a truly enlightened and benevolent ruler for the rest of his reign because he came to see the emptiness in distinctions between social class and recognized his obligation to rule well and justly, treating everyone equally.

In fact, one of the primary goals of many religious traditions is to get us to 'wake up' from our dreamlike experience of the world. Again, Chuang Tzu writes, 'Only after he wakes does he know it was a dream. And someday there will be a great awakening when we know that this is all a great dream. Yet the stupid believe they are awake, busily and brightly assuming they understand things, calling this man ruler, that one herdsman—how dense!'[14] We like to believe that we are born automatically equipped to perceive reality as it truly is, but it is the contention of many religious traditions that this is not the case. Most of us have experienced glimpses of this throughout our lives. As Swami Vivekananda once remarked, 'Blows are what awaken us and help to break the dream. They show us the insufficiency of this world and make us long to escape, to have freedom.'[15] Shocking events and sudden tragedies in our personal lives can momentarily snap us out of the autopilot mode that governs our lives most of the time. But it is when we lose a loved one, for instance, that we are confronted with a weightier sense of reality and the corresponding strangeness of realizing that the majority of our life is essentially dreamlike.

---

[13]Ashtavakra in Ankit Sharma, 'Ways of the Jnanis – 1–King Janak's Dream,' *Center of Indic Studies*, 10 August 2020, https://cisindus.org/2020/05/04/ways-of-the-jnanis-1-king-janaks-dream/#:~:text=%E2%80%9CNeither%20this%20is%20real%20nor,knew%20this%20to%20be%20true.

[14]*Zhuangzi: Basic Writings*, trans. Burton Watson (New York: Columbia University Press, 2003), 43.

[15]Swami Vivekananda, 'Epistles', in *Complete Works of Swami Vivekananda*, Digitally published by Partha Sinha, 27 November 2019, 1765.

Another religious tradition where this line of thinking is particularly prevalent is Buddhism. Indeed, the Buddha, following his enlightenment, became convinced that most people are living their lives as if they were asleep. He saw it as his mission to help people to wake up. Zen author Philip T. Sudo, echoing Vivekananda's reflection, affirms that tragedies can give us that little jolt and taste of being truly awake, but that it would be foolish to rely on those chance occurrences alone to achieve this goal.

> We all need to awaken, Zen says—to our true nature, to the timeless essence at our core that connects us to everything and everybody. So many of us are spiritually asleep, oblivious to the precious gift we have. We take life for granted, sleepwalking until a shattering event knocks us awake. Zen says, don't wait until the car accident, the cancer diagnosis, or the death of a loved one to get your priorities straight. Do it now. Let today's wake-up call signal the start of a new day—the first day of a new lifetime.[16]

The reality we awaken to, according to just about all religions, is that of a fundamental interconnectedness that is much deeper than we otherwise realize in our ordinary sleepwalking consciousness. Indeed, this is a critical truth to awaken to if we wish to strive towards a better future for humanity and our planet as a whole. It is the realization itself that is most important, and not the particular religious tradition or methods by which we arrive at it. As novelist Fyodor Dostoyevsky once remarked, 'What does it matter whether it was a dream or not, so long as that dream revealed the truth to me?'[17]

[16]Philip T. Sudo, *Zen 24/7: All Zen, All the Time* (New York: Harper Collins, 2009), 5.
[17]Fyodor Dostoyevsky, *The Idiot*, trans. Henry Carlisle and Olga Carlisle, Signet Classics edition (New York: Penguin Books, 2010), 271.

49

Suffering

Faith is the refusal to let go until you have turned suffering into a blessing.[1]

—Jonathan Sacks

One of the most difficult questions that religions struggle to resolve is the problem of evil. Theological attempts to explain the existence of evil and suffering in a world that was supposedly created intelligently and purposefully by a loving God are called 'theodicies'. In the wake of major tragedies and disasters, it is difficult to accept simplistic explanations like, 'everything happens for a reason', and, 'it is all part of God's plan'. One of the darkest tragedies to call into question the unsatisfactory nature of such explanations was the Holocaust, which was a catastrophic event of loss of life and human suffering that caused many people, Jews and non-Jews alike, to rethink their faith in an omnipotent and benevolent God. Karen Armstrong describes the ripple effects of this event on the religious psyche.

> Many Jews can no longer subscribe to the biblical idea of God who manifests himself in history, who, they say with [Elie] Weisel,

[1]Jonathan Sacks, *To Heal a Fractured World, The Office of Rabbi Sacks*, 224, accessed on 12 July 2022, https://rabbisacks.org/topics/faith-2/page/2/.s,.

> died in Auschwitz. The idea of a personal God, like one of us writ large, is fraught with difficulty. If this God is omnipotent, he could have prevented the Holocaust. If he was unable to stop it, he is impotent and useless; if he could have stopped it and chose not to, he is a monster.[2]

The idea of a God who could allow a tragedy of such monumental proportions to envelop so many faithful and innocent people is a tough pill to swallow. We have a deep yearning for fairness and justice, and an equally deep aversion to pain and suffering. As such, many of those who were determined to remain faithful had to rethink the very nature of God, such as Rabbi Harold Kushner.

> If God is a God of justice and not of power, then God can still be on our side when bad things happen to us. God can know that we are good and honest people who deserve better. Our misfortunes are none of God's doing, and so we can turn to God for help. We will turn to God, not to be judged or forgiven, not to be rewarded or punished, but to be strengthened and comforted.[3]

This is just one example of a meaning-making effort to reconcile deep suffering with faith, but there are many other possibilities. Religious responses to suffering need not be as black and white, either as accepting or rejecting God's will. Theodicies are usually more sophisticated than this. They do not shy away from or dismiss evil and suffering. Rather, they help us develop attitudes that allow us to endure, and possibly even benefit from, our suffering. We may suffer very deeply in the present, but we often look back and see that those moments of suffering were the very catalysts we needed in order to grow, learn and develop into the people we are today.

Literary works across religious traditions often include references and stories about God testing the faith and character of the righteous by inflicting suffering upon them. In the Qur'an, for instance, it is said, 'Be

---

[2]Karen Armstrong, *A History of God: The 4,000-Year Quest of Judaism, Christianity and Islam* (New York: Ballantine Books, 1994), 183.

[3]Harold S. Kushner, *When Bad Things Happen to Good People* (New York: Schocken Books, Dec 18, 2007), 61.

sure we shall test you with something of fear and hunger some loss in goods or lives or the fruits (of your toil) but give glad tidings to those who patiently persevere',[4] and, 'Do men think that they will be left alone on saying, "We believe", and that they will not be tested? We did test those before them, and God will certainly know those who are true from those who are false.'[5]

A well-known narrative illustration of this motif is the Book of Job in the Hebrew Bible. God sought to prove Job's depth of faith to Satan by allowing a series of tragedies to befall him, such as robbing him of his children, livestock, other property and even his own health. Still, Job did not lose his faith, proclaiming, 'Naked I came out of my mother's womb, and naked will I return there. Yahweh gave, and Yahweh has taken away. Blessed be Yahweh's name. In all this, Job didn't sin, nor charge God with wrongdoing.'[6] Having won this battle with Satan, God restored Job and his family to a life of prosperity. The implication here is that God watches us while we suffer and rewards us for persevering through it all. There is a close parallel to the story of Job in Hindu literature, in the story of a man named Maran.

> Now the Lord resolved to demonstrate that Maran was capable of pursuing such a course not only while his prosperity lasted, but also if he were to fall on hard times. Accordingly he planned that Maran's wealth should gradually diminish until it had all evaporated and he had been reduced to poverty. However, although his circumstances were thus straitened, the generosity of the lord of Ilaiyankuti was not straitened in the slightest. On the contrary, he sold his possessions and took out crippling loans, which enabled him to persevere in his sacred service as before.[7]

These stories attempt to make meaning out of one humanity's most perplexing questions: why do bad things happen to good people? While these stories may not provide satisfactory or direct answers to

[4]Qur'an, 2:155 (Yusuf Ali).

[5]Qur'an 29:2-3 (Yusuf Ali).

[6]Job 1:21-22 (World English Bible).

[7]'Periya Puranam' *in The Norton Anthology of World Religions: Vol. 1*, ed. Jack Miles (New York: W.W. Norton & Company, 2015), 333.

this question, they provide some solace for us when we must endure our own trials, offering a character with whom we can identify and towards whom we can look for hope and inspiration. As the Baha'i leader Shoghi Effendi writes, 'As we suffer these misfortunes, we must remember that the Prophets of God Themselves were not immune from these things which men suffer. They knew sorrow, illness and pain too. They rose above these things through Their spirits, and that is what we must try and do too, when afflicted.'[8] Indeed, all of the great prophets and saints had to undergo their own trials. The Buddha was assailed with temptations by the demon Mara who, as Buddhist monk and author Nyanaponika Thera puts it, is 'The personification of the forces antagonistic to enlightenment'.[9] Mara functions as a reminder to the rest of us that even the Buddha faced many struggles on his road to enlightenment, and that such struggles are a normal and necessary stage along any spiritual path.

Similarly, in the New Testament, we are told about the story of Jesus fasting for forty days and forty nights, after he 'was led up by the Spirit into the wilderness to be tempted by the devil'.[10] His unjust and painful death by crucifixion has served as one of the most iconic images of human suffering as well as the promise of salvation for millennia. Jesus is therefore seen as a source of strength and eternal life, encouraging Christians to persevere through their own suffering: 'We are pressed on every side, yet not crushed; perplexed, yet not to despair; pursued, yet not forsaken; struck down, yet not destroyed; always carrying in the body the putting to death of the Lord Jesus, that the life of Jesus may also be revealed in our body,'[11] and 'Not only this, but we also rejoice in our sufferings, knowing that suffering produces perseverance; and perseverance, proven character; and proven character, hope.'[12] For Christians, who believe Jesus was the

[8]Shoghi Effendi, *Directives from the Guardian* (New Delhi, India: Baha'i Publishing Trust, 1973), 68, Baha'i Reference Library: http://reference.bahai.org/en/t/se/DG/dg-181.html.

[9]Nyanaponika Thera, trans, *The Roots of Good and Evil: Buddhist Texts translated from the Pali with Comments and Introduction* (Buddhist Publication Society, 2008), 22.

[10]Matthew 4:1 (World English Bible).

[11]2 Corinthians 4:8-10 (World English Bible).

[12]Romans 5:3-4 (World English Bible).

son of God, his suffering is significant as a reminder that we are never alone in our suffering. One of the most important verses in the New Testament for Christians is John 3:16, which goes, 'For God so loved the world, that he gave his one and only Son, that whoever believes in him should not perish, but have eternal life.'[13] It shows that even God suffers with us out of compassion for humanity. In fact, the etymological source of the word 'compassion' is the Latin word 'compati', or 'to suffer with'.

One of the silver linings of personal suffering is an increased awareness and concern for the suffering of others. Rabbi Jonathan Sacks, in fact, goes so far as to say that, 'To be a Jew is to know that one cannot be indifferent when one's people are suffering.'[14] We are nodes on an interconnected web of life where the welfare of each of us is dependent on the welfare of all. In Confucian thought, 'ren' (often translated as 'benevolence') is an ideal human trait characterized by interconnectedness, empathy and altruism. Confucius described benevolence as the most important virtue and noted its close relationship to suffering: 'The benevolent man reaps the benefit only after overcoming difficulties.'[15] So too is suffering closely associated with 'bodhichitta' or the 'enlightenment-mind', as explained by Buddhist monk Pema Chödrön.

> An analogy for bodhichitta is the rawness of a broken heart. Sometimes this broken heart gives birth to anxiety and panic; sometimes to anger, resentment and blame. But under the hardness of that armor there is the tenderness of genuine sadness. This is our link with all those who have ever loved. This genuine heart of sadness can teach us great compassion. It can humble us when we're arrogant and soften us when we are unkind. It awakens us when we prefer to sleep and pierces through our indifference.[16]

Suffering can be redemptive as it can help us overcome our ego-selves

---

[13]John, 3:16 (World English Bible).

[14]Jonathan Sacks, 'The Chief Rabbi's Haggadah (Essays).' *The Office of Rabbi Sacks*, 16, accessed on 12 July 2022, https://rabbisacks.org/topics/jew/page/2/.

[15]Confucius, *The Analects*, trans. D.C. Lau, Penguin Classics edition (London: Penguin Books, 1971), 6:22.

[16]Pema Chödrön, *The Places That Scare You: A Guide to Fearlessness in Difficult Times* (Boston: Shambhala, 2002), 5.

and care more deeply for others. It interrupts the mundane nature of our lives and makes us look deeper into ourselves and think about what really matters. We are not our plans, our aspirations or our goals. The full force of this realization was a silver lining of the recent COVID-19 pandemic for many across the world.

Religions, therefore, do not ask us to turn a blind eye to suffering or to ignore its existence; on the contrary, they shine a light on the inevitability of suffering, as well as the roles we all play in creating, enduring and alleviating suffering. All the three major Indic religions, Buddhism, Hinduism and Jainism, share the concept of cosmic cause-and-effect, or karma. Essentially, all of our actions have consequences that catch up with us eventually. As the Hindu monk Swami Vivekananda explained, 'If I do an evil action, I must suffer for it; there is no power in this universe to stop or stay it.'[17] The term 'action' can even apply to the actions of our minds. As the Buddha taught, 'Our life is shaped by our mind; we become what we think. Suffering follows an evil thought as the wheels of a cart follow the oxen that draw it.'[18] Suffering is, thus, at the core of the Buddha's four 'Noble Truths': (1) life is inherently characterized by suffering; (2) suffering arises through desire or attachment; (3) suffering can be ended by letting go of attachments and desires; (4) the eightfold path can be attempted towards the cessation of suffering. As psychologist Rick Hanson writes, 'In Buddhism, it's said that suffering is the result of craving expressed through the Three Poisons: greed, hatred, and delusion.'[19]

One implication of all this is that we are the cause of our own suffering—not all of it perhaps, but a good deal of it. Aldous Huxley once wrote, 'Two thirds of all sorrow is homemade and, so far as the universe is concerned, unnecessary.'[20] As another well-known saying goes, pain

[17]Swâmi Vivekânanda, *Complete Works of Swami Vivekananda,* (digitally published by Partha Sinha, 27 November 2019), 49.

[18]*The Dhammapada,* trans. Eknath Easwaran, Classics of Indian Spirituality, Second edition (Tomales: The Blue Mountain Center of Meditation, 2007), 1.

[19]Rick Hanson, *Buddha's Brain: The Practical Neuroscience of Happiness, Love, and Wisdom* (Oakland, CA: New Harbinger Publications, 2010), 47-48.

[20]Aldous Huxley, *Island* (New York: Harper Perennial Modern Classics, 2009), 102.

is inevitable but suffering is optional.[21] As the Buddha points out in his second 'Noble Truth', our suffering is caused by our attachments to things we desire, and especially the attachment we have to the illusory nature of our ego selves.

Underlying our artificial ego selves, Hindus believe there is a deeper self, known as atman, which is imperishable. As one famous passage from the Bhagavad Gita states:

> Weapons do not cut the self, nor does fire burn it, nor do waters drench it, nor does wind dry it. The self is not to be pierced, nor burned, nor drenched, nor dried; it is eternal, all-pervading and fixed—unmoving from the beginning.[22]

This provides us with a different perspective, urging us to try and be aware of the separation of the soul, the body and the mind. If we are not attached to the body or the artificial ego self, for instance, we will be less afflicted by the suffering we bring upon ourselves by reacting negatively to difficulties in our lives.

The awareness that we are responsible for much of our suffering extends well beyond the religions of India. The Medieval Jewish scholar Maimonides summed it up well when he wrote, 'We suffer from the evils which we, by our own free will, inflict on ourselves and ascribe them to God, who is far from being connected with them!'[23] Similar to the sayings of the Buddha, the Baha'i leader 'Abdu'l-Bahá pointed towards greed and attachment to material things as the cause of our suffering: 'If we suffer it is the outcome of material things, and all the trials and troubles come from this world of illusion.'[24] Probably the most famous expression of recognizing our own role in the suffering we endure is the Serenity Prayer, which originated from the Christian theologian Reinhold Niebuhr.

---

[21]Variously attributed to the Buddha, the Dalai Lama, and Haruki Murakami

[22]*The Bhagavad Gita,* trans. Laurie L. Patton (New York: Penguin, 2014), 2:23-24.

[23]Moses Maimonides, *The Guide for the Perplexed,* trans. Michael Friedländer, Second Edition (London: G. Routledge & Sons, 1910), 268, digitized from Cornell University, 31 October 2012.

[24]'Abdu'l-Bahá, *Paris Talks,* eleventh edition (UK Bahá'í Publishing Trust, 1972), 110, Baha'i Reference Library, https://reference.bahai.org/en/t/ab/PT/pt-35.html

> God, grant me the serenity to accept the things I cannot change, courage to change the things I can, and wisdom to know the difference.[25]

Many misfortunes, both large and small, are unavoidable, but we can always choose how to respond to such events.

As Tyler J. VanderWeele, the director of the Human Flourishing Program at Harvard, notes, 'Suffering is not necessarily the opposite of flourishing [...] In the midst of suffering, we can still find ways to respond that promote at least some aspects of flourishing.'[26] A healthy attitude toward our trials can allow us to flourish even in the midst of suffering. This perspective corresponds closely with the advice and words of wisdom we have seen across the world's religions. Approaching suffering with open eyes can be painful, but doing so is the only way we can truly come to make meaning out of our suffering. Dr VanderWeele goes on to say:

> Our confrontation with suffering, and even death, provides an important opportunity for reflection. What is it that we value most? What relationships might be in need of forgiveness or reconciliation? How is it that we are to understand our lives and our own mortality?[27]

We can find appreciation for moments of suffering if we view them as periodic 'wake-up calls' that force us to re-evaluate what we are currently prioritizing in our lives. Are we living selfishly or magnanimously? Compulsively or consciously? Following the path of fear and hate, or that of love and compassion? Though we cannot avoid certain forms of suffering in our lives, we can always use these experiences as opportunities to better ourselves for our own sake and for the sake of others.

---

[25]Reinhold Niebuhr, The Serenity Prayer.

[26]Tyler J. VanderWeele, 'Flourishing Amidst Coronavirus,' *Psychology Today*, 26 March 2020, https://www.psychologytoday.com/us/blog/human-flourishing/202003/flourishing-amidst-coronavirus.

[27]Ibid.

50

Silence

Those who know don't talk/those who talk don't know.[1]

—Tao Te Ching

The unsaid can be a powerful and paradoxical means of coming to voice.[2]

—Michelle Voss Roberts

Life is characterized by change and movement. We constantly have work to attend to, and we rarely give ourselves the license to just sit and do nothing for an amount of time. Yet, periods of inactivity and silence are absolutely essential to restore us with the energy we need to carry on with our duties. Sleep is a prime example of this, but even while we are awake, a few minutes of silence can help us to clear our minds and re-establish focus.

Silence and restraint in speech have long been associated with some of the wisest prophets and sages throughout human history. The New Testament, for instance, recounts the silence of Jesus upon being condemned to death: 'When he was accused by the chief priests and

[1]Lao-Tzu, *Tao te ching*, trans. Red Pine (Port Townsend, Washington: Copper Canyon Press, 2009), Chapter 56, 112.

[2]Michelle Voss Roberts, *Tastes of the Divine* (New York: Fordham University Press, 2014), 144.

elders, he answered nothing. Then Pilate said to him, "Don't you hear how many things they testify against you?" He gave him no answer, not even one word, so that the governor marveled greatly.'[3] The New Testament also likens Jesus's lack of protest as the prophetic fulfillment of a passage from the Hebrew Bible: 'He was oppressed, yet when he was afflicted he didn't open his mouth. As a lamb that is led to the slaughter, and as a sheep that before its shearers is silent, so he didn't open his mouth.'[4] He understood the greater purpose of the sacrifice he was making on behalf of humanity, and he expressed this conviction and the mental fortitude necessary to carry it out through silence.

The prophets' silence has also been seen as a mark of wisdom, a true sign that they have had a direct apprehension of some insight that cannot be communicated through ordinary speech. One of the Buddha's monikers is meant to convey this, as scholar of religion Huston Smith explains: 'They called him Sakyamuni, "silent sage (muni) of the Sakya clan", symbol of something that could not be described.'[5] Indeed, this fits with the Buddha's teachings that each individual must walk his or her own path towards truth, as the greatest truths in life cannot be communicated through direct speech alone. This is quite similar to the teaching method employed by Socrates, who claimed not to know anything, but was deemed wise for his remarkable skill in 'pointing out the limits of language, and its inability to communicate moral and existential experience',[6] as Pierre Hadot puts it.

Across religions, many prophets, as well as the scriptures that encode their teachings, paradoxically use language to point towards the limits of language. The Taoist text Tao Te Ching—which happens to be the second-most translated text in the world after the Bible—sets such a tone in its very first lines: 'As for the Way, the Way that can be spoken of is not the constant Way.'[7] Behind everything we experience in the world is

---

[3]Matthew 27:12-14 (World English Bible).

[4]Isaiah 53:7 (World English Bible).

[5]Huston Smith, *The Illustrated World's Religions* (New York: HarperCollins, 1995), 65.

[6]Pierre Hadot, *Philosophy as a Way of Life*, ed. Arnold I. Davidson, trans. Michael Chase (Massachusetts: Blackwell, 1995), 163.

[7]Lao-Tzu, *Taoteching*, trans. Red Pine (Port Townsend: Copper Canyon Press, 2009), chapter 1.

something nameless and mysterious from which all of creation springs forth, and which is therefore the unifying principle of the universe. The vast array of seemingly differentiated individual objects and lifeforms only appear as separate entities to us because we have given them names. In order to apprehend the 'way' that underlies all of existence, we must essentially learn to think beyond ordinary language. Similarly, the Taoist sage Chuang Tzu writes, 'Heaven and earth possess vast beauties, but they do not speak of them. The four seasons have their unconcealed regularities, but they do not discuss them. Each of the ten thousand things makes its own perfect sense but does not explain it.'[8] This is closely mirrored by a reflection from Confucius in his Analects: 'Does Heaven speak? The four seasons pursue their courses, and all things are continually being produced, but does Heaven say anything?'[9] The 'way', heaven, God are words applied by various religions to point towards something that cannot be put into words, something that expresses itself through many forms in our world and has no language of its own. It is, therefore, only through direct experience of the world around us that we can really begin to have even a glimpse of such ultimate principles behind reality.

One of the means through which prophets and scriptures have tried to lead us through this doorway of insight is the instruction of contemplative practices like meditation, yoga and prayer. These promote a sense of clarity and stillness in the mind and body. As the Zen master Shunryu Suzuki writes, 'If your mind is empty, it is always ready for anything.'[10] Furthermore, as we are engaged in these practices, we are also engaged in silence. They might involve certain utterances, like mantras, but even still we remain silent and do not deviate from our ordinary way of speaking. Someone sincerely seeking to enter a contemplative state simply cannot do so without first being able to dwell in silence, as the Baha'i leader 'Abdu'l-Bahá points out: 'Bahá'u'lláh says there is a sign (from God) in every phenomenon: the sign of the intellect is contemplation and the sign of contemplation is silence, because it is impossible for a man to do

---

[8]*Zhuangzi: The Essential Writings,* trans. Brook Ziporyn (Indianapolis: Hackett Publishing, 2009), 86.

[9]Confucius, *Confucian Analects, The Great Learning The Doctrine of the Mean,* trans. James Legge (Pantianos Classics, 2017), 17:19.

[10]Shunryu Suzuki, *Zen Mind, Beginner's Mind* (Boston: Shambhala, 2011), 2.

two things at one time—he cannot both speak and meditate.'[11]

In addition to pointing out the benefits of silence, prophets and scriptures have always explained the detriments of excessive speech. The ancient rabbinic sage Simeon ben Gamaliel once said, 'I spent all my life among sages and found nothing better for a person than silence. He who talks too much brings on sin.'[12] This is reflective of passages from the Book of Proverbs in the Hebrew Bible, such as, 'Whoever guards his mouth and his tongue keeps his soul from troubles.'[13] Similarly serious warnings against excessive or improper speech are exhibited across many other religions as well. In a Buddhist text, the Aṅguttara Nikāya, it is said that, 'A person is born with an axe in their mouth. A fool cuts themselves with it when they say bad words.'[14] This imagery of material weapons and physical harm with regard to speech is a recurring motif. The Baha'i prophet Bahá'u'lláh taught that, 'The tongue is a smoldering fire, and excess of speech a deadly poison. Material fire consumeth the body, whereas the fire of the tongue devoureth both heart and soul. The force of the former lasteth but for a time, whilst the effects of the latter endureth a century.'[15]

The Prophet Muhammad also had much to say on the subject of guarding against faulty speech, highlighting the importance of weighing our words carefully before we speak. As he said, 'A man utters a word pleasing to Allah without considering it of any significance for which Allah exalts his ranks (in Jannah); another one speaks a word displeasing to Allah without considering it of any importance, and for this reason he

[11]'Abdu'l-Bahá, *Paris Talks*, eleventh edition (UK: Bahá'í Publishing Trust, 1972), 174, Baha'i Reference Library, http://reference.bahai.org/en/t/ab/PT/pt-55.html

[12]Avot, 1:17 in Hayyim Nahman Bialik and Yehoshua Ḥana Rawnitzki, *The Book of Legends: Sefer Ha-Aggadah*, trans. William Gordon Braude (New York: Schocken Books, 1992), 704.

[13]Proverbs 21:23 (World English Bible).

[14]Aṅguttara Nikāya, in *Numbered Discourses: A Translation of Aṅguttara Nikāya*, trans. Bhikkhu Sujato, (SuttaCentral, 2019), 10:89, https://suttacentral.net/an-guide-sujato?lang=en

[15]Bahá'u'lláh, *Gleanings From the Writings of Bahá'u'lláh* (US: Bahá'í Publishing Trust, 1990), 265, Baha'i Reference Library, http://reference.bahai.org/en/t/b/GWB/gwb-125.html

will sink down into Hell.'[16] Confucius and the Taoist sage, Chuang Tzu, also offered similar admonitions. The former said that, 'For one word a man is often deemed to be wise, and for one word he is often deemed to be foolish. We ought to be careful indeed in what we say.'[17] While the latter points out, 'A good completion takes a long time; a bad completion cannot be changed later.'[18]

The ancient prophets and sages would spend great amounts of time in the forest, the mountains or the desert—isolated locations—where they could silence their minds in order to focus their psychic energy on insights about life's great mysteries. Modern scientific studies have also revealed the cognitive and physical benefits of intentional periods of silence.

> Duke Medical School's Imke Kirste recently found that silence is associated with the development of new cells in the hippocampus, the key brain region associated with learning and memory. Physician Luciano Bernardi found that two-minutes of silence inserted between musical pieces proved more stabilizing to cardiovascular and respiratory systems than even the music categorized as 'relaxing'. And a 2013 study in the Journal of Environmental Psychology, based on a survey of 43,000 workers, concluded that the disadvantages of noise and distraction associated with open office plans outweighed anticipated, but still unproven, benefits like increasing morale and productivity boosts from unplanned interactions.[19]

One particularly popular practice of intentional silence today is Vipassana meditation, otherwise known as 'insight meditation'. This is an accessible practice even for people who have very busy lifestyles, as is evidenced by

---

[16]Riyad as-Salihin, Hadith 1515.

[17]*Confucian Analects, The Great Learning, The Doctrine of the Mean*, trans. James Legge (Pantianos Classics, 2017), 19:25.

[18]*Zhuangzi: Basic Writings,* trans. Burton Watson (New York: Columbia University Press, 2003), 57.

[19]Justin Talbot Zorn and Leigh Marz, 'The Busier You Are, the More You Need Quiet Time,' *Harvard Business Review*, 17 March 2017,https://hbr.org/2017/03/the-busier-you-are-the-more-you-need-quiet-time.

the growing popularity of the practice in places like the business world. Vipassana retreats are popular ten-day periods of intensive meditation while observing a strict vow of silence. The retreat was pioneered by Jack Kornfield (among others), who once said, 'To let go does not mean to get rid of. To let go means to let be. When we let be with compassion, things come and go on their own.'[20] By practising Vipassana, you separate yourself from your body and your mind, and you are able to examine your thoughts as an observer to decide which ones you can let go of and which ones you can attach your awareness to.

Compassion, the idea of letting go and deep insight are seen as virtues across religions. They can all be achieved through conscious observance of silence. Many Hindu saints, for instance, take the oath of remaining silent (called the 'maun vrat') for anywhere from a week to a month to attain purification of the mind, and often, they even retire to the mountains. But how many of us value silence seriously enough to consciously set aside even small amounts of time for the act? Even during the in-between times of our busy days—walking, commuting on a bus or train, cooking and cleaning—we drown out the silence with music or other distracting noises.

We find it uncomfortable to dwell in silence. The seventeenth-century French philosopher Blaise Pascal went so far as to say, 'All the unhappiness of men arises from one single fact, that they cannot stay quietly in their own chamber.'[21] C.S. Lewis also puts it as, 'We live, in fact, in a world starved for solitude, silence, and private: and therefore starved for meditation and true friendship.'[22] It may seem counterintuitive to think of silence and solitude as conducive to friendships and other interpersonal relations, but sitting in silence teaches us to be content in the absence of stimulation and enables us to give our full attention to a single thing, person or task at a time. This is an important skill in our modern world. Remember, there can be no music without silence interspersed with the sounds.

---

[20]Jack Kornfield, Twitter post, 12 February 2015.

[21]Blaise Pascal, *Pensées*, trans. W.F. Trotter (New York: Dover Publications, 2003), 39.

[22]C.S. Lewis, *The Weight of Glory: And Other Addresses* (New York: Harper Collins, 2001), 160.

51

Learning from Nature

There's a religion of nature and reason written in the hearts of every one of us from the first creation, by which all mankind must judge the truth of any institutional religion whatever.[1]

—Matthew Tindal

It knows everything, the river, a person can learn anything from it.[2]

—Hermann Hesse

The beauty of the natural world has always been a huge source of joy and inspiration for us as a species. The most important aspect of nature is that it loves diversity. There are 8.6 million species in nature. There are far more colours than we can visualize. When the modern man gets tired of city life, he seeks recuperation by retreating to a natural environment. And there is a religious lesson for all of us from nature's immense diversity—we should harness the diversity amongst us human beings.

---

[1]Matthew Tindal, *Christianity as Old as the Creation: Or, the Gospel, a Republication of the Religion of Nature. Volume 1* (New York: New York Public Library, 1730), digitized 12 July 2006, 60.

[2]Hermann Hesse, *Siddhartha*, trans. Stanley Applebaum (New York: Dover Publications, 1999), 57.

Keen observation of nature has led to some of humankind's greatest achievements, be it artistic, literary or scientific. For instance, we are all familiar with the story of Sir Isaac Newton who began investigating the nature of gravity after considering why apples fall towards the ground. Likewise, our religions also have much to say about nature. Many prophets and scriptures have been directly inspired by aspects of nature, which then become metaphors and parables in their teachings.

The clear quality of water reminds us to strive to maintain a clear mind and pure soul. Trees, with their broad trunks and numerous branches remind us of the fundamental unity that undergirds all diversity. The sky, like water, stands as another symbol of clarity and the clouds represent a tumultuous state of things when clarity is lost. The wind reminds us that we are always acted upon by forces we cannot see and that the source behind the way our lives unfold is beyond our conscious grasp.

The concept of God across most religions serves as an answer to the question of who or what is responsible for the creation of the universe. This, of course, means that the natural world stands as a reminder of God's existence. As expressed in the Hebrew Bible, 'Ask the animals, now, and they will teach you; the birds of the sky, and they will tell you. Or speak to the earth, and it will teach you. The fish of the sea will declare to you. Who doesn't know that in all these, Yahweh's hand has done this, in whose hand is the life of every living thing, and the breath of all mankind?'[3] We may not be able to physically see or interact with God, but nature allows us to perceive God indirectly. As the Baha'i Prophet Baha'u'llah writes, 'Nature in its essence is the embodiment of My Name, the Maker, the Creator. Its manifestations are diversified by varying causes, and in this diversity, there are signs for men of discernment. Nature is God's Will and is its expression in and through the contingent world.'[4] The characteristics and patterns of nature, therefore, serve as clues to understanding God's attributes, one of which is undeniably diversity.

---

[3]Job 12:7-10 (World English Bible).

[4]Bahá'u'lláh, *Tablets of Bahá'u'lláh Revealed After the Kitáb-i-Aqdas* (US: Bahá'í Publishing Trust: 1988), 141; Baha'i Reference Library: http://reference.bahai.org/en/t/b/TB/tb-10.html

There are so many species of life on earth, so many different environmental terrains and geological structures and even a large amount of variation among human beings. Every species has its place in an ecosystem, and this place aids in maintaining complex dynamics like the food web. Even removing a seemingly insignificant species (like fruit flies) can have rippling effects that damage many other species and the ecosystem as a whole. Clearly, diversity is a fundamental feature of creation. In the Qur'an, it is said that God creates 'gardens of grapes and olives and pomegranates each similar (in kind) yet different (in variety): when they begin to bear fruit and the ripeness thereof. Behold! In these things there are signs for people who believe'.[5] One way to interpret this 'sign' is to see that, just like these fruit-bearing plants, we too are a species comprised of similar yet varied communities. We tend to focus on our obvious differences as sources of conflict and disagreement, but if we focus on the 'fruits', we can see that every human culture and religion has something valuable to offer to the rest of humanity, and indeed, all are reflections of the same God.

The beauty and harmony of the natural world, of course, does not prove or disprove the existence of God, but it may provide the careful observer with a more concrete sense of the qualities often associated with God. Perhaps this is what C.S. Lewis was getting at when he wrote, 'Nature never taught me that there exists a God of glory and of infinite majesty. I had to learn that in other ways. But nature gave the word glory a meaning for me. I still do not know where else I could have found one.'[6] Both 'glory' and 'majesty' are terms that speak to the beauty of nature and how impressive its self-sustaining mechanics are. As Confucius once observed, 'All things are nourished together without their injuring one another. The courses of the seasons, and of the sun and moon, are pursued without any collision among them.'[7] Similarly, the Taoist sage Lieh Tzu explains:

---

[5]Qur'an 6:99 (Yusuf Ali).

[6]C.S. Lewis, *The Four Loves* (Mariner Books: New York, 2012), 755.

[7]Confucius, 'The Doctrine of the Mean,' in *Volume 1 of The Chinese classics: Confucian analects. The great learning. The doctrine of the mean.* trans. James Legge, (London: Trubner & Co., 1861), 30:3, digitized 17 April 2015 by University of California, Berkeley, 291.

> Old man sky never says a word, but we can see that everything has its place in the universe. Nature has a lot to teach us. All you need is to open your eyes and look. The changes you see in nature follow a course. The four seasons behave in a regulated way. In truth, all human matters follow the same principles as the workings of heaven and earth.[8]

Once again, we can glean truths by direct observation of nature. These truths have great importance for our own species as we continually search for better ways to live harmoniously with one another.

Religions are all about fostering interpersonal and intra-personal harmony. We yearn for a world of peace beyond conflict and division resulting from differences between human communities. And the many prescriptions and guidelines for individual practices and behaviours found throughout the scriptures of the world's religions demonstrate an awareness that this interpersonal harmony can only be achieved once we have each taken personal responsibility for establishing harmony within ourselves. Here, too, nature can serve as a valuable guide.

The religious traditions native to India and China have relied upon Ayurveda and traditional Chinese medicine (TCM) for thousands of years to maintain proper health, according to principles derived from particular understandings of the natural world and our place in it. The Sanskrit word, Ayurveda, translates to 'knowledge of life and longevity'. These traditions are too complex to describe here in detail, but they share an understanding of the body that corresponds to five natural elements. In Ayurveda, the earth, water, fire, air, and ether are elements similar to the Ancient Greek system of 'humors' and TCM also follows the elements, such as wood, fire, earth, metal and water. Ayurveda and TCM also share an emphasis on the balancing of opposing forces or characteristics that occur in nature, like hot balanced with the cold, hard with the soft, etc.

These systems also emphasize that it is our internal state—the state of our minds—which often gets in the way of us living peacefully and contentedly. But the mind is elusive. The Bhagavad Gita mentions that 'the mind is ever straying, troubling, strong and unyielding; I think

---

[8]*Lieh-tzu: A Taoist Guide to Practical Living,* trans. Eva Wong (Boston: Shambhala, 2001), 26.

holding it back is as hard to bring about as holding back the wind'.[9] Similarly, the New Testament of Christianity employs this metaphor of the wind to express the elusive nature of the Holy Spirit: 'The wind blows where it wants to, and you hear its sound, but don't know where it comes from and where it is going. So is everyone who is born of the Spirit.'[10] Just as we cannot see or touch the wind directly, so too can we not directly grasp the mind or God. But we can comprehend these forces indirectly by observing their effects upon ourselves and the external world. The French author Guy de Maupassant expresses this point vividly in one of his short stories, again through the analogy of wind.

> Do we see the hundred thousandth part of what exists? Look here; there is the wind, which is the strongest force in nature, which knocks down men, and blows down buildings, uproots trees, raises the sea into mountains of water, destroys cliffs and casts great ships onto the breakers; the wind which kills, which whistles, which sighs, which roars—have you ever seen it, and can you see it? It exists for all that, however.[11]

Sometimes, the most powerful and impactful forces are invisible. This is true of the natural world and in our own personal lives as well.

Different religions refer to the divinity within us using different names: the mind, the soul, the holy spirit and so on. But they all have prescribed similar practices for comprehending and harnessing this vital internal force: such as prayer, meditation and other contemplative practices that bring our egos in abeyance and promote careful observation of what lies beneath it. These practices can sometimes feel daunting and frustrating, particularly when we do not see results right away, but as the Zen master Shunryu Suzuki points out, those very moments of frustration provide us with key clues about our internal nature, just as the obstructing forces of nature work to paradoxically illuminate that which they are obstructing.

---

[9]*The Bhagavad Gita,* trans. Laurie L. Patton (New York: Penguin, 2014), 6:34.
[10]John 3:8 (World English Bible).
[11]Guy de Maupassant, *The Horla and Others: Best Weird Science Fiction and Ghost Stories*, ed. M. Grant Kellermeyer (Fort Wayne, Indiana: Oldstyle Tales Press, 2013), 30.

> Even though you do not feel anything when you sit, if you do not have this zazen [meditation] experience, you cannot find anything; you just find weeds, or trees, or clouds in your daily life; you do not see the moon. That is why you are always complaining about something. But for Zen students a weed, which for most people is worthless, is a treasure.[12]

Because the natural world is something concrete that we all participate in and co-inhabit, allegories based on nature become a universal language that can convey lessons that are otherwise abstract. This collective language allows for shared meaning-making about our human condition across time and geographical locations.

[12]Shunryu Suzuki, *Zen Mind, Beginner's Mind* (Boston: Shambhala, 2011), 112.

52

Awe

One cannot help but be in awe when he contemplates the mysteries of eternity, of life, of the marvelous structure of reality. It is enough if one tries merely to comprehend a little of this mystery every day. Never lose a holy curiosity.[1]

—Albert Einstein

Awe is deeply ingrained in our human nature as a way of experiencing the world. It can fill our lives with joy, excitement and fulfillment. In the eyes of a child, everything is worthy of awe, since everything is so new. But there are still plenty of reasons for us to feel awe as adults. Travelling the world can fill us with awe as we experience new cultures and new ways of living, ones that we never would have imagined. Being in nature can fill us with awe as we witness the great beauty of the earth's different landscapes, vistas and geological formations like waterfalls, rainbows, mountains, the northern lights. These things have been known to be everlasting sources of awe throughout human history.

Human history itself is filled with awe-inspiring phenomena—from masterful paintings, sculptures, music and other works of art our species

[1]Albert Einstein, 'Memoirs of William Miller', Life magazine, *PBS Nova,* 2 May 1955, https://www.pbs.org/wgbh/nova/einstein/wisd-nf.html.

has produced, to the astound architectural achievements like the Great Pyramids, the Taj Mahal, and a whole host of other complex and ornate castles, temples and more. Even the human body has been a deep source of awe for countless doctors, scientists and artists, all of whom have devoted a huge part of their lives to keenly studying every anatomical and physiological detail.

In more recent history, we also experience awe when we are thinking about things that modern science has uncovered, that otherwise are outside of our own day-to-day experience. We feel awe when we attempt to fathom the vastness of space, or the minute scales into which all matter can be broken down, or even the trillions of microorganisms that dwell among (and even inside) us. Upon gazing at the earth from the moon, Neil Armstrong, overcome by awe, simply remarked, 'I felt very, very small.'[2] And fellow astronaut Jim Lovell mused, 'The vast loneliness up here of the Moon is awe-inspiring, and it makes you realize just what you have back there on earth. The earth from here is a grand oasis to the big vastness of space.'[3]

Religious awe is similar. There are religious reasons to be awed by the physical world that we experience, and there are reasons to be awed by the magnificence of God and the spiritual world that is not as tangible to our physical senses. All religions want us to be in awe of God, to remember that there are wonders in the universe that lie far beyond our own capacities to control or even comprehend it. Scholar of religion, Robert C. Fuller, in his book *Wonder*, makes the case that the human capacity for experiences of awe and wonder is at the heart of all religions, and indeed, at the heart of human ingenuity itself.

> Religion, through the ritualization of wonder, sustains cultural paradigms that establish powerful, pervasive, and long-lasting moods and motivations. Moreover, wonder continually revitalizes

---

[2]Neil Armstrong, NASA Earth Observatory, accessed on 12 July 2022, https://earthobservatory.nasa.gov/images/91494/right-here-right-now.

[3]Jim Lovel, transcript of audiotapes of the Apollo 8 telecast, *National Archives, Records of the National Aeronautics and Space Administration, 24* December 1968, page 274/2, https://www.archives.gov/exhibits/eyewitness/html.php?section=25#:~:text=Jim%20Lovell%3A%20The%20vast%20loneliness,the%20big%20vastness%20of%20space.

> such paradigms by connecting them with belief in a general order of existence, a cosmic frame of reference. It is thus not just our appetite for wonder but also our ability to ritualize wonder that fuels humanity's adaptive capacities.[4]

The ritualization and cultural paradigms of religions have been shaped over time. But they are rooted in the original experiences of awe reported by the prophets who claim to have communed with God in some way. Religions also cultivate a sense of awe around the prophets themselves.

One of the most influential descriptions of awe in religion comes from the Christian theologian Rudolf Otto who, in a book called *The Idea of the Holy*, coined the term 'mysterium tremendum' to capture the indescribable nature of religious experience, of being in the presence of God or something divine.[5] He claims it is something mysterious and tremendous in its actuality and impact. As Otto put it, it's 'the "wholly other" "heavenly" thing, set in contrast to the world of here and now, "the mysterious" itself in its dual character as awe-compelling, yet all-attracting, glimmering in an atmosphere of genuine "religious awe"'.[6] One famous example of this kind of religious awe in Christianity is that of Saul, who in the Hebrew Bible was the first monarch of Israel. In the New Testament, he persecutes those in his kingdom who have come to believe in Jesus as the son of God. But on his way to the city of Damascus, he had his famous experience:

> As he traveled, he got close to Damascus, and suddenly a light from the sky shone around him. He fell on the earth, and heard a voice saying to him, 'Saul, Saul, why do you persecute me?' He said, 'Who are you, Lord?' The Lord said, 'I am Jesus, whom you are persecuting. But rise up and enter into the city, then you will be told what you must do.' The men who traveled with him stood speechless, hearing the sound, but seeing no one. Saul arose from the ground, and when his eyes were opened, he saw no one.[7]

---

[4]Robert C. Fuller, *Wonder: From Emotion to Spirituality* (Chapel Hill: University of North Carolina Press, 2006), 67-68.

[5]Rudolf Otto, *The Idea of the Holy*, trans John W. Harvey (Oxford: Oxford University Press, 1958)

[6]Ibid, 82.

[7]Acts, 3-8 (World English Bible).

Saul is so overwhelmed by this experience that he comes to believe in Jesus as the son of God, is then baptized and becomes Paul the Apostle, arguably the second most important figure in Christianity after Jesus himself.

The feeling of awe towards God is a huge theme in the scriptures of all the three Abrahamic religions. The Hebrew Bible proclaims, 'Let all the earth fear Yahweh. Let all the inhabitants of the world stand in awe of him.'[8] And in the Qur'an it is said, 'To Allah belongs whatever is in the heavens and whatever is on the earth. And we have instructed those who were given the scripture before you and yourselves to fear Allah.'[9] The people 'who were given the scripture before you' are Christians and Jews, with whom Muslims share many of the same prophets and stories. Adherents of all three religions are taught to 'fear' God. This is very similar to the way Otto describes God in terms of the 'mysterium tremendum': being in the presence of God can inspire awe and bliss, but it can also evoke reverence and fear due to the sheer power of God.

Religious awe is often described in a similarly dualistic manner in other religions as well. In Hinduism, for instance, one of the most-sought-after religious experiences is darshan, or having a direct vision of a deity. This can be a very positive and enlightening experience, but at the same time, many Hindu deities have frightful appearances, such as the Goddess Kali. Kali is viewed as the divine mother of all creatures, but she is also a Goddess of death and is frequently depicted wielding a sword in one hand and a severed head in another. Hence, the awe of witnessing Kali can be characterized both by bliss and by fear.

Another example of this in Hinduism can be found in the Bhagavad Gita, when Krishna reveals himself to Arjuna as an avatar of Vishnu and gives Arjuna the power to see his true form. Krishna exclaims, 'See the Adityas, the Vasus, the Rudras, the twin Ashvins, and the Maruts—these many wonders which have never been seen before, Son of Bharata',[10] prompting Arjuna to be 'seized by awe'.[11] We are told that, 'If a thousand

[8]Psalms, 33:8 (World English Bible).

[9]The Qur'an, 4:131 (Yusuf Ali)

[10]*The Bhagavad Gita,* trans. Laurie L Patton (New York: Penguin, 2014), 11:6.

[11]Ibid, 11:14.

suns had risen in the sky all at once, such brilliance would be the brilliance of that great self [of Vishnu].'[12]

This, too, is an experience reminiscent of the 'fear of God' from the Abrahamic religions. Even Otto himself remarks on the similarity of religious awe across many different religions, including Hinduism.

> The Sanskrit term Asura is the 'aweful' or 'dreadful' in the sense in which Jacob used the word, the eerie or uncanny. Later, in Indian religion, it is used as the technical expression for the lower forms of the spectral, ghostly, and daemonic. But at the same time it is from the primeval times a title of the sublimest of all the gods of the Rig-Veda, the weirdly exalted Varuna. And in the Persian expression Ahura-mazda, it becomes the name of the one and only eternal godhead itself.[13]

Rudolf Otto, therefore, draws parallels between the Abrahamic religions (the biblical prophet Jacob), Hinduism (Varuna) and Zoroastrianism (Ahura-mazda). These are very different religions but they all exhibit similar examples of religious awe in the presence of God.

The expression 'fear of God' might sound bleak, and even contradictory. Why are we supposed to fear a God that's supposed to be all-loving? But the great prophets and scriptures of religions are not saying that we should live our lives perpetually in fear of God, always walking on eggshells trying to make sure we don't do anything to anger God. Rather, the deeper meaning is that fear is also one side of religious awe, and this very fear can lead us to something much greater and more liberating.

Think about how scary it must have been for people in Copernicus' time to learn that our earth was not at the centre of the universe. And yet, that awe-inspiring fact enabled them (and us) to learn so much more about our universe and our place in it over the following centuries. Similarly, it must have been quite frightening when our microscopes enabled us to see all the microorganisms that exist around us. But that discovery led to germ theory, which has saved countless lives due to

---

[12]Ibid, 11:12.

[13]Rudolf Otto, *The Idea of the Holy*, trans John W. Harvey (Oxford: Oxford University Press, 1958), 128.

the advancements in medicine and practices that it ushered in. In much the same way, the prophets of the major world religions were saying that their revelations would forever transform the world because they involved earth-shattering truths that were so far beyond people's normal day-to-day experiences. Their claims were far reaching. They said that God incarnated on earth as a man, or that there are many deeper layers of consciousness that most of us have never tapped into, or that we have all lived many past lives. These are scary ideas with huge implications that may cause fear, but they also have many beautiful implications that have the potential to make us into better people.

As Buddhist monk Thich Nhat Hanh writes, 'Life is filled with suffering, but it is also filled with many wonders, such as the blue sky, the sunshine, and the eyes of a baby. To suffer is not enough. We must also be in touch with the wonders of life. They are within us and all around us, everywhere, anytime.'[14] Prophets, spiritual leaders and ordinary people from many walks of life have always pointed towards nature—God's physical creation that we are all part of—as a tremendous and uplifting source of awe. John Muir, the mountaineer who helped create the national park system in the United States, compared the awe he experienced in nature to the Christian sacrament of baptism because of how new and beautiful it made everything seem.[15] The pioneering conservationist Rachel Carson wrote, 'The more clearly we can focus our attention on the wonders and realities of the universe about us, the less taste we shall have for destruction.'[16]

Scientists and psychologists continue to study emotions and experiences of awe and wonder to record their effects on people and their potential for transforming society as a whole.

A team of psychologists in 2021 conducted research into the subject and it led them to consider how the promotion of compassion and feelings of interconnection elicited by awe can be instrumental in our world today:

---

[14]Thich Nhat Hanh, *Being Peace,* (Berkeley: Parallax Press, 2005).
[15]Robert C. Fuller, *Wonder: From Emotion to Spirituality* (Chapel Hill: The University of North Carolina Press, 2006), 49.
[16]Ibid, 106-07.

> Awe may promote prosocial instincts through the recognition of one's place in a vast interconnected world and be particularly beneficial in this age of rapid technological progress and social unrest [...] The [COVID-19] lockdowns may produce novel experiences of awe and opportunities to transcend the self in the consideration of the common good; such a capacity may be critical to the challenges imposed by the pandemic. Indeed, people may begin to cultivate awe through an intention and volition toward a more fully integrated way of being. Ultimately, this would allow people to experience the world as meaningful and awesome.[17]

Global events, much like the COVID-19 pandemic, profoundly disrupts and changes the lives of everyone on earth. These events bring with them a lot of pain and loss, but they can also be opportunities for us to experience the kind of awe that helps to reorient our perspective on the reality of our shared human nature and interconnectedness, as well as to reconsider the importance of love, compassion and cooperation.

Similarly, scholar of religion Michelle Voss Roberts posits that, 'The interpersonal dimension of spiritual disciplines also contains the transformative seeds of wonder. When we experience deep interpersonal connections we awaken to a larger reality; and when we connect with a participant in another religious tradition we obtain a taste of their larger reality.'[18] By allowing ourselves to explore unfamiliar religions, we can experience the sense of awe that comes from a direct connection with people we once saw as completely separate and different from ourselves. Such experiences are especially awe-inspiring when we realize how much we can learn from one another. And this kind of awe that promotes acceptance, togetherness and cooperation can be a great tool towards building a more peaceful world.

---

[17]Susan K. Chen & Myriam Mongrain, 'Awe and the interconnected self,' *The Journal of Positive Psychology*, Vol 16, no.6, 770-778, DOI: 10.1080/17439760.2020.1818808, 2019.
[18]Michelle Voss Roberts, *Tastes of the Divine* (New York: Fordham University Press, 2014), 184.

53

Light

No one, when he has lit a lamp, covers it with a container, or puts it under a bed; but puts it on a stand, that those who enter in may see the light.[1]

—New Testament

So powerful is the light of unity that it can illuminate the whole earth.[2]

—Baha'u'llah

In many religions, God or some other higher power is likened to light. Just like God, light is mysterious, omnipresent and it brings everything to life. We cannot always directly see the source of light, but without it we would not be able to see anything at all. The Christian writer C.S. Lewis writes:

> Man even at his highest sanctity and intelligence has no direct 'knowledge about' (savoir) the ultimate Being—only analogies. We

---

[1]Luke 8:16 (World English Bible).

[2]Bahá'u'lláh, *Gleanings From the Writings of Bahá'u'lláh* (US: Bahá'í Publishing Trust, 1990), 288, Baha'i Reference Library,_http://reference.bahai.org/en/t/b/GWB/gwb-132.html

cannot see light, though by light we can see things. Statements about God are extrapolations from the knowledge of other things which the divine illumination enables us to know.[3]

In this sense, God is like a lamp, illuminating an otherwise dark pathway. This is an analogy that recurs across religions. In the Qur'an, for instance, it is said that, 'God is the light of the heavens and the earth. The parable of His light is as if there were a niche and within it a lamp: the lamp enclosed in glass: the glass as it were a brilliant star: lit from a blessed tree, an olive, neither of the east nor of the west, whose oil is well nigh luminous, though fire scarce touched it: light upon light!'[4] According to the Baha'i prophet Baha'u'llah, even religion itself can be seen as 'a radiant light and an impregnable stronghold for the protection and welfare of the peoples of the world, for the fear of God impelleth man to hold fast to that which is good, and shun all evil'.[5]

Additionally, the prophets of religions—God's representatives on earth—are likewise described as guiding lights or lamps. According to the New Testament, Jesus spoke to them, saying, 'I am the light of the world. He who follows me will not walk in the darkness, but will have the light of life.'[6] In Hinduism, 'avatars', much like Jesus, are understood to be human incarnations of God on earth. In the Bhagavad Gita, the avatar Krishna explains, 'They who are always joined to yoga, who are part of me, and filled with kindness, to them I give the yoga of insight. By that yoga, they come to me. Since I move in sympathy with them, while dwelling in myself, I destroy their darkness born of ignorance with the bright lamp of wisdom.'[7] Religions, therefore, display a common tendency to describe their prophets as embodiments of teachings rather than just simple orators relaying a message—they are the living light that emanates directly from God or some other higher source.

---

[3]C.S. Lewis, *The Four Loves* (Mariner Books: New York, 2012), 826.

[4]Qur'an 24:35 (Yusuf Ali).

[5]Bahá'u'lláh, *Tablets of Bahá'u'lláh Revealed After the Kitáb-i-Aqdas* (US Bahá'í Publishing Trust: 1988), 125, Baha'i Reference Library, http://reference.bahai.org/en/t/c/CP/cp-12.html

[6]John 8:12 (World English Bible).

[7]*The Bhagavad Gita,* trans. Laurie L. Patton (New York: Penguin, 2014), 10:10-11.

This metaphor also is employed to refer to knowledge and the transmission of wisdom on a smaller, more concrete scale of regular life and interpersonal relations. We are constantly learning from others, and those who stand out as authorities in our lives are like prisms, who refract light for us to absorb. In the Hebrew Bible, for instance, one guideline of advice for young people is to 'keep your father's commandment, and don't forsake your mother's teaching. [...] For the commandment is a lamp, and the teaching is a light. Reproofs of instruction are the way of life'.[8] Prophets may bring new wisdom into the world for an entire civilization, but this wisdom is passed down generations through spiritual exemplars—priests, mystics, sages, etc. It also, of course, is passed from parents to their children through lessons of conduct, rituals and ceremonies. In the case of Judaism, lit candles are a major presence during meals on Sabbath and other holy occasions, such as Hanukkah, also known as 'the festival of lights'.

In the case of Confucianism, it is the 'gentleman' who is seen as the model human being, one who embodies virtues like compassion, a thirst for knowledge and a constant desire for self-improvement and self-transformation. As one passage in Confucius's Analects puts it, "The gentleman's errors are like an eclipse of the sun and moon in that when he errs the whole world sees him doing so and when he reforms the whole world looks up to him."[9] When a powerful religious figure mends his way, it is an even stronger source of inspiration for others as it underscores that no one is infallible and everyone can make mistakes. Recognizing right from wrong is an ongoing quest and one can improve their actions to reset the course on the righteous path at any time.

While all religious traditions do stress the importance of following prophets and teachers and other models, they also remind us that the same light that was emitted by such teachers resides within each of us as well.

This is also the meaning behind the Bhagavad Gita's teaching that, 'ignorance is destroyed by knowledge of the Self within. The light of this

---

[8]Proverbs 6:20-23 (World English Bible).

[9]Confucius, *The Analects*, trans. D.C. Lau, Penguin Classics edition (London, England: Penguin Books, 1971), 19:21.

knowledge shines like the sun, revealing the supreme Brahman.'[10] Light has to do with revealing the true essence of our minds, which is where the God within us can be found. The Baha'i prophet Baha'u'llah explains through a similar analogy:

> The soul of man should be likened unto this sun, and all things on earth should be regarded as his body. So long as no external impediment interveneth between them, the body will, in its entirety, continue to reflect the light of the soul, and to be sustained by its power. As soon as, however, a veil interposeth itself between them, the brightness of that light seemeth to lessen.[11]

In a concrete sense, the same light shines over us all in the form of the sun. The sun is a constant reminder that we are all one, which is why we see it as a common motif across many religions.

Usually, it is the veil of our egotistical selves that prevents us from perceiving the soul, or the authentic self, residing within each of us. And whereas the egotistical self gives us all the impression of separateness and division from one another, the soul—like the sun—is common to all, uniting humanity under a single light. As the great Bengali poet Rabindranath Tagore wrote, 'In the night we stumble over things and become acutely conscious of their individual separateness. But the day reveals the greater unity which embraces them. The man whose inner vision is bathed in an illumination of his consciousness at once realizes the spiritual unity reigning supreme over all differences.'[12] Unity, however, does not mean sameness—it simply offers a different perspective on viewing our differences. The historian of religion Jeffrey Kripal points out: religion 'is a shared light that is refracted through various historical prisms and psychological filters, which end up producing a veritable

---

[10]*The Bhagavad Gita*, trans. Eknath Easwaran, Second Edition (Tomales: Nilgiri Press, 2007), 5:16.

[11]Bahá'u'lláh, *Gleanings From the Writings of Bahá'u'lláh* (US: Bahá'í Publishing Trust, 1990), 154-55, Baha'i Reference Library. http://reference.bahai.org/en/t/b/GWB/gwb-80.html.

[12]Rabindranath Tagore in Jeffrey J. Kripal, *Comparing Religions*, illustrated edition (West Sussex: John Wiley & Sons, 2014), 369-70.

rainbow of different meanings and interpretations'.[13]

Spiritual leaders from many different religions point this out as well. The well-known Indian guru and popular author, Jaggi Vasudev, more commonly known as Sadhguru, explains, 'As many colors of the rainbow are an outcome of one pure light, the many religions of the world are an expression of one divine source.'[14] Quite similarly, the Sufi mystic and famous poet Rumi writes, 'All religions, all this singing, one song. The differences are just illusion and vanity. The sun's light looks a little different on this wall than it does on that wall, and a lot different on this other one, but it's still one light.'[15] We tend to focus on differences as something bad, something that keeps us separated from one another, rather than something that enriches us all. But when we fail to see the unity underlying our differences, it becomes more difficult to appreciate those differences for what they are: different layers that make the whole of humanity so much richer. The imagery and analogies involving light across religions get these points across and help us think deeply about what it would mean to see ourselves as all part of the same shared light.

In conclusion we should also consider scientific evidence that has revealed that most of the material world remains invisible to the human eye. Visible light, for instance, is not the sole illuminating energy of the universe, as pre-scientific common sense decreed. It is instead an infinitesimal sliver of electromagnetic radiation, comprising wavelengths of 400 to 700 nanometers (billionths of a meter), within a much wider spectrum (that ranges from gamma waves that are trillions of times shorter, to radio waves that are trillions of times longer) than the human visual range. As this vast spectrum was not only unseen, but completely unknown for most of human history, it is perfectly reasonable to assume

---

[13]Jeffrey J. Kripal, *Comparing Religions*, illustrated edition (West Sussex: John Wiley & Sons, 2014), 241.

[14]Sadhguru, 'Millennium World Peace Summit: Sadhguru's blessing addressed to the delegation of the Millennium World Peace Summit, convening at the United Nations, 28 August 2000,' *Isha*, 2 November 2017, https://isha.sadhguru.org/us/en/sadhguru/mission/millennium-world-peace-summit

[15]Jalaluddin Rumi, 'One Song,' trans. Coleman Barks, *SufiSpirit*, http://sufispirit.com.au/feature/rumi-sufi-poetry-one-song/, accessed on 12 July 2022.

that there is still much that is real and ever-present in our world, which we cannot see and do not even know about. This leaves lots of room for ongoing efforts of meaning-making.

54

Authentic Self

The great person is one who does not lose the child's mind.[1]

—Mencius

I have always been mesmerized by small children at play. They are so completely engaged in the moment, and seem to be living authentically, immersed in their play, without any care as to who might be watching. They never hesitate to show their emotion or affection, letting it flow unhindered, whether through a joyful hug or a loud bellyful laugh. These bundles of curiosity are like small sponges, soaking up everything that is presented to them and all that they seek and discover. Like a flower that needs the correct balance of air, water and sun to fully blossom, children only want to love, learn and play—and are in a state of flourishing when they engage in these three essential pursuits. If the key to flourishing is as simple as deeply engaging in loving, learning and playing, then why don't we do this? This is for one simple reason: as adults, we are governed by false narratives that are dominant in our societies. We allow these false narratives to dictate our lives because we live compulsively, instead of consciously; we are driven by societal forces that want to make us other than who we truly are.

[1]*Mencius*, trans. Irene Bloom (New York: Columbia University Press, 2011), 88.

Flourishing is something we see as outside of ourselves, an elusive destination to reach, instead of understanding that it is a choice that determines how we live our lives. There is a beautiful parable in ancient Hindu texts: a deer runs around as she is captivated by the smell of musk, not realizing that the musk she is smelling is inside her. We are like the deer; unaware that we can manufacture happiness and meaning inside us through acts of loving, learning and playing while engaging with the phenomenal world outside.

In the Bhagavad Gita, Krishna proclaims, 'This supreme Self is beginningless, deathless, and unconfined; although it inhabits bodies, it neither acts nor is tainted.'[2] This corresponds to the Hindu concepts of atman and brahman—that our authentic selves (atman) are microcosmic manifestations of the singular divine ground of reality (brahman).

However, most of us go through life unaware of the reality and profound superiority of our authentic self, which is occluded by our artificial ego-selves. Prophets, philosophers, sages and other figures across religions and traditions have tried to raise awareness of this. Referring to the ancient Greek schools of philosophy, for instance, historian of philosophy Pierre Hadot describes this line of reasoning: '[Philosophy] raises the individual from an inauthentic condition of life, darkened by unconsciousness and harassed by worry, to an authentic state of life, in which he attains self-consciousness, an exact vision of the world, inner peace, and freedom.'[3] Equally, philosopher Richard Rorty, referring to his near-contemporary Martin Heidegger, writes, 'Heidegger called the hope for authenticity, the hope to become one's own person rather than merely the creation of one's education or one's environment.'[4] The lesson to learn is that, so long as we are operating through our socialized self rather than our authentic self, we live compulsively and not consciously; in other words, the decisions we make are based solely on predetermined scripts and expectations of particular societies we are born into, and we

---

[2]*The Bhagavad Gita,* trans. Stephen Mitchell (New York: Harmony Books, 2000), 13:31.

[3]Pierre Hadot, *Philosophy as a Way of Life,* ed. Arnold I. Davidson, trans. Michael Chase (Massachusetts: Blackwell, 1995), 83.

[4]Richard Rorty, 'Philosophy as a Transitional Genre,' in *Pragmatism, Critique, Judgment: Essays for Richard J. Bernstein,* ed. Seyla Benhabib and Nancy Fraser (Cambridge: MIT Press, 2004), 7.

therefore have very little agency to experience and interact with the world through open eyes.

For me, the dots started to connect after having spent three years steeped in the rich intellectual world of Harvard University. I realized the distinct truth. There are two selves—an authentic self that we are born with, and a socialized self that we construct as we become integrated in society. I realized that, during this process, I had gradually and unconsciously strayed away from prioritizing the three desires of my authentic self. I was too busy with my duties as a professional. The artificial desires of my socialized self were starving me of my deeply natural needs for love, learning and play. I discovered the flourishing framework that I now call 'LLP'—Love, Learn and Play.

One of the goals of most religious and wisdom traditions is to help people to return to our authentic selves by clearing away the cobwebs of the socialized self, which hinders our growth. Achieving this is less a matter of acquiring something new, and more a matter of remembering who we are. Plato referred to this process as 'anamnesis', remembering who we really are. This is similar to the idea of Brahman in the case of Hinduism, or remembering our connection to God in the case of the Abrahamic religions. This idea is expressed in the short yet profound phrase, 'Tat twam asi' ('Thou are that', or, you are that ultimate reality), a concise summary of the Hindu philosophy. The veil of maya (ignorance or partial knowledge) hides our true selves from us. The process of a spiritual life is to recognize that authentic self. Israeli philosopher and rabbi David Hartman writes, 'The student of Torah is like the amnesia victim who tries to reconstruct from fragments the beautiful world he or she once experienced. By learning Torah, man returns to his own self.'[5] We also see similar notions expressed in other religions as well. The Taoist sage Chuang Tzu observed, 'Everyone in the world knows how to raise questions about what they don't know, but none know how to raise questions about what they already know. [...] All creatures, down to the smallest wriggling and fluttering insects, have thus lost touch with their inborn natures.'[6]

---

[5]David Hartman, *Love and Terror in the God Encounter: The Theological Legacy of Rabbi Joseph B. Soloveitchik, Volume 1* (Woodstock: Jewish Lights Publishing, 2001), 59.
[6]*Zhuangzi: The Essential Writings,* trans. Brook Ziporyn (Indianapolis: Hackett Publishing, 2009), 66.

Once again, religions agree in describing the authentic self as something that we must return to by purifying us of our current selves. This is what the phrase 'Tazkiya-e-nafs' signifies in Islam—the process of purifying the human self. As is written in the Qur'an, 'Whoever purifies himself does so for the benefit of his own soul; and the destination (of all) is to God.'[7] This is also why there is such a heavy emphasis on guidelines for modesty in Islam (and in many other religions). We see this in the New Testament of Christianity, for instance: 'Let your beauty be not just the outward adorning of braiding the hair, and of wearing jewels of gold, or of putting on fine clothing; but in the hidden person of the heart, in the incorruptible adornment of a gentle and quiet spirit, which is very precious in the sight of God.'[8]

Other practices, like prayer, meditation and yoga, can help us achieve purification as well. The Indian guru Yogananda explains, 'The goal of yoga science is to calm the mind, that without distortion it may hear the infallible counsel of the Inner Voice.'[9] The Buddhist monk and popular author Thich Nhat Hanh notes, 'Mindfulness is the kind of light that shows us the way. It is the living Buddha inside of each of us. Mindfulness gives birth to insight, awakening, compassion, and love.'[10]

Indeed, this description of the authentic self (in this case, the Buddha's nature) is another commonality across religions: the authentic self is characterized by wakefulness, compassion, and love; these are all traits where the ego self falls short. Our ego selves prefer easy-to-follow scripts over wakefulness, and selfish desires over empathetic expressions of love. This is why the Baha'i Prophet Bahá'u'lláh taught that we must 'Burn away, wholly for the sake of the Well-Beloved, the veil of self with the flame of the undying Fire, and with faces joyous and beaming with light, associate with your neighbour'.[11] The Baha'i leader Shoghi Effendi

---

[7]Qur'an 35:18 (Yusuf Ali).

[8]1 Peter 3:3-4 (World English Bible).

[9]Paramahansa Yogananda, *Autobiography of a Yogi* (Auckland, New Zealand: The Floating Press, 2009), 260.

[10]Thich Nhat Hanh, Twitter post, 21 January 2018.

[11]Bahá'u'lláh, *Gleanings From the Writings of Bahá'u'lláh* (US: Bahá'í Publishing Trust, 1990), 316, Baha'i Reference Library, https://reference.bahai.org/en/t/b/GWB/gwb-147.html.

further explains this as: 'The complete and entire elimination of the ego would imply perfection—which man can never completely attain—but the ego can and should be ever-increasingly subordinated to the enlightened soul of man. This is what spiritual progress implies.'[12] It is virtually impossible, and perhaps not even beneficial, to strip the ego self away entirely. After all, as Harvard psychologist and author Mark Epstein remarks, 'Some amount of ego or self is very important. But we also need the ability to observe our own mind, thoughts, and feelings. This is the second important thing. That's something that both meditation and psychotherapy encourage, in different ways.'[13] The problem is not the ego itself, but how much we depend upon the autopilot mode that the ego affords us. The socialized ego self and the authentic self exist in each of us, but we can improve ourselves and our relations with each other by listening more to the latter.

We let ourselves be seduced by the immediate thrill that we get out of acquiring more money, fame and power; we start to see these achievements as our goals, while in reality they can never be more than a means to help us in pursuing our three deepest longings i.e., loving, learning and playing. As the Dalai Lama explains, 'Ultimately, the reason why love and compassion bring the greatest happiness is simply that our nature cherishes them above all else. The need for love lies at the very foundation of human existence. It results from the profound interdependence we all share with one another.'[14] Neuroscience has recently revealed that the existence of mirror neurons forms the physiological source of our capacities for empathy and compassion. Our evolution, as a species, was driven largely through social cooperation, which is why parts of our cognitive apparatus like this remain with us. We were naturally selected to love. Beneath our egotistical selves lie

---

[12]Shoghi Effendi, 'letter to an individual believer,' *Baha'i Library Online,* 14 December 1941, https://bahai-library.com/compilation_psychology_knowledge_self.)

[13]Mark Epstein in Jill Radsken, 'Driven by ego? This book's for you,' *The Harvard Gazette,* 16 January 2018, https://news.harvard.edu/gazette/story/2018/01/harvard-trained-psychiatrist-offers-escape-route-for-the-ego-driven/.

[14]Tenzin Gyatso, The Fourteenth Dalai Lama, 'Compassion and the Individual,' accessed on 12 July 2022, https://www.dalailama.com/messages/compassion-and-human-values/compassion.

our authentic selves, which naturally long towards loving, learning and playing.

Life is beautiful when we are open, authentic and present to the fullness of ourselves. It is not something we must hide from each other; the insights and experiences that come through the authentic self allows us to give and receive from each other. As Harvard Divinity School alumni Casper ter Kuile and Angie Thurston stated in an interview, 'The ultimate millennial word is authenticity. And so one of the things that contributes to that feeling of "is this an authentic thing" is the idea of not just consuming something but co-creating it.'[15] Authenticity is important, not just at the individual level, but also at the level of leadership. Over the last decade, people have developed a deep distrust of leaders in America, and have been clamoring for new kind of leadership. When the Advisory Council of Stanford Business School was asked the question, 'What is the most important quality for leaders to develop for the next decade?' most of them said: 'Self-awareness and authenticity.'

[15]Casper ter Kuile and Angie Thurston, 'Video: Religion for a New Generation,' *Harvard Divinity School News,* 2 April 2020, https://hds.harvard.edu/news/2020/04/02/video-religion-new-generation.

55

Putting It All Together: Religions as a Meaning-Making Framework

[T]he search for meaning and purpose is rooted in biology to the extent that goal striving is a biological imperative of all zoological organisms.[1]

—Eric Klinger

We look for and find patterns in our world and in our lives, then weave narratives around those patterns to bring them to life and give them meaning. Such is the stuff of which myth, religion, history, and science are made.[2]

—Michael Shermer

[1]Eric Klinger, 'The search for meaning in evolutionary perspective and its clinical implications,' *The Human Quest for Meaning: A Handbook of Psychological Research and Clinical Applications, ed.* P.T Wong and P. S. Fry, American Psychological Association, 27–50, https://psycnet.apa.org/record/1998-06124-002.

[2]Michael Shermer, 'Chicken Soup for the Evolutionist's Soul', *Los Angeles Times*, 6 February 2000. https://michaelshermer.com/2000/02/chicken-soup-for-the-evolutions-soul/

The preceding chapters vividly display the fascinating commonalities between apparently different religions. It may be quite hard to believe in their similitude because we're usually taught to focus on the uniqueness of our religion. I am still in awe of the number of universal themes that we found in our research. And I think there are still more out there that we haven't covered. Most people are surprised to hear of so many commonalities.

Upon reflection, I ask myself, 'Why should we be surprised?' All religions, after all, have been attempts to address human beings' fundamental need to make meaning of life by exploring the mysteries of nature and asking existential questions. All prophets have tried to guide us to find meaning in life and lead a fulfilling life.

During my studies at Harvard, I gathered nuggets of wisdom from each of the diverse courses that I took. But the one that weaved it all together for me was the course by Robert Kegan on Adult Development. His course highlighted two key concepts: 'meaning-making' and 'different orders of mind', with which we make meaning. This framework immediately explained to me the commonalities and diversities we experience in religious behaviours across time and geographies. It was like the feeling of satori, the opening of the third eye. Meaning making has been our common quest of humanity, experienced through different contexts, different cognitive abilities, different levels of education, and different orders of mind, which affect how we make meaning, resulting in diversities. Hence, I decided to devote an entire chapter on this.

In his book *The Evolving Self* (1982) Kegan puts into perspective how fundamental the concept of meaning-making is in terms of how we interact with the world. 'It is not that a person makes meaning', he writes, 'as much as that the activity of being a person is the activity of meaning-making.'[3] The sense of our own impermanence, coupled with our seemingly inconsequential role in a vast and indifferent universe, makes us wonder why we are here and how we should live our lives; it makes us question what our meaning and purpose is as human beings.

An important aspect of Kegan's description of meaning-making is

[3]Robert Kegan, *The Evolving Self: Problem And Process In Human Development* (Cambridge: Harvard University Press, 1982), 11.

that nobody has the final answer. The totality of human experience defies full description by any single language, culture, religion or any other category of humanity.

> Even in the midst of charged and often irritable relations between men and women, East and West, we have the opportunity to drop back to consider the whole of which we are a part. When we do, something quite beautiful and moving appears: a single community of people who together give expression to the full complexity of being alive; a universality which each of us can find reflected in ourselves (the woman in every man, the Easterner in every Westerner).[4]

The diversity of beliefs we see across humanity does not indicate that some of us are 'right' and everyone else is 'wrong'. Our effort to imagine the unimaginable, to know the unknowable, to describe the indescribable—this is the power of the human spirit as it achieves its fullness of expression through a plurality of forms.

From a neuroscientific point of view, meaning-making refers to the processes by which our brains confront and alleviate uncertainty during the course of our everyday lives. From a grand existential perspective, we are uncertain of our place in the universe. We were born without choice and we must die without choice, and this sense of our own impermanence coupled with our seemingly inconsequential role in a vast and indifferent universe makes us wonder, among other questions, why we are here and how we should live our lives: what our meaning and purpose are as human beings.

As civilizations across the world became more complex, so too did our meaning-making capacities, as expressed in more complex and unified forms of the divine. Animism was the norm for a while across the world (where all aspects of the natural world were believed to be endowed with an animating spirit), but eventually the manifold aspects of our existence became packaged together as so many manifestations of the same single being or force: God. The various Semitic deities

[4]Robert Kegan, *The Evolving Self: Problem And Process In Human Development* (Cambridge: Harvard University Press, 1982), 209–10.

coalesced into the Abrahamic God, Yahweh, just as the Hindu concept of many anthropomorphic Gods and Goddesses was cast in a new light with the concept of 'Nirakar', or a formless God.

Our collective meaning-making processes as human beings have varied across time and place. At each point in history, our cultural worldviews have been made up of provisional truths about the world that are constantly being updated—through modelling, remodelling and optimization—as we gain new information, in a process that Thomas S. Kuhn termed as 'paradigm shifts' in his famous book *The Structure of Scientific Revolutions* (1962). The worldviews of each culture and historical era have differed according to a variety of factors that influence how meaning is made, including (1) cognitive development; (2) our sensory capabilities; (3) levels of education; (4) cultural and historical context; (5) individual cognitive capacities.

Cognitive Factors

We share 99 per cent of our DNA with other apes, and yet our brains are three times as large as theirs. This is the result of a seven-million-year process of evolution. As our brains expanded in size, so too did our cognitive capacities, enabling us as a species to develop novel ways of making meaning. As hunter-gatherers about two million years ago, we had to make meaning out of the behaviours of animals in order to hunt effectively and avoid being preyed upon. We had to make meaning out of fluctuating weather patterns to determine when to stay in place and when to move, or decipher patterns out of stars in the night sky to help with navigation. And still our brains kept growing, until about 200,000 years ago when Homo Sapiens first emerged. Since then, our brain size has remained about the same, but the shape and physiology of our brains has continued changing as a result of increasingly complex social behaviours and meaning-making activities, such as language, art and, of course, religion.[5]

These new forms of meaning-making were enabled, in large part,

[5]John Hawks, 'How Has the Human Brain Evolved?' *Scientific American*, 1 July 2013, https://www.scientificamerican.com/article/how-has-human-brain-evolved/

by the emergence of agriculture about 10,000 years ago. The broader movement from hunter-gatherer societies to farming-based societies—in other words, the emergence of agriculture and the food surplus it produced—was a revolutionary step in the history of human meaning-making. With surplus food, crucially, came leisure and a surplus of psychic energy, over and above the requirements to meet our biological needs. This is an important component in what distinguishes us from animals, who spend most of their cognitive energy on meeting their biological needs. When people looked up at the sky and the stars, they were not just trying to navigate their way back home or predict the weather. They were spending more time wondering about the existential questions that have captivated us as a species ever since: Who or what is responsible for the existence of the world around us? Who or what created us, and for what purpose? Who or what is the cause of the laws of nature, natural disasters, and so on? What happens after we die? How should we organize our societies and our individual lives in response to these questions?

Profound existential questions later went on to form the backbone of most religions. These then became human universals, and were deeply embedded from our evolutionary pasts into our neural makeup. Meaning-making in human history was deepening.

Sensory Capabilities

Another very basic factor affecting meaning-making is our sensory capabilities, our natural means of interfacing with the physical world. We know that we do not see, hear, smell, taste or feel any more than a small fraction of what is out there in the world.

Hawks can see much further than us, for instance; bees can see ultraviolet light, which is invisible to us; mantis shrimps can have four or five times as many colour receptors in their eyes than us. Our dogs hear sounds at pitches too high for us to notice, and bats can navigate in the dark through the use of sound waves. Many animals, including elephants and bears, have a much more complex sense of smell. The tiny hairs on a spider amplify its sense of touch, and catfish have ten times as many taste buds as us. Our ancestors were limited to the apparatus of their bare

Acknowledgements

First of all I want to acknowledge the debt to my parents who brought us up inter-religiously while being deeply immersed in our own religion. They taught us human values above all religious beliefs and to respect all religions.

This upbringing would not translate into this book but for the fellowship I got at Harvard's Advanced Leadership Initiative (ALI), which afforded me to take over thirty classes soaking in the intellectual diversity and depth of Harvard. My personal thanks to Rosabeth Moss Kanter whose tireless passion made the ALI possible. The concept of the book started as a project which we were supposed to undertake as ALI fellows.

Next on my list is David Hempton, Dean of Harvard Divinity School, who enthusiastically encouraged me to undertake this project and extended research status to me at Harvard to enable me to complete my work.

My professors Francis Clooney, Richard Parker, and Fernando Reimers at Harvard and Scotty McLennan at Stanford who encouraged me to pursue the book whenever I had some doubts. Professor Clooney read my drafts thoroughly and was generous with his time in writing a foreword to the book for which I am immensely grateful.

Next in line is Donald Frederick, who transitioned from Harvard's Human Flourishing Program to be the first colleague at UEF and with whom I brainstormed the original framework for this book and who helped me recruit Allen Simon from Harvard Divinity School. My thanks to Allen Simon who devoted almost five years of his life researching and helping me with writing this book. He undertook another difficult job making sure that we attribute quotes and other content diligently. If we have missed any proper reference, please accept our thanks and know that all income from this book will go to our foundation, UEF.

Thanks to Manny Singh who made profuse comments on the first draft and to my sister Anu Thareja for finally proofreading the manuscript.

Finally to Namita Devidayal, who introduced me to Rupa Publications and to my editor Dibakar Ghosh, who so enthusiastically endorsed this publication.

Bibliography

'Abdu'l-Bahá. *'Abdu'l-Bahá on Divine Philosophy*. Compiled by Elizabeth Fraser Chamberlain. Boston: Tudor Press, 1918. Baha'i Library Online. http://bahai-library.com/abdulbaha_divine_philosophy&chapter=all.

——— *Bahá'í World Faith—Selected Writings of Bahá'u'lláh and 'Abdu'l-Bahá ('Abdu'l-Bahá's Section Only)*. US Bahá'í Publishing Trust, 1976. Baha'i Reference Library. http://reference.bahai.org/en/t/c/BWF/bwf-103.html.

——— 'Deepening Our Knowledge and Understanding of the Faith, The Importance of.' *Compilation of Compilations*, Volume 1 (1991). Baha'i Library Online: http://bahailibrary.com/compilation_importance_deepening#37.

——— *Foundations of World Unity*, sixth printing. US: Bahá'í Publishing Trust, 1979. Baha'i Reference

Library. http://reference.bahai.org/en/t/c/FWU/fwu-29.html.

——— *Paris Talks*. Eleventh Edition. UK Bahá'í Publishing Trust, 1972. Baha'i Reference Library. http://reference.bahai.org/en/t/ab/PT/pt-31.html.

——— *The Promulgation of Universal Peace*. Second Edition. US Bahá'í Publishing Trust, 1982.

Baha'i Reference Library. http://reference.bahai.org/en/t/ab/PUP/pup-111.html.

——— *Selections From the Writings of 'Abdu'l-Bahá*. Bahá'í. World Centre, 1982. Baha'I Reference Library. http://reference.bahai.org/en/t/ab/SAB/sab-145.html.

——— *Tablets of Abdul-Baha Abbas*. Bahá'í Publishing Committee, 1909 edition. Baha'i Reference Library. https://reference.bahai.org/en/t/ab/TAB/tab-240.html.

Aitken, Robert, trans. *The Gateless Barrier: The Wu-Men Kuan (Mumonkan)*. New York: North Point Press, 2016.

'Aṅgulimālīya Sūtra.' In Shabkar, *Food of Bodhisattvas: Buddhist Teachings on Abstaining from Meat*. Translated by Padmakara Translation Group. Boston, MA: Shambhala Publications, 10 August 2004.

Armstrong, Karen. *A History of God: The 4,000-Year Quest of Judaism, Christianity and Islam*. New York: Ballantine Books, 1994.

Armstrong, Neil. Quoted by NASA Earth Observatory https://earthobservatory.nasa.gov/images/91494/right-here-right-now.

Ashtavakra. Quoted in Ankit Sharma. 'Ways of the Jnanis – 1 – King Janak's Dream.' Center of Indic Studies. 10 August 2020. https://cisindus.org/2020/05/04/ways-of-the-jnanis-1-king-janaks-dream/

Augustine of Hippo. 'Homily 7 on the First Epistle of John.' *Nicene and Post-Nicene Fathers, First Series.* Vol. 7. Translated by H. Browne. Edited by Philip Schaff. Buffalo: Christian Literature Publishing Co., 1888. Revised and edited for New Advent by Kevin Knight. http://www.newadvent.org/fathers/170207.htm.

Babylonian Talmud (Ḥul. 7b). Jewish Virtual Library. https://www.jewishvirtuallibrary.org/providence.

Bahá'í International Community. 'Valuing Spirituality in Development.' A concept paper presented to the "World Faiths and Development Dialogue" hosted by the President of the World Bank and the Archbishop of

Canterbury at Lambeth Palace. London, UK. February 18, 1998. Baha'i International Community. https://www.bic.org/statements/valuing-spirituality-development#I.

Baha'i Universal House of Justice. 'Ridvan Message'. 2010. https://universalhouseofjustice.bahai.org/ridvan-messages/20100421_001.

——— 'Scholarship, Bahá'í: Statements from the World Centre.' *Bahá'í Studies Review, 3:2.* (1993). https://bahai-library.com/compilation_scholarship_bsr.

Bahá'u'lláh. *Gleanings From the Writings of Bahá'u'lláh.* US Bahá'í Publishing Trust, 1990. Baha'i Reference Library. http://reference.bahai.org/en/t/b/GWB/gwb-110.html.

——— *The Importance of Obligatory Prayer and Fasting.* A Compilation Prepared by the Research

Department of the Universal House of Justice. May 2000. https://www.bahai.org/library/authoritative-texts/compilations/importance-obligatory-prayer-fasting/1#098356618.

———*The Kitáb-i-Íqán.* US Bahá'í Publishing Trust, 1989. Baha'i Reference Library. http://reference.bahai.org/en/t/b/KI/ki-1.html

——— *Prayers and Meditations by Bahá'u'lláh.* Pocket-size edition. US Bahá'í Publishing Trust, 1987. Baha'i Reference Library. https://reference.bahai.org/en/t/b/PM/pm-181.html.

——— *Tablets of Bahá'u'lláh Revealed After the Kitáb-i-Aqdas.* US Bahá'í Publishing Trust: 1988. Baha'i Reference Library. http://reference.bahai.org/en/t/b/TB/tb-10.html

——— *Trustworthiness: A Cardinal Bahá'í Virtue.* Universal House of Justice Research Department: August 1990. https://www.bahai.org/library/authoritativetexts/compilations/trustworthiness/trustworthiness.pdf?4fda74d6

Basho, Matsuo. *The Narrow Road to the Deep North and Other Travel Sketches.* Penguin Classics edition. Translated by Nobuyuki Yuasa. New York: Penguin Books, 1966.

Berger, Peter L. *The Sacred Canopy: Elements of a Sociological Theory of Religion.* New York: Open Road Integrated Media, 2011.

Bialik, Hayyim Nahman and Yehoshua Hana Rawnitzki. Ed. *The Book of Legends: Sefer Ha-Aggadah.* Trans. William Gordon Braude. New York: Schocken Books, 1992.

Bloom, Irene, trans. *Mencius*, 7B,32. New York: Columbia University Press, 2011.

Bodhi Bhikkhu. *In the Buddha's Words: An Anthology of Discourses from the Pali Canon.* Somerville: Wisdom Publications, 2005.

——— 'Nibbana (Nirvana).' 1981. In 'Why did the Buddha teach the Noble Truth of suffering?' *Handful of Leaves.* YouTube Video. 29 September 2021. https://www.youtube.com/watch?v=m8zEWml3000.

Bolte Taylor, Jill. *My Stroke of Insight: A Brain Scientist's Personal Journey.* New York: Plume Books, 2009.

Borg, Marcus J. *The Heart of Christianity: Rediscovering a Life of Faith.* New York: HarperCollins, 2003.

Boroditsky, Lera. 'How language shapes the way we think.' TEDWomen 2017. TED. https://www.ted.com/talks/lera_boroditsky_how_language_shapes_the_way_we_think/transcript.

Boyer, Pascal. *Religion Explained: The Evolutionary Origins of Religious Thought.* New York: Basic Books, 2001.

Broghammer, Francie Hart. 'Death By Loneliness.' Real Clear Policy. 6 May 2019. https://www.realclearpolicy.com/articles/2019/05/06/death_by_loneliness_111185.html

Bruit Zaidman, Louise and Pauline Schmitt Pantel. *Religion in the Ancient Greek City.* Trans. Paul Cartledge. Cambridge: Cambridge University Press, 1992.

Buber, Martin. *I and Thou.* New York: Simon & Schuster, 1996.

Budde, Mariann Edgar. 'Trump's Visit to St. John's Church Outraged Me.' *The New York Times.* 4 June 2020. https://www.nytimes.com/2020/06/04/opinion/trump-st-johns-church-protests.html.

Bush, George W. Quoted in Jena McGregor. 'The most memorable passage in George W. Bush's speech rebuking Trumpism.' *The Washington Post.* 20 October 2017. https://www.washingtonpost.com/news/on-leadership/wp/2017/10/20/the-most-memorable-passage-in-george-w-bushs-speech-rebuking-trumpism/

Campbell, Joseph. *The Hero with a Thousand Faces.* The Collected Works of Joseph Campbell Series edition. Novato, CA: New World Library, 2008.

Chang, Ruth H. 'Understanding Di and Tian: Deity and Heaven from Shang to Tang Dynasties.' *Sino-Platonic Papers.* Number 108 (2000): iv-50. Edited by Victor H. Mair.

Chen, Susan K. & Myriam Mongrain. 'Awe and the interconnected self.' *The Journal of Positive Psychology*, 16:6 (2021). 770-778. DOI: 10.1080/17439760.2020.1818808.

Chen, Ying, Sion Kim Harris, Everett L Worthington Jr, and Tyler J VanderWeele. 'Religiously or Spiritually-Motivated Forgiveness and Subsequent Health and

Well-Being among Young Adults: An Outcome-Wide Analysis.' Journal of Positive Psychology. 14 (5). 649-658. *PubMed.* 13 September 2018. https://pubmed.ncbi.nlm.nih.gov/31360213/.

Chin, Annping, trans. Confucius. *The Analects*. New York: Penguin, 2014.

Ching, Julia. *Confucianism and Christianity: A Comparative Study.* Tokyo: Kodansha International, 1977.

Chödrön, Pema. *The Places That Scare You: A Guide to Fearlessness in Difficult Times.* Boston: Shambhala, 2002.

Chopra, Deepak. 'How meditation can help anxiety.' Stanford University Wu Tsai Neurosciences Institute. 14 September 2015. https://neuroscience.stanford.edu/news/how-meditation-can-help-anxiety.

Chu Hsi. *The Su chin-ssu-lu,* 2:17. In *Further Reflections on Things at Hand: A Reader.* Trans. Allen John Wittenborn. Lanham, Maryland: University Press of America, 1991. The Church of Jesus Christ of Latter-day Saints. *Articles of Faith,* Article 11. https://www.churchofjesuschrist.org/study/manual/gospel-topics/articles-of-faith?lang=eng.

Cleary, Thomas, trans. *The Book of Master Lie.* 2009.

Cleary, Thomas, trans. *The Flower Ornament Scripture: A Translation of the Avatamsaka Sutra.* Boston: Shambhala Publications, 1993.

Clooney, Francis X., SJ. 'The Good Samaritan: In a time of violence, Jesus calls us to be neighbors to everyone who needs us.' *Harvard.edu blog.* 10 July 2016. https://projects.iq.harvard.edu/francisclooney/blog/good-samaritan-time-violence-jesus-calls-us-be-neighbors-everyone-who-needs-us.

———. 'Have We Forgotten How to Repent - and to Forgive?' *Harvard.edu blog.* 7 December 2017. https://projects.iq.harvard.edu/francisclooney/blog/have-we-forgotten-how-repent-and-forgive.

——— Interview with Wendy McDowell. Harvard Divinity School. December 2009.

Craiutu, Aurelian. 'Moderation May Be The Most Challenging and Rewarding Virtue.' Edited by Sam Haselby. *Aeon.* 17 July 2017. https://aeon.co/ideas/moderation-may-be-the-most-challenging-and-rewarding-virtue.

Csikszentmihaly, Mihaly. *The Evolving Self: A Psychology for the Third Millennium.* New York: Harper Perennial, 1994.

———. *Flow: The Psychology of Optimal Experience.* New York: Harper Collins, 1991. The Dalai Lama [Tenzin Gyatso]. 'Compassion and the Individual.' His Holiness the 14th Dalai Lama of Tibet. https://www.dalailama.com/messages/compassion-and-human-values/compassion.

———. *The Compassionate Life.* Boston: Wisdom Publications, 2003.

———. *Dalai Lama: A Policy of Kindness.* Edited by Sidney Piburn. Delhi: Motilal Banarsidass, 2002.

———. 'The Dalai Lama on the Value of Pilgrimages.' *Newsweek.* 20 April 2007. https://www.newsweek.com/dalai-lama-value-pilgrimages-97425.

———. 'Nobel Peace Prize Acceptance Speech.' Oslo, Norway. 10 December 1989.

https://www.nobelprize.org/prizes/peace/1989/lama/26133-the-14th-dalai-lama-acceptance-speech-1989/.

———. 'Feb 2.' *The Path to Tranquility: Daily Wisdom.* Edited by Renuka Singh. New York: Penguin, 2002.

———. 'Oprah Talks to The Dalai Lama.' O, *The Oprah Magazine.* August 2001. https://www.oprah.com/omagazine/oprah-interviews-the-dalai-lama/all.

———. Quoted in Alice Thompson. 'Westerners are too self-absorbed.' 1 April 2006. https://www.telegraph.co.uk/news/worldnews/asia/burmamyanmar/1514537/Westerners-are-too-self-absorbed.html.

———. Quoted in 'The Dalai Lama receives Mahatma Gandhi International Award in Bodh Gaya.' *Dalailama.com.* 4 January 2012. https://www.dalailama.com/news/2012/homepage-news-the-dalai-lama-receives-mahatma-gandhi-international-award-in-bodh-gaya-the-dalai-lama-receives-mahatma-gandhi-international-award-in-bodh-gaya/amp.

———. Quoted in Mitchell Landsberg. 'Dalai Lama suggests Osama bin Laden's death was justified.' *The Los Angeles Times.* 4 May 2011. https://www.latimes.com/local/la-xpm-2011-may-04-la-me-0504-dalai-lama-20110504-story.html.

Dalmia, Gaurav. 'Leadership lessons from Indian philosophy.' *The Times of India.* 9 October 2020. https://timesofindia.indiatimes.com/blogs/toi-edit-page/leadership-lessons-from-indian-philosophy/.

Darwin, Charles. *The Descent of Man, and Selection in Relation to Sex.* New Jersey: Princeton University Press, 1981.

———. *On the Origin of Species: By Means of Natural Selection Or the Preservation of Favored Races in the Struggle for Life.* New York: Cosimo, Inc., 2007.

De Chardin, Pierre Teilhard. 'The Evolution of Chastity.' *Toward the Future.* Trans. René Hague. San Diego, California: Harcourt, 1975.

Doniger, Wendy. *Hinduism. The Norton Anthology of World Religions: Vol. 1.* Ed. Jack Miles. New York: W.W. Norton & Company, 2015.

———. *The Hindus: An Alternative History.* London: Oxford University Press, 2010.

———. *The Implied Spider: Politics and Theology in Myth.* New York: Columbia University Press, 1998.

———, trans, *The Rig Veda.* New York: Penguin, 2005.

Dostoyevsky, Fyodor. *The Idiot.* Translated by Henry and Olga Carlisle. New York: Signet Classics, 2010.

Dunn, Elizabeth. 'Helping others makes us happier—but it matters how we do it.' *TED2019.* April 2019. https://www.ted.com/talks/elizabeth_dunn_helping_others_makes_us_happier_but_it_matters_how_we_do_it.

Durkheim, Emile. *The Elementary Forms of Religious Life,* Translated by Karen E. Fields. New York: The Free Press, 1995.

Easter, Michael. *The Comfort Crisis.* Quoted in Michael Easter. 'The Secret to Happiness? Thinking About Death.' *Outside.* 13 May 2021. https://www.outsideonline.com/outdoor-adventure/exploration-survival/secret-happiness-think-about-dying-comfort-crisis-easter/

Easwaran, Eknath, trans. *The Bhagavad Gita*. Second Edition. Tomales: Nilgiri Press, 2007.

——— trans. *The Upanishads*. Tomales, CA: Nilgiri Press, July 2007.

——— trans. *The Dhammapada*. Second Edition. Canada: Nilgiri Press, 2007.

Effendi, Shogi. *Bahá'í News*, no. 71. The National Spiritual Assembly of the Bahá'ís of the United States and Canada. West Englewood, New Jersey. February 1933. Accessed via Baha'i Works. https://bahai.works/Baha%27i_News/Issue_71/Text.

———. *Directives from the Guardian*. New Delhi, India: Baha'i Publishing Trust, 1973. Baha'i Reference Library. http://reference.bahai.org/en/t/se/DG/dg-181.html.

———. Letter to an individual believer, 14 December 1941. "The Bahá'í Life: Excerpts from the Writings of the Guardian On." Baha'i Library Online. https://bahai-library.com/compilation_bahai_life.

———.'Science and Technology.' Compiled by Research Department of the Universal House of Justice. Baha'i Library Online. https://bahai-library.com/compilation_science_technology

Einstein, Albert. Letter to the family of Michele Besso. March 1955. Christie's. https://www.christies.com/features/Einstein-letters-to-Michele-Besso-8422-1.aspx

———. Quoted in Life Magazine. *PBS Nova*. 2 May 1955. https://www.pbs.org/wgbh/nova/einstein/wisd-nf.html.

———. Quoted in Walter Sullivan. 'The Einstein Papers. A Man of Many Parts.' *The New York Times Archives*. 29 March 1972. https://www.nytimes.com/1972/03/29/archives/the-einstein-papers-a-man-of-many-parts-the-einstein-papers-man-of.html.

———. Quoted in 'Professor Einstein Declares His Faith in Spinoza's God.' The Archive of the Jewish Telegraphic Agency: 28 April 1929. https://www.jta.org/1929/04/28/archive/professor-einstein-declares-his-faith-in-spinozas-god.

Eliot, T.S. 'Little Gidding.' *Four Quartets*. Columbia University. http://www.columbia.edu/itc/history/winter/w3206/edit/tseliotlittlegidding.html

Emerson, Ralph Waldo. *The Collected Works of Ralph Waldo Emerson*. Musaicum Books, 2018.

Emoto, Masaru. *The Hidden Messages in Water*. New York: Simon & Schuster, 2011.

Epstein, Mark. In Jill Radsken. 'Driven by ego? This book's for you.' *The Harvard Gazette*. 16 January 2018. https://news.harvard.edu/gazette/story/2018/01/harvard-trained-psychiatrist-offers-escape-route-for-the-ego-driven/.

Erikson, Erik H. *Identity: Youth and Crisis*. New York: W. W. Norton & Company, 1994.

François, Myriam. 'I felt violated by the demand to undress': three Muslim women on France's hostility to the hijab.' *The Guardian*. 27 July 2021. https://www.

theguardian.com/world/2021/jul/27/i-felt-violated-by-the-demand-to-undress-three-muslim-women-on-frances-hostility-to-the-hijab

Friedländer, Michael, trans. *The Guide for the Perplexed: Mamonides*. Second edition. London: G. Routledge & Sons, 1910. Digitized from Cornell University, 31 October 2012.

Fromm, Erich. *The Art of Loving*. Fiftieth Anniversary Edition. New York: HarperCollins, 2006.

Fukuyama, Francis. 'Liberalism and Its Discontents.' *American Purpose*. 5 October 2020.https://www.americanpurpose.com/articles/liberalism-and-its-discontent/.

Fuller, Robert C. *Wonder: From Emotion to Spirituality*. Chapel Hill: University of North Carolina Press, 2006.

Gandhi, M. K. *An Autobiography, Or, The Story of My Experiments with Truth: A Table of Concordance*. Mumbai,

India: Jaico Books, 2008.

———. *Hindu Dharma*. Diamond Pocket Books Pvt Ltd, 2017.

———. Quoted in J.T.F. Jordens. *Gandhi's Religion: A Homespun Shawl*. New York: St. Martin's Press, 1998.

Ganguli, Kisari Mohan trans. *Mahabharata*, Anusasana Parva 113.8. Sacred Texts. https://www.sacred-texts.com/hin/m13/m13b078.htm#fn_255.

Gibran, Kahlil. *Sand and Foam: A Book of Aphorisms*. New York: Alfred A. Knopf. 1959.

Giles, Lionel, trans. *Taoist Teachings*. Ashland, Ohio: Library of Alexandria, 2009.

Gilovich, Thomas. *How We Know What Isn't So*. New York: Simon & Schuster, 2008.

Goldberg, Philip. *Spiritual Practice for Crazy Times: Powerful Tools to Cultivate Calm, Clarity, and Courage*. New York: Hay House, 2020.

Golding, William. *Lord of the Flies*. New York: Penguin, 1954.

Goldman, Samuel. 'Harvard's new chaplain is an atheist. Is that a contradiction?' *The Week*. 27 August 2021. https://theweek.com/life/religion/1004181/harvards-new-chaplain-is-an-atheist-is-that-a-contradiction? utm_campaign=afternoon_newsletter_20210829&utm_source=afternoon_newsletter&utm_medium=email&refid=8A308B74CC87F45B2F2D12F28F2F25D0.

Gombrich, E. H. "The use of art for the study of symbols." *American Psychologist*, 20(1). 1965. 34–50.

Gooding, David and John Lennox. *The Bible and Ethics*. Coleraine, N. Ireland: Myrtlefield House, 2015.

Gorfinkle, Joseph I., trans. *The Eight Chapters Of Maimonides On Ethics*. New York: Columbia University Press, 1912.

Hadot, Pierre. *Philosophy as a Way of Life*. Edited by Arnold I. Davidson. Translated by Michael Chase. Massachusetts: Blackwell, 1995.

Hanson, Rick. *Buddha's Brain: The Practical Neuroscience of Happiness, Love, and Wisdom*. Oakland: New Harbinger Publications, 2009.

Harari, Yuval Noah. *Sapiens: A Brief History of Humankind*. New York: HarperCollins, 2015.

Hartman, David. *Love and Terror in the God Encounter: The Theological Legacy of Rabbi Joseph B. Soloveitchik, Volume 1*. Woodstock: Jewish Lights Publishing, 2001.

Havel, Vaclav. 'Address to US Congress.' 22 February 1990. The Vaclav Havel Library Foundation. https://www.vhlf.org/havel-quotes/speech-to-the-u-s-congress/.

Hazrat Inayat Khan. *The Sufi Message Volume 1: The Way of Illumination*. Delhi: Motilal Banarsidass, 2011.

———. *The Sufi Message Volume 2: The Mysticism of Music, Sound and Word*. Delhi: Motilal Banarsidass, 2009.

Hesse, Hermann. *Siddhartha*. Trans. Stanley Applebaum. New York: Dover Publications, 1999.

Hillel the Elder, Babylonian Talmud, Shabbat 31a, Jewish Virtual Library, https://www.jewishvirtuallibrary.org/rabbi-hillel-quotes-on-judaism-and-israel.

Hofmann, Hans. *Search for the Real: And Other Essays*. Edited by Sara T. Weeks and Bartlett H. Hayes. Cambridge, MIT Press, 1967.

Hofmann, Stefan G., Paul Grossman, and Devon E. Hinton. 'Loving-Kindness and Compassion Meditation: Potential for Psychological Interventions.' *Clinical Psychology Review*. 30 November 2011. 31 (7): 1126–1132. https://www.ncbi.nlm.nih.gov/pmc/articles/PMC3176989/.

Horace. *The Odes*. Book II: X. Trans. A.S. Kline. 2003. Poetry in Translation. https://www.poetryintranslation.com/PITBR/Latin/HoraceOdesBkII.php#anchor_Toc39742784.

Hugo, Victor. *William Shakespeare*. Trans. Melville B. Anderson. Chicago: A.C. McClurg and Co., 1891.

Hume, Robert Ernest, trans. *Brihadaranyaka Upanishad*, 2. 5. 15. Oxford: Oxford University Press, 1921.

Huxley, Aldous. *Island*. Perennial Modern Classic edition. New York: HarperCollins, 2009.

———. *Point Counter Point*. Champaign, Illinois: Dalkey Archive Press, 1996.

———. 'The Rest is Silence', in *Music at Night and Other Essays* by Aldous Huxley. London: Chatto and Windus, 1957.

Hsi K'ang. *Philosophy and Argumentation in Third-Century China: The Essays of Hsi K'ang*. Trans. Robert G.

Henricks. New Jersey: Princeton University Press, 1983.

Idries Shah. *Tales of the Dervishes: Teaching Stories of the Sufi Masters Over the Past Thousand Years*. London: The Octagon press, 1982.

Ibn Al 'Arabi. *The Tarjuman al-Ashwaq*. Trans. Reynold A. Nicholson. 1911. https://www.sacred-texts.com/isl/taa/taa14.htm.

Ibn Qayyim al-Jawziyyah. Quoted in 'The Sayings of Ibn Qayyim al-Jawziyyah.' Trans. Ikram Hawramani. 2017. Ikram Hawramani's Website.Top of Form===https://

myjewishlearning.com/article/pirkei-avot-ethics-of-the-fathers-chapter-4/.
Rabbi Moshe ben Maimon ('Maimonides'). *De'ot: The Laws of Personal Development*. Translated by Eliyahu Touge. Chabad. https://www.chabad.org/library/article_cdo/aid/910343/jewish/Deot-Chapter-Three.htm.
Radhakrishnan, Sarvepalli. *The Hindu View of Life*. Quoted in 'Religious Experience.' *Encyclopedia.com*. 23 May 2018. https://www.encyclopedia.com/history/biographies/turkish-and-ottoman-history-biographies/religious-experience.
Radhakrishnan, Sarvepalli., trans. *The Principal Unpanisads*. London: George Allen and Unwin Ltd., 1955.
Rahula, Walpola. *What the Buddha Taught*. New York: Grove Press, 1974.
Ramirez-Ruiz, Enrico. 'Your body was forged in the spectacular death of stars.' *TED@NAS*. November 2019. https://www.ted.com/talks/enrico_ramirez_ruiz_your_body_was_forged_in_the_spectacular_death_of_star s?language=en
Ravichandran, Vasuman. 'Indrajala: The Infinite Web.' *Medium*. 25 June 2020. https://vasuman.medium.com/indrajala-the-infinite-web-5e08a0499f87.
Red Pine, trans. Lao-Tzu. *Taoteching*. Port Townsend: Copper Canyon Press, 2009.
Reuell, Peter. "Songs in the key of humanity." *The Harvard Gazette*. 26 January 2018. https://news.harvard.edu/gazette/story/2018/01/music-may-transcend-cultural-boundaries-to-become-universally-human/.
Riesebrodt, Martin. *The Promise of Salvation: A Theory of Religion*. Translated by Steven Rendall. Chicago: University of Chicago Press, 2010.
Rockhill, William Woodville, trans. *Udanavarga*. London, England: Psychology Press, 2000.
Rorty, Richard. 'Philosophy as a Transitional Genre.' *Pragmatism, Critique, Judgment: Essays for Richard J. Bernstein*. Edited by Seyla Benhabib and Nancy Fraser. Cambridge: MIT Press, 2004.
———. Quoted in Jürgen Habermas. 'Philosopher, poet and friend.' 6 December 2007. *Sign and Sight*. http://www.signandsight.com/features/1386.html.
Roser, Max and Esteban Ortiz-Ospina. 'Literacy.' *Our World in Data*. 20 September 2018. https://ourworldindata.org/literacy.
Rumi, Jalaluddin. 'One Song,' Translated by Coleman Barks. *SufiSpirit*. http://sufispirit.com.au/feature/rumi-sufi-poetry-one-song/.
Russell, Bertrand. 'How to Grow Old.' *Portraits From Memory and Other Essays*. New York: Simon & Schuster, 1956.
Sacks, Jonathan. 'Archive: Quotes.' *The Office of Rabbi Sacks*. https://rabbisacks.org/quotes/.
———. *The Chief Rabbi's Haggadah (Essays)*. 4 March 2003. *The Office of Rabbi Sacks*. https://rabbisacks.org/topics/jew/page/2/.
———. *The Home We Build Together*. 31 October 2007. *The Office of Rabbi Sacks*. https://rabbisacks.org/quotes/acts-kindness-chessed-3/.
———. *Not in God's Name: Confronting Religious Violence*. New York: Schocken Books, 2017.

———. *To Heal a Fractured World*. 8 March 2006. *The Office of Rabbi Sacks*. https://rabbisacks.org/topics/faith-2/page/2/.

Sadhguru [Jaggi Vasudeva]. *Inner Engineering: A Yogi's Guide to Joy*. Random House Publishing Group, 2016.

———. 'Millennium World Peace Summit: Sadhguru's blessing addressed to the delegation of the Millennium World Peace Summit, convening at the United Nations, 28 August 2000.' *Isha*. 2 November 2017, https://isha.sadhguru.org/us/en/sadhguru/mission/millennium-world-peace-summit.

Sagan, Carl. *Cosmos*. Season 1, episode 1. "The Shores of the Cosmic Ocean." Directed by Adrian Malone. Aired 28 September 1980, on PBS.

Schlieter, Jens. 'Master the Chariot, Master Your Self': comparing chariot metaphors as hermeneutics for mind, self and liberation in ancient Greek and Indian sources.' *Universe and Inner Self in Early Indian and Early Greek Thought*. Edited by Richard Seaford. Edinburgh, Scotland: Edinburgh University Press, 2016.

Scholem, Gershom. *Major Trends in Jewish Mysticism*. Reissue Edition. New York: Schocken Books, 2011.

Schopenhauer, Arthur. *The World as Will and Representation*. Volume 1. Trans. E. F. J. Payne. New York: Dover Publications, 1969.

Schumacher, Ernest Friedrich, 'Buddhist Economics,' Schumacher Center for a new economics, https://centerforneweconomics.org/publications/buddhist-economics/.

Schwartz, Howard, ed. *Tree of Souls: The Mythology of Judaism*. Oxford: Oxford University Press, 2007

Shantideva. *The Way of the Bodhisattva: A Translation of the Bodhicharyavatara*. Revised Edition. Trans. Padmakara Translation Group. Boston: Shambhala, 2011.

Shermer, Michael. 'Chicken Soup for the Evolutionist's Soul.' *Los Angeles Times*. 6 February 2000. https://michaelshermer.com/2000/02/chicken-soup-for-the-evolutions-soul/

Shinran. 'On Jinen Honi.' Quoted in Masao Abe. *A Study of Dogen: His Philosophy and Religion*. Albany: SUNY Press, 1992.

Siddiqui, Wajihuddin. *Commonalities and Similarities in World Religions*. Karachi: Royal Book Company, 2018.

Smith, Huston. *The Illustrated World's Religions*. New York: HarperCollins, 1995.

Spinoza, Baruch. *The Essential Spinoza: Ethics and Related Writings*. Cambridge, MA: Hackett Publishing, 2006.

Spurgeon, Charles Haddon. *Gleanings Among the Sheaves*. New York: Sheldon and Co., 1869.

Sri Nisargadatta Maharaj. *I am that*. Mumbai: Chetana Publishing: 1973.

Sri Ramakrishna. *The Gospel of Sri Ramakrishna*. Trans. Swami Nikhilananda. New York: Ramakrishna-Vivekananda Center, 1942.

Seneca, Lucius Annaeus. *Seneca's Morals of a Happy Life, Benefits, Anger And*

Clemency. Translated by Sir Roger L'estrange. Chicago: Belford, Clarke & Co., 1882. Project Gutenberg.

Shakespeare, William. 'As You Like It.' Edited by Samuel Thurber, Jr. and Louise Wetherbee. Boston: Allyn and Bacon, 1922. *Shakespeare Online*. 10 August 2010. http://www.shakespeare-online.com/plays/asu_5_1.html.

Shapiro, Rami. 'Religions are like languages.' *ProgressiveChristianity.org*. 21 May 2012. https://progressivechristianity.org/resources/religions-are-like-languages/.

St. Athanasius. *On the Incarnation*. Quoted in *English Translation of the Catechism of the Catholic Church for the United States of America*. 8 September 1997. *Catholic Culture*. https://www.catholicculture.org/culture/library/catechism/cat_view.cfm?recnum=2153

St. Augustine of Hippo. 'On Lying, Retractations, Book I.' *Moral Treatises of St. Augustine*. Trans. Rev. H. Browne. Augsburg, Bavaria, Germany: JazzyBee Verlag, 2012.

———. 'Homily 7 on the First Epistle of John.' Trans. H. Browne. *Nicene and Post-Nicene Fathers, First Series*, Vol. 7. Ed. Philip Schaff. Buffalo, NY: Christian Literature Publishing Co., 1888. Revised and edited for New Advent by Kevin Knight. http://www.newadvent.org/fathers/170207.htm.

Sujato Bhikkhu, trans. 'Aṅguttara Nikāya.' *Numbered Discourses: A Translation of Aṅguttara Nikāya*. SuttaCentral. 2019.

Suzuki, David. *The Sacred Balance: Rediscovering Our Place in Nature*. Vancouver: Greystone Books, 2009.

Suzuki, D.T., trans.'Lankavatara Scripture.' *A Buddhist Bible*. Edited by Dwight Goddard. Boston, MA: Beacon Press, 1994.

Suzuki, Shunryu. *Zen Mind, Beginner's Mind*. Boston: Shambhala, 2011.

Swami Adiswarananda. *The Vedanta Way to Peace and Happiness*. Woodstock: SkyLight Paths Publishing, 2007.

Swami Chidananda. 'The saint and the scorpion.' *The Times of India*. 16 May 2011. https://timesofindia.indiatimes.com/the-saint-and-the-scorpion/articleshow/6451408.cms.

Swami Sri Yukteswar Giri. In Paramahansa Yogananda. *The Autobiography of a Yogi: The classic story of one of India's greatest spiritual thinkers*. London: Arcturus Publishing, 2016.

Taherzadeh, Adib. *The Revelation of Bahá'u'lláh, Volume 1*. Oxford: George Ronald, 1976. Baha'i Library Online. https://bahai-library.com/taherzadeh_revelation_bahaullah_1.

———. *The Revelation of Bahá'u'lláh*, Volume 3. Oxford: George Ronald, 1976. Baha'i Library Online. https://bahai-library.com/taherzadeh_revelation_bahaullah_3.

Tagore, Rabindranath. *The Religion of Man*. Mansfield Centre: Martino Publishing, 2013.

Taylor, Jill Bolte. *My Stroke of Insight: A Brain Scientist's Personal Journey*. New York: Plume Books, 2009.

Teresa of Avila. *The Interior Castle*. Translated by Kieran Kavanaugh and Otilio Rodriguez. New Jersey: Paulist Press, 1979.

ter Kuile, Casper and Thurston, Angie. 'Video: Religion for a New Generation.' *Harvard Divinity School News*. 2 April 2020. https://hds.harvard.edu/news/2020/04/02/video-religion-new-generation.

Thanissaro Bhikkhu, trans. 'Aṅguttara Nikāya', 4:36. *Dhamma Talks*. https://www.dhammatalks.org/suttas/AN/AN4_36.html.

——, trans. 'Aṅguttara Nikāya', 4:62. *Dhamma Talks*. https://www.dhammatalks.org/suttas/AN/AN4_62.html.

——, trans. 'Saṁyutta Nikāya', 12:44. *Dhamma Talks*. https://www.dhammatalks.org/suttas/SN/SN12_44.html.

——, trans.'Saṁyutta Nikāya', 45:2. *Dhamma Talks*. https://www.dhammatalks.org/suttas/SN/SN45_2.html.

——, trans. 'Sutta Nipāta', 1:8. *Dhamma Talks*. https://www.dhammatalks.org/suttas/KN/StNp/StNp1_8.html.

Thapar, Romila. *Asoka and the Decline of the Mauryas*. Delhi: Oxford University Press, 1997.

Thera, Nyanaponika. *The Heart of Buddhist Meditation*. San Francisco: Weiser Books, 2014.

———., trans. *The Roots of Good and Evil: Buddhist Texts translated from the Pali with Comments and Introduction*. Buddhist Publication Society, 2008.

Thich Nhat Hanh. *Being Peace*. Berkeley, California: Parallax Press, 2005.

———. 'Building a Community of Love: bell hooks and Thich Nhat Hanh.' *Lion's Roar*. 24 March 2017. https://www.lionsroar.com/bell-hooks-and-thich-nhat-hanh-on-building-a-community-of-love/.

———. *Living Buddha, Living Christ: 20th Anniversary Edition*. New York: Penguin, 2007.

Tindal, Matthew. *Christianity as Old as the Creation: Or, the Gospel, a Republication of the Religion of Nature. Volume 1* (1730) Digitized from the New York Public Library, 12 July 2006.

Tolle, Eckhart. *A New Earth: Awakening to Your Life's Purpose*. New York: Penguin, 2005.

Tremlin, Todd. *Minds and Gods: The Cognitive Foundations of Religion*. Oxford: Oxford University Press, 2006.

Tutu, Desmond. *No Future Without Forgiveness*. New York: Doubleday, 1999.

Twain, Mark. *Life on the Mississippi*. New York: Harper & Brothers, 1883. Digitized from Harvard University, 23 June 2008.

Tyson, Neil deGrasse. 'Your Ego and the Cosmic Perspective.' *Big Think*. 25 May 2013. YouTube Video, 2:38, https://www.youtube.com/watch?v=x3sPsbv3fnY.

Ulluwishewa, Rohana. 'Spirituality, Universal Love and Sustainable Behaviour.'

Annals of Behavioral Neuroscience. Volume 1. September 2018. https://www.researchgate.net/publication/327932215_Spirituality_Universal_Love_and_Sustainable_Behaviour.

Unger, Roberto Mangabeira. *The Religion of the Future*. Cambridge: Harvard University Press, 2014.

Universal House of Justice. 'The Promise of World Peace.' Haifa, Israel: Bahá'í World Centre, October 1985. Baha'i Reference Library. http://reference.bahai.org/en/t/uhj/PWP/pwp-5.html.

VanderWeele, Tyler J. 'Flourishing Amidst Coronavirus.' *Psychology Today*. 26 March 2020. https://www.psychologytoday.com/us/blog/human-flourishing/202003/flourishing-amidst-coronavirus.

———. 'Forgiveness: An Important Aspect of Flourishing.' *Psychology Today*. 27 June 2019. https://www.psychologytoday.com/us/blog/human-flourishing/201906/forgiveness-important-aspect-flourishing.

———. 'How Parental Love Impacts Flourishing Later in Life.' *Psychology Today*. 28 June 2019. https://www.psychologytoday.com/us/blog/human-flourishing/201906/how-parental-love-impacts-flourishing-later-in-life.

Vivekananda, Swami. 'Is Vedanta The Future Religion?' Delivered in San Francisco. *Ramakrishnavivekananda*. 8 April 1900.https://www.ramakrishnavivekananda.info/vivekananda/volume_8/lectures_and_discourses/is_vedanta_thefuture.htm.

———. *Karma-Yoga and Bhakti-Yoga*. Revised edition. New York: Ramakrishna-Vivekananda Center, 1955.

———. *The Vedanta Philosophy: An Address Before the Graduate Philosophical Society of Harvard University*. 25 March 1896. New York: Vedanta Society, 1901.

——— *Complete Works of Swami Vivekananda*. Digitally published by Partha Sinha. 27 November 2019.

———. *Personality Development*. Kolkata, India: Advaita Ashrama, 2015.

———. Quoted in Sister Gayatriprana. *Swami Vivekananda's History of Universal Religion and Its Potential for Global Reconciliation*. Illinois: Cook Communications, 2020.

———. *The Vedanta Philosophy: An Address Before the Graduate Philosophical Society of Harvard University*. March 25, 1896. New York: Vedanta Society, 1901.

———. *Vivekananda, World Teacher: His Teachings on the Spiritual Unity of Humankind*. Edited by Swami Adiswarananda. Woodstock: SkyLight Paths Publishing, 2006.

Voss Roberts, Michelle. *Tastes of the Divine*. New York: Fordham University Press, 2014.

Waldinger, Robert. 'What makes a good life: lessons from the longest study on happiness.' *TEDxBeaconStreet*. November 2015. https://www.ted.com/talks/robert_waldinger_what_makes_a_good_life_lessons_from_the_longest_study_on_happiness/transcript

Wallace, David Foster. 2005 Commencement Speech at Kenyon College. Gambier, Ohio, 2005. Kenyon College Archive. http://bulletin-archive.kenyon.edu/x4280.html.

Watson, Burton, trans. *The Lotus Sutra*. New York: Columbia University Press, 1993.

———, trans. *Zhuangzi: Basic Writings*. New York: Columbia University Press, 2003.

Watts, Alan. *Out of Your Mind: Tricksters, Interdependence, and the Cosmic Game of Hide-and-seek*. Boulder: Sounds True, 2017.

Welby, Justin. BBC Radio interview. Quoted in Henry McDonald. 'C of E should rethink portrayal of Jesus as white, Welby says.' *The Guardian*. 26 June 2020. https://www.theguardian.com/uk-news/2020/jun/26/church-of-england-justin-welby-white-jesus-black-lives-matter.

Wilson, E.O. *Consilience: The Unity of Knowledge*. New York: Knopf Doubleday Publishing Group, 1998.

———. *The Meaning of Human Existence*. New York: Liveright Publishing, 2014.

———. *The Social Conquest of Earth*. Illustrated ebook edition. New York: W. W. Norton & Company, 2012.

Wong, Eva, trans. *Lieh-tzu: A Taoist Guide to Practical Living*. Boston: Shambhala, 2001.

Wright, Robert. *The Evolution of God*. New York: Little, Brown and Company, 2009.

———. *Why Buddhism is True: The Science and Philosophy of Meditation and Enlightenment*. New York: Simon & Schuster, 2017.

Yogananda. *Autobiography of a Yogi*. Auckland, New Zealand: The Floating Press, 2009.

———. *Demystifying Patanjali: The Yoga Sutras (Aphorisms): The Wisdom of Paramhansa Yogananda Presented by his direct disciple, Swami Kriyananda*. Nevada: Crystal Clarity Publishers, 2013.

Zajonc, Arthur. *Meditation as Contemplative Inquiry: When Knowing Becomes Love*. Massachusetts: Lindisfarne Books, 2009.

Ziporyn, Brook, trans. *Zhuangzi: The Essential Writings*. Indianapolis: Hackett Publishing, 2009.

Zorn, Justin Talbot and Leigh Marz. 'The Busier You Are, the More You Need Quiet Time.' *Harvard Business Review*. 17 March 2017. https://hbr.org/2017/03/the-busier-you-are-the-more-you-need-quiet-time.